A HISTORY OF
ENGLISH EDUCATION

From 1760

A HISTORY OF
ENGLISH EDUCATION
From 1760

H. C. BARNARD
Emeritus Professor of Education in the University of Reading

"L'histoire, qu'est-ce autre chose qu'une
analyse du présent, puisque c'est dans le passé
que l'on trouve les éléments dont est formé
le présent?"

ÉMILE DURKHEIM

UNIVERSITY OF LONDON PRESS LTD

SBN 340 08816 8

First published 1947
Second edition copyright © 1961 H. C. Barnard
Sixth impression (with amendments) 1969

University of London Press Ltd
St. Paul's House, Warwick Lane, London E.C.4

Printed in Great Britain
by Fletcher & Son Ltd, Norwich, and bound by
Richard Clay (The Chaucer Press) Ltd, Bungay, Suffolk

PREFACE

AN account of the educational history of this country since 1760, compressed within the compass of 351 pages, must of necessity be little more than a bare outline; and this implies that general statements have sometimes to be made which really call for amplification, modification, or explanation. It is hoped, therefore, that those who have the opportunity may be led by the reading of this outline account to consult more detailed and substantial works on the subject. For this reason fairly full references have been made in the footnotes in order to give some indication of the sources which are available; and a list of the works which are quoted, or to which reference is made, has been collected in Appendix III. In the *Cambridge History of English Literature*, vol. ix, pp. 568–74, and vol. xiv, pp. 590–610, there are very full bibliographies of books dealing with education published in the eighteenth and nineteenth centuries. These were compiled by Prof. J. W. Adamson, and they are of the greatest value to the student who wishes to make a more detailed study of the educational history of this period.

I would like gratefully to express my indebtedness to Mr. P. S. Taylor, Chief Education Officer for Reading, to my colleagues Miss H. S. Kermode, Mr. H. Armstrong, and Mr. V. Mallinson, and to my wife, all of whom read this volume in proof and made helpful comments. I wish also to thank Mr. H. E. M. Icely, formerly Reader in Education in the University of Oxford, who gave me some valuable suggestions with reference to the earlier part of the book, and Dr. I. E. Campbell and Miss M. E. Jones, who kindly checked certain details for me.

1947   H. C. B.

When this book was first published in 1947 it was entitled *A Short History of English Education from 1760 to 1944*. Since then it has been reprinted several times, and the suggestion has therefore been made to me that I should write a supplementary chapter, in

v

order to "bring it up to date." I have felt rather diffident about doing this. In the history of English education the year 1944 forms a definite *terminus ad quem*, and I did not want to spoil the symmetry of my lay-out. Also most of the subsequent developments are still in process, and it is not easy or satisfactory to attempt to write history while it is still in the making. No sooner are statements recorded than they tend to be out of date. However, the demand for the book seems to show that it has some value, particularly perhaps for students; and if a supplementary chapter is likely to increase its usefulness there may be some justification for adding this. I have therefore made the attempt, though there must inevitably be many loose ends.

1961   H. C. B.

CONTENTS

PREFACE v

INTRODUCTION xi

PART A

Education during the latter part of the eighteenth century and at the beginning of the nineteenth

I.   ELEMENTARY EDUCATION 2

II.   SECONDARY EDUCATION 12

III. UNIVERSITY AND FURTHER EDUCATION . . 24

IV.   EDUCATIONAL THEORY 32

V.   PHILOSOPHICAL, POLITICAL, ECONOMIC, AND RELIGIOUS THEORIES AFFECTING EDUCATION . 42

PART B

Education during the first part of the nineteenth century

VI.   ELEMENTARY EDUCATION 52

VII. STATE INTERVENTION IN EDUCATION . . . 63

VIII. SECONDARY EDUCATION 71

IX.   UNIVERSITY EDUCATION 81

X.   THE BEGINNINGS OF TECHNICAL AND SCIENTIFIC EDUCATION 88

PART C

Education in the middle period of the nineteenth century

XI.   TENTATIVE STATE ACTION IN ELEMENTARY EDUCATION 98

XII. STATE SUPERVISION IN ELEMENTARY EDUCATION . 107

XIII. THE EDUCATION ACT OF 1870 115

XIV. UNIVERSITY EDUCATION 120

XV. SECONDARY EDUCATION 126

XVI. THE DEVELOPMENT OF SCIENCE IN EDUCATION . 135

XVII. MID-CENTURY THEORY AND PRACTICE . . . 144

XVIII. THE EDUCATION OF GIRLS AND WOMEN . . 156

PART D

Education during the latter part of the nineteenth century

XIX. ELEMENTARY EDUCATION DURING THE SCHOOL
BOARD PERIOD 168

XX. TECHNICAL AND FURTHER EDUCATION . . . 177

XXI. THE TRAINING OF TEACHERS . . . 184

XXII. UNIVERSITY AND SECONDARY EDUCATION . . 195

XXIII. A NATIONAL SYSTEM OF EDUCATION . . . 204

PART E

Education since 1902

XXIV. THE WORKING OF THE 1902 ACT 214

XXV. THE DEVELOPMENT OF THE SPECIAL SERVICES . 223

XXVI. A NEW CONCEPTION OF "SECONDARY" EDUCATION 231

XXVII. PUBLIC AND PRIVATE SCHOOLS 240

XXVIII. UNIVERSITIES AND THE TRAINING OF TEACHERS . 249

XXIX. THE PROGRESS OF SECONDARY EDUCATION . . 259

XXX. TECHNICAL AND CONTINUATIVE EDUCATION . . 271

XXXI. HELPING THE ADOLESCENT 281

XXXII. THE WAR AND THE 1944 ACT 291

XXXIII. RECENT EDUCATIONAL THEORY 306

XXXIV. EDUCATION SINCE 1944 318

APPENDIX I. SCHOOLMASTER'S LICENCE TO TEACH
(1769). 335

APPENDIX II. A LIST OF DATES 336

APPENDIX III. BIBLIOGRAPHY 345

INDEX 353

INTRODUCTION

THE life of a nation is so complex that any attempt to single out a particular aspect of its history is bound to be more or less artificial. Forces of many kinds—political, intellectual, religious, social, economic—act and react, so that the task of disentangling one particular thread is often difficult; and the result is sometimes to give a wrong emphasis or perspective to the special topic which is being considered. For this reason a study of educational history *in vacuo* loses a great deal of its potential value. It is obvious that the educational system of a country is closely bound up with contemporary social and economic conditions and can be understood only in relation to them. One has also to remember that the term 'Educational History' itself can embrace a variety of subjects. It includes, for example, the building-up of the actual administrative structure of the educational system—often marked by the passing of Education Acts or the issuing of official reports. There is also the development of educational theories and principles, whether or not these are expressed in professional practice. We can discuss the history of institutions, such as schools or universities, or the life-work of individual teachers and educationists. We can follow the changing conception of the curriculum and the progress of teaching techniques. All these subjects are closely interrelated, and together they make up the content of educational history. But they can never be completely isolated from the general history of a nation, of which they form only one aspect, and particularly from its social and economic history.

To obtain a clear view of our special subject against this wider background is not always an easy task; but it must at any rate be attempted if one is to avoid a narrow and distorted view of what educational history should mean. In studying a period, therefore, such as that which is discussed in this book, it will be wise to have at hand a more general history. In this way the correlations may the more easily be made and the proper perspective maintained.

Because of this close association of educational history with the wider field of social and economic history it will be advisable to set the stage by describing briefly the social and economic changes which took place in England during the latter part of the eighteenth century. But first, perhaps, we should attempt a justification for starting an account of educational development in this country from the date 1760, the year of the accession of George III. The reason is that, in a broad sense, 'modern times' begin for us at about this period. Hitherto the population of the towns had been relatively small, and most of our people lived in villages which were still to quite a considerable extent self-sufficing. The old 'open-field' system was still practised in many places. The government of the country was oligarchic. Archdeacon Paley, writing in 1785, says: "We have a House of Commons composed of 548 members, in which number are found the most considerable landholders and merchants of the kingdom; the heads of the army, the navy, and the law; the occupiers of great offices in the State; together with many private individuals, eminent by their knowledge, eloquence, or activity. Now, if the country be not safe in such hands, in whose may it confide its interests?"[1] But although the government was largely in the hands of the nobility and the county families, the people generally were content with the existing state of things and were not imbued with ideas of progress and change. The country on the whole was prosperous; wages tended to be good and prices low. Yet this very prosperity and ease of life led to a relaxation of manners and morals. The eighteenth century is by no means so dark a period as it is sometimes painted, but it was disfigured by drunkenness, cruel sports, gambling, and immorality. Some of Hogarth's pictures provide a commentary on this state of society, and Gay's drama *The Beggar's Opera* satirises the corruption of contemporary life. The Church, which for the most part was sunk in lethargy, did little to check these evils. The French observer Montesquieu, who was himself an admirer of England, said:

[1] Quoted by Dicey, *Law and Opinion in England*, pp. 73, 74.

"There is no religion in England. . . . If one speaks of religion, everyone laughs."[1]

After 1760 the economic condition of England underwent a swift and marked change. This change, which is known as the Industrial Revolution, involved the development of large-scale manufactures and capitalistic industry, the rise of the factory system, and the growth of large towns. It was associated also with the progress of enclosures. The abolition of the 'open-field' system had begun as far back as the sixteenth century—even earlier—but by 1760 the chief counties affected were Devon and Cornwall, Kent and Sussex, Essex and Suffolk, and those along the Welsh border. About half of the whole area of England was still unenclosed. In order to stimulate the home production of corn the process was greatly increased during the second half of the eighteenth century and the first half of the nineteenth. In the reigns of Anne and the first two Georges there had been only 245 private Bills for enclosure; during the reign of George III (1760–1820) there were no less than 3,266 such Bills, besides a General Enclosure Act in 1801. The old cultivated strips, separated by turf balks, were cleared away and the modern fenced fields were substituted. With the new system went the introduction of the rotation of crops, and stock-breeding was also improved. All this helped England to survive the economic struggle with Napoleon. But enclosure was a costly process, for it was very expensive to procure the necessary private Acts of Parliament. It was therefore largely the work of capitalists and tended to benefit them. On the other hand, it had the effect of depressing the peasant; he was no longer self-sufficing, for he lost his meadow and grazing rights, and it was difficult—and often impossible—to allot him a plot of ground equivalent in quality and convenience to the scattered strips which he had lost. The compensation given to the dispossessed commoner or small-holder usually took the form of money, but this was often inadequate to enable him to purchase another farm. Arthur Young said in 1801: "By nineteen Enclosure Bills in twenty the poor are injured, and in some grossly

[1] 'Notes' in Œuvres, vol. vii, p. 184. Cf. also 'Advertisement' to first edition of Butler's Analogy. But they were both thinking primarily of the 'upper classes.'

injured."[1] Thus the peasant became dependent on what he could earn as wages; but towards the end of the eighteenth century— the time of the French wars—these had reached very low levels, and that at a time when food was especially dear.

In an attempt to deal with this situation it was suggested that wages should be assessed by law and that the price of labour should be proportionate to the price of wheat, which was about 30s. a quarter in 1750 and had risen to 119s. 6d. in 1801. This was not easy to effect, and therefore during a period of severe distress which occurred in the last decade of the eighteenth century an- other expedient was devised. At Speenhamland, now part of Newbury in Berkshire, the justices in 1795 decided to grant relief to starving labourers on a sliding scale for each member of the family; this scale was based on the price of bread and it went to supplement inadequate wages. The scheme was widely adopted; but its effects were to depress wages, to discourage initiative and self-help, and to multiply the children of paupers. A committee which reviewed the working of the scheme in 1824 said: "There are but two motives by which men are induced to work: the one, the hope of improving the condition of themselves and their families; the other, the fear of punishment. The one is the principle of free labour, the other the principle of slave labour. The one produces industry, frugality, sobriety, family affection, and puts the labouring class in a friendly relation with the rest of the community; the other causes, as certainly, idleness, impru- dence, vice, dissension, and places the master and labourer in a perpetual state of jealousy and mistrust. Unfortunately, it is the tendency of the system of which we speak to supersede the former of these principles, and to introduce the latter."[2]

Another factor which contributed to the Industrial Revolution was the development of machinery and the use of steam. Down to the first half of the eighteenth century many industries, such as spinning, weaving, furniture or basket making, were carried on in cottages. In some trades this domestic system and the capitalist

[1] *Annals of Agriculture*, vol. 36, p. 538.
[2] Quoted by Cunningham, *The Growth of English Industry and Commerce*, pp. 720–1.

system existed side by side; but the cottage industries did give re-
munerative employment to women and children and so helped to
supplement the labourer's wages. But the invention, during the
second half of the century, of machines for dealing with textiles
led to the setting up of factories and the ousting of domestic
workers. At the same time power was applied to machinery—at
first water-power and then steam; so that by the early part of
the nineteenth century the transference of industry from domestic
conditions was fairly complete.

The effects of this change were considerable. There was a
rapid increase of population, helped by the Speenhamland pau-
perisation of the agricultural labourer and also to the greater
chance of survival due to advance in medical science. With it
went a redistribution of the population, stimulated by the improved means of communication. There was a movement from
southern England to the coalfield areas of Lancashire, the West
Riding, Staffordshire, and Glamorgan. A great influx into the
towns began from the country districts. In 1760 no town outside
London had more than 50,000 inhabitants, except Bristol and
possibly Norwich.[1] The new population concentrated in the
towns of the industrial areas, which grew with incredible quick-
ness and with little regard to planning or control. Sanitation and
water-supply were alike inadequate. We have still a legacy of
this unregulated urban growth in the depressing slums, with their
back-to-back houses, of the great industrial towns of the North.
It is important to note that this rapid and uncontrolled expansion
implied a shortage of schools in the new manufacturing areas.
For this reason the Factory Acts, the first of which was passed in
1802, almost always contain some reference to the provision of
rudimentary education for children employed in mills. These
children were indeed often employed under appalling conditions,
with long hours and very low wages, and with little regard to
their intellectual or moral well-being. Yet the parents usually
acquiesced because they were dependent on what their children
could earn. The demand for child labour in the mills was stimulated by the fact that one adult could tend a machine with the

[1] See Toynbee, *The Industrial Revolution in England*, p. 36.

help of several children. To secure a sufficient number of recruits
factory owners imported parish-apprentices from workhouses.
Some of the employers were humane and enlightened, but too
often the children were most cruelly treated, for there was no
inspection or safeguard.[1]

It may be asked: Why were such things allowed? There were,
as we shall see, serious attempts to deal with these evils, and not
everyone was lethargic or cynical. But some sort of theoretical
justification for acquiescence was afforded by the current political
theory of *laissez-faire*, which implied opposition to government
interference and a belief in free competition and the unrestricted
liberty of the individual. The school of doctrinaire economists
who proclaimed this theory owed much to Adam Smith, whose
Wealth of Nations was published in 1776; but it was developed
during the earlier part of the nineteenth century by such writers
as Ricardo, Malthus, and John Stuart Mill. A Committee of
the House of Commons gave expression to the doctrine in
a Report issued in 1806: "The right of every man to employ
the capital he inherits or has acquired according to his own
discretion without molestation or obstruction, so long as he
does not infringe on the rights or property of others, is one of
those privileges which the free and happy Constitution of this
Country has long accustomed every Briton to consider as his
birth-right."[2]

Thus *laissez-faire* played into the hands of the capitalist and
afforded a comfortable economic doctrine to justify his exploitation of the advantages which he enjoyed. The governing classes,
to salve their consciences, preached—and indeed practised—
private charity; the suffering poor were encouraged to exercise
self-help, or, failing that, resignation. "Let compassion be shown
in action," said Burke, "the more the better according to every
man's ability, but let there be no lamentation of their condition.
. . . Patience, labour, sobriety, frugality, and religion should be

[1] This point is well illustrated by Prof. Frank Smith in his *History of English
Elementary Education*, pp. 13–15. See also Thomas, *Young People in Industry*, 1750–
1945.
[2] Quoted in Cunningham, *The Growth of English Industry and Commerce*, III,
p. 739.

recommended to them."[1] This belief in self-help and voluntary effort for social welfare also seemed to be justified by the rapid rise of men of vigour and character who worked themselves up and became wealthy manufacturers. Such examples suggested that the existing order of things afforded sufficient opportunity for individual effort, and it militated against plans for providing educational or social reform on a national scale and through the agency of the State.

[1] *Works*, vol. vii, p. 377 (*Thoughts and Details on Scarcity*).

B

PART A

EDUCATION DURING THE LATTER PART OF THE EIGHTEENTH CENTURY AND AT THE BEGINNING OF THE NINETEENTH

Chapter I

ELEMENTARY EDUCATION

Private Schools, Charity Schools, Schools of Industry, and Sunday Schools.

THE social setting described in the Introduction provides the background against which will be described the various types of educational institution which were available in England during the latter part of the eighteenth century, and many of which survived until well into the following century. In this account we may, for the sake of convenience, employ the terms 'elementary' or 'primary' and 'secondary,' though it should be understood that they were not in contemporary use in this country.[1] It should also be noted that the State did not aid or control any of these educational agencies. They were carried on by private individuals, though in many cases—as will be seen—under the ægis of the Church.

Of elementary schools we can distinguish several different types. There was first of all the 'dame school,' usually kept by an elderly woman whose weekly fee for each pupil was a few pence. A picture of such an institution is given in William Shenstone's often-quoted poem *The Schoolmistress*, which made use of Alexandrines in imitation of Spenser. The poem dates from 1742, but there were schools in existence for more than another century of which the description would still hold good:

> *In ev'ry village mark'd with little spire*
> *Embow'r'd in trees and hardly known to fame,*
> *There dwells, in lowly shed, and mean attire,*
> *A matron old, whom we Schoolmistress name;*
> *Who boasts unruly brats with birch to tame;*
> *They grieven sore, in piteous durance pent,*

[1] The terms *primaire* and *secondaire* came from France and (so far as I am aware) appeared for the first time in a Report presented to the Legislative Assembly by Condorcet in 1792.

Aw'd by the pow'r of this relentless dame;
And oft-times, on vagaries idly bent,
For unkempt hair, or task unconn'd, are sorely shent.

Nearly seventy years later the poet Crabbe describes a town dame school of much the same type:

Yet one there is, that small regard to rule
Or study pays, and still is deemed a school;
That where a deaf, poor, patient widow sits
And awes some thirty infants as she knits—
Infants of humble, busy wives, who pay
Some trifling price for freedom through the day.[1]

Another description of a dame school comes from Charles Kingsley's *Water Babies*, which was published as late as 1863 and owes much to a tour by the author in the Yorkshire Dales in the late fifties. Tom, the chimney-sweeper's boy, came down over Harthover Crag into Vendale and was given shelter by an old lady who kept the village dame school. "At her feet sat the grandfather of all cats; and opposite her sat, on two benches, twelve or fourteen neat rosy chubby little children, learning their Chris-cross row." That is a much pleasanter picture than the other two; and an article on 'The Dame School Forty Years Ago,' by a 'Working Man,' which appeared in the *School Board Chronicle* of May 11th, 1872, speaks in the highest terms of a school of this type which the author entered at the age of four. He compares it favourably with the National School to which he was sent later. But it is obvious that on the whole dame schools were little more than baby-minding establishments and that the education which they gave was extremely rudimentary.[2]

An institution which gave some kind of elementary education to rather older children was the common day school, or private day school. The master was often a man who had failed at other employments or was handicapped by some physical deformity.

[1] Crabbe, *The Borough*, Letter xxiv.
[2] According to the *Report* of the Newcastle Commission (1861), "Dames' schools are very common both in the country and in towns." They were declared to be "generally very inefficient." (See vol. i, pp. 28 and 29.)

In the poem by Crabbe, already quoted, we have a description of a common day school in the 'Borough':

> Poor Reuben Dixon has the noisiest school
> Of ragged lads, who ever bow'd to rule;
> Low is his price—the men who heave our coals
> And clean our causeways send him boys in shoals.
> To see poor Reuben, with his fry beside—
> Their half-checked rudeness and his half-scorned pride—
> Their room the sty in which th' assembly meet
> In the close lane behind the Northgate Street;
> To observe his vain attempts to keep the peace
> Till tolls the bell and strife on both sides cease—
> Calls for our praise; his labour praise deserves
> But not our pity; Reuben has no nerves;
> 'Mid noise and dirt and stench and play and prate
> He calmly cuts the pen or views the slate.

It seems that the masters in such schools were often ignorant, and sometimes even cruel and dissolute. Yet not all common day schools were inefficient. Joseph Lancaster, of whom more will be said later, worked out his monitorial system in such a school.

The dame school and the common day school provided a rudimentary education for the children of those who could pay fees—though the weekly charge was always a very small one. But the social conditions which have been described in the Introduction made it obvious that something would have to be done for the very poor. So long as the theory of the divine stratification of society was held, the chief impetus to provide popular education was humanitarian or religious. Fear was sometimes another motive. The governing classes in England were much jolted by the French Revolution, which was indeed a startling challenge to privilege. At first it had been welcomed by many in this country as a victory for constitutional freedom, but subsequent excesses alienated English sympathy. The Revolution was violently denounced by Burke, who referred to the common people as the 'swinish multitude.' He was answered by Tom Paine in his

Rights of Man, which became the gospel of the radical movement. But feeling in England was so strong that Paine escaped imprisonment only by flight to France. A few years later, when the sufferings of the working classes were increased by the French wars, there was a fresh upsurge of radicalism and republicanism, especially in the new industrial areas. Disorders occurred in some of the big manufacturing towns, and in 1796 the mob in Manchester created a riot at a theatre during the singing of the National Anthem. Thus, over and above the idea of popular education as a humane or religious duty, there was a feeling that some modicum of education would prove a safeguard and would combat vice, irreligion, and subversive tendencies among the poor. They must be taught to live upright and industrious lives in that station of life unto which it should please God to call them. This helps to explain the great stress which was laid on so-called 'religious' education in philanthropic schools for the poor.

An answer to the problem was found in the charity schools. Schools of this type had been started by the Society for Promoting Christian Knowledge as early as 1699. These schools were associated with parishes, and catered mainly for day pupils, although some had boarders. The catechising of the children was performed by the clergy; the masters and mistresses were required to be members of the Established Church and also "to be of meek temper and humble behaviour; to have a good government of themselves; and to keep good order." In *Sketches by Boz*, published by Dickens in 1836, there is a pathetic picture of the parish schoolmaster. He is represented as a man who had sustained many misfortunes and financial reverses, and had finally been driven to apply for parish relief. But a churchwarden who had known him in happier times obtained the situation for him. "Time and misfortune have mercifully been permitted to impair his memory, and use has habituated him to his present condition." It is obvious that all parish schoolmasters were not of this type, and as Miss M. G. Jones points out: "The men and women who earned their livelihood as (charity) school teachers have suffered hardly at the hands of contemporaries and of posterity."[1] But on

[1] Jones, *The Charity School Movement*, p. 102.

the whole they were of much the same class as the proprietors of the common day schools, to whom reference has already been made.

The curriculum of the charity schools—so far as they could be said to have one—included religious instruction (which usually meant learning the catechism by heart), and reading. In some cases writing and arithmetic were added. But apart from 'religion' the main stress was on industrial occupations, for the children were designed to become labourers or domestic servants and were therefore encouraged to develop 'habits of industry.' Spinning, sewing, knitting, gardening, and even ploughing were taught. No fees were paid, for the charity schools were supported sometimes by legacies and endowments, but usually also by voluntary contributions. The needs of the charity schools were kept before the public by the attendance of the children at church, where seats in the gallery were reserved for them. On certain Sundays charity-school sermons were preached and special collections were made. From 1704 onwards an annual service attended by charity-school children from London and Westminster was held; and from 1782 to 1877, when the custom ceased, this took place in St. Paul's Cathedral.[1] Some thousands of children were present and the occasion was regarded as an important one. William Blake makes a moving reference to it in his *Songs of Innocence*:

> *O what a multitude they seem'd, these flowers of London town!*
> *Seated in companies they sit with radiance all their own.*
> *The hum of multitudes was there, but multitudes of lambs,*
> *Thousands of little boys and girls raising their innocent hands.*

The charity schools did important work during the eighteenth century. By about 1760 they were educating some 30,000 children, but they tended to decline in efficiency, if not also in numbers, as the century progressed. Besides the Church of England schools there were some nonconformist and Roman Catholic charity schools; but these had no central co-ordinating

---

[1] In 1860 a proposal was made to transfer this service to the Crystal Palace! Fortunately it was not carried out. See *Punch*, June 9th, 1860.

body, like the S.P.C.K., to stimulate their zeal. By the end of the century charity-school methods were being criticised as mechanical, and the catechising by parish clergy as perfunctory. Mrs. Trimmer, writing in 1792, says: "Notwithstanding the plan is still in force which was originally concerted for the purpose of giving the children educated by charity a comprehensive knowledge of Christianity and to exercise them betimes to the practice of piety, it must be acknowledged that the education of children brought up in the charity schools is, in general, very defective in these particulars."[1] She complains that teachers are incompetent, reading books are too difficult, and the Bible and Prayer Book are taught by rote, so that children rarely understand what they are required to repeat. The charity schools paved the way for the monitorial schools which arose early in the nineteenth century, and of which something will be said later. But, for all their limitations, they made a real contribution to popular education. They were part of a movement which was not confined to England. A German named Francke (1663–1727) had started similar schools. He is associated with a movement called Pietism, which defined religion in terms of humanitarianism. The object of his educational efforts was to provide religious training for poor and neglected children, and to this he added practical instruction. Thus Pietism had close affinity with the nobler motives which prompted the charity-school movement in this country. Francke was in close correspondence with the S.P.C.K., and his views and his work were well known to the promoters of our own charity schools.

Yet another type of free education for the very poor was afforded by the schools of industry. Something of this kind for pauper children had been advocated as far back as 1697 by the English philosopher Locke. He says: "The children of labouring people are an ordinary burden to the parish, and are usually maintained in idleness, so that their labour also is generally lost to the public till they are twelve or fourteen years old. The most effectual remedy for this that we are able to conceive, and which we therefore humbly propose, is, that, in the fore-mentioned new

[1] *Reflections on the Education of Children in Charity Schools*, p. 19.

law to be enacted, it be further provided that working schools be set up in every parish, to which children of all such as demand relief of the parish, above three and under fourteen years of age, whilst they live at home with their parents, and are not otherwise employed for their livelihood by the allowance of the overseers of the poor, shall be obliged to come."[1] Little came of this proposal until the latter part of the eighteenth century. But under the impact of the Industrial Revolution and the rise of the factory system 'working schools' of this kind began to be opened, to which children were admitted from an early age. There they were taught to spin, wind, knit, plait straw, sew, cobble shoes, and do gardening jobs. The sale of the products of their labour paid the expenses of the school and provided the children with meals. We even read of cases where a small surplus was returned to the pupils in the form of wages. Provision was made for religious instruction—which, for reasons already explained, was regarded as of paramount importance—and sometimes also for the teaching of reading; but beyond this there was little or no intellectual instruction.

In some places pauper children were removed from the workhouse and sent to schools of industry, or the schools were confined to workhouse children. In 1796 Pitt proposed that children whose parents were in receipt of poor relief should be compelled to attend schools of industry; but this plan was not put into practice. The general effect of these measures was to depress the status of schools of this type, and they were also handicapped by competition with child labour in factories. Employers tended to object to them because they diminished the supply of this labour, and parents found that they could profit better from the earnings of their children if they worked in mills. An organisation called the Society for Bettering the Condition and Increasing the Comfort of the Poor, which was founded in 1796, tried to foster schools of industry, and also started friendly societies, soup kitchens, and savings banks; but these efforts were far from solving the problem of popular education. A return of 1803 showed that there were 188,794 children aged five to fourteen in

[1] See Locke, *On Education*, ed. Quick, Appendix A.

receipt of parish relief, but of these only 20,336 were in schools of industry and receiving education.[1]

Another contribution to the elementary education of the poor was made by the Sunday schools. The break-up of home education and the employment of children in factories were condoned or even welcomed because of the current *laissez-faire* theories and the demand of manufacturers for child labour and of parents for their children's earnings. But factory work left one day in the week free, and this made possible the Sunday-school movement. It is associated particularly with Robert Raikes, though he did not originate it. He was a well-to-do newspaper owner in Gloucester, and he used his resources to open schools for the undisciplined and illiterate children who were employed in local pin factories all the week, and let loose on Sundays. The scheme proved successful and it spread. It was made known through the agency of the *Gentleman's Magazine* and other journals of the day, and it soon captured the popular imagination. In 1785 was founded the Society for Establishment and Support of Sunday Schools in the different Counties of England. It formed local committees which were composed half of churchmen and half of nonconformists—a noteworthy fact in view of future religious difficulties in English education. The aims of the Sunday schools were religious and social rather than intellectual. The rules of the Society include this instruction: "Be diligent in teaching the children to read well. . . . Neither writing nor arithmetic is to be taught on Sundays." Professor Halévy has reminded us that Protestantism is the religion of a book, and "read well" in this context obviously refers to reading the Bible or a religious manual. This explains why so often in elementary popular education at this period the curriculum is confined to religious instruction, reading, and manual work, but includes no other form of intellectual instruction. Sunday-school children were also taken to church or chapel. The teachers were originally paid a small fee for their Sunday duties; but as the movement progressed the number of voluntary teachers greatly increased and the paid teacher tended to disappear. The interest and support of the

[1] *Report* of Society for Bettering the Condition of the Poor (1809), p. 307 n.

'upper classes' were secured by making them 'visitors' of Sunday schools. A great deal was done by some of these philanthropists, such as Mrs. Sarah Trimmer and the sisters Hannah and Martha More. In some cases the schools were opened at times during the week and their curriculum was extended to include practical work.

The Sunday schools had a rapid success. In 1787 they had 250,000 pupils in Great Britain; in 1801 there were 156,490 in London alone. They even tended to choke out the day schools, owing to the fact that manufacturers encouraged their child-employees to attend them, lest they might lose their labour otherwise.[1] Attending a school on Sunday did not interfere with labour in the mill during the week, and a modicum of education might have a civilising and stabilising effect on the worker. The Sunday-school movement also affected adults, and in some places writing and arithmetic were taught even in these schools to those who had left the ordinary Sunday school where they had learnt to read. J. R. Green in his *Short History of the English People* says: "The Sunday schools established by Mr. Raikes were the beginning of popular education";[2] and in a sense this is true. These schools are of great importance because they provided the chief means of humanising and educating the great mass of children who, after the Industrial Revolution, provided labour in factories. "In the new factory towns, amidst the social degradation and anarchy produced by violent economic change prolonged through twenty years of war, they were the sole organs of a community that transcended the fierce antagonism of misconceived class interests. In them the masters, foremen, and workers of the factory met on the common ground of mutual service."[3]

---

[1] Southey goes so far as to complain that the Sunday schools have been made "subservient to the merciless love of gain. The manufacturers know that a cry would be raised against them if their little white slaves received no instruction; and so they have converted Sunday into a Schoolday." (Letter to Lord Ashley, February 7th, 1833.) It was estimated that at the time when he wrote there were as many as one and a half million children attending Sunday schools in Great Britain.

[2] Chap. x, 'Modern England'; sect. i.

[3] G. Unwin, *Samuel Oldknow and the Arkwrights*, p. 41, quoted by Frank Smith, *A History of English Elementary Education*, p. 63.

But the Sunday schools did even more than this. They initiated the idea in this country of universal education applied to children of all ages and free of cost. At the same time they gave to our educational system a religious and denominational colouring which still survives.

Before concluding this outline account of elementary education in the second half of the eighteenth century and the early part of the nineteenth, something should be said of an important contribution made by the so-called 'circulating schools' in Wales. These were started in 1737 by the Rev. Griffith Jones, vicar of Llanddowror, near Carmarthen. He realised that the existing Welsh parochial schools were too few and inefficient, and he therefore established schools for teaching the poor to read the Bible in the vernacular and to obtain religious instruction from catechisms. The teachers travelled from place to place, staying three or six months in each locality, and the lessons were given in any vacant building—for example, a church, chapel, or empty house. The schools were open to adults as well as to children and were available in the evening as well as in the day-time. The movement was helped by the S.P.C.K. which gave Bibles and other books as well as financial support, and also by the donations and subscriptions of sympathisers, not only from Wales, but also from England. At Griffith Jones's death in 1761 no less than 3,495 of these circulating schools had been organised, and by 1777 the total had risen to 6,545. But the scheme was mismanaged by his successors, and his schools died out towards the end of the eighteenth century, to be replaced by the Sunday schools which from the very beginning increased rapidly in Wales.

Chapter II

SECONDARY EDUCATION

Endowed Schools, Public Schools, and Private Schools.

WE have now to describe secondary education during the period under consideration. This was given in the endowed school and the private school; but more information is available about the former than about the latter.

The endowed school, or grammar school, is an institution of considerable ancestry which can indeed be traced back to Roman times. Strictly speaking, it was a school where the classical languages (for this was the technical meaning of the term 'grammar') were taught. The endowed schools owed their origin to pious founders of various types. In the earlier days they had been mainly bishops or churchmen. Some of these schools were refounded at the Reformation. Sometimes the school had been provided by a Guild or a City Livery Company. In Tudor times the founders were mainly yeomen or merchants or men of title; and in some cases—as at Lady Manners' School, Bakewell—the school came into existence owing to the liberality of a woman. Eton and Winchester were in a sense unique, and for this reason are perhaps specially entitled to the name 'public schools.' Eton was founded in 1440 by Henry VI, and Winchester, which owes its origin to William of Wykeham, is still older (1382). Both are associated with colleges—Eton with King's, Cambridge, and Winchester with New College, Oxford; and both schools are themselves collegiate foundations and are still known as Eton *College* and Winchester *College*. Like the colleges of Oxford and Cambridge, they are societies of people living together for the promotion of a common purpose—in this case, education. Thus from the very beginning Eton and Winchester have been boarding schools. But most of the other old 'public' schools are town grammar schools which have outgrown their purely local associations, though a few (e.g. Westminster and King's School, Canterbury) have developed out of pre-Reformation monastic or cathedral schools.

Rugby may be taken as an example of a 'glorified' grammar school. In 1567 a certain Lawrence Sherriff, who had prospered as a citizen and grocer of the City of London, left some funds for the founding of a school at his native place, Rugby, which was then a small village containing barely a hundred houses. It was designed for local boys—"the children of Rugby and Brownes-over (a neighbouring village) and next for such as bee of other places thereunto adjoyneing."[1] There were to be no fees, and an almshouse was to be attached to the school. An "honest, discreet and learned man being a master of arts" was to be engaged to teach in this "free grammar school." But as the endowment increased in value the school grew wealthy and new buildings were erected. The development of communications and the influence of a great headmaster made it possible to turn a small local free grammar school into a famous boarding school which drew its pupils from all parts of the country. Attempts have been made to justify this transformation in the face of the founder's original intention. The phrase *pauperes et indigentes* is often used in foundation deeds to describe those who are to benefit under educational endowments. It might therefore seem that schools like Rugby—Harrow and Shrewsbury have had a similar history—applied for the benefit of the sons of wealthy parents funds which were originally intended to be devoted to the education of the poor and indigent boys of a specified town or locality. Mr. A. F. Leach in his *Schools of Mediæval England*,[2] when dealing with Winchester College, contends that *pauperes et indigentes* does not mean 'paupers,' but rather—to use a modern phrase—'those in need of financial assistance.' There is something to be said for this view, although the bulk of the pupils of the grammar school which had developed into a public school would still not come under this description. It remains true that public schools like Rugby and Harrow—and, in fact, most of those of old foundation—have

[1] See Rouse, *A History of Rugby School*, Appendix I, p. 360.
[2] Pp. 206–8. Leach's view is strongly contested in Wilkins and Fallows, *English Educational Endowments*, published by the W.E.A. See also Fleming *Report* on *The Public Schools* (1944), p. 8.

gone far beyond the intentions of the original founders. Down to the latter part of the eighteenth century the only exclusively boarding public schools in the kingdom were Eton and Winchester.

It is interesting to note that, so far as the grammar schools were concerned, the masters were supposed to hold a teaching licence which was granted by the Bishop of the diocese. This is a custom of some antiquity; it dates from at least the Middle Ages and it is not confined to this country. The 77th Canon of the *Book of Common Prayer* (1604) lays it down: "No man shall teach either in publick school or private house, but such as shall be allowed by the Bishop of the diocese, or Ordinary of the place, under his hand and seal, being found meet as well for his learning and dexterity in teaching, as for sober and honest conversation, and also for right understanding of God's true religion; and also except he shall first subscribe to the first and third Articles aforementioned simply, and to the two first clauses of the second Article." As late as 1795 in the case of *Rex* v. *the Archbishop of York*, it was held that "masters of grammar schools must be licensed by the ordinary who may examine the party applying for a licence as to his learning, morality and religion."[1] There was no doubt as to the legal position—though it should be noticed that the requirement of a licence to teach applied to masters in grammar schools and not apparently to those in elementary schools.[2] But by the end of the eighteenth century the Church had lost some of its interest in education, and the licence to teach was not always required. It was not finally abolished until the passing of the Endowed Schools Act in 1869.

The curriculum of the grammar school was indicated in its title. There had been a time when the classical languages, to which this term 'grammar' refers, were the key to almost all human knowledge, and when power to write and speak Latin well was the most purely vocational and utilitarian equipment with which the grammar school could supply its pupils. But, although that was no longer the case, the curriculum of the en-

---

[1] A copy of a schoolmaster's 'Licence to Teach' is given in Appendix I, p. 335.
[2] See De Montmorency, *State Intervention in English Education*, p. 172.

dowed grammar and public schools at the end of the eighteenth century was still much the same as it had been at the time of the Renaissance. It consisted mainly of Latin and Greek, to which at Merchant Taylors' Hebrew was added for the senior boys. The methods of teaching also were largely traditional. In *Tom Brown's Schooldays* there is a detailed description of the "time-honoured institution of the Vulgus, commonly supposed to have been established by William of Wykeham at Winchester, and imported to Rugby by Arnold."[1] It is true that schoolmasters tend to be a conservative race, and some schools are even yet museums of obsolete or obsolescent practices.

But there was a theoretical justification for the retention of Latin and Greek long after they had any practical value for those set to learn them, or any 'carry-over' into the ordinary life of the ordinary pupil. It was furnished by what in modern psychological phraseology is called 'formal training' and the 'transfer of training.' It has been maintained that the study of certain subjects affords a mental discipline; by such a process the mind of the child is trained and helped to perform the different and multitudinous tasks which it will have to tackle in later life. It was claimed that Latin and Greek are *par excellence* subjects of this kind; and the claim was advanced as the chief argument against those who questioned the utilitarian value of the Classics in education. A headmaster giving evidence before a Royal Commission in the middle of the nineteenth century said: "Classical studies are for all boys a gymnastic of the very best kind." More recently the theory has been invoked on behalf of the study of scientific subjects. The Report of the Prime Minister's Committee on Natural Science in Education (1918) says: "As an intellectual exercise science disciplines our powers of mind. . . . It quickens and cultivates directly the faculty of observation."[2] Modern psychological investigation has greatly modified the force of the 'formal training' and 'transfer' theory;[3] yet even today it is not infrequently put forward as if it were a self-evident truth. The fact remains that, so far as any theoretical basis was

[1] Hughes, *Tom Brown's Schooldays*, pt. ii, chap iii.   [2] *Op.* cit. § 5.
[3] See, for example, Appendix V (by Prof. H. R. Hamley) in the Spens *Report*.
C

supplied to justify a traditional practice, this doctrine held sway in the grammar and public schools throughout the period which we are considering. They continued to give their chief attention to what in the current school idiom was called 'business'—i.e. the Classics.

In the case of some of the grammar schools—and especially of those in country districts—there was little local demand for a curriculum of this kind. All that the headmaster had to do was to draw his salary, which was provided by the endowment. In 1795 Lord Chief Justice Kenyon described the English grammar schools as "empty walls without scholars and everything neglected except the receipt of the salaries and emoluments."[1] That state of affairs was not unknown for many years to come. As late as 1866 the headmaster of Whitgift School, Croydon, had held office for thirty years and during that time had not had a single pupil. Yet, bad as it was, something perhaps can be said to extenuate such a situation. In 1805 the Lord Chancellor Eldon ruled that the governing body of Leeds Grammar School, which was desirous of adding to the classical curriculum arithmetic, writing, and modern languages, was incompetent to do this. It was held to be illegal because the school had been founded (like Rugby) as a free *grammar* school; and Eldon decided that a grammar school must teach 'grammar'—i.e. the classical languages—and nothing else. Any addition to the curriculum would involve a misapplication of the school's endowments. This important judgment was not overset till the passing of the Grammar Schools Act in 1840. It implied that an endowed school could refuse to teach anything but Latin and Greek, or that, even if it had been founded as a free school, the headmaster could exact his own private terms for the teaching of other subjects. Perhaps this is the origin of the 'extras' which used to figure on school bills. In any case—as has been said—Latin and Greek were the school's 'business'—the real purpose of its existence; any other subject was outside the curriculum proper and was often taken on a half-holiday. Arithmetic was the chief 'extra' of this kind. The attitude towards such subjects, as Adamson appositely points out, was similar to

[1] See De Montmorency, *State Intervention in English Education*, p. 180.

that of the modern grammar school towards typewriting and shorthand.

In defence of this state of things it can be said that in some cases and with some pupils the teaching of the Classics was not unsuccessful. It certainly produced scholars and statesmen of the type of Burke and Pitt, Chatham and Peel and Gladstone. It is also true that the teaching of non-classical subjects consisted mainly of rote-work—the getting by heart of long lists of dates or capes and bays. Yet, however strong were the forces of conservatism and the belief in the fortifying virtues of the good old classical discipline, there was also plenty of criticism. As early as the end of the seventeenth century the philosopher Locke had censured over-emphasis on grammar and rote-work in the teaching of Latin, and he called attention to the neglect of the mother-tongue and other subjects. In the period at present under consideration some of the most drastic criticisms came from the pen of Sydney Smith and were published in the *Edinburgh Review*. In an essay[1] entitled *Too much Latin and Greek*, published in 1809, he says: "A young Englishman goes to school at six or seven years old; and he remains in a course of education till twenty-three or twenty-four years of age. In all that time, his sole and exclusive occupation is learning Latin and Greek: he has scarcely a notion that there is any other kind of excellence."

It was not only the curriculum of the public and grammar schools which was criticised. In many of these schools the boarding arrangements were primitive and the food very poor. At Eton the boys had to wash at the pump and the dormitories were damp. Discipline, again, was often very harsh. John Keate, headmaster of Eton from 1809 to 1834, though only about five feet high, won a reputation as a flogger. On one day in 1832, in his sixtieth year, he flogged eighty boys. These drastic punishments were largely necessitated by the huge size of the forms. Keate took all the Upper School at once—198 boys.[2] When he retired in 1834, having brought the numbers in the Upper School at

[1] It was a review of R. L. Edgeworth's *Professional Education* (see *infra*, p. 41). Sydney Smith, *Essays*, p. 91.
[2] See Maxwell Lyte, *A History of Eton College*, p. 386.

Eton up to 570, there were still only nine masters. Under such conditions the only way to keep order was by terror. The assistant masters were not expected to help with discipline, and the senior boys were often ringleaders in disorder. It is hardly surprising, therefore, that there were frequent rebellions and barrings-out. At Winchester there were several rebellions in the last quarter of the eighteenth and first quarter of the nineteenth centuries. In 1793 the boys held the College buildings for two days and, fired no doubt by the news from revolutionary France, set up the red cap of liberty. In 1818 another rising at Winchester had to be put down by two companies of soldiers with fixed bayonets. At Rugby in 1797 the boys blew up the door of the headmaster's study with gunpowder. Soldiers had to be called in and the Riot Act was read. The last serious school rebellion on record occurred at Marlborough as late as 1851.

These excesses were partly due to the fact that little provision was made for the boys' free time. Organised games were in their infancy and received little encouragement, as an occupation of educative value, from the school authorities. It was Butler, headmaster of Shrewsbury from 1798 to 1836, who said that football was fit only for butcher boys; but he was probably thinking of the game as played by hooligans in the streets. We have it on record that at Eton in the second part of the eighteenth century such games as battledore, tops, and hoops were still played. Gray, in his ode on a *Distant Prospect of Eton College*, had written this in 1748:

> *Say, Father* Thames, *for thou hast seen*
>   *Full many a sprightly Race,*
> *Disporting on thy Margent green*
>   *The Paths of Pleasure trace.*
> *Who foremost now delight to cleave*
> *With pliant Arm thy glassy Wave?*
>   *The captive Linnet which enthrall?*
> *What idle Progeny succeed*
> *To chase the rolling Circle's Speed*
>   *Or urge the flying Ball?*

It has often been pointed out that the tag about the Battle of Waterloo having been won on the playing-fields of Eton has no reference to the educative value of organised games. It relates literally to the *fights* which took place at Eton and which—as can be seen from *Tom Brown's Schooldays*, or *Eric*, or any other school story of the period—were characteristic not only of the late eighteenth century but also far down into the nineteenth, and doubtless are even yet not extinct. But an even less desirable result of leaving boys so much to their own devices and of not encouraging interests for their spare time was that the moral tone of the boarding schools, at any rate, was not usually good and was often very bad. Bullying was not uncommon. *Punch*, as late as 1854,[1] has a caustic article on "Bullying at Public Schools" and refers to an "aggravated assault at Rugby by two ruffians of 16 or 17 on a little fellow, apparently between 10 and 11." Thring, writing from his own memories of Long Chamber at Eton after eight o'clock at night, says: "Cruel at times the suffering and wrong; wild the profligacy."[2] Drinking, gambling, and even worse excesses were not uncommon. This was, of course, to some extent a reflex of the prevalent moral atmosphere of contemporary society, and some reference to this point was made in the Introduction. Sydney Smith in an essay published in 1810 speaks of the prevalence in the public schools of his day of "a system of premature debauchery" and suggests that they "only prevent men from being corrupted by the world by corrupting them before their entry into the world." But it should be remembered that criticisms of this kind applied mainly to the big boarding schools, and to a far less degree to the ordinary grammar schools, in which most of the pupils were day boys.

The endowed public and grammar schools were not the only type of institution which provided secondary education during this period. There were also private schools. They have left few records or histories and the best pictures of them can be obtained

[1] Vol. xxvi, p. 107. In November 1872 *Punch* again criticised very strongly the cruelty of 'tunding' small boys by the prefects at Winchester. The custom was characterised as "preposterous."

[2] Parkin, *Life and Letters of Edward Thring*, p. 23. Gladstone said that Eton during his schooldays (1821–7) was "the greatest pagan school in Christendom."

from novels—as, for example, those of Thackeray and Dickens. There were always parents who were unwilling to allow their children to mix with the sons of tradesmen at the town endowed school, or too poor to send their boys to a public boarding school, or too apprehensive of the moral dangers and roughness of life to be found there. Thus there was a large demand for the private school, often the property of a clergyman headmaster. It is possible that Dr. Blimber's academy in *Dombey and Son* is a not very exaggerated picture of such a genteel school. In *Vanity Fair* the school attended by Dobbin and Rawdon Crawley is viewed more from the pupil's point of view. At the other end of the scale we have in Squeers' Dotheboys Hall an example of the private school at its worst. These schools varied greatly, both in kind and quality, but in all of them the pupils were much more supervised than in the public schools. The curriculum was modelled on that of the endowed school, but it was not tied by a dead hand—as in the case of Leeds Grammar School, to which reference has been made. This meant that there was greater room for subjects other than the Classics. Again, many of the parents were merchants, business men, or concerned with the rising manufacturing industries; and they created a demand for instruction of the so-called 'useful' kind. Arithmetic, drawing, history and geography, and modern languages more easily found a place in the private school. Much of the information was imparted from books of the catechism type. *Mangnall's Questions*, first published in 1800, is a good example. It survived for nearly a hundred years. The present writer was taught from it at a private school in the nineties of the last century.

There was, however, the possibility of experiment in the private school, and we therefore find occasionally such institutions of a definitely progressive type. Outstanding are those conducted by the Hill family.[1] These were started by Thomas Wright Hill, the father of Rowland Hill, to whom we owe the penny postage, and of Matthew Davenport Hill, who was a criminal law reformer. After some preliminary experiments the

---

[1] There is an excellent account of these schools in Archer, *Secondary Education in the XIX Century*, pp. 90–6. See also *Plans of Government at Hazelwood School* (1825).

Hill family opened a school in 1819 at Hazelwood, near Birmingham, and it was transferred in 1833 to Bruce Castle, Tottenham. Although these schools date from the early years of the nineteenth century, they embody some of the most modern and 'progressive' educational principles. The syllabus was not overloaded. It consisted mainly of the Classics, mathematics, English and French; but, in addition, there was a long list of 'voluntary labours'—options in which a pupil could express himself according to his own individual aptitudes or inclinations. The list included drawing, etching, painting, modelling, printing, surveying, and music. The scheme was systematised by requiring each pupil to complete a given piece of work before any account of it was taken. Marks in the form of dummy coins were given for places in class and for the performance of pieces of optional work; and they were lost for bad work or bad conduct. Thus both in bookish and non-bookish activities the pupil could obtain merit, and marks were credited to him; and the spur of competition was used to encourage the non-academic, as well as the academic, boy. An even greater innovation was that the discipline of the school was administered through the boys themselves. The pupils elected a committee, which drew up the school rules. If anyone infringed these he appeared before a judge and jury, all of whom were boys. Fines could be inflicted on offenders, and they were paid in the dummy coins which had been earned for work. Other punishments were loss of privileges, 'sending to Coventry,' and, in the last resort, confinement in the dark—the French *cachot*. But in every case the penalty was assessed and imposed on the culprit by his own school-fellows. The numerous school societies and social activities—as at 'Churnside'[1] in our own days—were also run by committees composed of the boys themselves. It was a notable experiment, though, being at the time little known, it had few imitators. Yet the system of the Hills has been criticised on the grounds that it tended to produce precocity—"We were premature men," says an old pupil. The over-earnest teacher is perhaps too much inclined to force his plants and make them bloom before their time.

[1] See Simpson, *Sane Schooling*.

The endowed public and grammar schools were available almost exclusively for boys; but most of the girls of the upper and middle classes, who were not educated at home by governesses, attended private schools. A glimpse of one—the school in which Becky Sharp taught—can be obtained in the early pages of *Vanity Fair*. In these girls' schools the pupils learnt to read and write, and some stress was often laid on the domestic arts. But the more socially distinguished the school, the greater was the emphasis on accomplishments which were supposed to give girls something with which to occupy their minds and to make them attractive— for marriage was regarded as the only real career open to them. And so the curriculum was extended to include a smattering of French and Italian, painting and embroidery, singing and instrumental music. All this was supplemented with unco-ordinated facts of general knowledge taught mainly from catechisms. Jane Austen in *Emma* gives a picture of a well-run middle-class girls' school from the latter part of the eighteenth century: "Mrs. Goddard was the mistress of a school—not of a seminary, or an establishment, or anything which professed, in long sentences of refined nonsense, to combine liberal acquirements with elegant morality upon new principles and new systems—where young ladies for enormous pay might be screwed out of health into vanity—but a real honest, old-fashioned Boarding school, where a reasonable quantity of accomplishments were sold at a reasonable price, and where girls might be sent to be out of the way and scramble themselves into a little education, without any danger of coming back prodigies. Mrs. Goddard's school was in high repute, and very deservedly; for Highbury was reckoned a particularly healthy spot; she had an ample house and garden, gave the children plenty of wholesome food, let them run about a great deal in the summer, and in winter dressed their chilblains with her own hands. It was no wonder that a train of twenty young couples now walked after her to church."[1]

It will be realised that, even in a school of the type of Mrs. Goddard's, there was no real attempt to develop the intellect of the girls. Women were, in fact, very generally considered to be

[1] *Emma*, chap. iii; quoted in Percival, *The English Miss*, pp. 86–7.

as a sex intellectually inferior to men—a questionable theory which may even today be rife in some quarters. Mme de Genlis in her *Adèle et Théodore* (1782), one of the most popular books on education in France and England alike, says: "Women are born to a life both monotonous and dependent. In their case genius is a useless and dangerous endowment which takes them out of their natural state."[1] Sydney Smith, in his essay on *Female Education* (1810), takes a much more advanced and, for the time, unusual view: "Why the disproportion in knowledge between the two sexes should be so great, when the inequality in natural talents is so small; or why the understanding of women should be lavished upon trifles, when nature has made it capable of better and higher things, we profess ourselves not able to understand. The affectation charged upon female knowledge is best cured, by making that knowledge more general: and the economy devolved upon women is best secured by the ruin, disgrace, and inconvenience which proceeds (*sic*) from neglecting it."[2] It was only an outstanding feminist like Mary Wollstonecraft, authoress of *Thoughts on the Education of Daughters* (1787) and *A Vindication of the Rights of Women* (1792), who advocated that the course of study should not be determined by the sex of the pupil, and that boys and girls should be educated together. She was greatly influenced by political and educational theories which were fermenting in contemporary France. For the prevailing dependence, superficiality, and affectation among women she seeks to substitute a healthy independence and a desire to share in the work of the world as the companions and co-operators of men. In short, she was more than a hundred years before her time.

[1] *Adèle et Théodore*, letter ix.   [2] Sydney Smith, *Essays*, p. 207.

Chapter III

UNIVERSITY AND FURTHER EDUCATION

Beginnings of Reform at Oxford and Cambridge. Nonconformist Academies;
Joseph Priestley.

UNTIL well within the nineteenth century Oxford and
Cambridge were still the only universities in England.
During the period at present under review they were, in
some ways, in much the same case as the endowed public and
grammar schools. They had made but little advance since the
Renaissance—in fact, there had even been a decline; for with the
revival of learning there had awakened a new enthusiasm for
classical humanism, for the life and spirit of ancient Greece and
Rome. But that impetus had long since spent itself, and, although
great scholars were never altogether lacking, the universities as a
whole had become conventionalised and traditionalised. Instead
of being places of learning they had degenerated to a large extent
into a preserve for the idle and the rich.

Like the endowed grammar schools, the colleges at Oxford and
Cambridge had, for the most part, been founded primarily for the
benefit of poor students who received assistance from endowments. But by the eighteenth century there had grown up the
practice of receiving large numbers of fellow-commoners or
gentlemen-commoners who paid fees and who greatly outnumbered the 'poor scholars.' Undergraduates of noble birth had
the privilege of wearing an embroidered gown of purple silk,
and a college cap with a golden tassel. They were further distinguished from the common herd by being entirely excused the
examinations which led to a degree. Even so, the standard of
these tests was extremely low. In a pamphlet dating from 1773
and written by Dr. John Napleton, Vice-Principal of Brasenose,
the author says: "The public exercises are in truth for the most
part performed in so negligent a manner, that it is equally impossible that they should contribute to the advancement of learning,

to the improvement of the candidate, or to the honour of the University."[1]

Vicesimus Knox, who was headmaster of Tonbridge School from 1778 to 1812 and had previously been a fellow of St. John's College, Oxford, in one of his *Essays*, which has often been quoted, also gives a full and vivid description of the perfunctory requirements for the Oxford degree. He refers to them as a "set of childish and useless exercises" which "raise no emulation, confer no honour and promote no improvement."[2] Knox was a trenchant critic of the universities of his day. In a treatise entitled *Liberal Education*, which appeared in 1789, he gives a startling account of the depths to which they had declined. The section (no. xliii) which deals with "The Present State of the University of Oxford" is headed with the words *Omnia ruunt in pejus*. "Many of those houses," he says, "which the piety and charity of the founders consecrated to religion, virtue, learning, everything useful and lovely, are become the seats of ignorance, infidelity, corruption, and debauchery."[3] University discipline, as administered by proctors and deans, is concerned with externals and trivial regulations, and many of the statutes which the matriculant swears to observe have become utterly obsolete. "With respect to the state of morals, I firmly believe that in no department a worse state exists."[4] The universities were, of course, open to none but members of the Church of England, but the prescribed religious exercises were 'hasty and irreverent.' The tuition is described as pedantic and inefficient, and it "stands in great need of alteration."[5] Residence is far too easily excused; at Oxford an undergraduate can qualify for the degree requirements by spending only thirteen weeks of the year at the University. The rest of the time he can give to field-sports in the country or less desirable dissipation in London. Yet the expenses tend to be far too high, and the standard is set by the idle rich, who form a large proportion of the students. "Who is there that requires to be

[1] Napleton, *Considerations on the Public Exercises for the First and Second Degrees in the University of Oxford*, p. 1.
[2] Vicesimus Knox, *Essays*, no. lxxvii.
[3] Vicesimus Knox, *Liberal Education*, p. 204.
[4] *Op. cit.*, p. 179.   [5] *Op. cit.*, p. 177.

informed that the lower orders imitate the higher; and that by the contagion of example, extravagance becomes universal?"[1] Yet all these abuses are condoned by the authorities, and the universities have become places where great numbers are maintained "who neither study themselves nor concern themselves in superintending the studier of others."[2] We can realise the force of Knox's demand when he says: "Let them therefore be reformed and rendered really useful to the community, or let them be deserted."[3]

In a subsequent letter (1789), addressed to Lord North, the Chancellor of the University of Oxford, Vicesimus Knox sets out detailed suggestions for the reform of the abuses which he had already described in his other works. It seems that Cambridge had hardly descended to such low levels; according to Gibbon she "appears to have been less deeply infected than her sister with the vices of the Cloyster."[4] But Knox and Napleton were not the only champions of university reform at this time. Between 1771 and 1787 there was an agitation to free B.A.s from the statutory statement of adherence to the Church of England. It is not, perhaps, surprising that it failed; but more successful were attempts to reform the curriculum and the tests for degrees. In 1780 Cambridge instituted a written examination in the Senate House. There was still only one tripos, and it consisted mainly of mathematics, which was the chief characteristic of the Cambridge course at this time. At Oxford some advance was made during the last twenty or thirty years of the eighteenth century by three progressive heads of colleges who were strong enough to wear down conservative opposition. In 1800 they carried the 'Public Examination Statute,' which provided for a written examination, as at Cambridge, but also retained the *viva-voce* test. At Oxford Classics formed the staple of the examination, though some mathematics was included. A little later the two honours schools were divided, and a separate pass degree was also instituted. The honours schools soon won a high place in public esteem. A 'first'—and especially a 'double first' in both Classics and mathe-

---

[1] *Op. cit.*, p. 212.   [2] *Op. cit.*, p. 150.   [3] *Op. cit.*, p. 154.
[4] Quoted by Trevelyan, *British History in the Nineteenth Century*, p. 26.

matics—was supposed to mark a man out for high distinction in Church or State. Peel took such a degree in 1808, and Gladstone in 1831. The widening of the curriculum is also shown by the institution at Cambridge during the eighteenth century of a number of new professorships, several of them in scientific subjects. At Oxford the Radcliffe Observatory was founded in 1772, and the professorship of Anglo-Saxon dates from 1795. These facts do not necessarily imply a corresponding broadening of the course taken by the ordinary undergraduate, but at any rate the standards were rising and the outlook was extending.

The two universities were not the sole institutions in England at this period which provided further education; and some reference must now be made to the nonconformist academies. It will be clear from what has been said that almost all forms of education in this country at this time were to a great extent controlled, either directly or indirectly, by the Church of England. Protestant dissenters and Roman Catholics were by law excluded from Oxford and Cambridge. The public schools were church foundations; the headmaster was usually in orders and the chapel services were those of the Established Church. It was much the same with the grammar schools, and even with many of the private schools for middle-class boys. Dr. Blimber and Dr. Swishtail were obviously doctors of divinity and therefore clergymen. As regards elementary education, eleven-twelfths of the charity schools in 1760 were under the control of the parish clergy, and the children of the schools of industry were normally required to attend the parish church on Sundays. In the field of the elementary education of the poor, however, and in the Sunday schools, the nonconformists had always a clearer field and a larger share than in most forms of higher education; and this fact may underlie the 'religious difficulty' of the nineteenth century which affected elementary far more than secondary education. At the same time it was hardly to be expected that nonconformists would be content to allow secondary and further education to lie wholly in the hands of the Church of England; and the nonconformist academies provided the answer to this.

To explain their existence it is necessary to go back a little before the beginning of the period which is at present being considered. The Act of Uniformity (1662) not only excluded dissenters from the universities, but—as has been seen—it required every schoolmaster and private tutor to subscribe to the Liturgy of the Established Church and to hold a licence to teach granted by the bishop of the diocese. This was followed in 1665 by an Act which forbade nonconformists to teach in any public or private school under a penalty of £40. There were similar provisions in an Act of 1713 to 'prevent the Growth of Schism.'[1] But later there was some reaction against these Acts, and the licence to teach was interpreted as applying primarily to grammar schools. This left the field of elementary education open to dissenters, and, as we have already seen, by the latter part of the eighteenth century they ran their own Sunday schools and in some places had charity schools. But the universities were still closed to them, and the endowed public and grammar schools were still the preserve of the Church of England. The object of the nonconformist academy, therefore, was to supply for dissenters a place of higher and further education, and one of its functions was to train candidates for the ministry.

Some of the earliest nonconformist academies had been opened by clergy who had been ejected by the Act of Uniformity. They were among the best intellects of the time and they brought a seriousness and competence to their educational work which were often lacking in the universities. The result was that on the whole the academies reached a higher stage of efficiency than the universities, and were free from many of the moral dangers to which reference has already been made. For these reasons not only dissenters, but also members of the Church of England, often sent their sons to nonconformist academies, both because of the good education which they gave and because, as a rule, no religious tests were imposed upon entrants. Thomas Secker, who was Archbishop of Canterbury from 1758 to 1768, had been a pupil at a nonconformist academy at Tewkesbury early in the century —so also was Bishop Butler, who wrote *The Analogy of Religion*, though he had originally been a Presbyterian. The academy

[1] It is given in Leach, *Educational Charters*, pp. 542-4.

course usually lasted for four years and was of university standard. Instruction was given not only in Classics, logic, philosophy, theology, and Hebrew, but also in mathematics and natural science, and sometimes even in medicine. As an example of a nonconformist academy we may take one of the most famous— that at Warrington, founded about 1757. Though it lasted only until 1783, it had 393 students during its short career. Of these 22 read medicine, 24 law, 52 divinity, and 98 commerce; 197 are unspecified. The commercial course was designed for those who were destined to become merchants or bankers or to take leading positions in industrial concerns. The unspecified courses seem to refer to a generalised unvocational education, such as would be suitable for those designed to be tradesmen or shopkeepers, or to enter the army, or to become country gentlemen. Thus there was in the nonconformist academy a greater breadth as regards both curriculum and social outlook as compared with that of the contemporary University of Oxford or Cambridge.

There is one name which is particularly associated with the work of the nonconformist academies during the period under review—that of Joseph Priestley (1733–1804). His own early history illustrates the educational opportunities open to the dissenter at this time. He was educated first at a free school and then by a Congregational minister; and afterwards, having decided to become a minister himself, he entered an academy at Daventry. Later he became a tutor at the Warrington Academy. It was here that he developed his interest in science. He lectured on this subject and carried on research. In 1764 he became an LL.D. of Edinburgh, for a Scottish university could, of course, give a dissenter a degree. In 1766 he was elected an F.R.S. He achieved a reputation as the discoverer of oxygen and other gases; but his interests were far from being confined to science. He taught Latin, Greek, French, Italian, philosophy, theology, and even made incursions into politics. It was while holding his tutorship at Warrington that he wrote his *Essay on A Course of Liberal Education for Civil and Active Life* (1765), and he followed this up in 1778 with his *Observations relating to Education*. He contends that "the chief and proper object of education is not to form a shining and popular character, but an useful one, this being also the only foundation of real happiness."[1] While he advocates a different type of education specially fitted to the needs of each class in society, he believes that the pursuit of truth and practice of virtue must underlie all education. One can trace alike the non-conformist divine and the man of science in his recommendations. His aims were to a great extent exemplified in the academies themselves. Priestley is no opponent of the Classics, but he realises the value of the vernacular. He himself wrote a *Rudiments of English Grammar* for the use of schools. He also considers a knowledge of French very necessary. Mathematics "ought to be indispensable in every plan of liberal education."[2] The study of history is advocated and geography is associated with it; and it is also desirable that every future citizen should be given some acquaintance with the constitution, laws, and commerce of his country. It was on the basis of this wide general curriculum that the specialised courses in divinity, law, medicine, and science were to be built.

It is possible that the importance of the nonconformist acade-mies in English education has not always been sufficiently recog-nised. They doubtless varied in size and efficiency, in the breadth of their curriculum and the ability of their teachers; and the academy at Warrington and Priestley the scientist may represent the high-lights of the general movement. But there were other excellent academies and first-rate teachers in them, and they kept the torch of true education burning at a time when the two national universities were dormant. The noncomformist acade-mies employed rational teaching methods, they encouraged free-dom of inquiry, they strove to satisfy the needs of the upper middle classes for a practical, modern education which the universities and the public schools made no attempt to supply. They are, indeed, the forerunners of our modern universities which have grown up in commercial or industrial centres. Yet, significant as they are, their career was a short one. They begin soon after the Act of Uniformity—i.e. in the latter decades of the

[1] *Observations*, pp. xiii–xiv.
[2] *Essays*, p. 13.

seventeenth century—but they decline and for the most part disappear towards the end of the eighteenth.

Their decay was due to various reasons. The very freedom of inquiry, which they had made possible and even encouraged, led to a spread of unitarian opinions, and that caused alarm among orthodox nonconformists. Priestley himself favoured these views, and the academy at Warrington was started on frankly rationalistic lines. To combat this tendency some of the academies began—like the universities—to impose a religious test upon all students who entered. This at once split the academies up into narrow sectarian groups, reflecting the various facets of dissent; it tended to restrict their aim and outlook and to introduce inter-denominational rivalry. It also excluded the Church of England students, who—as has been said—in an earlier day had come freely to the academies, attracted by the wider and wiser curriculum and the better moral conditions which were offered. But while these tendencies were at work, Oxford and Cambridge, benighted though they still were, began to awaken from their long torpor. As has been said, they initiated some reforms in their curriculum and their statutes. There was even a movement from inside them for the abolition of religious tests, and although it was not successful it showed the way the wind blew. It seems that at Cambridge dissenters were sometimes allowed to matriculate and reside as undergraduates, though they could not graduate or hold fellowships. Moreover, we are almost in sight now of the movement which led to the foundation of the University of London in 1828, which from the beginning never had any tests and originally left religion entirely outside its curriculum.[1]

[1] For early-nineteenth-century proposals to found a Dissenting University and their relation to the origin of the University of London, see Bellot, *University College, London*, 1826–1926, pp. 20–4.

D

Chapter IV

EDUCATIONAL THEORY

Rousseau Pestalozzi, and Fellenberg; and their influence on English educational thought.

EDUCATIONAL theory is often in advance of educational practice. Sometimes there is little contact between the two because those who theorise have not tested or applied their principles in the actual work and life of the school. Yet even the pure theorist not infrequently has a message for the practitioner who is busied in the daily routine of teaching and has little time to stand aside and look at his work in a detached way; and some of the greatest advances in education have been due to thinkers who had little or no contact with the school itself. That was perhaps more generally true in the past than it is today. During the period with which we are at present concerned teachers of all types tended to be fettered by tradition and convention, or by routine and narrowness of outlook; though, as we have seen and as we shall see again, there were always a few who could rise above the general level and take a higher viewpoint. But the chief impetus to progress came largely from independent thinkers who regarded education either as something due to the individual as an individual, or as a national concern. The fact that many of them were not Englishmen does not lessen their influence upon educational reform in this country. In this chapter and the following one, therefore, we shall discuss some of the theories of education the spirit of which was beginning to stir among the dry bones, and was destined in due course during the nineteenth century and down to our own times to awaken them into life.

For centuries it had been customary to regard the child not so much as an independent personality, with its own special characteristics which determine its development and indicate its treatment, but rather as a miniature adult—a man 'writ small.' This can be illustrated by the fact that in their dress children were exact copies of adults, as can be seen in the pictures and tomb-figures of the seventeenth and eighteenth centuries. And so the education of children tended to be less concerned with what children actually are, and more with what, according to pre-conceived adult standards, they ought to be. The manners and behaviour of children were modelled on the conventions which their elders observed, and few books were written especially for children. The child's education was similarly affected. In the elementary-school curriculum there was little to *interest* him or to provide scope for his natural activities; while the secondary school had a régime which was really suited to an adult mind. If the education of a child could succeed in forcing him to anticipate in the formal school subjects the ordinary achievements of someone a few years older than himself, both he and the system were com-mended. There is in St. Mary's Church, Nottingham, a memorial to Henry Plumptre, who died in 1718 at the age of ten. It proudly proclaims that: "In these few tender years he had to a great degree made himself master of the Jewish, Roman and English History, the Heathen Mythology, and the French Tongue, and was not inconsiderably advanced in Latin." We have not yet fully learned the unwisdom of forcing clever children like hot-house plants; but at any rate the whole weight of educational theory is against this practice, and a real attempt has been made to suit the curriculum to the child, and not the child to the curriculum.

Educational thinkers like Comenius and John Locke in the seventeenth century had already realised that the child himself should be the determining factor in the educational process, but they are by no means typical of their age. A more emphatic and arresting statement of this truth was made by the French writer Jean-Jacques Rousseau (1712–78). His importance in educational history is not simply that he wrote a treatise called *Émile*, which was published in 1762. His influence, and the influence of those whom he influenced, is at work today in every school in this country and wherever Western civilisation has penetrated. He it was who set it finally beyond question that education must accommodate itself to the child, and that the child must not be accommodated to a predetermined, adult-centred system of education. *Émile* is an amazing book, full of exaggerations and inconsistencies and paradoxes; but the mere fact that Rousseau was so provocative and original a writer secured him a wide audience and stirred people to think seriously about the questions which he raised.

Émile has had so much influence on educational thought and practice in this country that it will not be out of place to give some attention to the book itself, and also to the views and activities of some of Rousseau's followers who have also left their mark on English education. Rousseau lays it down that education must be progressive—i.e. it must be accommodated to the various stages of the child's development. When D'Arcy Thompson went to Christ's Hospital in 1835 at the age of seven and a half, there was put into his hands a 'portentously bulky' Latin grammar. "The syntax rules, in the edition presented to me, were, for the first time, rendered mercifully in English; those for gender and quantity remained in the old Latin; and the Latin was communicated in a hideously discordant rhythm. Over a space of years we went, systematically through and through that book; page after page chapter after chapter. It was all unintelligible; all obscure."[1] It was against that sort of régime that Rousseau had made his protest. He even goes on to make the rather startling claim that up to the child's twelfth year he should be given no definite and formal instruction, either intellectual or moral. And he bases his contentions on the fundamental doctrine that education must be 'natural.' It is not always easy to see what exactly Rousseau, and his followers, mean by the term 'nature'; but he seems to regard the action of man as something outside 'nature' and often in opposition to it.

The first sentence of *Émile* in W. H. Payne's English translation reads: "Everything is good as it comes from the hands of the Author of Nature; but everything degenerates in the hands of man."[2] Rousseau holds the doctrine of original goodness, which

[1] D'Arcy W. Thompson, *Daydreams of a Schoolmaster*, p. 4.
[2] "Tout est bien, sortant des mains de l'Auteur des choses: tout dégénère entre les mains de l'homme." Note the word which Payne translates 'Nature.'

is just as misleading as the doctrine of original badness, for children in themselves are not necessarily either good or bad according to adult theories of morality. But, starting from this original-goodness theory, Rousseau has great faith in education according to 'nature.' For instance, he hates towns and would have his pupil Émile brought up in the country away from the contaminating influences of civilisation, which is an artificial product for which man is responsible. He advocates the complete contrary of the educational practice of the day, which has already been illustrated in many of the contemporary schools to which reference has been made. "Take the very reverse of the current custom and you will nearly always do right."[1]

Rousseau divides the intellectual development of the child into three periods. He tends to draw the line too sharply between these periods and to forget that the whole of the child's life is one continuous development. He does not consistently apply his own requirement that education should be 'progressive.' The first stage up to the age of twelve is the 'negative' period. Rousseau starts from the cradle. He condemns swaddling clothes because they hinder the natural movements of the body. The child is to be brought up 'hard'; he is to go bare-foot and is not to be allowed a light in the dark. His education consists in what he can find out for himself; the teacher's work is merely to put the pupil on the way to make his discoveries and so to assist nature. Education is to be effected entirely through the medium of objects and must not be verbal at this stage; for that reason history and literature are forbidden. Rousseau is doubtless justified in stressing the importance of education through sense experience, and in pointing out that one can appeal only to a limited degree to the reason in the case of young children. But the emphasis tends to be one-sided; at the age of twelve Émile would remain little better than an animal with a stock of experiences.

Again, Rousseau pretends to follow nature in isolating the young child from society and putting him in the charge of a tutor—which means, incidentally, that his system could never be adopted generally. He even removes him from his family, which

[1] Payne, Rousseau's *Émile*, p. 60.

is a 'natural' institution if ever there was one. When Émile arrives at the age of twelve this 'negative' period ends and the 'age of intelligence' begins. Even now Rousseau is anxious not to over-work the pupil, and he would not approve of Henry Plumptre's precocious genius. He believes in the Socratic method of telling the pupil directly as little as possible, but encouraging him to find out things for himself. The system was rediscovered a century or so later and given the imposing title of 'heurism.' Rousseau even goes so far as to condemn books, with the excep-tion of *Robinson Crusoe*, which he regards as a kind of treatise on 'natural' education. But the intellectual studies which he recom-mends are not those which were common in contemporary schools; they must be *useful*—for example, astronomy (which probably means little more than finding one's way by the sun and the stars), geography without the assistance of maps made by someone else, object-lessons, a modicum of natural science and of history. At the age of fifteen Émile is to be apprenticed to a trade "less for the sake of knowing the trade than for overcoming the prejudices which despise it."[1] Finally, from fifteen to twenty comes the education of the sentiments. After puberty the passions begin to awaken and Émile is at last introduced into the society of his fellows and helped to learn his duties towards them. Educa-tion is now moral and religious; Émile must eschew evil and do good, but this must be inculcated through contact with his fellows. Now, too, he can study the ways of men in literature, history, and art. At the age of eighteen the existence of God is revealed to him because he is capable of forming an abstract conception which before was impossible. If Émile had been a normal child he would probably have begun to ask questions about a First Cause long before this age. It may be sound educa-tionally to give the child a concrete, anthropomorphic idea of God, such as he can understand, when his mind first awakens to these problems, and to ætherialise and philosophise the idea as he grows older.

Throughout his treatise Rousseau is thinking of a boy—Émile; but as a kind of appendix to it he adds a fifth book on the educa-

[1] *Op. cit.*, p. 178.

tion of Sophie, who is to be Émile's helpmeet when his education is over. She is to be brought up, not by a tutor in the isolation of the country, but by her mother in the home. She is not allowed to become too intellectual, but she may mix with the world and even go to balls and theatres. Rousseau advocates more liberty for girls than for married women—the opposite of what happens in France, "where girls live in convents and women frequent the world."[1] This may be just another example of Rousseau's inherent tendency to challenge contemporary custom and tradition in education. But his whole conception of Sophie is that she is designed solely for Émile; the end of woman, according to him, is to please man, and she is not regarded as an independent being. The fifth book adds nothing to the value of Rousseau's treatise.

It is the spirit rather than the letter of *Émile* which gave life. Its details could never have been fully or widely applied, but it expressed a protest against contemporary educational theory and practice; and in spite of its exaggerations and extravagances— perhaps, because of them—it exerted a great influence. The followers of Rousseau were innumerable, and so were those who opposed him or who took his theories and altered or improved them. One of those who did much to popularise and develop and modify Rousseau's ideas and who—though mainly indirectly— had much influence on education in this country was the Swiss Pestalozzi (1746–1827). He was born at Zürich and educated at the university there. From 1774 to 1780 he tried to run a farm at Neuhof, and in connection with it started a school for destitute children where agricultural labour might be combined with elementary education. This was, in fact, a school of industry, but it could not be made self-supporting and it had to be closed. In 1798 Pestalozzi was asked by the Government to open a school for homeless orphans at Stans, on the Lake of Lucerne. Here he introduced lessons in the three 'R's,' together with industrial work and physical education, which included both play and drill. In 1799 he was given charge of an infant school for boys and girls, aged five to eight, and by this time he had produced most of the books in

[1] *Op. cit.*, p. 282.

which his educational views are set forth. These had excited considerable attention and brought Pestalozzi into touch with some of the most progressive thinkers of the time. Finally, from 1805 to 1825, Pestalozzi conducted a school at Yverdon which became an object of interest to educationists throughout Europe. It was visited, among others, by Robert Owen and Henry Brougham, of whom more will be said later. But Pestalozzi was no administrator; there were financial difficulties as well as public and private misunderstandings, and the Yverdon institute declined until it had to be closed.

We can gather some general idea of Pestalozzi's educational theories from his books, for he was a prolific writer. He expounds his methods and principles chiefly in *Leonard and Gertrude* and *How Gertrude teaches her Children*. He regards education as the development and cultivation of the possibilities native to the human being—a theory which, as we have seen, was certainly not being put into practice in the majority of contemporary schools. The educator's duty is to assist 'nature's march of development' so as to secure a natural, symmetrical, and harmonious progress. From this Pestalozzi deduces that education must be religious, since man has a divine origin and end and is therefore by *nature* concerned with religion—he goes far beyond Rousseau in this respect; education must also develop the *whole* man—"the head, the hand and the heart"; and it must encourage and guide self-activity, because it is life and experience which educate. We might be describing the principles which underlie the modern nursery-school régime.

Pestalozzi also lays it down that education must be based on *Anschauung*—a term which is often translated 'intuition,' but more nearly means 'observation' or 'sense-impression.' This is not the place to develop Pestalozzi's philosophy of education; but it should be said that he applies his doctrine of *Anschauung* even to the sphere of morals. What he means is that ethical teaching should not be based on precepts or codes or catechisms, on which too much reliance was placed by contemporary practice. The child must learn of the goodness of God or the rightness of truth and kindness from his actual experience; and the educator's job is not to inculcate or propagandise, but so to direct the child that he may obtain this experience. As Pestalozzi himself said, he taught neither morality nor religion, but he strove to arouse the sentiment of each virtue before pronouncing its name. And because morality is ultimately concerned with social relationships, children can best learn it in the home. Pestalozzi did his utmost to reproduce the home atmosphere even in his school for destitute orphans at Stans. "Every assistance," he says, "everything done for them in their need, all the teaching that they received, came directly from me; my hand lay on their hand, my eye rested on their eye. My tears flowed with theirs, and my smile accompanied theirs. Their food was mine, and their drink was mine. I had nothing, no housekeeping, no friends, no servants; I had them alone. I slept in their midst; I was the last to go to bed at evening, and the first to rise in the morning. I prayed with them, and taught them in bed before they went to sleep."[1]

There are many obvious points of contrast between the views of Pestalozzi and of Rousseau; but it is equally obvious that the former owes much to the latter. Both agree in believing in the child as a child, and in basing education on his nature and needs, and not on some preconceived theory. But Pestalozzi is more human than Rousseau; his emphasis on the home and on brotherly love shows that. His whole life was devoted to the service of poor children. The inscription on his tombstone reads: "Alles für andere; für sich nichts."

Another Swiss educationist, Philipp von Fellenberg (1771–1844), who was for a time associated with Pestalozzi and much influenced by him, had more direct effect on educational ideas in this country than had Pestalozzi himself. In 1799 Fellenberg opened a school for poor children at Hofwyl, not far from Berne. It was an avowed attempt to put Pestalozzi's theories into practice, and it had much in common with the Neuhof experiment. But it was eventually developed so as to include an intermediate school for the sons of farmers, and an upper school for 'better-class' pupils. Fellenberg emphasised the need for suitable preparation in all classes of society; upright leaders and employers

[1] See Green, *Educational Ideas of Pestalozzi*, p. 185.

were just as necessary as reliable and honest workers. For the children of peasants in the 'Poor School' great stress was laid on agricultural work and only two hours a day were given to such intellectual labours as the three 'R's,' nature study, drawing, and singing. So that this too was in a sense a 'school of industry'; but it was organised for purely educational ends and not designed to make profit. In the intermediate school a scientific and theoretical training was given, which, though practical and industrial, included a good deal more intellectual work than did the 'Poor School.' The upper school taught Classics, modern languages, science, drawing, music, physical drill, and practical work. Hofwyl also included a training college for teachers and a summer school for the improvement of village schoolmasters. But it was all one establishment and one society. Thus it was designed as a small-scale copy of the world itself with its class distinctions which Fellenberg regarded as divinely ordained. But he laid great stress on religious and moral education and, like Pestalozzi, he believed that true moral training comes from social contacts—the relations between the individual pupils in their common life. This is the theory upon which good modern schools are run; and if it is contrasted with the practice of most of the contemporary schools in this country, which has already been described, the importance of such practical theorists as Pestalozzi and Fellenberg may be realised.

The educational influence of Rousseau and his followers was at first felt more on the Continent than in England. But their theories excited much interest here also. Thomas Day (1748–1789), the author of *Sandford and Merton*, even went so far as to bring up two orphan girls—a blonde and a brunette—on Rousseau-ian lines, with the idea of marrying the one which turned out better. In the end he married neither. More important were Day's friend R. L. Edgeworth (1744–1817) and his daughter Maria, who did much to popularise in this country, and to adapt, the ideas of Rousseau. R. L. Edgeworth married four times and had eighteen children, of whom Maria was the eldest; so that he had at hand plenty of raw material for educational experiment. In 1798, in collaboration with his daughter Maria, he produced

Practical Education; and he followed this with *Professional Education* in 1809. He tries to apply and to modify the theories of Rousseau, though his work is also greatly influenced by the English philosopher Locke. Edgeworth agrees with Rousseau that we should study the child himself, and shape the curriculum and our teaching methods to the child's needs as we discover them during his growth. Learning should be made attractive and memory work diminished; occupations should be rendered interesting and varied, and self-activity encouraged. Edgeworth advocates the acquirement of positive knowledge through observation and the cultivation of habits of attention. He lays great stress on handwork and gives a prominent place to utility as a standard for estimating the value of any particular study. This point is exemplified in the very title of his treatise—'*Practical*' *Education*.

Chapter V

PHILOSOPHICAL, POLITICAL, ECONOMIC, AND RELIGIOUS THEORIES AFFECTING EDUCATION

The Enlightenment and the Revolution. Adam Smith and Malthus.
Wesleyanism.

IN the last chapter we have discussed some of the more important theories which were being put forward by educational thinkers and practitioners in the latter part of the eighteenth century. They were spread partly by the influence of books and partly by the example of the experimental institutions in which attempts were made to put them into practice. But we can also discern contemporary philosophical, political, economic, or religious theories which are not specifically educational, but which, none the less, tended to affect the course of educational ideas and ultimately also the practice of the schools themselves.

A great deal of the most potent philosophical and political thinking of the time was being done in France. The movement known as the 'Enlightenment' had its roots in England, and Locke is an early representative of it; but it is particularly marked and particularly interesting in France, perhaps because of its relation to the Revolution. It sought its illumination from the light of reason; authority and tradition were pushed aside or discarded altogether. Free play was demanded for the individual judgment and a protest was made against anything metaphysical or transcendental or beyond the interpretation of ordinary experience. This was the viewpoint of the famous French *Encyclopædia* (published 1751–65), which aimed at making recent scientific discoveries available in such a manner as to destroy superstitious notions about nature. The editor was Diderot; and Voltaire, Rousseau, and Montesquieu were among the contributors. The *Encyclopædia* caused much fluttering in orthodox circles; for it was a small step from this advocacy of reason to an opposition to vested interests, superstition, and tyranny. A state of society was pictured, free from clerical influence and ruled by universal benevolence; everyone would have equal rights and be able to attain the fullest self-realisation. Pushed to their logical conclusion, these doctrines had very important educational consequences; they implied that education should be withdrawn from the control of the Church (which, of course, in contemporary France, no less than in England, was paramount in every branch of education), and that a State system should be set up.

That step was advocated by La Chalotais in his *Essai d'Éducation Nationale* (1763). He was a lawyer. The Society of Jesus had been expelled from France in 1762 and the local *parlements* were drawing up educational schemes designed to fill the gaps caused by the closing down of the Jesuit colleges. The plan put forward by La Chalotais is one of these schemes—and the best known. The very title gives the author's position—*Éducation 'Nationale'*; secular education is a State concern. He says: "I claim the right to demand for the nation an education that will depend upon the State alone because it belongs essentially to it; because every nation has an inalienable and imprescriptible right to instruct its members; and finally because the children of the State should be educated by the members of the State."[1] Teachers are to be laymen. Moral instruction may be given in the schools, but religious teaching is to be left to the home and the churches. Thus with La Chalotais there emerges the conception of the lay, secular, State school, which has since become a reality in France. It was an idea which profoundly affected English Liberal views on education during the nineteenth century.

Although the Encyclopædists demanded a system of secular schools controlled by the State, they were not all in complete sympathy with 'universal' education—i.e. popular and compulsory. But there were some educationists of the time who went the whole way. Rolland d'Erceville,[2] for example, another lawyer, who in 1768 presented his *Compte Rendu* to the *Parlement de Paris*, says: "Everyone ought to have the opportunity to receive

---

[1] La Chalotais, *Éducation Nationale*, translated by F. de la Fontainerie in *French Liberalism and Education in the Eighteenth Century*, p. 53. See also Barnard, *The French Tradition in Education*, chap. vii.

[2] The name is sometimes spelt 'Roland.'

the education which is adapted to his need. Education cannot be too widely diffused."[1] These projects for "education—universal, compulsory, gratuitous, and secular"—were much debated in the National Assembly during the French Revolution. The movement was prolific in educational schemes, though its actual achievements were less remarkable. But at every stage politics and education were closely connected, and that meant that people in England who were affected by the political doctrines of the Revolution tended also to be affected by its educational theories. For example, those among the middle and upper classes in this country who, as the Revolution progressed, were horrified at the excesses of the mob and who deplored the spread of republicanism and deism or atheism, were inclined to blame the withdrawal of the old restraints and therefore to oppose any extension of popular education which might encourage further licence. On the other hand, among those in this country who saw some good underlying what the Revolution stood for, there grew up a body of opinion which favoured State action in popular education, or which wanted to separate secular from religious teaching or to make school attendance compulsory. Not every reformer adopted the complete programme, and secular education, in particular, has never been officially adopted in this country. But, as an example of a highly respectable advocate of the rest of the formula—'universal, compulsory, and gratuitous'—we may take the poet Wordsworth. He was at Cambridge when the French Revolution broke out, and he spent two long vacations in France. As is not infrequent among undergraduates, he reacted considerably towards the Left.

> Bliss was it in that dawn to be alive,
> But to be young was very Heaven![2]

Even though Wordsworth outlived some of his youthful enthusiasms he did not abandon the views on popular education which are particularly associated with the Revolution. As late as 1814 he gave expression to them in the last two books of the *Excursion*. They probably influenced English opinion in this

[1] *Recueil*, p. 25.   [2] Wordsworth, *Prelude*, bk. xi, 108–9.

direction as much as, if not more than, the writings of contemporary economists and political philosophers. The following lines are particularly significant:

> O for the coming of that glorious time
> When, prizing knowledge as her noblest wealth
> And best protection, this imperial Realm,
> While she exacts allegiance, shall admit
> An obligation, on her part, to teach
> Them who are born to serve her and obey;
> Binding herself by statute to secure
> For all the children whom her soil maintains
> The rudiments of letters, and inform
> The mind with moral and religious truth.[1]

Besides theorists like Wordsworth there were the more definitely advowed economic or political thinkers. Adam Smith (1723–1790), for example, had travelled in France during the sixties of the eighteenth century, and had been much influenced by the Enlightenment and the Encyclopædists. In 1776 appeared his *Wealth of Nations*. In it he points out that the common people, the labouring poor, are engaged on deadening, routine tasks which cause them to degenerate both physically and morally; he is already aware of the effects of the Industrial Revolution to which reference has been made. He says: "A man without the proper use of the intellectual faculties of a man is, if possible, more contemptible than even a coward, and seems to be mutilated and deformed in a still more essential part of the character of human nature. Though the State was to derive no advantage from the instruction of the inferior ranks of the people, it would still deserve its attention that they should not be altogether uninstructed. The State, however, derives no inconsiderable advantage from their instruction. The more they are instructed, the less liable they are to the delusions of enthusiasm and superstition, which among ignorant nations frequently occasion the most dreadful disorders. An instructed and intelligent people, besides, are always more

[1] Wordsworth, *The Excursion*, bk. ix, 293–302.

decent and orderly than a stupid one. They feel themselves, each individually, more respectable and more likely to obtain the respect of their lawful superiors. They are more disposed to examine, and are more capable of seeing through, the interested complaints of faction and sedition, and they are, upon that account, less apt to be misled into any wanton or unnecessary opposition to the measures of government. In free countries, where the safety of government depends very much upon the favourable judgment which the people may form of its conduct, it must surely be of the highest importance that they should not be disposed to judge rashly or capriciously concerning it."[1] Adam Smith therefore advocates a minimum of instruction for everyone —reading, writing, and mathematics. Physical training is prescribed so as to counteract the adverse effects of indoor occupations. "For a very small expense the public can facilitate, can encourage, and can even impose upon almost the whole body of the people, the necessity of acquiring these most essential parts of education." To achieve this end he proposes the establishment of district schools, maintained partly at public expense and partly by fees. Attendance is to be made only indirectly compulsory by the institution of an examination for entrance to a trade or profession. Adam Smith is often regarded as an out-and-out exponent of *laissez-faire*; but here he appears as an advocate— though perhaps a little half-hearted—of the free and universal State education, which was being preached by the most advanced theorists in contemporary France.

Thomas Paine (1737–1809), the pamphleteer of the revolutionary party in England, went further still. His *Rights of Man* (1791–2) was described as "an answer to Mr. Burke's attack on the French Revolution." Paine asserts that "a nation under a well-regulated government should permit none to remain uninstructed."[2] He proposes to substitute for poor relief a grant of £4 a year for each child under fourteen years of age, "enjoining the parents of such children to send them to school, to learn reading, writing, and common arithmetic. . . . By adopting this

---

[1] Adam Smith, *Wealth of Nations*, bk. v, chap. i, pt. iii, art. 2.
[2] Paine, *Rights of Man*, pt. ii, 'Combining Principles and Practice,' p. 131.

method, not only the poverty of the parents will be relieved, but ignorance will be banished from the rising generation, and the number of the poor will hereafter become less, because their abilities by the aid of education will be greater."[1] For parents, "who, though not properly of the class of poor, yet find it difficult to give education to their children."[2] an allowance of ten shillings a year should be made in respect of each child, in order to meet the expense of schooling, and in addition half a crown for the purchase of paper and spelling-books. The actual provision of schools Paine leaves to individual effort and so avoids putting on the State any responsibility for the kind of instruction which is given.

William Godwin (1756–1836), on the other hand, who married Mary Wollstonecraft, does not believe in any kind of State interference in education. In his *Enquiry concerning Political Justice* (1793) he regards government as an evil, and denounces its laws, regulations, and punishments. He thinks that a State system of education would check the growth of free opinion and perpetuate dogma and tradition. Thus it was possible for the ferment of the French Revolution to work against, as well as for, popular education.

Some reference should be made to T. R. Malthus (1766–1834), author of a famous *Essay on Population* which appeared in 1798. He opposes the doctrine of human equality which had been proclaimed by the Revolution in its slogan "Liberté; Égalité; Fraternité." He asserts that inequality is a patent fact and is a result of the natural law that increasing population tends to outstrip the means of subsistence. This operates as a check and involves a great deal of misery. Indiscriminate charity is no solution; each individual must exercise restraint and foresight, and in order to do that he must be educated; hence the necessity for public instruction. "We have lavished immense sums on the poor, which we have every reason to think have constantly tended to aggravate their misery." [Malthus is thinking of poor-relief as administered by the Speenhamland scheme which dates from 1795.[3]] "But in their education and in the circulation of those important political

---

[1] *Op. cit.*, p. 127.   [2] *Op. cit.*, p. 131.   [3] See *supra*, p. xiv.

E

truths that most nearly concern them, which are perhaps the only means in our power of really raising their condition and of making them happier men and more peaceful subjects, we have been miserably deficient. It is surely a great national disgrace that the education of the lowest classes of people should be left entirely to a few Sunday schools, supported by a subscription from individuals who can give to the course of instruction in them any kind of bias which they please. And even the improvement in Sunday schools (for, objectionable as they are in some points of view, and imperfect in all, I cannot but consider them as an improvement) is of very late date."[1] Malthus therefore believes that popular education is the surest means of safeguarding against the "false declamation of interested and ambitious demagogues." He even suggests that the principles of political economy should be taught in the schools of the poor, so that they may acquire the right, scientific outlook.

The stagnation and apathy of much of the Church of England during the latter part of the eighteenth century have already been mentioned; but there were, none the less, during this period some religious movements which had their influence on education. John Wesley (1703–91) had been educated at Charterhouse and afterwards became a fellow of Lincoln College, Oxford. From about 1740 onwards he travelled about the country, preaching justification by faith and directing people's attention to the simple truths set out in the gospels. He was most successful in the centres of crowded population in the new manufacturing areas; and Methodism did much to civilise and educate their inhabitants. It also helped to further the Sunday-school movement. Raikes, who—as we have seen—was its chief exponent, began his work in 1780; but already in 1769 a Methodist minister had started a Sunday school at High Wycombe in Buckinghamshire. Methodism's stress on a personal religion founded on the Bible implied certain intellectual requirements; the individual must be taught to read and understand and search the inspired Scriptures if he was to be able to make them a personal possession and so achieve salvation. It was for this reason that Protestantism generally

[1] Malthus, *Essay on Population*, vol. iii, pp. 203–4 (bk. iv, chap. ix).

tended to encourage popular education; the same phenomenon can be seen in the educational history of, for example, Germany, Holland, and Scotland.

Again, the democratic organisation of Methodism, with its local preachers and lay administrators, helped to train up among the workers a generation which later was to take a lead in the struggle for political reform. As Trevelyan well says: "Many of the more self-respecting of the new proletariat found in the Baptist or Wesleyan chapel the opportunity for the development of talents and the gratification of instincts that were denied expression elsewhere. The close and enthusiastic study of the Bible educated the imagination more nobly than it is educated in our age of magazines, novelettes, and newspapers. And in chapel life working-men first learnt to speak and to organise, to persuade and to trust, their fellows. Much effort that soon afterwards went into political, trade-union, and co-operative activities was then devoted to the chapel community. It was in little Bethel that many of the working-class leaders were trained. In a world made almost intolerable by avarice and oppression, here was a refuge where men and things were taken up aloft and judged by spiritual and moral standards that forbade either revenge or despair."[1] It was not only through the work of the academies that during this period nonconformity was making an important contribution to English education.

Methodism at first made its headway among the poor. The upper classes remained hostile to it, and the Church of England choked it out, so that it joined its vigour and enthusiasm to that of the older dissenting bodies. But eventually Methodism reacted even on the more exalted circles inside the Church of England itself. Those who were influenced by the movement which it started included the poet Cowper, the authoress Hannah More, who with her sisters founded successful village schools in the Mendip district, and William Wilberforce, who is well known in connection with the abolition of the slave trade in 1806. All these were zealously affected in good works; but although their evangelicalism brought philanthropy and uprightness into

[1] Trevelyan, *British History in the Nineteenth Century*, p. 160.

quarters where they had been little known before, it had its inconsistencies. It was alive to the sufferings of the slaves overseas, but tended to take a biased view of the misery of the poor in this country. It suggested that this was due, not to callous and grasping landlords and employers, but to irreligion or lack of submission to authority. Inequalities of fortune in this world must be accepted without demur because they would be redressed in the next. Thus the attitude of evangelicalism, for all its piety and good works, tended to be condescendingly philanthropic. The best that we can say of it—and this is a good deal—is that it emphasised the importance of high standards of personal conduct, and it inculcated in the upper classes a new sense of responsibility towards social and educational reform. It paved the way for, and is largely responsible for, the rise of the voluntary movement in English education in the early part of the nineteenth century.

EDUCATION DURING THE FIRST PART OF THE NINETEENTH CENTURY

Chapter VI

ELEMENTARY EDUCATION

The Monitorial System: Bell and Lancaster. Robert Owen, Wilderspin and Stow.

IN Part A of this book an attempt has been made to give an account of education in England during the latter part of the eighteenth century and on the threshold of the nineteenth. There is a dark background to the picture—the degradation and sufferings of the poor, especially in the large towns. The educational ideal of the time was the training of the poor to an honest and industrious poverty which knew its place and was duly appreciative of any favours received. But, as has been seen, there were many forces for change at work, and conspicuous among them was the philosophical movement for freedom, inspired largely by Rousseau and subsequent thinkers in France and elsewhere, and expressed in this country by many social and philanthropic campaigns. Thus even among people who were not particularly interested in the political and economic aspects of the problem there was a growing recognition of the neglect and danger into which the children of the poor had fallen, and a search for some means to remedy this situation.

What seemed to be the solution to the problem was discovered early in the nineteenth century. A scheme emerged for providing popular education on a large scale and by a method which fitted in well with the economic and industrial ideas of the time. This method is known as the monitorial, or mutual, system, and in its essence it consisted in setting children to teach children. It was not entirely new; it must have been used in families from time immemorial. It had even been put into practice at the public schools, for the præpositors and prefects at Winchester and Eton were not only policeman and informers, but also at times pupil-teachers. A record relating to Eton and dating from 1530 says: "The Vth. forme learn the versyfycall rules of Sulpicius gevyn in ye mornyng of some of the VIth. forme, and this Vth.

forme gevyth rulys to the fowrth."[1] But the introduction of the method on a large and organised scale is due to two men, Andrew Bell and Joseph Lancaster, who seem to have hit upon the device by accident and to have made their discovery independent of each other.

Bell (1753–1832) was a clergyman of the Established Church. While serving as a missionary in Madras he had been forced by shortage of staff, in a school of which he had charge, to put classes in the care of some senior pupils. When he returned to England he published pamphlets describing his experiments, and his scheme was tried out successfully in some parochial charity schools. Meanwhile Joseph Lancaster (1778–1838), who was a Quaker, had opened a private school in Southwark. As the numbers increased he moved to larger premises in Borough Road and made use of monitors as a means of helping to keep all the children occupied. "When a child was admitted, a monitor assigned him to his class; while he remained, a monitor taught him (with nine other pupils); when he was absent, one monitor ascertained the fact, and another found out the reason; a monitor examined him periodically, and when he made progress a monitor promoted him; a monitor ruled the writing paper; a monitor made or mended the pens; a monitor had charge of the slates and books; and a monitor-general looked after all the other monitors."[2] By such means the number of children ultimately in the charge of a single adult could be greatly increased. All that the master did was to organise, to reward or to punish, and to 'inspire' the monitors. It is possible that in working out the scheme Lancaster was helped by the published account of Bell's experiments in Madras—though this has been questoned.[3] Some influential members of the Society of Friends interested themselves in Lancaster's school, and before long its numbers were over 800, while

[1] Quoted by Leach in *Encyclopædia of Education* (ed. Foster Watson), vol. iii, p. 1332. See also Maxwell Lyte, *A History of Eton College*, pp. 139 and 142.

[2] Salmon, *Joseph Lancaster*, p. 7. There is a full account of the organisation of a monitorial school, with illustrations, in Birchenough, *History of Elementary Education in England and Wales*, pp. 283–96. See also Binns, *A Century of Education*, chaps. i and ii.

[3] But see Lancaster's own acknowledgment of his debt to Bell in *Improvements in Education*, pp. 64–5.

the annual cost of educating each child was barely a guinea and could be further reduced if the numbers increased, because the 'overhead' expenses remained practically stationary. Lancaster gave an account of his work in *Improvements in Education*, which was published in 1803. His school in the Borough Road became one of the sights of London. "Foreign princes, ambassadors, peers, commoners, ladies of distinction, bishops and archbishops, Jews and Turks, all visited it with wonder-waiting eyes."[1] Donations poured in, and even the King became an annual subscriber to the funds.

In the monitorial school the headmaster was in sole charge. He taught the monitors only, and they passed on the instruction which they had received. The subject-matter was carefully graded, but it was very elementary. The whole technique was mechanical; there was no opportunity for the asking of questions nor, of course, for the development of individuality. In fact, the system was one of mass production in education. Professor Adamson quotes a contemporary writer, who says: "The grand principle of Dr. Bell's system is the division of labour applied to intellectual purposes. . . . The principle in manufactories and schools is the same."[2] In short, it substituted machinery for personality and forced facts into the pupils' memory in a purely mechanical way. Yet up to a point it worked. The children did learn something; they were taught to be quiet and orderly; and above all the system was cheap. This argument was used by Samuel Whitbread, who in 1807 introduced a Parochial Schools Bill into the House of Commons. Among its provisions was the establishment of rate-aided parochial schools "because within a few years there has been discovered a plan for the instruction of youth which is now brought to a state of great perfection; happily combining rules, by which the object of learning must be infallibly attained with expedition and cheapness."[3] The measure proposed to provide two years of free schooling

---

[1] Corston, *Life of Lancaster*, p. 11.
[2] See Adamson, *English Education*, 1789–1902, p. 24. The quotation is from Bernard, *Of the Education of the Poor*, pp. 34–35 and 36.
[3] *Hansard*, vol. viii, 984, 1051.

for children between the ages of seven and fourteen who could not pay fees.

Opposition was strong, not only on the ground of the cost of the proposal, but because it was feared that it would undermine the monopoly of the Church in education. When the Bill came before the House of Lords, the Archbishop of Canterbury said that "it would go to subvert the first principles of education in this country, which had hitherto been, and he trusted would continue to be, under the control and auspices of the Establishment."[1] There was also a feeling that the spread of education might make the lower classes discontented. In the Commons debate Mr. Davies Giddy said: "However specious in theory the project might be of giving education to the labouring classes of the poor, it would be prejudicial to their morals and happiness; it would teach them to despise their lot in life, instead of making them good servants in agriculture and other laborious employments. Instead of teaching them subordination, it would render them fractious and refractory, as was evident in the manufacturing counties; it would enable them to read seditious pamphlets, vicious books, and publications against Christianity; it would render them insolent to their superiors; and in a few years the legislature would find it necessary to direct the strong arm of power towards them."[2] That perhaps was typical of the attitude of the landowners and farmers towards popular education, and Whitbread's Bill did not pass. But it is an important sign of the times, for it was the forerunner of a series of proposals which culminated in the Elementary Education Act of 1870.

Meanwhile the monitorial schools were giving rise to a controversy which was destined to rage all through the nineteenth century; its echoes have hardly yet died away. Lancaster was a nonconformist, Bell a clergyman of the Church of England. Lancaster's system, though it included Bible teaching, was frankly unsectarian; and its rapid success alarmed the Church party. The controversy flared up, owing to the activities of Mrs. Sarah

[1] *Hansard*, vol. ix, 1178 (Aug. 11th, 1807).
[2] *Ibid.*, vol. ix, 798 (July 13th, 1807).

Trimmer, who had already shown her interest in education by founding a Sunday school at Brentford and by writing books for children and for teachers. In 1805 she published a book in which she accused Lancaster of having borrowed everything of value in his system from Bell, and asserted that the development of his schools was a menace to the "System of Christian Education founded by our pious Forefathers for the Initiation of the Young Members of the Established Church in the Principles of the Reformed Religion."[1] There was a great outcry. Her views were condemned by the Whigs and the *Edinburgh Review*,[2] and upheld by the Tories, the Church, and the *Quarterly*. We are already embarked on the 'religious difficulty' which almost ever since has been the chief obstacle to the evolution of elementary education in this country. The cleavage between Bell and Lancaster was emphasised by the formation of two societies. In 1811 was founded the "National Society for promoting the Education of the Poor in the Principles of the Established Church throughout England and Wales." It took over the charity schools which had been sponsored since the early days of the eighteenth century by the S.P.C.K. Considerable financial support was forthcoming. The Universities of Oxford and Cambridge each gave £500, and by 1830 some 346,000 children were receiving an elementary education in Church schools assisted by the National Society. As a condition of receiving aid from the Society it was necessary to follow the monitorial system as laid down by Bell, to give the pupils instruction in the Liturgy and Catechism of the Church of England, and to take them to church regularly on Sundays. At the same time there was, in some schools at least, a conscience clause which allowed nonconformist children to be withdrawn from religious instruction.

The Royal Lancasterian Association was formally constituted in 1810. Four years later it was renamed The British and Foreign School Society. Lancaster—like Pestalozzi—was no man of business; and he was also extravagant and given to display; but

---

[1] Part of the title of her book.

[2] In the *Edinburgh Review* of 1806 there is a slashing review of Mrs. Trimmer's book by Sydney Smith—himself a clergyman of the English Church.

with the help of men like Brougham, Whitbread, William Wilberforce, and James Mill, his schemes were developed and his methods began to spread to the Continent and to the colonies. This fact explains the word 'Foreign' in the title of the society. A training school for teachers was opened at Borough Road. It still exists, though it was moved to new premises at Isleworth in 1890.[1] It had a model school attached to it. All the elementary schools aided by the British and Foreign School Society were open to children of any denomination, for in them no distinctive sectarian religious teaching was given; but the pupils were required to attend a place of worship on Sundays.

It may be said with justice that Bell and Lancaster between them created the English elementary school of the nineteenth century. They determined its mechanical methods, its low standards, its large classes and mass production, its emphasis on cheapness, its low ideals of education. But its system of dividing the pupils into groups—instead of the master teaching a few pupils separately while the rest wasted their time—was something of an innovation which has proved of permanent value. Also the monitorial schools did popularise elementary education, and therefore, for all their shortcomings, they achieved a great social work. The National Society and the British and Foreign School Society have survived to the present day.

In addition to the activities of these two societies there were other early-nineteenth-century movements for the education of the poor. One of the most important is that which was started by Robert Owen (1771–1858).[2] He was born at Newtown in Montgomeryshire, and showed such early precocity that at the age of seven he was helping his schoolmaster. He left school at eleven and was apprenticed to a draper—one Mr. McGuffog. He had already decided that "there must be something fundamentally wrong in all religions as they had been taught up to that period."[3]

---

[1] The women's side had been transferred to Stockwell in 1861. This training college is also still in existence.

[2] There is a good account of Robert Owen and his work in *Social and Political Ideas of the Age of Reaction and Reconstruction* (ed. Hearnshaw), chap. v.

[3] Owen, *Life of Robert Owen*, p. 5.

He soon showed great business ability and rapidly forged ahead. In 1790 he became a cotton spinner in Manchester, and in 1799 bought for himself and his partners some cotton mills at New Lanark, near Glasgow. He withdrew from this venture in 1829, and from then until his death he was continually engaged in propaganda on behalf of co-operation and socialism, using his private fortune for the diffusion of his ideas. He believed that man is entirely the creature of circumstance—environment controls development, and therefore social problems can be solved by providing environment of the right kind. "Any character," he says, "from the best to the worst, from the most ignorant to the most enlightened, may be given to any community, even to the world at large, by the application of proper means; which means are to a great extent at the command and under the control of those who have influence in the affairs of men";[1] and again: "Human nature is one and the same in all . . . by judicious training the infants of any one class in the world may be readily transformed into men of any other class."[2] Owen takes no account of innate qualities or heredity, and therefore for him education is all-powerful. These ideas were by no means new. A French philosopher Helvétius (1715–71), for example, had already uttered the famous dictum "L'éducation peut tout."

Robert Owen tried to put his ideas into practice by organising his rough and ignorant factory community at New Lanark under a kind of paternal government. He fixed the minimum age for employment there at ten, and provided free schools for his workers' children between the ages of five and ten. These schools were at first worked mainly on the Lancasterian plan; but Owen got into touch with some of the most progressive educationists of his day both here and on the Continent, and his schools were never mere mechanical monitorial institutions. Lessons were given in the three 'R's,' geography and history, nature study, dancing, singing and drill. Punishment was avoided, and stress was laid on mutual goodwill and social service. In 1816 he also opened an infant school—the first in Great Britain and the fore-

[1] Owen, *First Essay on the Formation of Character*, p. 3.
[2] *Idem, Fourth Essay on the Formation of Character*, p. 72.

runner of the modern nursery school. Children as young as one and a half years were received. Instruction was given mainly by conversations or by objects displayed—e.g. pictures of animals. The infants were occupied with dancing and singing and games. Owen provided classes in the evening, after working hours, for his apprentices, of whom he had some five hundred, and the schools were also used as a social centre for the employees in their leisure time. It is not surprising that New Lanark was visited by social reformers from all parts of the world.

Education was only one means which Robert Owen advocated for the reform of society; but his socialistic views in general and his attempt to found an ideal community at New Harmony, in America, are rather outside the scope of the present volume. In 1813 he published *A New View of Society*. In it he plans the establishment of industrial communities which shall be self-contained, educationally organised, and self-supporting on co-operative lines. He seems—perhaps like many socialists—to be over-sanguine as to the practical efficiency of the governmental action which is to engineer and control this scheme; and his views were bound to conflict with the pronounced individualistic theories which were current at this time. He also estranged public sympathy by his hostility to Christianity. But his achievements at New Lanark were of very great significance, and Owen also helped to bring English education into touch with the fruitful experiments which were being made on the Continent. In 1818, for example, he visited Pestalozzi at Yverdon and Fellenberg at Hofwyl. The latter pleased him so much that he sent his two elder sons to be educated there.

Stimulated by the example of New Lanark, a committee which included James Mill, Brougham, and Zachary Macaulay started a school on Owen's lines in Westminster in 1818, and a similar one in Spitalfields in 1820. The latter was put in the charge of Samuel Wilderspin (1792–1866). In 1823 he published a treatise *On the Importance of Educating the Infant Children of the Poor*, and this led to the founding in the following year of the London Infant School Society. Its object was to provide schools for children aged two to six, whose only source of education up to that time had been the very inefficient dame schools. Wilderspin was appointed 'agent' of this society, and he travelled all over the country in its service. In 1836 the Home and Colonial Infant School Society was formed in order to provide training for teachers in infant schools. For long its college had buildings in the Gray's Inn Road, London, but in 1903 it moved out to Wood Green. It was closed during the economy period of the 1930's.

Wilderspin has much in common with Pestalozzi, although he claims to have worked out his educational schemes before he had read the works of the Swiss reformer. He says: "The great secret of training children was to descend to their level and become a child; the error had been to expect in infancy what is only the product of after years."[1] He stresses kindness, patience, sympathy. We must approach the head through the heart—not *vice versa*. He also sees the educational value of amusement, activity, and change. He calls the playground the "uncovered schoolroom," and its occupations are to him as important as those of the classroom. "I would rather see a school where they charged two-pence or three-pence per week for each child, having a playground, than one where the children had free admission without one."[2] It should be supplied with apparatus for games and planted with trees and flowers. All this is a commonplace of educational theory—if not of practice—nowadays; but the contrast is great between Wilderspin's theories and those which underlay the contemporary dame school. He also disliked the mechanised methods of the monitorial system; but he was inclined (like many schoolmasters before and since) to be pedantic. He is said to have invented the ball-frame for teaching elementary arithmetic; but this may be questioned, for the *abacus* was used by the ancient Greeks. But he exaggerates the importance of memory work, and much of the information which he gives is of little value. He is also not exempt from the contemporary habit of pointing a moral. There are some examples of this practice in Wilderspin's *The Infant System*. This is how he correlates tables with temperance:

[1] Wilderspin, *Importance, etc.*, p. 44.   [2] Idem, *The Infant System*, p. 101.

Two pints will make one quart,
  Four quarts one gallon, strong:—
Some drink too little, some too much,—
  To drink too much is wrong.

Eight gallons one firkin make,
  Of liquor that's called ale:
Nine gallons one firkin of beer
  Whether 'tis mild or stale.

With gallons fifty-four
  A hogshead I can fill,
But I hope I never shall drink much,
  Drink much whoever will.[1]

The infant-school movement was also making some independent progress in Scotland. There it was associated particularly with David Stow (1793–1864). He was a Glasgow merchant, who made up his mind to improve the condition of the poor children in his city. In 1816 he started a Sunday school; but soon, realising that this of itself was insufficient, he founded, in 1826, the Glasgow Infant School Society and got into touch with Wilderspin. The movement was followed up with an attempt to train teachers. In 1836 the Glasgow Normal Seminary was opened; in it teachers were instructed in their craft, and their professional training followed their general education, contrary to the usual custom in training colleges. Stow always stressed the difference between mere instruction and what he called 'training'—i.e. education in its widest sense, including both moral and intellectual development. And so he prefers to call his teachers 'trainers,' as indicating their wide responsibility. 'Training,' according to Stow, was a highly skilled craft, "awakening thought, stimulating and directing enquiry and evolving the energies of intellect."[2] He therefore condemns the mechanical monitorial

[1] Wilderspin, *The Infant System*, p. 258. Another example of these 'arithmetical songs' is given in Frank Smith, *History of English Elementary Education*, p. 96. See also Wilderspin's *Manual*, in which these verses are "set to original and select music."
[2] Stow, *The Training System*, p. 5.

system; but he believes very much in what he calls the 'sympathy of numbers'—which, in actual practice, seems to have meant little more than answering in chorus. He also advocates 'picturing out'—i.e. giving verbal pictures which may stimulate the child's imagination. He says that, by using simple terms and ideas within the range of the child's experience, he can be "made to perceive as vividly by the mental eye as he would real objects by the bodily eye."[1]

Bell, Lancaster, Robert Owen, Wilderspin, David Stow—all these have contributed to make English elementary education; nor were ideas from the Continent without their effect, for Rousseau, Pestalozzi, and Fellenberg had a powerful, if indirect, influence. But progress was slow. In spite of the work of the pioneers, there were many obstacles to overcome—the mechanised routine and passive receptivity of the monitorial schools, the excessive reliance on rotework and verbalism, jealousy between the churches and the growth of the 'religious difficulty,' the eagerness of industrialists to obtain child labour, the fear of the governing classes that popular instruction might result in discontent and revolution. From time to time vestiges of these obstacles to educational progress are even yet discernible. But the effort to overcome them has never relaxed; and that continued and increasing effort is an important feature of all the subsequent educational history of this country.

[1] *Op. cit.*, chap. xvi; for examples see chap. xxxvii.

Chapter VII

STATE INTERVENTION IN EDUCATION

Factory Acts and Elementary Education. Early Education Bills: Whitbread, Brougham, and Roebuck.

IN spite of the Government's policy of non-intervention in education and its too-ready satisfaction with the efforts of cheap day schools and Sunday schools, there was some general misgiving as to the position of workhouse children who were being carried off into virtual slavery in the mills. The condition of child workers in some of the factories was so bad that even the most uncompromising advocates of *laissez-faire* felt that there would be some justification for intervention on behalf of the future well-being of the population. Children were not free agents, and therefore even those who thought that adults should be left free to make their own bargains were ready to legislate for the protection of child workers. Most of these in the Lancashire cotton factories had been workhouse children, who were imported in batches from their parishes and 'apprenticed' to the mill-owners; but the parish authorities were very negligent about the conditions under which this was done, and their chief concern seems to have been to get rid of their charges. The children were ill-fed and housed under insanitary conditions; the hours of employment were excessive and night work was not uncommon; there was no provision, or even opportunity, for intellectual and moral training.

The first measure on behalf of these victims of the Industrial Revolution was the work of Sir Robert Peel, father of the future Prime Minister, who was himself a cotton manufacturer. In 1802 he introduced the Health and Morals of Apprentices Bill, which, in spite of opposition from mill-owners, was passed into law. It is important as being the first Factory Act, and it initiated the whole modern system of State regulation in industry; but its scope was limited. It applied only to the apprentices sent from workhouses by public authorities to be employed in the larger cotton and woollen mills. The Act restricted their working hours to twelve a day; night work was forbidden; the factory premises were to be kept clean and properly ventilated, and they were to be whitewashed inside once a year. There was also *inter alia* a provision that during some part of the working day apprentices should be instructed in the three 'R's' and that religious teaching should be given for an hour on Sundays. The children were to be taken to church at least once a month and prepared for confirmation when they were old enough. Thus, almost by accident, educational legislation was introduced as part of a measure designed to improve the lot of a relatively small section of the nation's children. But it was the thin end of the wedge, and the forerunner of the legislation which culminated in the Education Act of 1870. All the same, in itself Peel's Act was not very effective. The methods of enforcing it were quite inadequate, and in any case it applied only to parish apprentices and not to those 'free' children who were sent by their parents to work in factories. Moreover, the whole apprenticeship system in mills was abolished in 1814, so that the Act ceased to apply.

A more ambitious scheme was put forward in 1807 by Samuel Whitbread, in his Parochial Schools Bill, to which reference has already been made.[1] It was part of a larger Poor Law Reform Bill, and it aimed at providing free elementary education for pauper children of all kinds—not merely those who were employed in factories. But it was emasculated by the House of Commons and rejected by the House of Lords. However, in 1815, Sir Robert Peel made a new attempt, this time on behalf of the 'free' children who worked in the mills. A Select Committee was appointed to investigate 'the State of the Children employed in the manufactories of the United Kingdom.' The reports made to it revealed the appalling conditions under which many child workers lived. Some of them toiled for over a hundred hours a week. A working day of fourteen or fifteen hours—even sixteen —was not unknown. The time for meals and sleep was utterly inadequate; the punishments were often brutal. But in spite of this

[1] See supra, p. 54.

evidence there was much opposition to Peel's new Bill on the part of the manufacturers. The measure was drastically cut down before it was passed by the Commons in 1818, and the final Factory Act, which became law in 1819, was only a shadow of Peel's original proposals. It applied only to children in cotton mills; but in them the employment of workers under nine years of age was prohibited, and those between nine and thirteen were not to work for more than twelve hours a day. As with the Apprentices Act of 1802, the measure was very inadequately enforced, and both employers and parents combined to render it inoperative.

Samuel Whitbread died in 1815, but his place in Parliament as protagonist in the cause of popular education was taken by Henry Brougham (1778–1868). Owing to his efforts a parliamentary committee was appointed in 1816 'to inquire into the Education of the lower Orders.' Its report revealed a great lack of educational facilities, and a very irregular attendance on the part of those children who did go to school. Brougham followed this up with a demand for an inquiry into the whole question of educational endowments. It was suggested that in many cases these were being abused, and that if they were rightly redistributed, they could be used to finance a system of popular education throughout the country, without entailing a burden on the taxpayer. At this there was a good deal of resentment; even some of the great public schools were asked to give an account of their trusteeship—much to their indignation. But the main result of all this activity was Brougham's Parish Schools Bill of 1820, "for the better Education of the Poor in England and Wales." The schools were to be erected at the expense of the manufacturers. The cost of maintenance was to fall on the rates, though school fees of 2d. to 4d. a week were to be paid by such parents as could afford them; and the application of the redistributed educational endowments was to be a further source of revenue. Schoolmasters were to be members of the Church of England and appointed by the parish vestry. The clergyman could also veto their appointment and dismiss them. He was to have unlimited 'right of entry' to the school and the duty of determining the curriculum. Brougham's proposals, like those of Whitbread, had in view a *national* system of education; but it is not surprising that they aroused very strong opposition among dissenters and Roman Catholics; even the supporters of the Established Church were lukewarm. The Bill was accordingly withdrawn.

The parliamentary committee had collected statistics which may not be very reliable, but had been used by Brougham in support of his Bill. According to these, there were in 1820 some 500,000 children in the unendowed schools, of whom 53,000 were being "educated, or rather not educated," at dame schools. There were also 165,432 pupils in the endowed schools. In some of the counties, particularly where there was much child labour, the proportion was very low—1 in 24 in Lancashire, and 1 in 26 in Middlesex, "beyond all dispute the worst educated part of Christendom." In Westmorland the children at school formed 1 in 7 of the total population. This worked out at an average of about 1 in 14 or 15 of the population over the whole country—or 1 in 16 if the dame schools were not counted in. Brougham reckoned that the proportion ought rightly to be 1 in 8; and if the figures are at all reliable, there was obviously a considerable deficiency in the schooling available. One has also to remember that the average school life at the time was short—perhaps not more than one and a half or two years. But, for all that, there had been considerable improvement since the beginning of the century, largely due to the efforts of the National Society and the British and Foreign School Society. Brougham himself said, in a speech in the House of Commons: "The average means of mere education was only in fact one-sixteenth in England; yet even this scanty means had only existed since the year 1803, when what were called the new schools, or those upon the systems of Dr. Bell and Mr. Lancaster, were established. Those schools were in number 1,520, and they received about 200,000 children. Before 1803, then, only the twenty-first part of the population was placed in the way of education, and at that date England might be justly looked on as the worst-educated country of Europe."[1] Thus it was argued that under the existing voluntary

[1] *Hansard*, N.S.2, 1820, col. 61.

system popular education, though it had still far to go, was making progress. Even Brougham, though he wished to multiply schools and increase their population, was no advocate of free education. "It was his great object that, whilst measures were adopted for bringing education home to the doors of all, all should still pay a little for it."[1]

All through the 1820's the power of liberal thought was growing. The year 1825 saw the formation of the Society for the Diffusion of Useful Knowledge.[2] It was the outcome of a pamphlet by Brougham, entitled *Observations on the Education of the People*, and its object was to popularise science and general knowledge by the publication of instructive books at a low price. In 1828 was founded the secular University of London, of which more will be said in a later chapter. The repeal of the Test Acts in the same year recognised the civil rights of nonconformists, for hitherto they had been excluded from holding national or municipal offices. This was followed in 1829 by the Catholic Emancipation Act, which gave similar rights to Roman Catholics. Finally, in 1832, came the Reform Bill, which gave the franchise to the 'ten pound householders' in the boroughs, and so redistributed seats that the large centres of industrial population, now converted into new boroughs, were represented in Parliament. Thus the middle classes and the manufacturing towns now sent their members to the House of Commons. This was only a stage in the direction of complete popular representation; but it is intensely significant, because it was carried through by the force of "popular will against the strenuous resistance of the old order as entrenched in the House of Lords."[3] Thus, by the Reform Act of 1832, the balance of power in the Commons passed to the newly enfranchised middle classes, and popular education therefore was regarded more than ever as a matter of urgency.

[1] *Op. cit.*, col. 77.
[2] In 1816 Bentham had published a book called *Chrestomathia*, which proposed to set up a school to give instruction which would be 'conducive to useful knowledge.' A good account of the scheme is given in Adamson, *English Education, 1760–1902*, pp. 102–5.
[3] Trevelyan, *British History in the Nineteenth Century*, p. 241. In this book there is a dramatic account of the whole struggle. See pp. 232–42.

This feeling was voiced in Parliament in 1833. John Arthur Roebuck (1801–79) had taken Brougham's place as champion of popular education in the House of Commons, for the latter had been translated to the Upper House as Baron Brougham and Vaux. "Education," said Roebuck, "means, not merely these necessary means or instruments for the acquiring of knowledge, but it means also the so training or fashioning the intellectual and moral qualities of the individual, that he may be able and willing to acquire knowledge, and to turn it to its right use."[1] He viewed education in the light of the growth of democracy: "I wish the people to be enlightened, that they may use the power well which they will inevitably obtain." He stressed the fact that France, Prussia, and Saxony had already introduced systems of compulsory popular education. And so he put forward the motion that "the House, duly impressed with the necessity for a due Education of the People at large, and believing that to this end the aid and care of the State are absolutely needed, will, early during the next Session of Parliament, proceed to devise means for the universal and national Education of the whole People."[2]

The plan which he advocated was more thorough-going than that of either Whitbread or Brougham. "In general terms, I would say, that I would oblige, by law, every child in Great Britain and Ireland, from, perhaps, six years of age to twelve years of age to be a regular attendant at school. If the parents be able to give, and actually do give their children elsewhere sufficient education, then they should not be compelled to send them to the national school. If, however, they should be unable or unwilling to give them such instruction, then the State should step in and supply this want, by compelling the parent to send the child to the school of the State."[3] Roebuck proposed to set up schools of four types—infant schools, schools of industry, evening schools in towns for adolescents and adults, and normal schools for training teachers. For administrative purposes the country was to be divided into a number of school districts, in each of which the voters should elect a school committee. The

---

[1] *Hansard*, vol xx, 142.   [2] *Commons Journal*, vol. lxxxviii, p. 615.
[3] *Hansard*, Third Series, vol. xx, col. 153.

whole national system was to be under the control of a Cabinet
Minister. The cost would be met partly by "school pence,"
paid by parents who could afford them, but chiefly from taxation
and from existing endowments, which were to be reapplied to
this purpose. The education to be given was to be "as liberal as
prudence would permit." In the schools of industry it would
include not merely the three 'R's,' but also art, music, hygiene,
natural history, civics, and training in some trade.

It is hardly surprising that so ambitious and so expensive a
scheme did not find acceptance; but there was a long and keen
debate on the Bill, which is some evidence of the growing
popular interest in education. The Government showed that it
was not altogether indifferent to the subject by voting in 1833 a
sum of £20,000 for the erection of school-houses. There was
some sort of precedent for this in that a vote had been made a
few years previously for the building of churches. The resolution
ran as follows: "That a sum, not exceeding twenty thousand
pounds, be granted to His Majesty, to be issued in aid of Private
Subscriptions for the Erection of School Houses, for the Education of the Children of the Poorer Classes in Great Britain, to the
31st day of March 1834; and that the said sum be issued and paid
without any fee or other deduction whatsoever."[1] Though
trivial in itself, this vote is of great significance as showing the
future trend of English education. It was the first Government
grant in aid of education.[2] That grant has been renewed and increased, and its application extended each year since 1833. By
1846 it amounted to £100,000 and by 1859 to £836,920. But
the purpose of the original grant should be noted. It was issued
"in aid of Private Subscriptions." In practice it was paid over to
the National Society and the British and Foreign School Society—
two private institutions—to help them to build schools. It was
decided that the local subscriptions for this purpose must be
equivalent to at least half the grant made in any particular case,

[1] *Commons Journal*, vol. lxxxviii, pp. 692-3.
[2] Unless one counts the parliamentary grant, part of which was to provide
schoolmasters' salaries, which was voted in 1649. See De Montmorency, *State
Intervention in English Education*, p. 104.

and the Society which benefited had to undertake the maintenance of any schools that were erected. Preference was given to applications from large cities and towns, and for schools with accommodation for not less than 400 pupils. Thus the grant tended to encourage the building of schools in comparatively well-to-do and populous areas, while the poorer, and therefore more necessitous, country districts were neglected. No other conditions were laid down. No standards for building were required; there was no inspection to see that the schools were adequately maintained after they had been built; no enquiries were made as to the efficacy of the instruction which was to be given in them. The scheme was obviously designed as a tentative one, and although the grant was renewed in succeeding years, the applications for assistance far exceeded the funds which were made available.

An important contribution to the gratuitous education of children of the poorest classes was made by the Ragged School Union which was founded in 1844. Schools for such children were opened in the slum districts not only of London, but also of other large cities in England and Scotland. The Union owed much to the work of its first president Lord Ashley (afterwards Earl of Shaftesbury). In 1914 its title was changed to The Shaftesbury Society. Since the introduction of a compulsory and gratuitous system of national education, it has devoted itself to philanthropic and religious work of various kinds, including holiday homes, Sunday schools, and residential schools for crippled children.

Chapter VIII

SECONDARY EDUCATION

Public Schools: Samuel Butler, B. H. Kennedy, and Thomas Arnold.

THE unsatisfactory state of the endowed public and grammar schools during the second half of the eighteenth century has already been described in Chapter II. It cannot be
said that there was much improvement during the first three or
four decades of the nineteenth century. According to Mr. Marvin, in his *Century of Hope*,[1] "it has been estimated that the condition of our public or higher schools was worse between 1750 and
1840 than at any time since King Alfred." Be that as it may, the
narrow classical curriculum, the unsatisfactory housing and
boarding conditions, and the low moral tone continued to be
characteristic of them. But criticism was growing, and it came
from many different quarters. Utilitarianism, as expounded by
Jeremy Bentham and the two Mills, became popular in the early
nineteenth century. Its aim was "the greatest happiness of the
greatest number." It judged the rightness of an act, not by its
motive, but by its result on the pleasure or pain of those affected
by it.[2] The philosophic radicals who held this creed were intolerant of effete schools and colleges, which were upholding a
traditional and apparently useless curriculum. The elder Mill, in
his article on 'Education' in the *Encyclopædia Britannica* (1825),
says: "An institution for *education*, which is hostile to pro-
gression, is the most preposterous, and vicious thing, which the
mind of man can conceive."[3]

Other criticisms came from the evangelicals. In spite of their
limited outlook, the movement with which they were identified
has (as Trevelyan says), "brought rectitude, unselfishness and
humanity into high places,"[4] and its influence was therefore

[1] P. 204.
[2] See J. S. Mill, *Utilitarianism*, and especially p. 22 of the Routledge edition.
[3] James Mill on *Education* (ed. Cavenagh), p. 67.
[4] *British History in the Nineteenth Century*, p. 54.

exerted on those classes who sent their sons to the public schools. They were not likely to approve of the vices which boys were said to learn there, and which were stigmatised by Sydney Smith and many another writer after him. Again, there was growing up a class of factory-owners and manufacturers who had forged ahead and made their money in industry. Such parents were critical of the curriculum and the educational facilities which were offered to their children in the public and grammar schools. They wanted value for money here as in everything else, and—as has already been pointed out[1]—they often, for this reason, preferred a private school. In view, therefore, of their deficiencies and the criticisms that were levelled at them from so many sides, the public schools might well not have survived, had they not been reformed during the course of the nineteenth century. But they *were* reformed, and they *did* survive. That this happened is due largely to the efforts of two great headmasters—Samuel Butler of Shrewsbury and Thomas Arnold of Rugby.

Samuel Butler (1774–1839)—grandfather of the author of *Erewhon*—had been educated at Rugby and at St. John's College, Cambridge. He was elected to the headmastership of Shrewsbury in 1798, at the age of twenty-four. It was an ancient institution which had been refounded in the reign of Edward VI as a town grammar school. At the time when Butler arrived there were very few boys; but a new scheme had just come into force and the reconstituted governing body gave their headmaster valuable support. His chief reforms concerned teaching methods. He abolished what Carlyle stigmatised as 'gerund-grinding.' Boys had been set to learn by heart the rules of grammar and syntax from antique text-books written in Latin; reference has already been made to the experience of D'Arcy Thompson at Christ's Hospital.[2] Every possible variation and exception were given, and the rules themselves were set out with incredible complexity. The compilers had forgotten that—as Quintilian[3] said—it is one of the virtues of a grammarian to be ignorant of some things.

---

[1] See *supra*, p. 20.   [2] See *supra*, p. 34.

[3] "Mihi inter virtutes grammatici habebitur aliqua nescire." Quintilian, *Inst. Or.*, chap. viii, § 21.

Butler at long last cleared all this away and required his boys to learn only what was really necessary. He promoted emulation and gave life to lessons by using a system of marks. He held regular examinations and based promotions on merit. Mathematics was taught to those who needed this subject. Benjamin Hall Kennedy, who was a pupil at Shrewsbury under Butler and became his successor there as headmaster, says: "History and geography were never neglected. . . . He was, of course, an excellent scholar and no ordinary teacher; but his crowning merit was the establishment of an emulative system, in which talent and industry always gained their just recognition and reward in good examinations. This it was that made his school so successful and so great. Added to this, he always advised and recommended private reading."[1]

Another of Butler's reforms was to give a certain share of authority to some of the senior boys—'prepostors,'[2] as they were called. Thus he anticipated Arnold, who is generally credited with the introduction of the prefect system into the modern public school. It was all part of his general policy to make boys "in intellectual as well as in moral matters *self-reliant*." His methods were justified by their results. Shrewsbury boys swept the board in the scholarship and honours examinations at Oxford and Cambridge. The school's reputation grew rapidly and the numbers greatly increased. In 1842, three years after Butler's death, the *Quarterly Review* said of him: "If the silent but most practical reformation which has been at work in our public schools for many years ever attracts the notice it deserves, then the time will come when men will take an interest in tracing the steps of the improvement; and they will hardly fail to give honour due to that scholar who first set the example in remodelling our public education, and gave a stimulus which is now acting on almost all the public schools in the country."

Butler's methods were carried on by his successor, Benjamin Hall Kennedy (1804–1889), an old Salopian, who was headmaster

---

[1] Letter quoted in *Life and Letters of Samuel Butler*, vol. i. p. 252.
[2] On Butler's spelling of this word see *Life and Letters of Samuel Butler*, vol. i, p. 206.

of Shrewsbury from 1836 to 1866. He had won the Porson Prize
at Cambridge while still a boy at school, and during his university
career he carried off practically every distinction in Classics that
was open to him. As a schoolmaster, therefore, he naturally laid
great stress on this subject, and he was the author of the *Public
School Latin Primer*, which had a long career, though it did not
escape criticism as being too detailed. None the less, Kennedy
introduced mathematics and French as subjects in the ordinary
curriculum. He (unlike Butler[1]) encouraged organised games
and started a school choir. In passing, it is interesting to notice that
Kennedy had a dispute with the burgesses of Shrewsbury, which
illustrates a point to which reference has already been made.[2]
They contended that the term *libera schola grammaticalis*, as used in
the original charter of Edward VI, meant literally a 'free grammar
school,' available without fee to the sons of townsfolk. Kennedy
issued a pamphlet in which he expressed his views on this point.
"All who are well read in the terminology of mediæval law," he
says, "know that this term means a royally chartered school, a
school free from all superiority, save that of the Crown." The
quarrel went on for some time, but it was finally settled
in Kennedy's favour by the Public Schools Commission in
1862.[3]

There is little doubt that, in his reforms of Shrewsbury School,
Kennedy was to some extent influenced by his more famous
contemporary Arnold, of whom something must now be said.
Thomas Arnold (1795–1842) had a distinguished career at Winchester, and thence went up to Corpus Christi College, Oxford.
He was elected a fellow of Oriel at the age of twenty-one. This
college had become the headquarters of a group of keen and
critical scholars, who were known as 'noetics.' These "were a
select body somewhat inclined to mutual admiration, producing
little but freely criticising everything; they applied an unsparing
logic to received opinions, especially those concerning religious
faith, but their strength lay rather in drawing inferences and re-
futing fallacies than in examining and settling the premises from

[1] See *supra*, p. 18.   [2] See *supra*, p. 13.
[3] On this whole subject see How, *Six Great Schoolmasters*, pp. 111–13.

which their syllogisms were deduced."[1] Nurtured in such an atmosphere, Arnold was inclined to be critical and intolerant of mere tradition. For him the Classics were not simply material for linguistic exercises, but a stimulus to ethical, philosophical, and political thinking. Yet he was intensely religious. He was ordained in 1818, though he never did any parochial work. His views were extremely Protestant, and he was always an opponent of Tractarianism. In 1819 he left Oxford and settled at Laleham, near Staines, where he began to take in private pupils and coach them for entrance to the Universities. About this time also he married. He and his wife seem to have been successful and happy in their work. "The most remarkable thing which struck me at once on joining the Laleham circle was the wonderful healthiness of tone and feeling which prevailed in it. . . . Dr. Arnold's great power as a private tutor resided in this, that he gave such an intense earnestness to life. . . . In the details of daily business, the quantity of time that he devoted to his pupils was very remarkable. Lessons began at seven, and with the interval of breakfast lasted till nearly three; then he would walk with his pupils and dine at half-past five. At seven he usually had some lesson in hand; and it was only when we were all gathered up in the drawing-room after tea, amidst young men on all sides of him, that he would commence work for himself, in writing his sermons or Roman History."[2]

In 1827 the headmastership of Rugby School became vacant, and Arnold offered himself as a candidate for the post. In a testimonial from Dr. Hawkins, the Provost of Oriel, it was stated that if Mr. Arnold were elected to the headmastership of Rugby, he would change the face of education all through the public schools of England. Prophecies made in testimonials are not always justified by events; but the future proved that in this case, at least, Dr. Hawkins was right. Arnold was elected and entered upon his duties in August 1828. At the time of his arrival Rugby was certainly in no worse a condition than many of the English

[1] Brodrick, *History of the University of Oxford*, chap. xviii. See also Mark Pattison, *Memoirs*, pp. 79–80.
[2] Bonamy Price in Stanley, *Life of Thomas Arnold*, p. 39.

public schools, and in some respects it was probably better than most. Under the rule of his predecessor, Dr. Wooll, the school buildings had been rebuilt and the accommodation had been greatly improved. The numbers had increased, though they had fallen off latterly, probably owing to a raising of the school fees in 1813. The teaching and boarding arrangements had been improved, and a pension scheme had been started for the benefit of the assistant masters.[1] The long list of distinguished Rugbeians who were members of the school during Wooll's headmastership is some proof that the school was far from inefficient. But, as W. H. D. Rouse says: "The system as Arnold found it at Rugby was not unlike to the administration of a conquered state. The Headmaster was an autocrat, dispensing punishments with no unsparing hand. He and his colleagues alike were looked on as the natural enemies of boyhood, set over them by a mysterious dispensation of Providence to interfere with personal liberty and enjoyment. To these rulers the boys rendered a grudging obedience, which ceased when it ceased to be enforced. They had their own organisation, by which the weaker were slaves of the stronger; and their own code of honour, mercilessly strict among themselves, but lax towards their masters. A lie told to a schoolfellow was a very different thing from a lie told to the master. Differences between themselves were settled by an appeal to brute force, not only amongst the younger, where it was natural, but amongst older boys already on the verge of manhood. Ideals of conduct were otherwise low, and intemperate indulgence of various kinds was not condemned by public opinion."[2] Thus it was not so much in the externals as in the whole tone and spirit and outlook of the school that Arnold recognised that reformation was needed. His chief claim to greatness lies in the fact that he effected this reformation, and that his ideas and ideals were widely accepted and imitated.

For Arnold education had a twofold basis—religion and a liberal culture. The school chapel gave him an opportunity of

[1] In 1811 there were nine assistant masters for 381 boys. Contrast conditions at Eton in 1834—see *supra*, p. 18.
[2] Rouse, *A History of Rugby School*, p. 224.

influencing the whole school, and he used it to the full.[1] On his appointment as headmaster, he got himself also made school chaplain, for he felt it essential that the head should stand in a pastoral relationship to his boys. He also exerted enormous influence on the school by means of his Sixth Form, whom he treated as 'gentlemen.' Stanley, his biographer and one of his old pupils, says: "There grew up a general feeling that it was a shame to tell Arnold a lie—he always believes one."[2] But if his trust proved to be misplaced, he took no further risks; and any offender whose influence he felt to be deterimental to the school he ruthlessly expelled. Much of the improvement in tone was due, not merely to Arnold's personal influence and direct action, but also to better organisation. He introduced separate studies, smaller dormitories, and more adequate supervision. This was a real gain. Reference has already been made to conditions in Long Chamber at Eton when Edward Thring was a pupil there from 1833 to 1841.[3] "After 8.0 o'clock at night," he says, "no prying eye came near till the following morning; no one lived in the same building; cries of joy and pain were equally unheard; excepting a code of laws of their own, there was no help or redress for anyone."

Even at Rugby and in the days of Arnold such practices as tossing in blankets and roasting of small boys before an open fire were not unknown—as readers of *Tom Brown's Schooldays* will remember. But Arnold never acquiesced in such evils as these, and it was in order to deal with them that he developed the prefect system, the origin of which is so often associated particularly with him and with Rugby. In an article which he contributed to the *Quarterly Journal of Education* he speaks of "the power given by the supreme authorities of the school to the Sixth Form, to be exercised by them over the lower boys, for the sake of securing a regular government amongst the boys themselves, and avoiding the evils of anarchy; in other words, of the lawless tyranny of physical strength."[4]

[1] See his 'Selected Sermons preached in Rugby Chapel,' in Findlay, *Arnold of Rugby*, pp. 122–97.
[2] Stanley, *Life of Thomas Arnold*, p. 100. [3] See *supra*, p. 19.
[4] *Quarterly Journal of Education*, vol. ix, pp. 286–7.

Arnold also reformed the school curriculum. He believed in methods of instruction which would stimulate self-activity and train the power of self-expression, and which at the same time would be adjusted to the needs of individual pupils. As an ex-fellow of Oriel, and a 'noetic,' he believed strongly in the educational value of the Classics, but he took no traditional or conventional view as to the method of teaching them. One of his biographers, Sir Joshua Fitch, says of him: "In his teaching of languages he was the first Englishman who drew attention in our public schools to the historical, political, and philosophical value of philology and of the ancient writers, as distinguished from the mere verbal criticism and elegant scholarship of the preceding century."[1] Arnold also advocated the claims of history as a school subject and was, in fact, the first modern teacher of it. It was a branch of study which had always interested him. While still at Laleham he had written a series of articles on Roman History for an encyclopædia, and he later published a work on the same topic in three volumes. From 1841 to 1842 he was professor of Modern History at Oxford, holding this office in conjunction with his headmastership. To Arnold, history is the record of God's dealings with man.[2] Human progress is divinely directed. The Jews, the Greeks, and the Romans were the three chosen people of ancient times, and their history converges on that of Christianity. The State is the appointed means of drawing men nearer to God. Aristotle—whom Arnold greatly admired—had said that man is a 'political animal'; thus individual perfection and the perfection of society go hand in hand. Men's relations to God underlie and explain their association in the Church; their relations to one another underlie and explain their association in the State. Thus the more closely Church and State are associated, the more nearly will human perfection be attained. Arnold stands for "the great principle that Christianity should be the base of all public education in this country." It was for this reason that in 1838 he resigned from the Senate of the University of London, when it was proposed to institute a voluntary examination in

[1] Fitch, *Arnold of Rugby*, p. 78.
[2] Arnold was a great admirer of Vico. See Lionel Trilling, *Matthew Arnold*, p. 51.

theology, which, he felt, showed that Christianity was regarded as "no essential part of one system, but merely a branch of knowledge, which any man might pursue if he liked, but which he might also, if he liked, wholly neglect, without forfeiting his claim, according to our estimate, to the title of a completely educated man."[1]

Arnold was fortunate in his 'press,' for he has been 'written up' in three works which spread his fame far and wide—Stanley's *Life*, *Tom Brown's Schooldays*, and his son Matthew Arnold's poem *Rugby Chapel*. He was a great figure and a dominating personality; and such men tend to be idealised by their admirers. It has become something of a fashion in recent years to 'debunk' the heroic figures of an earlier age, and Arnold has not escaped the process. In Mr. Lytton Strachey's *Eminent Victorians*, he reappears as a tedious prig; and the former practice of ascribing every possible public-school reform to him has not altogether unjustly been termed the 'Arnold myth.' It is certainly true that some of the credit which is often given too exclusively to him ought to be shared with others. Reference has already been made to the important work of Butler and Kennedy; much also was done by other headmasters, many of them old pupils of Butler or Arnold. There resulted from this a movement to found new and more progressive schools during the forties and fifties of last century; examples are Cheltenham (1841), Marlborough (1843), Rossall (1844), and Wellington (1853).

It may well be that Stanley has exaggerated Arnold's single-handedness in the moral reform of the public schools and the extent of his personal influence on his pupils. But it is still true that Arnold's greatness lies in the fact that he saved the English public-school system and gave it a place in the esteem of the people of this country which it has not yet lost—and that in spite of continued criticism, much of which may be not wholly undeserved. Arnold carried out his reforms by the force of his own vigorous moral personality. His own high reputation increased the prestige of other headmasters and that of the profession generally; and this strengthened the position and independence of

[1] Letter to the Earl of Burlington, in Stanley, *Life of Arnold*, chap. viii. p. 485.

the endowed schools against State interference. Sir Michael Sadler says that if it had not been for Arnold, it is probable that English higher secondary education would have passed more or less completely under the control of the State.

Again—as has been indicated—Arnold's influence was exerted through members of his staff and old pupils who became headmasters of many of these public and endowed schools. He was very careful to appoint as his assistants men whom he could trust to carry out his ideals. "I want," he says, "a man who is a Christian and a gentleman, an active man, and one who has common sense, and understands boys. I do not so much care about scholarship, as he will have under him the lowest forms in the school; but yet, on second thoughts, I do care about it very much, because his pupils may be in the highest forms; and besides, I think that even the elements are best taught by a man who has a thorough knowledge of the matter. However, if one must give way, I prefer activity of mind and an interest in his work, to high scholarship: for the one may be acquired far more easily than the other."[1] Men of this type, trained and inspired by him, spread his ideas, not only in the public boarding schools, but in the big day schools like Manchester Grammar School and St. Paul's. The fact that Arnold was a liberal evangelical churchman and keen on interdenominational relations strengthened the school of thought which favoured unsectarian Christian teaching as a basis for religious instruction in schools attended by pupils drawn from a variety of religious bodies. Thus nonconformist parents were not unwilling to send their boys to what were nominally Church of England schools. This helped to keep the 'religious difficulty'— which was already complicating the development of our elementary education—out of the secondary schools. Professor Archer also points out that the example of Arnold helped to perpetuate the custom of preferring clergymen as headmasters of public and grammar schools—a custom which lingered on into the twentieth century and is not even yet quite extinct.

[1] See Stanley, *Life of Arnold*, chap. iii, p. 93.

Chapter IX

UNIVERSITY EDUCATION

Progress of Reform at Oxford and Cambridge. The University of London.

EDUCATIONAL reform at Oxford and Cambridge proceeded slowly during the first part of the nineteenth century. *The Adventures of Mr. Verdant Green*, which was first published in 1853, is admittedly a skit on the university life of the time, but it mirrors very faithfully the lack of serious purpose and of intellectual interests, the extravagance and the dissipation which characterised the career of too many undergraduates. When the *Edinburgh Review* attacked this state of things, the Universities found a champion in Copleston, who was Dr. Hawkins's predecessor at Provost of Oriel and was himself something of a reformer. Yet this is what Professor Archer says of him: "It is hard to realise that a man who was regarded by his contemporaries as among the ablest Oxonians of his day both intellectually and practically should, in carrying on a discussion, be so completely unable to distinguish the wood for the trees. He spends more time in defending himself from a charge of a small slip in his Greek than in meeting serious attacks on the Oxford system; he indulges in trivial attacks on the opponent's attorney; and he tediously replies to the charges sentence by sentence when a few decisive thrusts might have given him the victory."[1]

Yet there was some real improvement from within, chiefly in the widening of the curriculum, and the tightening-up of the examination system. Reference has already been made to the Oxford 'Public Examination Statute' of 1800.[2] The separation of the classical and mathematical honours schools, which made possible the achievement of a 'double first,' dates from 1807. 'Moderations'—a kind of intermediate examination at either a pass or honours standard—was not introduced until 1850; while the

---

[1] Archer, *Secondary Education in the Nineteenth Century*, p. 36.
[2] See *supra*, p. 26.

final honours schools of natural science, and law and history (afterwards separated), date from 1853. The Oxford Museum, due largely to Dr. Acland, was founded in 1855. At Cambridge, up to 1824 there was only one tripos, which consisted almost entirely of mathematical subjects. In that year a second tripos in Classics was established, but as it was open only to those who had already taken honours in the mathematical tripos its effectiveness was limited. This regulation was not repealed until 1850. Meanwhile, in 1848, two new triposes had been instituted—one in moral sciences, and the other in natural sciences. Thus it was practically the middle of the century before the modern examination system was really under way at either University. At Oxford the chief interest continued to be the Classics—or rather 'literæ humaniores'; at Cambridge it was mathematics.

But the great majority of college tutors and undergraduates were little affected by the changes which were slowly taking place. The college societies formed close oligarchies, and most of the teaching was done inside their walls. The lectures given by college tutors were little more than construing classes, like a translation lesson with a Classical Sixth Form in a public school. An intelligent and well-prepared undergraduate, when he came into residence, often found that he had covered much of the work already; and that encouraged idleness. Moreover, it was much more usual to take a pass degree than an honours school or a tripos—the reverse of the present custom at Oxford and Cambridge; and there was little inducement to tempt the student to leave the beaten track. At Oxford, as late as 1850, out of some 1,500 or 1,600 undergraduates, the average annual attendance at the modern history course was eight; at botany, six; at Arabic, Anglo-Saxon, Sanskrit, and medicine, none.

Apart from the changes in university organisation and routine, there were at work some less obvious forces, which none the less had considerable effect. The 'first Oriel school'—the noetics to which Arnold belonged—was succeeded by a very different 'second Oriel School' from which sprang the religious revival in the Church of England known as Tractarianism or the Oxford Movement. This began about 1833. In spite of the bickering and bitterness to which it gave rise in its early days, it did much to transform and transfigure the English Church. So far as education was concerned, it tended to strengthen the view that this is the duty of the Church. Thus its supporters were found on the side of the voluntary system and were opposed to the State-controlled school. The movement has therefore been criticised as reactionary and narrow in intellectual outlook; but at any rate it helped to awaken the Universities to a higher standard of personal behaviour and a greater sense of responsibility. Moreover, the very reactionary elements and Romeward tendencies in the Oxford Movement themselves stimulated a liberal reaction in the Universities which was in sympathy with the growing demands for reform from outside.

It remains true that Oxford and Cambridge, although they were slowly beginning to move and contained progressive elements, on the whole continued to be conservative and aristocratic. They were closely associated with the Established Church; they were mainly interested in Classics, theology, and theoretical mathematics, which were frankly not utilitarian, but based their claims to value on taste or culture or religion. The two Universities were also very expensive. The annual cost of sending a boy to Oxford or Cambridge in the 1830's was estimated at £200 to £250—which represented a good deal more then than it does today. So the appeal of the ancient Universities was mainly to the wealthy and upper classes, and no dissenter could enjoy their full privileges. On the other hand, there was a large and dissatisfied opposition to such a state of things. It included Liberals, nonconformists, Jews, Roman Catholics, secularists, men who were much more interested in the new science than in the old 'humanities,' and the successful manufacturers and business magnates who believed in a 'useful' rather than a traditional, and so-called 'cultural,' education. And so the democratic and utilitarian tendencies of the day allied themselves with the scientific and secularist movements in providing an entirely new institution of general and vocational higher education for the benefit of those to whom Oxford and Cambridge were closed by reason of religious tests or of expense or of unsuitability.

In *The Times* of February 9th, 1825, there appeared a letter addressed to Henry Brougham and written by the poet Thomas Campbell. The author pleaded for the establishment of a "great London University" designed primarily to provide education for the "middling rich," "the small, comfortable, able, trading fortunes." Campbell had already visited Bonn and Berlin, and he doubtless had the non-residential German university in mind; he had also discussed the matter with the politician Joseph Hume, who had been educated in one of the Scottish universities, which were run on similar lines. As a result of this letter, a meeting, presided over by the Lord Mayor, was held at the London Tavern. A prospectus was issued and an appeal launched. The outcome of this was the opening of a college in Gower Street in 1828. It was a proprietary institution, run by shareholders as a joint-stock company. Among the Whigs and Radicals who sponsored the new college were the utilitarian philosophers Jeremy Bentham[1] and James Mill, the statesman Brougham, the educationist Birkbeck, the politician Hume, and the historian George Grote. The 'University of London' was to be an undenominational teaching institution; there were no tests and theology was to be kept out of the curriculum. Arnold referred to it as "that godless institution in Gower Street."[2] The tendency of the embryo 'university' was towards modern studies and science. Its curriculum embraced languages, mathematics, physics, mental and moral science, law, history, political economy. Medicine was also an important subject from the beginning, and a hospital, attached to the college, was opened in 1834. The annual fees in the 'university' were low—£25 to £30 a year, a mere fraction of the cost of a course at Oxford or Cambridge. The founding of London University was an educational event of the first importance, though there were not many at the time who realised it. There were frequent jibes at Brougham and his 'Cockney College,' and it was nicknamed 'Stinkomalee' by Theodore Hook, because it was built on the site of a rubbish

[1] Bentham's skeleton is still kept in a case in the library at University College, Gower Street.
[2] See also *supra*, pp. 78-79.

dump; but by 1830 it had already over five hundred students, the majority of whom were reading medicine.

The success of the institution was due partly to the fact that it was non-residential and therefore cheap, and partly to its provision of subjects which were not taught, or inefficiently taught, at Oxford and Cambridge, but for which there was a real and growing demand. But its complete secularisation was a stumbling-block not only to members of the Church of England like Arnold, but to all who regarded religion as an essential constituent—or indeed, the basis—of education at all stages. It was therefore felt that a counterblast must be made, and this time the moving spirit was Dr. D'Oyly, a distinguished Cambridge man, and at the time Rector of Lambeth. A meeting was held on June 21st, 1828. The Prime Minister, the Duke of Wellington, was in the chair, and the Archbishops of Canterbury and York were among the galaxy of prelates on the platform. The following resolution was passed: "That it is the opinion of this meeting that a college for general education be founded in the metropolis, in which, while the various branches of literature and science are made the subjects of instruction, it shall be an essential part of the system to imbue the minds of youth with a knowledge of the doctrines and duties of Christianity as inculcated by the United Church of England and Ireland."[1] Subscriptions flowed in, and a long and narrow site end-on to the Strand, next to Somerset House, was secured. Here a building was erected, and in 1831 King's College, London, armed with a royal charter and with the Archbishop of Canterbury as 'visitor,' was opened. It included a higher department in which were taught "religion and morals, classical literature, mathematics, natural and experimental philosophy, chemistry, parts of natural history, logic, English literature and composition, the principles of commerce and general history. To these will be added instruction in modern foreign languages, and in subjects connected with particular professions, as medicine and surgery, jurisprudence, etc."[2] There was also a lower department which consisted of "a school for the reception of day

[1] See Hearnshaw, *Centenary History of King's College, London*, p. 41.
[2] *Op. cit.*, p. 79.

scholars," which, though totally distinct from the higher department, afforded an education preparatory to it.[1] The institution
had a rather slow start. In the session 1831-2 there were 114 full-
time students, and 162 boys in the school. By 1836-7 these
numbers had risen to 183 and 380 respectively. But there followed
a period of expansion, and by 1843-4 there were 293 full-time
students and 465 boys.

Meanwhile the so-called 'University of London' was a university in name only, for it had not yet—like King's College—
been incorporated, and neither of them had power to grant
degrees. A petition was preferred in 1830, and the grant of in-
corporation was made in the following year; but there was a
good deal of opposition to the proposal that this institution should
be allowed to grant degrees—especially on the part of Oxford
and Cambridge. The question was raised both in the House of
Commons and the House of Lords. There were petitions and
counter-petitions to the Privy Council. At last, in 1836, a compromise was reached. The original Gower Street college was
renamed University College, London—a title which it still re-
tains. A new body, the University of London, was chartered with
powers to grant degrees in arts, laws, and medicine; and students
who had taken courses at either University College or King's
College could be admitted as candidates. Provision was made for
other institutions to be allowed subsequently to submit candidates
if they were of sufficient status. The Senate of the newly formed
University included Henry Brougham, Michael Faraday, and
Thomas Arnold. The last-named, as we have seen, resigned in
1838, because he could not induce the University to impose an
examination in Scripture, on Christian but not sectarian lines, for
all its candidates for degrees—an equivalent, apparently, of what
in Oxford used to be called the First Public Examination in Holy
Scripture.

[1] The 'London University' in Gower Street had also started a junior school.
This afterwards became known as 'University College School,' and it occupied
the south wing of the College until it was moved out in 1907 to new buildings at
Hampstead. Hearnshaw (*op. cit.*, p. 80) says that these two schools were models
"of a new type of secondary school destined to rise to great importance during the
nineteenth century—a type intermediate between the great residential public
schools and the old local grammar schools."

It was owing to the example of London that the education of the modern non-residential universities and university colleges in this country, founded during the nineteenth century, has been given its distinctive neutral, non-sectarian character. It had been intended originally to make London a teaching University; but in the event the actual teaching was done by the colleges—University College and King's College in particular. The Senate had no power to inspect affiliated colleges or to inquire into methods of teaching. Its only means of control was through its degree examinations. As time went on, other institutions were affiliated to the University. Many were scattered all over the country, and some of them were little more than secondary schools, so that affiliation ceased to have any real significance. Finally, by a charter of 1858, the Senate was empowered to dispense with 'certificates of studentship'—i.e. certificates showing that candidates for degrees had attended a course of study at an affiliated college; the only exception was in the case of medical students. Thus, with this exception, the University became an examining body pure and simple, admitting all comers to its examinations without any inquiry as to their training or preparation. The system of 'external degrees' was in full swing.

Chapter X

THE BEGINNINGS OF TECHNICAL AND
SCIENTIFIC EDUCATION

Birkbeck and the Mechanics' Institutes. Scientific Progress and the Royal
Institution. Whewell.

HIGHER education during the eighteenth century had
been associated almost entirely with the Universities.
They were to a large extent the preserves of a certain
class of society, and those who passed through them tended to
enter one of a small number of callings—chiefly the Church (and
with it teaching in the grammar and public schools), the law,
public life, the life of a country gentleman. But the social developments of the latter part of the century had created new demands
and stimulated new attitudes towards the fulfilling of them. The
Industrial Revolution and the invention of steam machinery
fostered an interest in mechanical subjects: mathematics, science,
drawing, and engineering took on a new importance. At the
same time the doctrines of the French Revolution were bound
sooner or later to lead to a demand by the working classes for
wider educational opportunities. There were endless new posts to
be filled in industry, and only those who had some technical
knowledge were qualified to fill them. Thus even the people
who did not approve of social and political equality—e.g. the
opponents of the movement which led to the Reform Bill of
1832—did not necessarily object to giving the workers some
specialised technical education which would make them more
effective in industry. To admit them to this would not imply any
kind of competition with the Universities, or with secondary
schools, because neither of them were in the least interested in
technical subjects. It was realised that, even if workmen were
given instruction beyond the modicum afforded by the elementary schools of the day, it would but serve to improve their
labour and their productiveness in industry; and this would be of

benefit to the employer. They would not be educated "above their class," because their education would not be of the kind to enable them to climb out of that state of life into which it had pleased God to call them, but would merely enable them to do their duty in that state of life more efficiently.

It was in this way that higher education for the working classes, and with it technical education, were born in this country. It was at an epoch when a great advance was being made in many branches of natural science, and when the results of this advance were being applied in industry. It was therefore to be expected that the higher instruction given to workers should be mainly concerned at first with science. As early as 1760 a professor at Glasgow, named Anderson, had begun to hold evening classes in science, which working men were encouraged to attend. In his will he left an endowment for a chair of natural philosophy at the University. Its first occupant was George Birkbeck (1776–1841), who held a degree in medicine. When he started his lectures in 1799 he found it necessary to have a good deal of apparatus, and while this was being made under his instructions he became acquainted with a number of Glasgow artisans. He found them so intelligent and so eager to learn that he resolved to start a course of lectures and experiments in mechanics "solely for persons engaged in the practical exercise of the mechanical arts, men whose situation in early life has precluded the possibility of acquiring even the smallest portion of scientific knowledge." The lectures proved a great success. After Birkbeck removed to London in 1804, the lectures were continued by the next occupant of the chair; and finally, in 1823, the members of the class organised it into a 'Mechanics' Institute.' Its purpose was defined as "instructing artisans in the scientific principles of arts and manufactures."[1]

The movement soon spread. Birkbeck, who was now a practising physician in London, took the lead in the establishment of a similar institute there (1823). He lent a large sum for building a lecture-room, and was elected first president of the institute. The movement was also fostered by a periodical called *The Mechanic's Magazine*. In 1824 alone 16,000 copies of it were

[1] See Delisle Burns, *A Short History of Birkbeck College*, chap. i.

sold. Another supporter was Brougham. Although his Parish Schools Bill had recently been withdrawn (1820), he had not yet lost his enthusiasm for popular education. It was shown in a pamphlet called *Practical Observations on the Education of the People* (1825).[1] It went through twenty editions in a year—a striking evidence of the interest in popular education taken by liberal opinion in the 1820's. His opponents talked about the 'education-mad party,' of which he was the leader, and of the 'steam-intellect society' which he was supposed to advocate. In his pamphlet Brougham says: "I begin by assuming that there is no class in the community so entirely occupied with labour as not to have an hour or two every other day at least to bestow upon the pleasure and improvement to be derived from reading—or so poor as not to have the means of contributing something towards purchasing this justification, the enjoyment of which, beside the present amusement, is the surest way to raise our character and better our condition." This sounds as if Brougham were advocating popular education, and not merely technical instruction for artisans. But the majority of his Whig followers were not really interested in the education of the lowest classes; they were too much obsessed with the virtues of individualism and the rather cold and theoretical utilitarianism of the times. In any case, Brougham's assumption was scarcely justifiable; most factory workers and agricultural labourers and miners had neither leisure nor surplus wages to devote even an hour or two every other day to the "pleasure and enjoyment to be derived from reading." The new artisans—the engineers and mechanics—were the one class among the workers who were likely to gain more than they lost by the Industrial Revolution, and to whom knowledge (i.e. scientific knowledge) would be of daily use. Many of these men worked their way up and eventually came to the forefront in mechanical invention. George Stephenson, son of a colliery fireman, was one of them.

Mechanics' institutes soon sprang up in many parts of the country. They were supported by subscriptions from the members and by donations from sympathisers. By 1850 there were

[1] See *supra*, p. 67.

610 institutions, with 102,050 members.[1] They were naturally most popular and numerous in the manufacturing districts, such as London, Lancashire, and Yorkshire; but there were a few successful institutes also in such rural centres as Lewes, Basingstoke, Chichester, and Lincoln. Each institute usually included a library, reading-room, and museum of models and apparatus. Lectures were provided on mathematics and its applications, and on natural and experimental science and drawing. Sometimes literary subjects, such as English and foreign languages, were included. Travelling lecturers and circulating boxes of books helped to keep the smaller institutes in touch with one another.

The mechanics' institutes played an important part in English education, and yet they were only partially successful. By 1850 two changes had become noticeable. Their membership consisted more of clerks and apprentices and middle-class people than of working men, for whose benefit they had been founded;[2] and, as a corollary of this, their syllabuses had tended to change. There was less purely technical instruction and more recreational activities and popular lectures. Discussions, debates, and even social functions, such as dances, tended to take the place of *ad hoc* courses designed to help artisans.

There were several reasons for this change. The artisans and working classes had not yet received an elementary education, which would form an adequate foundation on which to build a superstructure of technical education. Reference has already been made to the meagre limits of education provided by the monitorial schools and other elementary schools. It must also be remembered that some of the children of the poor hardly went to school at all and that the average length of school life was in any case only one and a half or two years. Moreover—as Adamson points out—a great obstacle to the spread of knowledge at this period was the high cost of newspapers, owing to the Government duty; from 1819 to 1836 there was a stamp-duty of 4*d.* a copy. In a Poor Law Commissioners' Report of 1834 there occurs

[1] See tables in Hudson, *History of Adult Education* (1850), pp. 222–36.
[2] Cf. "The Institution (Birkbeck) has for some years been little more than an association of shop-keepers and their apprentices, law copyists and attorney's clerks." Hudson, *History of Adult Education*, p. 52. See also Preface, p. vii.

this passage: "The dearness of newspapers in this country is an insurmountable obstacle to the education of the poor. I could name twenty villages within a circuit of a few miles in which a newspaper is never seen from one year's end to another."[1] Again, the fees for membership and classes in mechanics' institutes tended to be too high for those for whom they were originally designed. At the London Mechanics' Institute in 1823 the annual subscription was fixed at £1, and this seems to have been a fairly usual charge. In 1826 1,477 workmen paid this fee at the London Institute; but it would be a rather high fee for people of that type even today, and it must have been much more onerous in the Corn Law days, after the Napoleonic Wars, when wages generally were low. Thus the mechanics' institutes tended to decline in importance and to change in character. They were the forerunners of the atheneums, mutual improvement societies, clubs, and reading-rooms which were popular in mid-Victorian days. But some of them retained much of their original character and were stimulated into new life by the development of technical education during the second half of the nineteenth century. For example, the London Mechanics' Institution was the forerunner of the present Birkbeck College, which caters for evening students but is a constituent part of the University of London. In the broadest sense, the mechanics' institutes have laid the foundation for the development of our modern technical schools and colleges.

It has already been pointed out that the latter years of the eighteenth and early part of the nineteenth centuries were a time of great progress in science. Chemistry, for example, had been a subject of particular interest to the philosophical scientists of eighteenth-century France; Lavoisier's work was done mainly between 1770 and 1794. Interest in this subject had spread rapidly since Priestley's discovery of oxygen in 1774. The tradition was carried on in the next two generations by Sir Humphry Davy and Michael Faraday. To them also—and especially to Faraday—are due the researches into magnetism and induction which laid the basis for subsequent improvements in the application of electricity. The scientists of those times were to a much less degree specialists

[1] Quoted by Adamson. See *English Education*, 1789–1902, pp. 41–2.

than they are today. Geology was another subject which, as a science, dates mainly from this period. William Buckland (1784–1856), who became the first professor of geology at Oxford in 1819, did not succeed in allaying the alarm of heresy-hunters by his attempts to reconcile his researches on fossils with the cosmogony of Genesis. Even more important was the work of his pupil, Sir Charles Lyell (1797–1875), who was professor of geology at King's College, London, from 1831 to 1833, and who published about the same time a *Principles of Geology*, which remained a standard work on the subject throughout the nineteenth century.

Scientific discoveries, however, and the application of them to industry did not necessarily mean that they were, or could be, included in the school curriculum. The very range and diversity of the new subjects provided one of the chief obstacles. If a selection was to be made, what principles were to govern it? We are facing a similar problem today; biology has been admitted into many schools, but now geology and astronomy are claiming a place in an already overloaded curriculum. Again, the teaching even of elementary science requires some modicum of apparatus, and this was not always easy to obtain or construct. Thus those who most ardently advocated the teaching of science in schools were not always agreed either as to what the term *science* should include, or how the subject should be taught. Even as late as 1862 a Royal Commission, which was visiting the public schools, found that Rugby alone was making any serious attempt to teach natural science. Even there it had only just started; a few months previously it had set up a science laboratory and put it in the charge of a young and enthusiastic master, J. M. Wilson, who had recently come down from Cambridge, where he had been senior wrangler.

But more than thirty years before this something had been done to popularise scientific instruction among the people. In 1800 the Royal Institution had been founded "for diffusing the knowledge and facilitating the general introduction of useful mechanical inventions and improvements; and for teaching by courses of philosophical lectures and experiments the application of science to the common purposes of life." This aim links up on the one side with the contemporary development of scientific research and with the mechanics' institute movement on the other. Sir Humphry Davy had been professor of chemistry at the Royal Institution, and he was succeeded by Michael Faraday. In addition to his research work and his lectures to adults, Faraday started in 1827 courses of Christmas lectures for juveniles, and he continued these until 1862. Their scope can be gathered from the collections of lectures which have been published under the titles *The Chemical History of a Candle* and *On the Various Forces of Matter*. Thus the Royal Institution did much to promote an interest in science, especially among such young people as would be attending the type of school where Classics was the staple of the curriculum, and where there was little or no instruction in any kind of science.

As to the Universities, as has been said, the classical and abstract mathematical tradition was very strong in them. There were doubtless criticisms that their courses were not sufficiently 'practical'; but the university attitude, when it was explicitly thought out, was that they should teach people to *think*, and that the practical applications of mathematics and science were in no way part of their business. This view is taken by Whewell (1794–1866), one of the greatest mathematicians of the nineteenth century, Cambridge professor of mineralogy and a writer on astronomical subjects. He is prepared to admit science to the university course and encourage students to do research work, if they have the ability and necessary preliminary training; but he says: "habits of thought must be *formed* among other subjects"[1]— i.e. there must be a basic course in subjects which give a logical discipline to the mind. Among these he would include the Classics. "Greek and Latin," he says, "are peculiar and indispensable elements of a liberal education."[2] But Classics alone is not enough; it must be combined in university teaching with mathematical subjects because "we are, in that study, concerned with long trains of reasoning in which each link hangs from all the

[1] Whewell, *On the Principles of English University Education*, p. 42.
[2] *Op. cit.*, p. 34.

preceding."[1] So in his *Of a Liberal Education in General*, published in 1845, he makes various recommendations: school mathematics should be taught by practical methods; applied mathematics (mechanics and hydrostatics) should form part of the ordinary university course; the history of science should be studied so that the student may learn the difficulties which scientific investigators have encountered in their researches and how they have overcome them; there should be optional courses for more advanced students in order to stimulate them to research, and a post-graduate tripos in science should be introduced for the benefit of such students. The last of these recommendations was put into effect by the institution, in 1848, of the Cambridge Natural Science Tripos, which at first was open only to those who had already graduated. The Oxford Honours School of Natural Science dates from 1853, and was a degree course. At the University of London, largely owing to the efforts of Michael Faraday, a Faculty of Science came into being in 1859. The degrees of B.Sc. and D.Sc. were created. This was the first time that they had been used.

[1] *Op. cit.*, p. 13.

EDUCATION IN THE MIDDLE PERIOD OF THE NINETEENTH CENTURY

Chapter XI

TENTATIVE STATE ACTION IN ELEMENTARY EDUCATION

The Committee of Council for Education. Kay-Shuttleworth and the Training of Teachers. The 'Education Vote.'

IT was in 1833 that the Government had made its first educational grant, for in that year it had voted a sum of £20,000, which was paid over to the National Society and the British and Foreign School Society in order to supply half the cost of building new school houses. The other half was to be supplied by voluntary contributions. Mr. J. E. G. de Montmorency, a lawyer who wrote *State Intervention in English Education*, called it "an important and historic precedent," for henceforth the grant became an annual one, increasing in amount as time went on. In 1833 an investigation had been started into the elementary educational facilities which were available in the country. The results of this emphasised both the lack of schooling, especially in the large towns, and the poor condition of many of the schools which did exist. It appeared that out of every ten children of school age, four went to no school at all, three to Sunday schools only, two to inefficient dame schools or private day schools, and only one received a satisfactory education. The report led to a renewed demand by the 'education-mad' party for a State system of education, with a central controlling authority which would have powers to found schools, make Government grants, and superintend the distribution of other funds drawn from local taxation. In 1836 a Central Society of Education was formed to advocate these proposals. It was also suggested that a State training college for teachers should be set up, with model schools, in which the religious instruction would be divided into 'general' (i.e. undenominational), given by the teachers, and 'special' (i.e. denominational), given by ministers of the different religious bodies, who were to have 'right of entry.' There were several Bills on these lines in the thirties, but they all struck on the same rock—the religious difficulty. The problem was to satisfy several interests which seemed to be irreconcilable. In the first place, the Church of England claimed the traditional right to dominate public education, and a fresh stimulus was being applied by the Oxford Movement, which was arousing in the Church a new sense of its dignity and a new faith in its mission. Against this the dissenters not unnaturally claimed the right to educate their own children; while there was a growing liberal opinion which believed that there should be no religious education in State schools.

In the face of these difficulties the Crown in 1839 set up a Committee of the Privy Council "for the consideration of all matters affecting the education of the people," and "to superintend the application of any sums voted by Parliament for the purpose of promoting public education." Thus a central administrative authority for national education—the forerunner of the present Ministry—was established, not by Act of Parliament, but by Royal Prerogative. A vote of protest was lost by only five votes (280 to 275), and the education grant for 1839 (£30,000 for Great Britain) was passed by only two votes. The first secretary of this Committee was Dr. Kay (1804–77), who later became Sir James Kay-Shuttleworth and one of the most important figures in English educational history. He had graduated in medicine at the age of twenty-three, and had worked in the slum areas of Manchester. There he studied the conditions under which the workers had to live—the disease, dirt, and discomfort which were the inevitable lot of the victims of the Industrial Revolution. By his writings he had drawn public attention to these evils, and in 1835 he was appointed an assistant Poor Law Commissioner. He had for long regarded education as the key to reform, and had advocated schools, libraries, mechanics' institutes, and instruction in science and domestic economy, as means of helping the workers to help themselves. His work as a poor-law official convinced him more strongly than ever that the education of the poor was a national responsibility. He made a study of schools, both in the homeland and in some European countries where the problem of educating the children of the poor had been receiving special attention. He was particularly impressed with David Stow's school in Glasgow, and with the work of Wehrli, who was one of Fellenberg's assistants at Hofwyl and had there been successfully training teachers to work in schools for the very poor. Kay succeeded in putting into effect the methods and principles which he advocated.

At Norwood there was a poor-law school to which some of the London unions had farmed out their workhouse children. It was really a school of industry run on monitorial lines, but so far as it went it was not unsatisfactory. Kay in 1838 secured a grant of £500 per annum from the Home Office. He used this at Norwood to pay teachers imported from Stow's Normal Seminary at Glasgow, and to build workshops and provide apparatus. A system of pupil-teaching was introduced. Half the time was spent in handicrafts, and the girls were taught domestic work. The institution was obviously modelled very largely on Fellenberg's 'Poor School' at Hofwyl. It was rapidly successful and attracted many visitors.

It is easy now to see why, in 1839, Kay was selected to be the secretary of the newly formed Committee of Council for Education. The scheme for setting up a State training college for teachers[1] had had to be abandoned; but a sum of £10,000, which had been voted for the purpose, was divided between the National Society and the British and Foreign School Society. The Committee also made Government inspection a condition of all educational grants, and extended the application of grants to some schools not run by these two societies, provided that daily Scripture reading was included as part of their curriculum. In order to circumvent the 'religious difficulty' a concordat was arrived at in 1840; two inspectors for the Church of England schools were appointed by the Archbishops, who were to issue instructions on religious teaching and receive copies of their inspector's reports on this; but the Committee of Council retained control of these inspectors as regards secular subjects. In general, the inspector's duty was considered to be the collection of accurate information

[1] See *supra*, p. 98.

and to give advice and encouragement, if asked to do so, rather than to interfere; he was "to abstain from any interference with the instruction, management or discipline of the school."[1] This is a conception of the inspector's functions which unfortunately did not last.

Kay had a high conception of the part which the school should play in the life of the community. It was to be the focus of the activities of the area which it served—like the Cambridgeshire village college of the present day. A minute of the Committee (1840) says: "The parochial or village library can nowhere be so conveniently and usefully kept as at the school house under the charge of the schoolmaster; and the buildings afford abundant facilities for this purpose. The office of Secretary to the Benefit Society of the parish or village would in no respect injuriously interfere with the schoolmaster's duties; as the meetings of the society would probably be held in the evening. The schoolroom is, in all respects, conveniently arranged for such meetings, and would be a place of assemblage for the working classes, preferable to the tavern, where these meetings are too commonly held."[2]

Kay's experience at Norwood had made it obvious to him that no substantial progress could be effected in popular education without properly qualified teachers. The weakness of the monitorial system was becoming manifest and some attempt to train an adequate number of teachers was imperative if a national system of any kind was to be set up. Since the project for a State training college had been wrecked, owing to disagreements as to the religious instruction to be given in its model schools, Kay and a friend of his, E. C. Tufnell, decided to establish a training college at their own risk. The Battersea Normal School, opened in 1840, owed much to Wehrli's training college. "The task proposed was, to reconcile a simplicity of life not remote from the habits of the humble classes, with such proficiency in intellectual attainments, such a knowledge of method, and such skill in the art of teaching, as would enable the pupils selected to become

[1] See Frank Smith, *A History of English Elementary Education*, p. 183.
[2] Minutes, February 20th, 1840, p. 48; quoted by Frank Smith, *The Life of Sir James Kay-Shuttleworth*, p. 98.

efficient masters of elementary schools."[1] By January 1841 there were thirty-three students, of whom twenty-four were young pupils under a scheme of apprenticeship, while the others were more mature candidates taking a course which lasted a year or more. The Vicar of Battersea offered his parish schools for the practical training of the students and superintended their religious instruction. There were many practical activities; the syllabus included gymnastics and excursions, and the students did their own house-work and tended their garden. Kay himself gave lectures on the theory and practice of education, and everything was done to discourage the rule-of-thumb, monitorial methods, which were inculcated in the British and Foreign School Society's training college at Borough Road. A spirit of experiment and free enquiry was encouraged. In 1842 the Government made a grant of £1,000 towards the expenses which had already been incurred in founding and running the College, and the Prince Consort became its patron.

Battersea soon became a pattern for other training colleges. The National Society in 1841 founded St. Mark's, Chelsea; and it also opened a women's college at Whitelands in the same neighbourhood. By 1845 there were no less than twenty-two church training colleges in England and Wales. For nearly fifty years to come the training of elementary-school teachers was carried out entirely in residential colleges, run by voluntary societies, on the lines laid down by Kay at Battersea, and subsidised by the State. His college remained a private venture for four years, but it was then taken over by the National Society, on the condition that it should be carried on as nearly as possible along its original lines. The rapid development of training colleges in the forties shows an increasing realisation of this period of the limitations of the monitorial system, and of the truth that educational efficiency in the last resort depends on competent teachers.

The application of public funds to popular education, which had begun in 1833, tended to exacerbate the 'religious difficulty' which was implicit from the days when the Bell and Lancaster

[1] See Frank Smith, *A History of English Elementary Education*, p. 180.

monitorial schools were founded and Mrs. Sarah Trimmer raised the issue between them.[1] There were still those who thought that national education was the exclusive concern of the national church. Archdeacon Denison, for example, was a truculent exponent of this form of religious totalitarianism. He pointed out that the National Society had been founded to educate "the children of the poor, *without any exception*, in the doctrine and discipline of the Established Church." Those who took a more liberal view advocated either a 'comprehensive' system in which schools would be connected with some religious body, and would teach a distinctive creed, but in which rights of conscience were respected; or else a 'combined' system in which secular instruction would be given by the teachers and any distinctive religious training which was provided would be in the hands of visiting ministers of the particular denominations. The 'combined' system is a solution which has never commended itself to the people of this country.

However much politicians and ecclesiastics might wrangle on the 'religious difficulty,' it was obvious that something would have to be done. The condition of the working classes in the thirties was giving concern. Unemployment and dear food had helped to foster the Chartist agitation (1838–9), which had collapsed amid rioting and insurrection. There were many who felt that the education—and especially the religious education—of the poor might prove some sort of safeguard against tendencies to violence. In the early 1840's an enquiry was made into the conditions under which children in factories and mines were being employed. The revelations which resulted were absolutely revolting. The Government were therefore moved to produce a Factory Bill (1843), which was sponsored by the Home Secretary, Sir James Graham. Children between the ages of eight and thirteen, in textile mills and workhouses, were to have at least three hours' instruction a day and were not to work for more than six and a half hours. Schools were to be maintained out of the poor rate and Government loans were to be available for the erection of schools. The schoolmaster was to be a member of the

[1] See *supra*, p. 56.

Established Church and his appointment by the school trustees would be subject to the approval of the bishop; the trustees themselves were to include the parish clergyman and the church-wardens. The religious instruction was to be that of the Church of England, and the children were to attend the parish church on Sunday. Thus most of the control of the schools would be given to the Established Church; but the scheme was a 'comprehensive' one, for a conscience clause made it possible for nonconformist parents to withdraw their children from catechism and attendance at church. Even so, dissenters were hardly likely to accept a scheme which put the management of the rate-aided education of the poor under the control of the Church of England. The Government offered concessions; but a vigorous opposition went on all over the country and the Bill had to be withdrawn. Thus a State system of education was postponed for nearly thirty years.

The result did, however, tend to stimulate voluntary effort. A new party arose, called the Voluntaryists and consisting mainly of Congregationalists. Their tenets were that all education must have a religious basis; that State interference in education is unwarrantable; and that the spread of education must therefore depend on individual effort and self-help. Freedom and competition, it was said, are the best safeguards for improvement. This was, in fact, the doctrine of free trade as applied to education. The Voluntaryists raised funds and opened schools, of which there were 364 by 1851; not one of them was receiving any kind of State or rate aid. But even among the nonconformists it began soon to be realised that voluntaryism was a mistake. "The voluntary principle is inapplicable in education, because it is precisely those who need education most that are least capable of demanding it, desiring it, or even conceiving it."[1]

We have already seen the noteworthy attempts which Kay (or Kay-Shuttleworth, as he must now be called) had been making to foster the training of teachers, for he realised that this was vital to the whole cause of popular education. In 1846 a scheme which he had drawn up was announced by the Committee of Council on

[1] Quoted from Edward Baines in Birchenough, *History of Elementary Education*, p. 86.

Education. The details are important. Stipends were to be offered to selected boys and girls indentured as pupil-teachers for a five-years' apprenticeship, from the age of thirteen to eighteen. Grants were to be made to the teachers who trained them and the pupil-teachers were to be examined annually by Her Majesty's Inspectors. Broadly speaking, the pupil-teachers received seven and a half hours' instruction every week, before or after school hours, and they were occupied for five and a half hours every day in teaching or some kindred activity. At the end of the apprenticeship pupil-teachers could compete for Queen's Scholarships, to be held at a training college; while unsuccessful candidates were to be given a preferential claim for minor appointments in the Civil Service. An annual grant was to be made to training colleges in respect of each ex-pupil-teacher student in training. College-trained teachers were to receive proficiency grants from the Government, in addition to a salary paid by the school managers; grants were also to be available in aid of gardens, workshops, and the like. Finally there was to be a pension scheme for teachers retiring after at least fifteen years' service.

This scheme was imitated in part from a pupil-teacher system, which Kay-Shuttleworth had already seen at work in Holland, and he hoped by means of it to supersede the use of the juvenile monitors of the Bell and Lancaster schools—'monitorial humbug,' as he called it. It seems probable none the less that he regarded the pupil-teacher system as merely a temporary and opportunist method of bridging the gap between the employment of monitors and the introduction of an efficient scheme for training adult teachers. But it was a definite step forward. In spite of extremist objections Kay-Shuttleworth's proposals met with considerable support. In 1847 an education vote of £100,000 was passed by a large majority, and from 1848 to 1850 it was raised to £125,000.[1] Thus the period of tentative State aid to education was now ended, and henceforward the Government was

[1] A minute of the Committee of Council (Dec. 3rd, 1839) had made grants available to schools connected with religious bodies other than the National and British Societies. The Catholic Poor School Committee (1847) was recognised for this purpose, and the "Management Clauses" of 1847 also included a scheme for the government of Roman Catholic schools.

committed to a definite policy in educational administration. In the debate on the education vote in 1847 the position had been summed up by Macaulay, who was a warm supporter of State education. He bases his arguments on the familiar contention that it is the duty of every Government "to take order for giving security to the persons and property of the members of the community," and that a system of popular education is the best means of securing this. It is therefore "the right and duty of the State to provide means of education for the common people." He shows the fallacy of the current analogy between free trade in economics and free trade in education; and he quotes statistics to prove that the criminal classes are the worst educated. This is a limited conception of the aims of popular education, but it was sufficient to justify a State system. In his peroration Macaulay appealed to "future generations, which, while enjoying all the blessings of an impartial and efficient system of public instruction, will find it difficult to believe that the authors of that system should have had to struggle with a vehement and pertinacious opposition, and still more difficult to believe that such an opposition was offered in the name of civil and religious freedom."[1]

[1] April 18th, 1847; Macaulay's *Speeches* (Everyman edition), pp. 349–69.

Chapter XII

STATE SUPERVISION IN ELEMENTARY
EDUCATION

Insufficiency of the Voluntary System. The Newcastle Commission. Robert Lowe
and 'Payment by Results.'

BY the middle forties it was generally recognised that the resources of voluntary effort were not of themselves sufficient to provide for the educational needs of the country. In 1846 Dr. Hook, the Vicar of Leeds, had published a pamphlet entitled *On the Means of Rendering more efficient the Education of the People*. He advocated the 'combined' system. The State should take over complete responsibility for elementary schools so far as secular instruction was concerned, and these schools should be supported from the rates; but on two afternoons a week ministers of the various denominations should have the 'right of entry' and give doctrinal instruction. Teachers were to hold certificates issued by the Government, and they were to be paid direct from this same source. The curriculum was to be broadened so as to include mathematics, drawing, geography, history, and music. The pamphlet aroused a great deal of controversy; but Kay-Shuttleworth realised that the 'comprehensive' scheme (i.e. a denominational school with a conscience clause) was the only kind which the nation would accept.

In 1850, however, the advocates of a 'secular' system founded the National Public Schools Association. Among its supporters it included men of various opinions who were united by their common impatience with the 'religious difficulty' and their belief in the importance of education. In 1850 they introduced a Bill which was sponsored by W. J. Fox, and which in some respects foreshadows the Education Act of 1870. It proposed that compulsory powers should be given to ratepayers to establish schools where there was a deficiency and to levy an education rate for the support of free and secular schools for children aged seven to thirteen. No provision was made for the existing denominational schools. The opposition of the denominationalists killed the Bill, for both the Church and the nonconformists were united in a common horror of secular education. Yet it was obvious that if a national system of popular education was to be secured, some means must be found to supplement State grants by local contributions. Several Bills with this aim were introduced. Sir John Russell's Borough Bill in 1853 proposed that school committees should be set up in boroughs in order to assist schools which were already in receipt—or eligible for receipt—of grants from the Committee of Council. This scheme was dropped, but there were three more unsuccessful Education Bills in 1855. That of Sir John Pakington (No. 2) envisaged the permissive establishment of local boards with power to aid existing schools and to set up new schools, the denominational colour of which was to be determined by the type of religion most prevalent in the area to be served—though, of course, a conscience clause was provided.

The inherent difficulty of the position with which all the abortive proposals were trying to cope was that voluntaryism of itself could not provide and finance a national system of education; rate-aid must therefore be invoked to supplement its resources from contributions and fees and to make up the not more than equivalent grant from the Committee of Council for Education. But rate-aid implies local control, and those who pay rates are of all shades of religious opinion. Not unnaturally, there were a large number of people who hotly disputed the claim of the Church of England to be responsible for national education—a claim based mainly on history and tradition; yet, except among the extreme secularists, it was generally agreed that popular education must have a religious basis. The State's contribution to education had been steadily growing since 1833, and with it voluntary effort had also grown. But it was not clear that the voluntary system with Government aid was proving capable of meeting national needs and of being so developed as to meet future needs. There were many parties and much conflict, and the dissatisfaction was general; but recognition of the importance of the education question was shown by the creation of an Education Department by an Order in Council dated February 25th, 1856. It absorbed the Privy Council's Committee for Education. The Lord President of the Council was nominally its chairman; but, as he was a peer, a Vice-President was also appointed, who was a member of the House of Commons and a member of the Government in power. He was thus responsible to the House for the expenditure of his Department and was in practice the head of it.

To investigate the complicated problems of national education, a Royal Commission was appointed in 1858, under the chairmanship of the Duke of Newcastle. Its aim was "to inquire into the Present State of Popular Education in England, and to consider and report what measures, if any, are required for the Extension of sound and cheap Elementary Instruction to all Classes of the People.'" In order to discover the "present state of popular education" ten assistant commissioners carried out an investigation in ten selected areas of differing types. It was found that a few monitorial schools still existed, but the pupil-teacher system was proving a success, though it was as yet in its initial stages. The policy of leaving popular education to the churches and the voluntary associations had in a way been justified, for it was estimated that 1 in 7·83 of the population was attending school.[1] It had been 1 in 14 or 16 forty years before, and 1 in 21 at the beginning of the century. But the great weaknesses of the system were the early leaving age (due to the demand for child labour) and the short duration and great irregularity of school life. It was estimated that only 29 per cent. of the children in inspected schools were over the age of ten, and only 19 per cent. over eleven.[2] The moral tone of the schools was said to be improving, but the education given was in many cases most elementary and superficial; and there was a tendency for teachers to neglect the younger children and hand them over to the pupil-teachers.

The Newcastle Commission reported in 1861 and made their recommendations for "the extension of sound and cheap

[1] See Newcastle Commission *Report*, vol. i, p. 87.
[2] *Op. cit.*, vol. i, p. 171.

elementary instruction." The adjectives are significant. Immense sums had been frittered away on the Crimean War, and the annually increasing education grant (it was £663,435 in 1858) was regarded with some alarm. As at other periods in our history in the face of expenditure on war, national education was regarded as a suitable field for economies. At any rate, value for money should be secured. The Commission thought that the system of State grants inaugurated in 1833 had not succeeded in effecting a "general diffusion of sound elementary education among all classes of the poor." They did not, however, advocate the withdrawal of the grants, but they wished rather to secure regular attendance, sounder teaching, and a wider curriculum for older pupils.

The existing system was not without value, but it had serious defects. The central government was paying for benefits which were mainly local, and the most needy areas got the least help, because they could not raise from voluntary sources the necessary half-cost of buildings and maintenance. Again, elementary subjects were badly taught, and the whole system was getting unwieldy and difficult to manage. The Commissioners therefore recommended a simplification. The State should pay capitation grants, with an additional grant for pupil-teachers, to schools which had a satisfactory report from Her Majesty's inspector. These grants should be supplemented by local grants from county and borough rates, based on the attainments of the pupils as assessed by examination by the inspector.[1] Thus was introduced the system of 'payment by results' which hampered the development of English elementary education for many years to come. There was no suggestion of abolishing school fees; the amount received from both State and local contributions was not to exceed the amount raised by fees and subscriptions. Nor was there any idea of introducing compulsory attendance, as had already been done in Prussia. "An attempt," it was said, "to replace an independent system of education by a compulsory system, managed by the Government, would be met by objections, both religious and political, of far graver character in this country

[1] See Newcastle Commission *Report*, vol. i, pp. 544–5.

than any with which it has had to contend in Prussia."[1] To administer the local grant county or borough boards were to be
elected, but they were to have no power in the management of the
schools, nor were they to concern themselves with the religious
teaching given there. Such, then, were the recommendations of
the Newcastle Commission. As one would expect, they had been
reached after much compromise, and they aroused a great deal of
criticism. The Government therefore felt unable to risk embody-
ing their proposals in an Education Bill.

Kay-Shuttleworth had retired in 1849. He had laid the foundations of English elementary education; he had stimulated public
interest and his pupil-teachers had put an end to the mechanical
monitorial system. To him education meant an inculcation of
habits, a training of skills, and a development of intelligence; the
school was to be a centre of social life and culture. His views were
very far in advance of those of most educational administrators of
his day. But by the time of the Newcastle Commission national
educational administration was in the hands of a very different
person. Robert Lowe had been Vice-President of the Education
Department since 1859. He was a Liberal free-trader and was prepared to apply to education his economic theories.

The late fifties and early sixties are a period in which the
belief in the value of examinations was greatly strengthened. It
was increasingly felt that they afforded a reliable way of selecting
merit and of avoiding nepotism. The Oxford and Cambridge
locals date from 1858; the Science and Art examinations from
1861. Open competition was gradually introduced into the Civil
Service from 1855 onwards. These facts have a bearing on Lowe's
conception of the administration of popular education. He
thought that if minor Civil Service appointments (e.g. postmen)
were thrown open to competition, poor people would be the
more ready to keep their children at school at their own expense,
in the hope of their securing a post of this kind by examination.
In short, the scheme squared with free-trade theories of demand
and supply. Lowe was therefore unwilling to accept the Newcastle Commission's recommendation that education grants

[1] *Op. cit.*, vol. i, p. 300.

I

should be paid from the rates; but he proposed to retain the denominational character of popular education and "the practice of giving grants from the central office in aid of local subscriptions." One of the chief weaknesses of the system, as revealed by the investigations of the Newcastle Commissioners, was low and irregular school attendance. It had been estimated that in 1858, of 2,213,694 children at school, 38·81 per cent. attended for less than one year.[1] Lowe tried to remedy this state of affairs by basing the Education Department's grants, not simply on the amount raised by local voluntary effort, but on the attendance of pupils under a certificated teacher, and subject to the results of an examination of each child in the 'three R's' by an inspector. "Hitherto," he said, "we have been living under a system of bounties and protection. Now we propose to have a little free trade." So the teachers' pension scheme, grants for apparatus, and pupil-teachers' stipends were withdrawn, and grants to training colleges were cut down. These measures were embodied in the 'Revised Code' of 1862—a document issued by the Education Department, and having statutory force. In reply to criticisms Lowe said of the new system: "If it is not cheap, it shall be efficient; if it is not efficient, it shall be cheap."[2]

'Payment by results' lasted with modifications for nearly forty years; it was not finally disposed of until the introduction of the block-grant system in 1900. It did certainly effect economies. In 1861 the education grant was £813,441; this fell to £636,806 in 1865. The immediate effect of the Revised Code was also a rise in average attendance. In 1862 this was 888,923; in 1866, 1,048,493. So long as Parliament acquiesced in child labour and refused to introduce compulsory schooling, the most that could be done was to give the child, who would probably leave school to go to work at about the age of twelve, or less, the minimum of elementary instruction. This was assessed under the Revised Code as ability to read a short passage from a newspaper, to take it down from dictation, and to do arithmetic up to bills of parcels. The scheme of work for the elementary school

[1] See *Report*, pp. 79 and 173.
[2] Speech, February 13th, 1862, *Hansard*, vol. 165, 229.

was also graded and organised far more definitely than had been customary hitherto. The syllabus mentioned above was for the leaving year—the Sixth 'Standard'; but each of the previous five standards had also a definite course of work leading up to it. The child entered Standard I at the age of about six; at the end of the year he was examined and passed on to the next standard. If he were successful in his examination, he could earn his grant, but he could not be presented more than once at the same grade. It was a rigid and mechanical method of promotion, but it did tend to stiffen up school organisation.

On the other hand, the shortcomings of the Revised Code were clearly seen by such educationists as Kay-Shuttleworth and Matthew Arnold; and subsequent history shows the justice of their condemnation of it. The examination system resulted—as it so often does—in over-pressure on the children, due to anxiety to produce 'results.' The teaching of the three 'R's' may have improved because teachers were tempted to concentrate on these grant-earning subjects and neglect other work; but this encouraged mechanical methods in teaching.[1] The New Code also tended to demoralise the teachers. Their position in the eyes of school managers, and therefore their very livelihood, might depend on the amount of grant earned by their pupils. Hence there was a temptation to falsify registers and hoodwink inspectors by making children learn off their reading book by heart. One of the inspectors stated that he used to try to counteract this practice by requiring pupils to read their book backwards. It is easy to realise how this situation led to a feeling of hostility—or, at any rate, of distrust, between teachers and inspectors. That feeling outlived the system of 'payment by results,' and it is hardly dead in some quarters yet. The quality of the teachers also declined owing to the New Code. The withdrawal of the pupil-teachers' grants caused a serious decrease in their numbers and efficiency, just at the time when the number of pupils was increasing. The result was a growth in the size of classes. There was less

[1] In the *Life and Remains of R. H. Quick* (pp. 128–57 *passim*) there are some interesting first-hand accounts of the teaching in elementary schools under the conditions imposed by 'Payment by Results.'

inducement and less opportunity for head teachers to train pupil-teachers, and thus the standard of admission to training colleges had to be lowered. This again reacted against the schools. "When the numbers in attendance reach a certain point and competent assistants are withheld, it is inevitable that one end or other of the school must be neglected and that the victimised portion will be that which is least likely to produce money for the examination grant."[1] Kay-Shuttleworth had some justification for his statement that "the Revised Code has constructed nothing; it has only pulled down."[2] But under his successor, R. R. W. Lingen, the system of 'payment by results' was emphasised, and relations between the Education Department and those responsible for teaching and school administration, which had been cordial in the days of Kay-Shuttleworth, tended to cool off. This helped to increase the unpopularity of the Department and the Code which it administered.[3]

[1] See *Report* of Committee of Council on Education, for 1866–7, pp. 394–5.

[2] *Memorandum on Popular Education*, p. 30; quoted by Frank Smith, *The Life of Sir James Kay-Shuttleworth*, p. 287.

[3] On Lingen, see the article in *British Journal of Educational Studies*, June 1968, pp. 138–68.

Chapter XIII

THE EDUCATION ACT OF 1870

ALTHOUGH attempts were made to tinker with the Revised Code, it soon became obvious that it would never succeed in providing an adequate system of popular education. But there was a growing realisation of the necessity for this. Even a convinced individualist like J. S. Mill said in 1859: "Is it not almost a self-evident maxim that the State should require and compel the education up to a certain standard of every human being who is born its citizen?"[1] Herbert Spencer and Thomas Huxley were also arousing public interest in education. Yet the actual state of the children in many parts of the country was still deplorable, owing to the demand for their labour. The non-contentious provisions of Graham's Bill of 1843 had been passed as a Factory Act in the following year, and this compelled the parents of children who worked in textile mills to make them attend school on three full days, or six half-days, in each week. Further regulations of 1864 and 1867 extended these provisions to non-textile factories and workshops. But evasion was easy; and in agriculture the employment of children in gangs was still common. The children were sent away to work for farmers who were short-handed, and were put in the charge of an overseer. It was a system which obviously was liable to abuse. Secularists and Voluntaryists alike realised the seriousness of these evils. Societies of various kinds were formed in big towns, such as Manchester, Birmingham, and Liverpool, to try to help deserving parents to pay school fees and to encourage them to send their children to school regularly.

In 1867 came the Reform Bill, which gave the vote to householders who paid rates. This enfranchised the artisans of the big

---

[1] *On Liberty*, chap. v, p. 157 (Routledge ed.).

industrial towns who had not been qualified as 'ten-pound house-holders' under the 1832 Reform Act. A lodger franchise was also added in Committee. Mr. Lowe, who did not approve of the Bill, said, in an oft-quoted epigram, "We must educate our masters."[1]

In the following year the Liberals came into power, under Mr. Gladstone, and the Education Department was put in the charge of W. E. Forster, a Quaker, a Radical, and a prosperous West Riding woollen manufacturer. He had married a daughter of Dr. Thomas Arnold, and, like his father-in-law, was deeply interested in education and in social questions. In the large towns of the North, such as Bradford, which Forster represented in Parliament, the population had outstripped the school provision; there was not only a lack of school places, but also an uneven distribution of schools. It was impossible for Forster and the Government which he represented to ignore the great existing voluntary system, though there were many Liberals and nonconformists who would have liked to see the establishment of a system of publicly controlled schools financed from State funds. But, as Gladstone himself said in the House: "It was with us an absolute necessity—a necessity of honour and a necessity of policy —to respect and to favour the educational establishments and machinery we found existing in the country. It was impossible for us to join in the language or adopt the tone which was conscientiously and consistently taken by some members of the House who look upon these voluntary schools, having generally a denominational character, as admirable passing expedients, fit, indeed, to be tolerated for a time, deserving all credit on account of the motives which led to their foundation, but wholly unsatisfactory as to their main purpose and therefore to be supplanted by something they think better. . . . That has never been the theory of the Government."[2] This attitude led to serious breaches inside the Liberal Party, but Gladstone and Forster stood their ground. In February 1870 Forster had introduced a Bill in which (in his own words), he proposed "to complete the present volun-

[1] For what Lowe really said, see *Oxford Dictionary of Quotations*, p. 572.
[2] *Hansard*, cciii, 746, July 22nd, 1870.

tary system, to fill up gaps, sparing the public money where it can be done without, procuring as much as we can the assistance of the parents, and welcoming as much as we rightly can the co-operation and aid of those benevolent men who desire to assist their neighbours."[1] Thus the 1870 Act was essentially a compromise. It did not create a new national system of education, or a completely compulsory system, or a free system. It left room for voluntary effort and school fees and private endowments.

The Bill divided up the country into 'school districts,' which were the municipal boroughs or civil parishes. London was a separate 'school district.' The Education Department was given power to investigate the available school accommodation in each district and to determine how much further accommodation, if any, was necessary. If there was a deficiency, the denominations were allowed a period of grace, until the end of the year 1870, in which to supply it, and they could apply for a parliamentary grant in aid of building, enlarging, improving, or fitting up an elementary school; but they were to get no help for this purpose from the rates. If they did not, or could not, supply the deficiency —'fill up the gaps,' as Forster had said—a new local authority, the school board, was to be set up. It was to be elected *ad hoc* by the ratepayers, and women were eligible for membership of it; it would hold office for three years. It would have powers to establish and maintain public elementary schools with rate aid, in addition to Government grant and school fees. The school board was also to be empowered to appoint an officer or officers to enforce the attendance of children between the ages of five and twelve, unless satisfactory arrangements for their education had already been made. Schooling was not to be made free. Section 17 of the Act laid it down that: "Every child attending a school provided by any school board shall pay such weekly fee as may be prescribed by the school board, with the consent of the Education Department; but the school board may, from time to time, for a renewable period not exceeding six months, remit the whole or any part of such fee in the case of any child when they are of opinion that the parent of such child is unable from poverty to

[1] *Op. cit.*, cxcix, 444, February 17th, 1870.

pay the same." In any case, "the ordinary payments in respect of the instruction from each scholar" were not to exceed ninepence a week.[1]

School boards were left to decide whether their schools should give religious instruction, but if it was provided, "no religious catechism or religious formulary which is distinctive of any particular denomination shall be taught."[2] This is the famous 'Cowper–Temple Clause'. Section 7 (1) moreover, stated that: "It shall not be required, as a condition of any child being admitted into or continuing in the school, that he shall attend or abstain from attending any Sunday school, or any place of religious worship, or that he shall attend any religious observance or instruction in religious subjects in the school or elsewhere, from which observance or instruction he may be withdrawn by his parent, or that he shall, if withdrawn by his parent, attend the school on any day set apart for religious observance by the religious body to which his parent belongs." In order to facilitate withdrawal from religious instruction, when desired, it was provided that this should be given either at the beginning or at the end of a school session. Even in a State-aided voluntary school no child was to be compelled to attend religious instruction, and the 'conscience clause' was obligatory on all schools which received Government grant. In both board schools and voluntary schools alike religious instruction was no longer inspected or enforced as a condition of grant, and this was made wholly in respect of secular instruction.

The school boards were abolished by the Education Act of 1902, but the dual system of education which was set up in 1870 still exists. The two types of school were clearly marked. The board schools were secular and non-denominational; they were provided by local authorities (i.e. the school boards), and they were maintained out of rates and Government grants. The voluntary schools, on the other hand, were for the most part denominational. They had been built by endowments or subscriptions, and were maintained partly from this source and partly by Government grants—but not by rates; and they were

---

[1] *Education Act*, 1870, § 3.   [2] *Op. cit.*, § 14 (2).

controlled by 'managers,' who were not elected, as were the members of the school boards. In both types of school it was still possible to charge fees. It should be noted that the school boards did not cover the whole country, but were set up only in places where voluntary effort was not sufficient to supply the local demand.

As has been said, the Act, which came into force on August 8th, 1870, was a compromise, and for that reason it incurred bitter criticism and opposition from several quarters. But for all that, it was a notable achievement, for it did gradually 'fill up the gaps' and so secure a more adequate supply of schools. But for it, England would have fallen behind among the nations of Europe. The noteworthy advance which Prussia, for example, had made since the beginning of the century, and her recent successes in the war against France, were attributed as much to her educational system as to her military organisation. Mr. G. M. Trevelyan makes the comment that "it was characteristic of the two nations that whereas the German people already enjoyed good schools, but not self-government, the rulers of England only felt compelled to 'educate their masters' when the working-men were in full possession of the franchise."[1] Finally, it should be recorded that one of the effects of the institution of school boards was to stimulate voluntary effort. During the 'period of grace'—a bare five months—3,342 applications for building grants were made; of these 1,333 were subsequently withdrawn, but of the remainder over 1,600 were allowed. In the years immediately preceding 1870 the number of applications had averaged about 150. Between 1870 and 1876 a million and a half new school places were provided; but of these two-thirds were due to the churches and only one-third to the new school boards.[2]

[1] *British History in the Nineteenth Century*, p. 353.
[2] The first 'board school' was opened at St. Austell, Cornwall, in December 1872.

Chapter XIV

UNIVERSITY EDUCATION

J. H. Newman and Mark Pattison. The Oxford and Cambridge Acts.

EDUCATIONAL activity in the middle decades of the nineteenth century was not confined to working out the problem of providing a national system of elementary schools. In university and secondary education there is also progress to show. University reform at this period owed much to John Henry Newman and Mark Pattison, though their methods of approach to it differed greatly. Newman (1801–90) had been a fellow of Oriel in the days of the 'noetics.'[1] He was later caught up in the Oxford Movement, and finally, after many spiritual wrestlings, which are recorded in his *Apologia pro Vita Sua*, he joined the Church of Rome in 1845. Nine years later he was sent to Dublin as rector of a Roman Catholic university which had just been established. This institution proved a failure, partly through lack of State recognition, and partly because Newman had little ability for organisation or administration. But his theories on university education are set out in *The Idea of a University*, which has more than a contemporary interest. Apparently Newman has in mind the Platonic ἰδέα, and his search is for an academic *Republic*. To him all knowledge is one; and as man's most fundamental relationship is to God, so theology is the most 'architectonic' of the sciences—the basis of all true education. It cannot be separated from the other forms of knowledge as a distinct subject. Mere intellectual education, therefore, is not necessarily good in itself. In a famous passage Newman says that if he had to choose between two university courses, one non-residential but intellectually exacting, and the other residential but intellectually disorganised, he would prefer the latter. Such a community "will constitute a whole, it will embody a specific idea, it will represent a doctrine, it will administer a code of conduct, and it will furnish

[1] See *supra*, p. 74.

principles of thought and action. It will give birth to a living teaching, which in course of time will take the shape of a self-perpetuating tradition or a *genius loci*, as it is sometimes called, which haunts the home where it has been born, and which imbues and forms, more or less, and one by one, every individual who is successively brought under its shadow."[1] The contrast between Oxford and the twenty-year-old University of London[2] is implicit in the whole passage, which does indeed sum up the true inwardness of university life. That the truth of Newman's contention is increasingly being realised is shown by the attempts of our modern 'provincial' universities to provide residential facilities for more and more of their students.

Yet Newman is no despiser of intellectual achievement. The arts and the sciences must play their part in a university education, but they must be regarded by a philosophic habit of mind which looks for relationships and co-ordinates knowledge. For knowledge is "something more than a sort of passive reception of scraps and details; it is a something and it does a something, which never will issue from the most strenuous efforts of a set of teachers, with no mutual sympathies and no intercommunion, of a set of examiners with no opinions which they dare profess, and with no common principles, who are teaching or questioning a set of youths who do not know them, and do not know each other, on a large number of subjects, different in kind, and connected by no wide philosophy, three times a week, or three times a year, or once in three years, in chill lecture-rooms or on a pompous anniversary."[3] And since it is the Church which supplies the underlying, unifying, 'architectonic' science, it is the Church which is to devise and superintend the organisation of the university. In short, the academic *Republic* for Newman is an idealised Catholic Oxford.[4]

Mark Pattison (1813–84) had been an undergraduate at Oriel, but in 1839 he became a Fellow of Lincoln and was ultimately Rector of this college until his death. In his early days he too was

---

[1] *The Idea of a University*, Discourse VI, § 9.
[2] *Op. cit.*, Discourse VI, § 8.   [3] *Op. cit.*, Discourse VI, § 9.
[4] He had also the University of Louvain in mind.

influenced by the Oxford Movement; but he afterwards reacted violently against it in the opposite direction to that which Newman took. He was ill at ease in the Church of England and a bitter critic of its representatives. (He contributed to the once famous *Essays and Reviews*, which were considered unorthodox and incurred episcopal condemnation.) This made him rather a lonely figure in the Oxford of his day; but he had a brilliant intellect and a broad, philosophical outlook.[1] He greatly interested himself in university reform,[2] and in particular he advocated the professorial, as contrasted with the tutorial, system of instruction. This method was customary in Germany and also in Scotland, where the universities had nothing comparable with the colleges of Oxford and Cambridge. The professorial system had been advocated by the *Edinburgh Review* in the early years of the century, and more recently by the founders of London University; but the giving of instruction by tutors was closely bound up with the existence of colleges—and both institutions were strongly entrenched in Oxford. Pattison did not go so far as to advocate the complete replacement of tutorial by professorial teaching; but his views, as can be understood, were by no means popular in Oxford, and his own personality did little to commend them. He is a trenchant critic of the low standards of the pass degree, which demanded little more than school studies.[3] He maintains that "the first and indispensable condition of the efficiency of the higher education is an intellectual activity, general, pervading, sustained; and that this activity be directed upon the central and proper object of human knowledge. . . . The instructor does not lay down principles, he initiates into methods; he is himself an investigator, and he is inviting the pupil to accompany him on his road."[4] To Pattison, therefore, research is a primary function of the university. The whole issue has been raised again in our own time by Mr. 'Bruce Truscot.'[5]

The champions of academic reform had made considerable

[1] There is a good picture of Mark Pattison in Tuckwell, *Reminiscences of Oxford*, chap. xiii. See also Greene, *Oxford Common Room*.
[2] See his *Suggestions on Academical Organisation, passim*.
[3] See *op. cit.*, p. 163   [4] *Essays*, vol. i, pp. 418 and 420.
[5] In *Redbrick University, passim*.

headway during the forties. As Mark Pattison himself said: "A restless fever of change had spread through the colleges—the wonder-working phrase 'University Reform' had been uttered. ... We were ready to reform a great deal—everything—only show us how to set about it and give us the necessary powers."[1] Both inside and outside the university this spirit was felt. In 1849 a memorial was presented to the Prime Minister, Lord John Russell. It was signed by members of both Oxford and Cambridge, and by Fellows of the Royal Society, and it urged that a Royal Commission should be issued to enquire into the state, discipline, and revenues of the two Universities. The investigation was carried out and the Commissioners reported in 1852. Those who visited Oxford had encountered considerable opposition, but their colleagues who went to Cambridge were more cordially received. The recommendations of the two Reports formed the basis of the Oxford University Act of 1854 and the Cambridge University Act of 1856. In both cases the aim was to clear away existing handicaps and to give the Universities a clear field to develop along their own lines without further State interference. One obstacle to reform lay in the fact that the Universities were still tied and bound by founders' regulations or ancient statutes. Oxford was still governed by enactments of Archbishop Laud, and Cambridge by those of Queen Elizabeth. The real power lay with the heads of colleges—with the Hebdomadal Board at Oxford and the Caput at Cambridge. These alone could initiate legislation, and there was a final veto in the hands of all M.A.s who had kept their names on the books. The Acts of 1854 and 1856 therefore widened the representation of the Hebdomadal Board and the Caput and gave greater power to other representatives of the University, both resident and non-resident. Measures could now be discussed in English instead of in Latin, as hitherto.

In the colleges most of the old local restrictions as to 'close' or 'founder's kin' scholarships and fellowships were removed, and these were thrown open to competition. Religious tests were removed for admission to the University or for taking the degree of B.A.—which, it should be noted, gave no right to any share in

[1] *Memoirs*, p. 245.

the government of the University. The test was not finally abolished for all degrees (except those in divinity) until 1871.[1] At the same time a number of new professorships were founded, and endowments of older ones were augmented from the revenues of certain colleges. The professors were also given a place of greater importance in university administration. The new system afforded some sort of approximation between the views of those who, like Sir William Hamilton or (to some extent) Mark Pattison, advocated the German or Scottish plan, and those of the Oxford Tutors' Association and other champions of the current tutorial method of instruction. The tutors were not displaced, but the professors could carry on research in and teach subjects which the colleges could not provide; also many professorships now had college fellowships attached to them, and this strengthened the link.

The Commissioners had drawn attention to the great and largely unnecessary expense of university life. One of the reasons why London University had been founded was to provide university facilities for those of limited means. In 1832 a university had also been established at Durham. Before the coming of the railways the country areas of Northumberland, Westmorland, Cumberland, and Durham were much cut off from communication with the rest of the country. The population was sparse and the clergy were for the most part very poor and inadequately educated. Bishop Van Mildert sought to remedy this state of affairs by helping to found the University of Durham. It was started in the Norman castle which fronts the cathedral, and it was run on the residential lines of Oxford and Cambridge, but at a much lower cost. Subsequently another college (Hatfield Hall) on still more economical lines was founded. It was at once crowded out and further accommodation had to be provided. It was thus obvious that there was a strong demand for university education at reasonable rates. The Oxford and Cambridge University Acts did something to meet this by making possible the opening of

[1] One is still admitted to the M.A. degree at Oxford "in nomine Domini, Patris Filii et Spiritus Sancti." There is an excellent Appendix on the history of the movement for the abolition of University Tests in Dicey, *Law and Opinion in England* (pp. 477–81).

private 'halls,' presided over by an M.A.; this was a reversion to a common practice in the Middle Ages. In the event this scheme was adopted only to a limited extent—as was also the subsequent admission of 'non-collegiate' or 'unattached' students living in licensed lodgings. But there is no doubt that extravagance became less fashionable at Oxford and Cambridge as the second half of the nineteenth century progressed. This was due largely to the development of secondary education and the throwing open of scholarships so as to widen the field from which candidates were drawn. It is also probable, as Professor Archer suggests,[1] that the development of sports at the Universities put an end to the exclusiveness of the hunting, shooting, and racing type of undergraduate. The Oxford and Cambridge boat race, as an annual event, dates from 1856; inter-collegiate boat races started about 1815 and were properly organised from about 1837.[2] Cricket (in top-hats) also developed in the forties. All these activities gave prominence in college to the undergraduate who can do things—and not to the man with the greatest wealth or the 'best family' or the most extravagant tastes; and this characteristic fortunately has remained true of both Oxford and Cambridge.

[1] *Secondary Education in the Nineteenth Century*, p. 157.
[2] See *Brasenose Quatercentenary Monographs*, vol. ii, no. xiv, i.

Chapter XV

SECONDARY EDUCATION

The Clarendon and Schools Inquiry Commissions.

THE close association between the Universities of Oxford and Cambridge and the public schools meant that an investigation of the state of the former inevitably drew public attention to the latter also. In spite of the growing importance of science and modern studies, which had been illustrated by the Great Exhibition of 1851 and in a hundred other different ways, the public-schools curriculum in most cases remained unaffected by contemporary progress; and it was realised that both France and Germany were ahead of us in the field of secondary education, as well as in that of elementary and technical education. Public opinion on this point is well exemplified by a leader in the *Illustrated London News* of May 4th, 1861. "No Latin or Greek," it says, "may make Master Jacky a dull boy; but Latin and Greek without anything else go far towards making Master Jacky a very dullard. Parents are beginning to feel this, and to ask whether a skinful of classical knowledge, with a little birching thrown in for nothing, be an equivalent for the two hundred a year they pay for the education of a boy at Eton. It is true that the young Hopefuls of the aristocracy *may* learn French, German, drawing, and mathematics at public schools—just as they may learn Berlin-wool work or the cornet-à-pistons—but these branches of polite education are treated as 'extras' and charged for accordingly."

The general tone of the public schools had certainly been raised by Arnold and those whom he influenced, but it was still felt that ignorance and idleness were far too common. It was for these reasons that in 1861 Lord Palmerston's Government set up a Royal Commission, under the chairmanship of Lord Clarendon, to inquire into the revenues, management, and curriculum of the nine chief public schools—Eton, Winchester, Westminster, Charterhouse, Harrow, Rugby, Shrewsbury, Merchant Taylors', and St. Paul's. The Commissioners carried out a thorough investigation and issued their report in 1864. They had something to say to allay public misgivings. They praised the discipline and moral tone of the schools and emphasised the progress that had been made during the previous twenty-five years; but the curriculum came in for serious criticism, and the ineffectiveness of much of the teaching was laid bare. "The course of study," says the *Report*, "has been enlarged, the methods of teaching improved, the proportion of masters to boys increased; the quantity of work exacted is greater than it was, though still in too many cases less than it ought to be. At the same time the advance in moral and religious training has more than kept pace with that in intellectual discipline. The old roughness of manners has in great measure disappeared. . . . The boys are better lodged and cared for, and more attention is paid to their health and comfort. Among the services which [the public schools] have rendered is undoubtedly to be reckoned the maintenance of classical literature as the staple of English education, a service which far outweighs the error of having clung to these studies too exclusively. A second and greater still is the creation of a system of government and discipline for boys, the excellence of which is admitted to have been most important in its effects on national character and social life."[1]

At the same time the Commissioners expressed the opinion that "in their course of study, sound and valuable in its main elements but wanting in breadth and flexibility, there are defects which destroy in many cases, and impair in all, its value as an education of the mind; and which are made more prominent at the present time by the extension of knowledge in various directions and by the multiplied reforms of modern life. . . . We have been unable to resist the conclusion that these schools, in very different degrees, are too indulgent to idleness, or struggle ineffectually with it, and that they consequently send out a large proportion of men of idle habits and empty and uncultivated minds."[2] In spite of the great emphasis which was laid on the Classics and the large proportion of the pupils' time spent in the study of them, the results, even in

[1] *Report of Public Schools Commission*, p. 56.   [2] *Op. cit.*, p. 55.

K

these subjects, were in many cases most unsatisfactory; while the inferior status afforded to other subjects in the curriculum encouraged the idea that they were comparatively unimportant and less worthy of attention. A change of attitude was urgently needed. "A young man . . . is not well educated if all his information is shut up within one narrow circle."[1]

The Commissioners advocated the reform of governing bodies and the remodelling of the curriculum on the lines of that of the German classical secondary school or *Gymnasium*. Classics and religious instruction were still regarded as the chief studies of the public school, but mathematics, French or German, and some instruction in natural science and music or drawing should be included. The recommendations of the *Report* were followed up by the Public Schools Act of 1868, which applied to all the schools which had been investigated, with the exception of Merchant Taylors' and St. Paul's. By its provisions each school was required to submit a scheme for a new and more representative governing body. This body was given full powers with regard to school fees, the curriculum, and the appointment or dismissal of the headmaster. The latter was responsible to the governing body, but he had the right to appoint his assistant masters and they had no appeal to the governors from his decisions. The seven schools affected by the Act were attended by some 3,000 pupils—the élite of the country's youth, and their governing bodies administered an aggregate annual income of about £65,000. The schemes drawn up by these bodies were to be submitted to and approved by the Queen in Council, but there was to be no continued responsibility for the schools, and they were not liable to Government inspection. The policy adopted was one of decentralisation and each school remained virtually independent.

The Clarendon Commission was followed in 1864 by the Schools Inquiry Commission, under Lord Taunton's chairmanship, and it reported in 1868. Its business was to investigate the schools which had not been considered by the Newcastle and Clarendon Commissions—i.e. schools other than the elementary schools and the public schools. For the purposes of this Com-

[1] *Op. cit.*, p. 30.

mission Matthew Arnold, son of Dr. Thomas Arnold and an inspector of schools, visited France, Germany, Switzerland, and Italy, and reported on their secondary education. Of the schools investigated by the Commissioners, nearly 800 were endowed and many were of great antiquity. They were not maintained by public moneys, either in the form of rate aid or of Government grant, and they were not proprietary—i.e. under private management. The administration of their endowments was quite outside the purview of the Education Department, and was the concern of the Charity Commission which had been set up in 1853. But the Taunton Commission also investigated 122 proprietary schools maintained by joint-stock companies. A number of schools of this type had recently come into existence. Some of these were day schools on the lines of Merchant Taylors' or St. Paul's; examples are University College School, originally founded in 1830 as London University School, and King's College School, dating from 1831. Others were boarding schools— e.g. Cheltenham (1841) and Malvern (1865). There were also the Woodard Schools—as, for instance, Lancing and Hurstpierpoint, founded in 1849 and 1851—which were due to the enthusiasm of Nathaniel Woodard. His aim was to provide institutions on the lines of the older public schools, but with greater economy, and by such means to foster Tractarianism. Again, there were the 'County Schools' (not in the modern sense)— boarding schools with moderate fees for "the education of boys of the middle class on the public-school system." West Buckland in Devon, and Dorchester, in Dorset, for example, had schools of this type, and the former still survives. These proprietary schools were not so expensive as the great public schools, and they tended to provide a more 'modern' education than the older endowed schools. The majority of the latter still by founders' statutes had to give a classical education. But, with the exception of a few old grammar schools like Tonbridge, Repton, and Uppingham (under Thring), which had worked their way up to public-school rank and sent a fair number of boys to Oxford and Cambridge, most of the endowed schools served small towns or agricultural areas where a rigidly classical curriculum was useless.

Such, then, was the situation with which the Taunton Commissioners had to deal. Their *Report* was issued in twenty-one volumes, and it included a full account of the conditions found in each of the 942 schools which were visited. Their general findings and recommendations are given in the first volume of this *Report*. They advocated that three types of school should be made available, with the leaving ages of eighteen to nineteen, sixteen and fourteen respectively.

The first would be for the sons of parents of ample means, or of good education but 'confined means'; the second for boys whose parents' means were 'straightened,' or who wished to enter professions requiring early special training (e.g. medicine, the Army, engineering); and the third for the sons of "the smaller tenant farmers, the small tradesmen, the superior artisans."[1] This third type of school was regarded as "the most urgent educational need of the country." The distinction between the three kinds of school, which corresponded "roughly, but by no means exactly, to the gradations of society,"[2] was made by the curriculum recommended for each of them. It was felt that there should be no attempt to displace the Classics in the first-grade school, but that the course should be broadened so as to include mathematics, modern languages, and science. In fact, what was needed was more schools of the type of those investigated by the Clarendon Commission, but with a wider curriculum and lower fees.

In the second grade of school, with a leaving age of sixteen, Latin at least should be retained, and to this should be added "a certain amount of thorough knowledge of those subjects which can be turned to practical use in business, English, arithmetic, the rudiments of mathematics beyond arithmetic, in some cases natural science, in some cases a modern language."[3]

It appeared clear to the Commissioners that parents who would send their sons to schools of the third grade would not wish for a technical or vocational education. "On this point there was an almost unanimous agreement in favour of general education."[4]

[1] *Report*, vol. i, p. 20.   [2] *Op. cit.*, p. 16.
[3] *Op. cit.*, p. 20.   [4] *Op. cit.*, p. 21.

The subjects of instruction could be classified under the headings of language, mathematics, and natural science. There was some difference of opinion among the Commissioners as to whether Latin should be taught in the third-grade schools, but it was felt that one language other than English should be included in their curriculum. Mathematics and drawing are important, but some doubt is expressed as to whether Euclid is a good text-book for beginners. Natural science, if facilities and skilled teaching are available, should form part of the course. In all three types of school alike religious instruction should be retained, but parents should have the right to withdraw their children from it should they wish to do so. The restriction of masterships to persons in holy orders should be abolished.

The *Report* goes on to discuss the organisation of secondary education. An 'Administrative Board' is needed as a central authority. This could be either a new body, or it might be constituted by enlarging the powers of the Charity Commission. It would deal mainly with educational endowments and would appoint "proper officers for the inspection of the endowed secondary schools."[1] There should also be in every Registrar-General's division[2] a 'provincial authority,' with an official district commissioner. He would inspect each endowed secondary school in his division at least once in every three years, and make a thorough report on it. Towns of 100,000 inhabitants, or over, might be allowed to "withdraw from the jurisdiction of the Provincial Boards and rank as provinces of themselves."[3] The individual schools would, of course, have their own governors who would fix the subjects of instruction, appoint the headmaster, and manage the endowment and expenses of the school. The management of secondary schools should be "in some reasonable measure" left under local control; but "in the internal management as a general rule the less the trustees interfere with the master the better."[4] It would be the duty of the provincial authority to decide the grade of each school in its area, and efficient private

[1] *Op. cit.*, p. 634.
[2] The country had been divided up into eleven districts by the Registrar-General for the purpose of the census.
[3] *Op. cit.*, p. 643.   [4] *Op. cit.*, p. 644.

schools could be registered according to their grade, and officially inspected and examined. Parliament should regulate the purposes to which endowments should be applied, and there should be greatly increased provision for girls from this source. "The exclusion of girls from the benefit of Educational Endowments would be in the highest degree inexpedient and unjust."[1] At the same time, gratuitous instruction should be given only to such children as are most capable of profiting by it. On the question of school expenses, it was maintained that if education is made too cheap it will not be valued; but fees should be kept low and fixed by governors. The hostel system in boarding schools was regarded as preferable to 'houses' run by masters for their own profit.

In order that the schools should be efficient, the Commissioners made recommendations with regard to the qualifications of their staff and the examination of their pupils. Some means was needed whereby competent teachers could be discriminated from those who were incompetent. The profession should be made "attractive to men of ability"—and this implied better salaries. The Commissioners considered, but turned down, the proposal to set up an *École Normale*, on the French model; and they therefore discouraged any form of professional training which "would almost inevitably give the Government an undue control over all the superior education of the country."[2] But it was recommended that certificates of competence should be given to teachers after due examination, which should test "not the candidate's knowledge only, but whether his knowledge is adapted both in form and substance to the uses of his profession."[3] The list of those who had qualified for these certificates would form a 'scholastic register,' on the lines of the Medical Register, which had been instituted in 1858. It was further suggested that teachers should be superannuated at the age of sixty, or sixty-five. The efficiency of the teaching would also be tested by a system of periodic inspections and examinations of schools by the officers appointed by the central administrative board. The university local examinations and those of the College of Preceptors seemed

[1] *Op. cit.*, p. 567.   [2] *Op. cit.*, p. 613.   [3] *Op. cit.*, p. 614.

"hardly easy enough to test the work of any large proportion of scholars";[1] and therefore each official inspector, aided by a panel of examiners, should test the schools in his district at some stated time which would not interfere with their normal time-tables. In order to standardise and regularise these examinations, there should be created a Council of Examinations, consisting of two members elected by each of the Universities of Oxford, Cambridge, and London, and six appointed by the Crown. They would nominate the examiners who formed the panel in each area presided over by the district Commissioner. This Council would also "make the necessary rules for the examination of candidates for the office of schoolmaster, appointing the examiners, and granting the certificates."[2]

The *Report* of the Schools Inquiry Commission is a document of the greatest interest because it contains many of the germs of the subsequent reorganisation of secondary education in this country. But those germs lay dormant for very many years, and the immediate effect of the Commissioners' four years of unremitting activity was very meagre. In 1869 Mr. Gladstone's Government passed the Endowed Schools Act. It gutted the *Report*. No local authorities were set up; there was to be no obligatory annual examination of pupils in endowed schools, although the Commissioners had said that this was "the pivot of all improvements" recommended by them; nor was there to be any registration of teachers. The Act confined itself to the problem of educational endowments. Three special Endowed School Commissioners were appointed to initiate schemes for the better application of these; and provision was to be made, so far as was possible, for extending to girls the benefit of endowments. Public schools and elementary schools were outside the control of the Commissioners, and so were secondary-school endowments less than fifty years old unless the governing body of the school concerned consented. Pupils were to be withdrawn from religious instruction if their parents made this request in writing, and schoolmasters were not to be required to be in holy orders. The Commissioners got to work, and in the event they obtained

[1] *Op. cit.*, p. 620.   [2] *Op. cit.*, p. 650.

parliamentary sanction for 902 schemes out of a total of 1,448 in the whole country.

The Public Schools Act of 1868 and the Endowed Schools Act of 1869 were far from realising to the full the recommendations of the Clarendon and Taunton Commissions. It can, however, be said that, as a result of them, most endowed secondary schools revived and the secondary education of girls was greatly stimulated. Some sort of "educational ladder"—a phrase coined by Huxley and appropriated by Forster—was set up, because some endowed schools had scholarships from elementary schools on the one side, and were beginning to send more and more pupils to the universities on the other. The curriculum, too, was broadened and teaching was improved. This had been fostered also by the institution of those local examinations to which the Schools Inquiry Commissioners had referred—those of the College of Preceptors (1853) and of Oxford and Cambridge (1858).[1] Yet the results were disappointing and the opportunity of setting up an organised system of secondary education was postponed for over thirty years. This was due largely to the aloofness of the wealthy and governing classes, and to the lack of any statesman to champion the cause of national education, as Brougham had done in the twenties. There was also a distrust of Government action on the part of those who still clung to the creed of individualism and *laissez-faire*. Headmasters, seeing the demoralising effects of 'payment by results' in the elementary schools, not unnaturally distrusted State interference in education. Moreover, there was not yet in existence an organised system of local government upon which the local control of education could be based; and there was no move to provide a body of Government inspectors of secondary schools who could cooperate with local authorities and governors of endowed schools in organising an educational system which would be adjusted to the needs of different districts.

[1] Candidates who passed the Oxford Senior Local (or 'Middle-Class') examination were granted the 'degree' of A.A. (Associate in Arts).

Chapter XVI

THE DEVELOPMENT OF SCIENCE IN EDUCATION

The Science and Art Department. Herbert Spencer and T. H. Huxley.

UNIVERSITY reformers and those who wished to see more science taught in schools were interested rather in pure science than in the practical applications of the subject; though there were critics who compared unfavourably the facilities for scientific research at the English universities with those at the universities of Germany. But, as was pointed out in a previous chapter, the mechanics' institutes tried to put elementary scientific instruction within the reach of those who could apply it in their daily work as artisans or operatives. These institutes were, in fact, the forerunners of our modern technical education. As early as 1836 the Privy Council Committee of Trade (now the Board of Trade) had obtained a Government grant of £1,500 for a Normal School of Design—i.e. for the teaching of art as applied to commerce and industry. Other similar schools, aided by Government grants, were later established in the provinces. In 1842 an attempt was made to set up within the Royal Institution a school of practical chemistry which was to be named after Sir Humphry Davy. This failed, but in 1845 the Royal College of Chemistry, under the presidency of the Prince Consort, was opened.

The Great Exhibition, held in 1851, disclosed the fact that in applied science Continental nations were ahead of us, and that there were many defects in British manufactures. In November of the same year an institution called 'The Government School of Mines and Science applied to the Arts' came into existence; and in 1852 a Department of Practical Art was established, which greatly improved the old Normal School of Design. A science division was added to this in the following year, and it became the Science and Art Department of the Board of Trade. It was transferred to the newly formed Education Department in 1856.

Meanwhile the Royal College of Chemistry and the Government School of Mines, after a period of amalgamation as the 'Metropolitan School of Science applied to Mining and the Arts,' were separated. They became what were known as the Royal College of Science and the Royal School of Mines, and were housed at South Kensington.

The Science and Art Department is important in the history of English education because, with the help of parliamentary grants, which it administered, it encouraged the teaching of science and art—and especially of science—throughout the country. These subsidies were known as 'South Kensington grants.' They were offered to school managers, teachers, and students who complied with the conditions laid down by the Department. At first the teaching of science, aided in this way, was carried on mainly in evening classes. In 1851 there had been only thirty-eight science classes, with 1,300 pupils, in the whole country; but by 1861 the numbers had risen to seventy science classes, with 2,543 pupils. The Department also instituted examinations for teachers, the first being held in 1859. Candidates who qualified could give science instruction in evening classes and were paid according to the number of their pupils who passed the examinations held by the Department. The weakness of the system lay in the fact that no arrangements were made for training these teachers. Thus there was a tendency for teachers who aimed at qualifying in science under the Science and Art Department to cram the subjects and to have little idea of their inherent educational value. Their chief aim was to secure a means of augmenting their meagre salaries, which were more meagre than ever after 1862, when 'payment by results' was introduced into the elementary schools. All this tended to handicap the progress of science as a really educative school subject, and to make those who cared about education suspicious of the claims which were advanced on its behalf.

None the less, the scientific movement in schools and universities alike, as well as the general public interest in science, received great impetus from the writings of some contemporary scientists. Darwin's *Origin of Species* (1859) caused a good deal of perturbation in orthodox circles; but broad-minded churchmen like Charles Kingsley could find a fascination in science (as he showed in *Madam How and Lady Why*) and could make it part of their religion. Kingsley in this respect is not typical of the Church of England of the middle nineteenth century. From an educational point of view, the chief importance of the *Origin of Species* and the movement which it exemplified lies in the fact that they aroused an interest in science and helped to popularise the subject, and so strengthen the claim to include it in ordinary school education. The chief advocates of this claim are Herbert Spencer (1820–1903), and T. H. Huxley (1825–95). The former's case is the better known, but the latter's is the more balanced and reasonable.

Herbert Spencer was by profession an engineer, but he developed into a scientist, psychologist, sociologist, and philosopher. Between 1854 and 1859 he had written a series of magazine articles, which were published in book form in 1861, under the title *Education—Intellectual, Moral and Physical*. There was little that was original in the book, but it was very widely read, and it helped to arouse public opinion to the necessity for educational reform. In view of the influence which it has had, it seems desirable to give some analysis of it; but every student of English educational history should read the original work.

In his first chapter, Spencer asks: "What knowledge is of most worth?" He omits to say what he means by *worth* or to whom it is of 'most worth.' He asserts—and this would probably be generally granted—that "to prepare us for complete living is the function which education has to discharge";[1] and that the only rational means of judging of an educational course is to decide in what degree it discharges that function. This leads Spencer to classify in order of importance the leading types of activity which constitute human life. There are five of these: (i) those which minister directly to self-preservation; (ii) those which indirectly achieve this object by enabling a man to gain a livelihood; (iii) those which concern the bringing up of offspring; (iv) those which concern proper relations with other people—i.e. good citizenship; (v) those which occupy leisure. In preparation for

[1] Spencer, *Education*, p. 9.

these activities an education in 'science'—in a broad and rather undefined sense—seemed to Spencer the one object of primary importance. But he does not envisage the problem from the point of view of the child and his needs. For example, in reference to his first class of activities, he would have the child be given an acquaintance with the principles of physiology. This is doubtless an interesting study, but there is little evidence that it necessarily 'ministers directly to self-preservation.' One may ask whether doctors as a class are more healthy than farm-labourers, or whether those who know most about their internal arrangements are not often the greatest hypochondriacs. Again, as regards Spencer's second heading, we cannot anticipate the child's future occupation. We are told that mathematics should be taught, because it will be useful to the future carpenter, builder, surveyor, or railway constructor; chemistry for the future bleacher, dyer, and calico-printer; astronomy for the navigator; sociology for the industrialist; and Spencer goes on to say: "That which our school courses leave almost entirely out we thus find to be that which most nearly concerns the business of life. Our industries would cease were it not for the information which men begin to acquire, as best they may, after their education is said to be finished."[1] This is a specious argument, but it is still frequently repeated. The fact remains that the child is a child, and not an embryo engineer or calico-printer or navigator or business man.

The history of technical education has illustrated the danger— or rather, the impossibility—of trying to base a training of this sort on an inadequate foundation of general education. This objection may be urged still more strongly in reference to Spencer's third class of activities—those connected with the bringing-up of offspring. He says that if an antiquary in the remote future were to look at a pile of our text-books or examination papers, he would say: "This must have been the curriculum for their celibates." To which one can only reply that children *are* celibates, and that it would be just as inappropriate to teach children the duties of parenthood as the fundamentals of a trade

[1] *Op. cit.*, p. 29.

or profession. Of course, much depends on the age or type of the child under consideration; and, in prescribing his curriculum, this is a point upon which Spencer never seems to be clear.

The fourth class of activities in order of importance comprises those which teach good citizenship. Spencer criticises the contemporary school-teaching of history. "Familiarity with court intrigues, plots, usurpations, or the like, with all the personalities accompanying them, aids very little in elucidating the causes of national progress."[1] This is a criticism not of history as a school subject, but of a particular method of trying to teach history. But Spencer can see no good in it, and would replace it by what he calls 'descriptive sociology'—"all the facts which help us to understand how a nation has grown and organised itself." These social phenomena can be understood only when the laws of life itself are understood. "Thus then," concludes Spencer, "for the regulation of this fourth division of human activities we are, as before, dependent on science." The argument is not very clear; there may be some justification for the statement that Herbert Spencer put forward a number of unscientific arguments to support the demand for the teaching of science in schools. Finally Spencer deals with leisure-time activities. He himself was but little susceptible to the influence of art or æsthetics. He regards accomplishments, fine arts, *belles lettres* as the "efflorescence of civilisation which should be wholly subordinate to that instruction and discipline on which civilisation rests."[2] It may be questioned whether this is true as regards the child. Æsthetic culture and the appeal to the emotions are, as a matter of fact, peculiarly suited to the child in its early stages. With the young child dancing, music, and drawing are natural methods of self-expression and should be the staple of the curriculum rather than subordinated to the training of the reason. Spencer says that, as these things "occupy the leisure part of life, so should they occupy the leisure part of education." But it may be urged that their influence is not something apart from the rest of education, but rather that it affects one's whole attitude to life. The clash between the vast intellectual progress which science has made, and the

[1] *Op. cit.*, p. 37.   [2] *Op. cit.*, p. 47.

barbarous uses to which the results of that advance have been put, is implicit in this criticism of Spencer's outlook. What most touches the affections and serves to implant worthy motives and high ideals is relegated to the least important category in education. The school if devoted, as Spencer seems to wish, to the inculcation of science and pure reason might be in danger of ceasing to be a place of sweetness and light and becoming instead a kind of mental gymnasium.

Someone has said that no treatise on education is complete without a gibe at Herbert Spencer; but it is only fair to set his views against their contemporary background. If we remember the curriculum of the public and grammar schools and of the elementary schools alike, we shall realise that there is much justification for his criticisms and claims. The fact that they were set out in so extravagant a fashion helped to call attention to them. Rousseau had done the same thing in his *Émile*. It is, in fact, generally true that reformers of all kinds have tended to overstate their case in order to emphasise it and draw attention to it.

Spencer's second chapter deals with method. He condemns learning by rote, of which there was far too much in the schools of his day, and he quotes Montaigne: "Sçavoir par cœur n'est pas sçavoir." The child should not be given the rule, but should make his own generalisations from the particulars which he observes—in short, he should act as a scientist does. "Children should be led to make their own investigations. They should be told as little as possible and induced to discover as much as possible." Again, early education should be made amusing and all education interesting. "Thus," says Spencer, "we are on the highway towards the doctrine, long ago enunciated by Pestalozzi; that alike in its order and its methods, education must conform to the natural process of mental evolution—that there is a certain sequence in which the faculties spontaneously develop, a certain kind of knowledge which each requires during its development; and that it is for us to ascertain their sequence and supply this knowledge."[1] Spencer seems to have studied Pestalozzi at second-hand through the writings of a German named Biber; but it is a

[1] *Op. cit.*, p. 79.

pity that he did not follow the Swiss educationist when he was writing his first chapter. He does not tell us what the natural order of development is; though we can hardly believe that he would seriously recommend the abstractions of comparative sociology or the details of how to bring up a family as the kind of knowledge naturally adapted to children who were to leave school at the age of twelve.

In his chapter on moral education Spencer puts forward the doctrine of the discipline of natural consequences which had been enunciated by Rousseau. It appeals to him as an advocate of scientific education because it emphasises the law of cause and effect; it also eliminates the personal element of authority and so removes a possible sense of injustice. Unfortunately 'natural discipline' sometimes visits a trivial offence with dire penalties; and in any case the value of such discipline depends on the child recognising clearly the causal connection between the sin and its punishment. Moreover, 'natural discipline' neglects the effect on other people. Happy, undeserving A may sin, but wretched, meritorious B may suffer as the result. In order to escape from the difficulties of this position, Spencer has to bring in the parent as a sympathetic friend who will advise and warn the child against the risks involved in this 'natural discipline'—and that is not discipline by natural consequences at all. But, apart from this, Spencer has some sensible things to say: parents should not expect moral precocity; they should be sparing of commands, but, having once commanded, should secure obedience. Their aim should be to make the child a self-controlling being, not a person governed by others.

Spencer's fourth chapter, which deals with physical education, is one of the most valuable parts of his treatise. He emphasises the superiority of spontaneous games over formal gymnastic exercises, and he combats the contemporary idea that violent exercises are 'unladylike' for girls. There is a famous passage in which he contrasts the playground of a boys' school during break with that of an "establishment for young ladies."

It is justifiable, perhaps, to discuss the views of Herbert Spencer at some length, because his treatise, for all its illogicalities and inconsistencies, is one of the few really potent English books on education. It is not merely the plea of a scientist for a larger place for his subject in the school curriculum. It represents the progressive, individualistic, utilitarian, mid-Victorian point of view, which was highly critical of contemporary educational methods. There is no suggestion whatever that the State should play any part in the provision or administration of education. Spencer believes that the sanctity of the individual human being must be kept inviolate; and, sociologist though he is, he does not recognise an obligation on society to provide educational facilities by which that individuality may be given its fullest development.

The case for science in education was put with greater logic and restraint by T. H. Huxley. He had a wide knowledge of his subject; he had qualified in medicine, he had visited New Guinea on a scientific expedition, he was a geologist, a naturalist, and an anatomist, and he was well read in French and German scientific literature. As a teacher he was magnetic and his own personality did much to popularise the teaching of science. For many years he was intimately connected with the Science and Art Department; he was Dean of the Royal College of Science and secretary of the Royal Society. To him science was a great enthusiasm, to be preached not for its utilitarian value—for what it was 'worth'— but for its own sake. He proclaimed the grandeur of its subject-matter—"the great and fundamental truths of nature and the laws of her operations"[1]—the greatness of the scientist's quest, the æsthetic pleasure and the spirit of adventure which scientific research affords, the value of the intellectual qualities which a study of science develops. That is an enthusiasm which anyone can share. Yet Huxley was no opponent of the humanities; they were not to him—as to Spencer—the mere frills and trimmings of a true education. But they must be truly *humanities*, and not simply a study of language and style—'gerund-grinding.' Thus Huxley was prepared to retain the Classics in the curriculum, if they were properly taught, but he would also include physical science (even in the elementary school), history, geography, English literature, drawing, and music. He declared himself in

[1] Huxley, *Collected Essays*, vol. iii, p. 87.

favour of "reading the Bible, with such grammatical, geographical, and historical explanations by a lay teacher as may be needful, with rigid exclusion of any further theological teaching than that contained in the Bible itself."[1] This is the Cowper-Temple clause in terms of the syllabus, and it is evident that Huxley had the newly formed board schools in mind; he was himself a member of the first London School Board. He justifies a system of compulsory elementary education and he advocates infant schools, continuation schools, and technical schools. He wishes to see an 'educational ladder' set up by the State; and in this he goes far beyond Herbert Spencer. But although the State provides the ladder, individuals must be left to make use of it through their own innate capacity, rather than be raised by State assistance into positions for which they are not really suited. Sir Michael Sadler says that Huxley "represents at its best a transitional phase in English speculation and practice in the sphere of ethics and politics."[2] He does indeed stand between the thoroughgoing individualism and *laissez-faire* of the early-nineteenth century and the State socialism of a later age. His writings on education are not so well known or so widely read as Spencer's polemic; but his influence on actual school practice, in view of his work as an educational administrator, was probably greater.

[1] *Op. cit.*, p. 398.
[2] Article on Huxley in Monroe's *Cyclopædia of Education*, vol. iii, p. 353.

Chapter XVII

MID-CENTURY THEORY AND PRACTICE

J. S. Mill, Matthew Arnold, Ruskin, F. D. Maurice, and Charles Kingsley.
Edward Thring.

OUTSIDE the sphere of Royal Commissions and State intervention there was a good deal of interest in education during the middle years of the nineteenth century. Among its chief exponents were John Stuart Mill, Matthew Arnold, Ruskin, Frederick Denison Maurice, and Charles Kingsley. Of each of them, therefore, something must be said.

J. S. Mill (1806–73), like Herbert Spencer, had no university training, and he never even went to school. He was a precocious child, and his education was conducted entirely by his father, James Mill. We can follow the process in the early chapters of his *Autobiography*. He began Greek at three, and Latin at eight. By the age of ten he had read all the usual classical authors and had also started mathematics. At twelve he was studying Aristotle and the Platonic dialogues. But James Mill took care that this should not be mere cramming. He shared his son's intellectual pursuits. They used to walk and discuss together, and the boy was encouraged to think problems out and to weigh evidence. He was given no religious training and grew up to be an agnostic; the elements of play and physical education also seem to have been lacking.

We are not surprised that, after a régime like this, the younger Mill had a severe mental breakdown at the age of twenty, and did not recover until after a prolonged period of rest and foreign travel. He then entered the service of the East India Company, as an official at their London headquarters; but he seems to have had plenty of leisure, for much of his time was devoted to study and he wrote extensively. His interest in philosophy and political theory led him to express views on education. He was a utilitarian and an individualist, but he does not—like

Herbert Spencer—assign to the State no part at all in national education. In his essay *On Liberty* (1859), he says: "Is it not almost a self-evident axiom, that the State should require and compel the education, up to a certain standard, of every human being who is born its citizen?"[1] But that does not necessarily imply that the State itself should furnish the means of education. "If the Government would make up its mind to *require* for every child a good education, it might save itself the trouble of *providing* one. It might leave to parents to obtain the education where and how they pleased, and content itself with helping to pay the school fees of the poorer classes of children, and defraying the entire school expenses of those who have no one else to pay for them. The objections which are urged with reason against State education do not apply to the enforcement of education by the State, but to the State's taking upon itself to direct that education: which is a totally different thing."[2]

Mills' most specific and best-known contribution to education is his *Inaugural Address* as Rector of St. Andrew's University, delivered in 1867. On the vexed question of the position of science in education—which had recently been raised by Herbert Spencer—Mill asserted that there was no real antagonism between it and literary training. "If there were no more to be said than that scientific education teaches us to think, and literary education to express our thoughts, do we not require both?"[3] Using this 'formal training'[4] argument, Mill advocates a full and complete education in both directions; mathematics and science must be included in the curriculum, as well as Latin and Greek; but he neglects modern languages, history, and geography— they can be acquired by 'private reading.' He condemns the schools of his time as inefficient shams; but he knew nothing of them at first hand. He is more indulgent to the universities, for he says that "they are doing better work than they have done within human memory."[5] That is probably true, for there had been considerable improvement even before

---

[1] Mill, *On Liberty*, chap. v. [2] *Ibid.*
[3] *James and J. S. Mill on Education* (ed. Cavenagh), p. 138.
[4] See *supra*, pp. 15-16. [5] *Op. cit.*, p. 187.

the Oxford and Cambridge Commissions of 1850, and the advance had continued. But here again, J. S. Mill knew the universities only from the outside, and he could hardly be impolite in a rectorial address. It remains true that he regards school and university alike as merely a 'teaching-shop' for purveying knowledge. They are not for him societies, living and developing organisms and sources of light and life. His attitude can be understood if one remembers his own upbringing.

Matthew Arnold (1822–88) was the eldest son of Thomas Arnold and brother-in-law of W. E. Forster. From 1851 to 1886 he was one of Her Majesty's Inspectors of Schools, and, in spite of his official position, he did not hesitate in his Reports from 1863 onwards to condemn the demoralising effects of the Revised Code.[1] For the purposes of both the Newcastle and the Taunton Commissions he investigated the state of education on the Continent of Europe, and he thus became a recognised authority on comparative education. He embodied the results of his observations in *Popular Education in France* (1861), *A French Eton* (1864), and *Higher Schools and Universities in Germany* (1868)—thus covering all aspects of his subject. His experience abroad impressed him with the inadequacy of middle-class schools in this country. The *lycée* or *collège* in France, and the *Gymnasium* in Germany, were part of the national State system of education; and Arnold felt that there was need for State intervention to supply similar schools here. "Organise your secondary education" was his slogan. Many of his recommendations found their way into the Report of the Schools Inquiry Commission. These would have given us a national system of secondary education, but they were set aside by Parliament when the Endowed Schools Act of 1869 was passed. Thus in spite of Matthew Arnold's eminence as an educationist and his labours as an official, his direct influence on English education was not so great as it might have been and as it deserved to be.

Indirectly his influence was considerable. Distinguished as he was as an educational administrator, his fame rests mainly on his

[1] See, for example, *Reports on Elementary Schools*, 1852–1882, pp. 91–8, 111–17, 123–37.

achievements as a poet and a man of letters. In *Culture and Anarchy* (1869) he sets forth his views on society, which he divides into 'barbarians, philistines, and populace.'[1] The 'barbarians' are the uneducated, or half-educated, aristocracy, the members of the Church, and the professional classes, who are hidebound by the traditions of their family or of their order or of the 'old school tie.' The 'philistines' were the class with whom Arnold had had most contact as a school inspector. At this period the church schools of the National Society were visited by clerical inspectors, and the lay officials of the Education Department were restricted to schools of other denominations. Thus the 'philistines' formed the sort of society that one meets in the novels of Mark Rutherford. They were the uncultivated, narrow-minded bourgeois who were out to make money, and who judged the value of art and literature from the crudest utilitarian standpoint. Finally, the 'populace' is the vast residuum—"the working-class which, raw and half-developed, has long lain half-hidden amidst its poverty and squalor, and is now issuing from its hiding-place to assert an Englishman's heaven-born privilege of doing as he likes, and is beginning to perplex us by marching where it likes, meeting where it likes, bawling what it likes, breaking what it likes."[2] These seemed to be the first-fruits of the Reform Act of 1867, which enfranchised the town workmen. Arnold "believed that order could only be ultimately secure when the whole people learnt self-discipline through culture—culture which 'seeks to do away with classes, to make the best that has been thought and known in the world current everywhere; to make all men live in an atmosphere of sweetness and light, where they may use ideas, as it uses them itself, freely,—nourished and not bound by them.' "[3] To that end we must work and organise.

Arnold was a leader in the reaction against individualism. Contrasting our meagre educational activities with those of France, Germany, and other Continental nations, he would extend the State's functions in promoting collective well-being by means of

[1] M. Arnold, *Culture and Anarchy* (ed. Cavenagh), p. 98.
[2] *Op. cit.*, p. 105. In 1866 the mob had pulled down the railings of Hyde Park in an attempt to hold mass meetings there in support of the Reform.
[3] *Op. cit.*, pp. xxiv–v; and see p. 70.

public education. But he is critical of the contemporary scientific movement, and he insistently voices the need for a literary and humane element in the training of the workers and the middle classes. To quote his own words: "To have the power of using, which is the thing wished, these data of natural science, a man must, in general, have first been in measure *moralised*; and for moralising him it will be found not easy, I think, to dispense with those old agents letters, poetry, religion."[1] The need for 'moralising' scientific knowledge has been brought home to us with devastating clarity during recent years. How best that 'moralising' may be effected is perhaps still an unsolved problem.

John Ruskin (1819–1900) was a prolific writer. None of his books treats specifically of education, but most of them contain many passages bearing on the subject. Most important from this point of view are *Unto this Last*, *Time and Tide*, and *Sesame and Lilies*. For twelve years Ruskin was Professor of Fine Art at Oxford, and he was actively associated with the Working Men's College in London. He was a destructive critic of the existing educational system, which seemed to him based on the principle of competition and to give a wrong outlook on life. To him Art was a moralising influence—not something apart and specialised, but a necessary part of the full development of human nature. It is essential to the full enjoyment of life and a natural medium of expressing oneself. "The right question to ask respecting all ornament is simply this—was it done with enjoyment—was the carver happy while he was about it?"[2] Thus to Ruskin Art is never merely a utilitarian accomplishment, but an essential instrument of education. It must be linked up, as it was in the Middle Ages, with craft, religion, and a love of nature. Handwork has a moral and educative value, and is no longer something 'banausic.' An education regarded in this way will help to break down class distinctions, and in *Unto this Last* (1860) Ruskin makes an appeal for a new social order based on justice and a recognition of the brotherhood of man. Hence he is led to demand free and com-

[1] M. Arnold, *Reports on Elementary Schools*, 1852–1882, p. 178. See also Archer, *Secondary Education in the Nineteenth Century*, p. 188. Cf. also the poem *Steam and Electricity* in *Punch* of September 16th, 1857.

[2] Ruskin, *The Seven Lamps of Architecture*, chap. v, § 24.

pulsory State education which shall be an ethical, more than an intellectual, process. "It consists essentially in giving Habits of Mercy and Habits of Truth."[1] "The great leading error of modern times is the mistaking of erudition for education."[2] That was the error of J. S. Mill and the Revised Code and the current and growing belief in the virtue of examinations.

To Ruskin education was "not a means to getting on in the world" but an end in itself. "The best elements of State Education should be calculated equally for the advantage of every order of person composing the State."[3] The laws of health should be taught so that the body may be "as beautiful and perfect as it can be." The whole atmosphere of the school should inculate "the two great mental graces" of reverence and compassion— reverence by attaching it to the right persons and things, and compassion by "making it a point of honour so that it shall be held as shameful to have done a cruel thing as a cowardly one."[4] The teaching of truth as a habit will enter into all parts of education. The subjects of the curriculum will be such as may develop these noble virtues—poetry, music, history, natural science, and mathematics. Schools must be "in fresh country, and amidst fresh air, and have great extents of land attached to them in permanent estate."[5] The school buildings should be worthy of their purpose—architecturally beautiful, well planned and healthy, furnished with pictures and amply provided with good books. One is reminded of a very famous passage from Plato's *Republic*: "Then will our youth dwell in the land of health, amid fair sights and sounds, and receive the good in everything; and beauty, the effluence of fair works, shall flow into the eye and ear, like a health-giving breeze from a purer region, and insensibly draw the soul from earliest years into likeness and sympathy with the beauty of reason."[6] That also was Ruskin's attitude, and one can realise how bitterly he would hate the contemporary system of 'payment by results,' with its cramming of the three 'R's' and its illiberal outlook. We have by now become converted to so

[1] Ruskin, *Time and Tide*, chap. xvi.
[2] *Idem, Stones of Venice*, vol. ii, appendix 7.
[3] *Idem, Time and Tide*, chap. xvi.   [4] *Ibid.*
[5] *Ibid.*   [6] Plato, *Republic*, iii, 401.

much of what Ruskin advocated, that it is easy to underestimate his importance as an educational reformer; but it is largely to his influence that we owe the development of art teaching in schools, interest in nature study, the extension of playgrounds and playing-fields, more imaginative methods of teaching history and litera-ture, the realisation of the educational value of handicrafts, and the medical and physical care of school children.

F. D. Maurice (1805–72) belonged to a Unitarian family, but he became a Church of England clergyman and in 1840 was elected to the chair of English Literature and History at King's College, London. He formed a friendship with Charles Kingsley and with Thomas Hughes, the author of *Tom Brown's Schooldays*. His chief interest was in social reform. He believed in the prin-ciples of Chartism, but he wanted to Christianise the movement. This was the origin of 'Christian Socialism.' Maurice was also interested in the co-operative movement which had been origi-nated by the Rochdale Pioneers in 1844.[1] He tried to start some co-operative industries—e.g. associations of tailors or bootmakers working together; but these were not successful. It therefore seemed to him that the principle of fellowship, expressed in a college where professional men and working men associated, might be more effective and would replace the superficial teach-ing of the mechanics' institutes. All this found expression in the foundation, in 1854, of the Working Men's College, in Red Lion Square. It still exists in Crowndale Road, St. Pancras. Its aim was to establish an institute where working men could gain, not merely a technical equipment, but a higher, liberal education in the humanities, and where they might share a social life and intercourse such as that which characterised the older Universities. "The name *College* had a significance on which Maurice loved to dwell. . . . A college was an association of teachers and learners; and that was what Maurice desired the Working Men's College to be. It was not to be an institution to which the uneducated might resort, to pick up knowledge which might be of pecuniary benefit to them. The idea of fellowship was to run through all its work; every teacher was to assume that he might gain as well

[1] See Trevelyan, *British History in the Nineteenth Century*, p. 277.

as impart, might learn as well as teach; every student was to be made to feel that in coming to the College he was entering into a society in which he might hope to become more of a citizen and more of a man."[1]

The movement attracted some of the ablest leaders of contemporary thought and public life—Ruskin, Dante Gabriel Rossetti, Ford Madox Brown, C. Lowes Dickinson, Charles Kingsley, John Hullah. There was systematic class-teaching in such subjects as history, literature, science, mathematics, natural history, and art. There were social meetings and sing-songs. Gymnastics were popular, and "Mr. Hughes, on at least one night a week, met all comers with 'the gloves.' "[2] Cricket was played on Primrose Hill or at Gospel Oak, and there were country walks on Sundays—and even expeditions to North Wales and Switzerland—with much botanising, entomologising, or geologising *en route*. At the rise of the Volunteer movement in 1859 the College formed its own Corps and achieved a creditable record of service. The institution was so successful that other working men's colleges were established elsewhere in the country; but they did not achieve equal success, perhaps because they lacked so distinguished and effective a teaching personnel. Maurice's real importance, from our point of view, is that he put education in the forefront of social reform. Modern developments, such as the Workers' Educational Association and the University Extension movement, owe much to the pioneer work of F. D. Maurice.

Charles Kingsley (1819–75), like Maurice, was a clergyman of the Established Church, and he was closely associated with Christian Socialism. He was an exponent of what Professor Archer calls the 'hygienic movement'; he advocated "sanitary and housing reform, the free sale of land and corresponding reform of the land laws, moral improvement of the family relations, public places of recreation."[3] A national system of education seemed to him the best method of achieving these ends, and he supported Forster's Bill of 1870. Like Spencer and Huxley, he

[1] *The Working Men's College*, 1854–1904, pp. 10–11 (article by J. Llewelyn Davies). See also Harrison, *A History of the Working Men's College*, 1854–1954.
[2] *Op. cit.*, p. 73.   [3] From Hughes's introduction to *Alton Locke*.

was interested in science, but not from utilitarian or even cultural motives. He does not feel that the advances in scientific knowledge of the middle nineteenth century are a danger to theology, but rather that they amplify and illuminate our knowledge of God and His ways. Thus to Kingsley a knowledge of science is an important weapon in the hands of the social reformer. Outbreaks of cholera are not "acts of God" or punishments for national shortcomings. They can be, and ought to be, prevented by the dissemination of knowledge, in the school and elsewhere, as to how to deal with them. Kingsley, therefore, is not only allied with F. D. Maurice as a social reformer, but he also shows another aspect of the scientific movement in education.

The five educational theorists of the middle nineteenth century, whose views have been summarised in this chapter, agreed in criticising the narrowness or formalism of existing educational institutions—especially as it was expressed in the elementary-school system of 'payment by results.' Even Matthew Arnold could do only a little to mitigate that system in actual practice; and it was therefore more easy at the time to apply progressive theory in the sphere where State interference was least felt—i.e. in the secondary school. Most conspicuous of those who attempted to do this was Edward Thring (1821–87). He had been educated at Eton, where he experienced the horrors of 'long Chamber.'[1] He afterwards went up to King's College, Cambridge, and was ordained in 1846. He served as a curate at St. James's Church, Gloucester, and taught in the national school of the parish. He also acted as examiner at Eton and Rugby, and for the Classical Tripos at Cambridge in 1858.

After a period of private coaching at Marlow, which helped him (like Arnold at Laleham) to realise the importance of treating his pupils as individuals, he was appointed headmaster of Uppingham in 1853. It was at the time a country grammar school with twenty-five boys and two assistant masters. In spite of difficulties with an obstructive governing body, Thring rapidly raised Uppingham to the status of a public school with its numbers limited to about three hundred, so that the headmaster could

[1] See *supra*, pp. 19 and 77.

know each boy individually. Financial problems were recurrent; but Thring was fortunate in his assistants, who helped him by building boarding-houses at their own expense and sharing the risks of the venture. He had tremendous driving force of personality—'the enthusiast, Mr. Thring,' as Henry Sidgwick rather slightingly called him. He believed that "every boy is good for something. If he can't write Iambics or excel in Latin prose, he has at least eyes and hands and ears. Turn him into the carpenter's shop, make him a botanist or a chemist, encourage him to express himself in music, and if he fails all round, here at least he shall learn to read in public his mother tongue and write thoughtfully an English essay."[1] So the curriculum must be broadened. Compulsory subjects like Classics, English, and mathematics were taken in the morning; but in the afternoon there was a wide range of optional subjects from which every boy could choose what interested him. These included modern languages, science, carpentry and metalwork, drawing and music. To the last-named subject Thring attached great importance, and with the help of one of his masters, Herr David, he built up a strong musical tradition in the school.

He was a convinced believer in the educational value of organised games. He started his headmastership by taking part in a school cricket match and making fifteen "by some good swinging hits, to the great delight of my few pupils."[2] He also had a gymnasium built, besides workshops and laboratories. He stressed the value of organisation—'machinery,' as he calls it. He realised what any experienced schoolmaster knows to be true—that a well-organised school tends to be a good school as regards tone and discipline. "There is a large percentage," he says, "of temptation, criminality, and idleness in the great schools—a moral miasma—generated by known causes, and as certainly to be got rid of even by mere mechanical improvements."[3] Therefore he believes in good buildings and equipment—the 'almighty wall,' as he calls it. "Never rest till you have got the almighty wall on your side, and not against you. Never rest till you have got all the

---

[1] See Rawnsley, *Edward Thring*, p. 82.
[2] Parkin, *Life and Letters of Edward Thring*, I, p. 79.   [3] *Op. cit.*, II, p. 117.

fixed machinery for work, the best possible. The waste in the teacher's workshop is the lives of men."[1] He was fond of saying: "Honour the work, and the work will honour you"; and these are the words inscribed on a tablet to his memory in the school chapel at Uppingham.

Thring regarded teaching as a skilled craft, and he was anxious that teachers should be interested in method. He puts forward his own suggestions in *Education and School* (1864) and in *Theory and Practice of Teaching* (1883). But he did not advocate the establishment of training colleges for secondary-school masters, for he was apparently not impressed by those already in existence for elementary-school teachers. He was also violently opposed to the *Report* of the Schools Inquiry Commission. He regarded it as "the heaviest blow education could have received." It is obvious that he felt that the recommendations of the Commissioners would be inimical to the success of Uppingham.[2] This was due almost entirely to the hard work and financial sacrifices of himself and his staff, and not to the efforts of the governing body of the school. Thring even threatened to resign; but the Commissioners, recognising that his was a special case, gave way in large measure to him. But there was considerable alarm among some of the headmasters of endowed schools. While the Endowed Schools Bill was before Parliament, they held a meeting to consider the situation. Thring suggested that such a gathering should be held every year, and invited his fellow-headmasters to meet at Uppingham in December 1869. Thus was born the Headmasters' Conference, which rapidly increased in size and importance and has ever since represented the 'independent' schools and remained suspicious of State interference. Finally, it should be noted that Thring was a keen advocate of higher education for girls and women and that he was the first public-school headmaster to start a school mission in the East End of London.

Thring interests us, not only because of his vivid and dynamic

[1] *Op. cit.*, II, p. 116.
[2] He had even made a formal protest in writing against the teaching in his school being inspected. See *Report*, vol. xvi, p. 133.

personality, but also because he is an exponent in practice of much of the progressive educational theory of his time. Like Matthew Arnold, he hates the cramping routine of 'payment by results' and the formal, illiberal conception of education which it illustrates; like Ruskin, he believes in the ennobling influence of a beautiful and ordered environment, and in the educative value of craftwork, art, and music; like Maurice, he realises the social function of education and the obligations of the wealthier classes towards their poorer brethren; like Kingsley, he is an advocate of muscular Christianity. To him physical training and games are an essential element in education, and he is certainly an exponent of the 'hygienic' movement. When an epidemic of typhoid, due to bad drainage, broke out in Uppingham, Thring did his utmost to get the lethargic local authorities to put things right, and he even stirred up the Local Government Board to act in the matter. In order to safeguard the health of his boys meanwhile he evacuated the school to Borth, on the shores of Cardigan Bay; and it remained there a whole year (1876–7), until it could return with safety to its original home.

Chapter XVIII

THE EDUCATION OF GIRLS AND WOMEN

Queen's College and Bedford College. Women at Cambridge and Oxford. Miss Buss and Miss Beale. Secondary Schools for Girls. Co-education.

THE education of girls and women during the nineteenth century is not a self-contained subject. It is closely bound up with a larger movement which aimed at giving women greater economic and political freedom. It should be noticed that the educational side of this movement is concerned mainly with the daughters of the middle and upper classes—i.e. with university and secondary education. In the elementary system of the country girls had benefited equally with boys. This is true of private or common day schools, of monitorial schools and schools of industry, of national schools and British and Foreign schools, of board schools and voluntary schools. There was no question of female disabilities in this sphere of education, for girls had just as much—or, rather, just as little—chance as boys. But when one turns to secondary and higher education, the picture is a different one. The endowed schools and the Universities had been founded to ensure a sufficient supply of "fit persons to serve God in Church and State"; and it rarely seems to have occurred to pious founders that women could be included in that category. As late as the middle of the nineteenth century the Universities were closed to women, and there were no public schools and only a few endowed schools for girls. The Clergy Daughters' School at Cowan Bridge had been founded in 1823 in an attempt to provide cheap education for girls; but if we may believe Charlotte Brontë, who was a pupil there,[1] the girls were badly fed and badly taught. Such private secondary schools as did exist were for the most part inefficient and pretentious—though there were exceptions. Many girls of the upper and middle classes did not attend a school, but were educated at home by governesses, often of Swiss, French, or

[1] It is pilloried as 'Lowood' in *Jane Eyre*.

156

German nationality—we meet them in the pages of contemporary novelists. There was little solidity or depth in the education which they gave.[1] Much stress was still laid on behaviour and deportment, but physical exercises and games were scouted. In fact, the real aim of a girl's education, so far as it went, was to make her superficially attractive because the only career open to her was marriage; any solidity of instruction or seriousness of intent in education would not "become a young woman," and the 'blue-stocking' was a familiar figure of ridicule or even horror.

However, a movement for reform was already stirring by the mid-century. It started from the direction of higher education, but it soon after affected secondary education. F. D. Maurice and Charles Kingsley were among the protagonists of the reform.[2] Maurice had a sister who was a governess. For this reason he became interested in the Governesses' Benevolent Institution, which had been founded in 1843 to aid governesses who needed financial assistance. Their Swiss and German rivals were in many cases equipped for their educational work by a special training and the possession of a teacher's diploma; and it was hoped, therefore, that the Institution might also hold examinations for some similar qualification. But the standard of educational attainment among potential candidates proved to be so low that it was evident that the first step would be to provide means for teaching the teachers. Maurice therefore enlisted the help of some of his brother professors at King's College, London, and as a result Queen's College

[1] Cf. E. B. Browning, *Aurora Leigh*, bk. i:

> "I learnt the royal genealogies
> Of Oviedo, the internal laws
> Of the Burmese empire,—by how many feet
> Mount Chimborazo outsoars Teneriffe,
> What navigable river joins itself
> To Lara, and what census of the year five
> Was taken at Klagenfurt—because she liked
> A general insight into useful facts. . . .
> I danced the polka and Cellarius,
> Spun glass, stuffed birds, and modelled flowers in wax,
> Because she liked accomplishments in girls."

The whole passage should be consulted.

[2] Ruskin also strongly advocated a better education for girls. See *Sesame and Lilies* 'Of Queens' Gardens,' especially §§ 80 and 81.

was founded in Harley Street in 1848. It was rather loosely organised and did little more than provide courses of lectures. Pupils were admitted as young as fourteen, but on the other hand there were women students of mature years. There was an evident desire to allay possible apprehensions that women might be over-educated. "We are aware," said Maurice in his Inaugural Address, "that our pupils are not likely to advance far in mathematics, but we believe that if they learn really what they do learn, they will not have got what is dangerous, but what is safe. . . . I cannot conceive that a young lady can feel her mind in a more dangerous state than it was, because she has gained a truer glimpse into the conditions under which the world in which it has pleased God to place her actually exists."[1] In the summer of 1855 Maurice also ran a course of 'Lectures to Ladies on Practical Subjects' at the Working Men's College. In the introductory address, given by Maurice himself, he outlines a 'Plan of a Female College for the Help of the Rich and the Poor.' Other lectures dealt with hospital and dispensary work, the country parish and district visiting, workhouses, sanitation, the law as it affects the poor. Maurice seems to have aimed at establishing a training centre for women who would volunteer for social work among the poor and nursing—those were the days of Florence Nightingale. Such women would undertake the work done by sisterhoods in Roman Catholic countries. Here, therefore, as well as in teaching, there would be opportunities of service to the community open to educated women.

Meanwhile, in 1849, Queen's College had been followed by another college of the more orthodox type—Bedford—which was established in London and endowed by Mrs. Reid. It was an undenominational institution, and it took University College, London, as its model. In 1869, the year when Bedford College was incorporated, the University of Cambridge instituted a Higher Local examination, open only to women candidates over the age of eighteen. This gave the students of such colleges as Bedford and Queen's something to aim at; for as yet there were no

[1] From *Introductory Lecture on the Objects and Methods of Queen's College* (March 29th, 1848); quoted by Zimmern, *Renaissance of Girls' Education*, pp. 23-3.

degrees open to women. In 1862, however, a proposal had been made to alter the charter of London University so as to admit women to graduation, and it was lost only by the casting vote of the Chancellor. But Miss Emily Davies, who was a doughty champion of the education of women and girls, and who had been secretary of a committee which aimed at securing the admission of women to university examinations, succeeded in starting a women's college in a house at Hitchin (1869) and induced the University of Cambridge to let her students work degree papers. Three years after the opening of the institution three of its students had fulfilled the conditions required by the University for an honours degree, and all those who entered for the test of the previous examination attained the pass standard. In 1873 Miss Davies's college was moved from Hitchin to Girton, two miles from Cambridge, and the foundress became its first 'mistress.'

Side by side with Miss Emily Davies another pioneer was at work. Miss A. J. Clough, who had already run schools at Liverpool and Ambleside, was trying to organise courses of lectures for women, given by university teachers, in various big towns in the North of England. It was an adumbration of the University Extension movement. Out of this grew a 'North of England Council for promoting the Higher Education of Women,' of which Miss Clough became the secretary. Finally, with the help of the Cambridge philosopher, Henry Sidgwick, Miss Clough took charge of a house of residence for women students in the University town; and this became the germ of Newnham College, Cambridge, which was opened in 1875, with Miss Clough as its first principal. Its aims were rather different from those of Girton. Miss Davies wished her students to be admitted to the ordinary university examinations under the same conditions as the men; there should be no special examination or lower standard for women. But at Newnham there were special courses designed for women only and intended specifically to advance feminine culture. If the students took an examination, it would be the Cambridge Higher Local—a kind of inferior female substitute for the degree examinations which were open to

M

men undergraduates only. Girton's point of view prevailed, and Newnham eventually adopted it. Women's claim to share the highest university studies with men was abundantly justified when students from their colleges could be bracketed equal with the senior classic or the senior wrangler. The force of this argument was too strong to be disregarded. In 1881 the Senate of the University of Cambridge formally admitted women students from Girton and Newnham to the Previous and Tripos examinations; a separate pass list was published and certificates were awarded to successful candidates. They were not, however, admitted to degrees or allowed to take the examinations for the ordinary degree.

The movement for the university education of women, so conspicuous at Cambridge, was gathering force elsewhere. In Oxford an 'Association for the Education of Women' had been founded with the object of "establishing and maintaining a system of instruction having general reference to the Oxford examinations."[1] The outcome was the foundation of Somerville College and Lady Margaret Hall, both of which date from 1879. St. Hugh's (1886) and St. Hilda's (1893) were subsequently added. Meanwhile, in 1878, London University, which was an examining and not a teaching body, at last opened its degrees to women. As a concession to popular sentiment the first 'graduettes' made their own hoods. When, between 1880 and 1887, the federal Victoria University was formed from the union of the colleges at Manchester, Liverpool, and Leeds, it was permitted by its charter to admit women, as well as men, to degrees. In 1892 the four Scottish Universities followed suit, and so did the federal University of Wales in 1893. Their example has since been copied by Trinity College, Dublin, and all the newer English universities. It was not until 1920 that Oxford admitted women students to full university status. They are eligible under the same conditions as men to be members of Convocation and Congregation, of the Hebdomadal Council, and of any university board or committee. They can act as university examiners and hold university fellowships and scholarships. It is curious that Cambridge, where the

[1] See Rogers, *Degrees by Degrees*, chap. i.

main battle for the university education of women was fought and won, should have been the last of the British universities to admit women to matriculation and to degrees on the same terms as men.[1]

We have now to trace the development of the secondary education of girls. Here again progress was due primarily to the determination of a few women of outstanding personality. Frances Mary Buss (1827–95) began her career as a teacher in a private school run by her mother. She also attended evening lectures at Queen's College. Her school increased rapidly in numbers and developed into the North London Collegiate School. Although still a private venture, it was put under the superintendence of the vicar and clergy of St. Pancras; but in 1871 Miss Buss transferred her property in the school to a body of trustees and it thus acquired a 'public' character.

At Queen's College she was contemporary with another pioneer of girls' education—Dorothea Beale (1831–1906).[2] Miss Beale remained at Queen's College giving some help in the teaching of mathematics; but after a not very happy year on the staff of the Clergy Daughters' School she was appointed, in 1858, headmistress of Cheltenham Ladies' College, which had been founded five years previously. Cheltenham was already becoming a favourite place of residence for retired people in easy circumstances, who sent their boys to Cheltenham College, which dates from 1841. But they had daughters as well as sons, and the Ladies' College was a kind of female counterpart of the boys' school, just as Queen's and Bedford had found their prototypes in King's and University. Miss Beale realised that girls, no less than boys, needed a solid education; it was not for nothing that she had been a tutor in mathematics. At first there were difficulties; parents objected to the thoroughness of the teaching and well-qualified mistresses were hard to come by. But Miss Beale won through. She had not merely a keen intellect, but also a deep religious sense and great ability as a teacher. All this in due

[1] They were admitted to 'titular' degrees in 1921; but for full membership of the University they had to wait until 1947.
[2] They did not actually meet till many years later—see her letter to Sir Joshua Fitch in Raikes, *Dorothea Beale of Cheltenham*, p. 413.

course bore fruit abundantly. By 1864 there were 130 pupils and a boarding-house had been opened; by 1883 there were 500 girls and ten boarding-houses. Miss Beale lived to see Cheltenham developed into an educational institution which was far more than a secondary school. It comprised several departments, all under the direction of the Principal. One of them prepared senior students for the general certificate and for university scholarships. Below this was a secondary school for girls between the ages of eleven and sixteen. Below this again were separate junior departments and a kindergarten. Thus the whole range of education was covered in one and the same institution. Moreover, St. Hilda's College was founded primarily as a hall of residence for those old girls of Cheltenham who wished to proceed to Oxford. The institution as a whole, though it has since in some respects been imitated, was without precedent in our educational history.[1]

It was not only through the example of their schools that the influence of Miss Beale and Miss Buss was felt. When the Schools Inquiry Commission was investigating the provision of education for girls, they were both invited to give evidence before it; and Miss Davies was also interrogated. They made the most of their opportunity. Eight Commissioners also investigated the girls' schools in selected districts. Their conclusions emphasise the value of the work upon which Miss Beale and Miss Buss were engaged. "It cannot be denied," says the *Report* of the Commission, "that the picture brought before us of the state of Middle-Class Female Education is, on the whole, unfavourable. The general deficiency in girls' education is stated with the utmost confidence, and with entire agreement, with whatever difference of words, by many witnesses of authority. Want of thoroughness and foundation; want of system; slovenliness and showy superficiality; inattention to rudiments; undue time given to accomplishments, and those not taught intelligently or in any scientific manner; want of organisation—these may sufficiently indicate the character of the complaints we have received in their most general

[1] See Clarke, *A History of Cheltenham Ladies College*, 1853–1953. The kindergarten and a Secondary Training department have now been closed down.

aspect."[1] One of the Commissioners adds: "We find, as a rule, a very small amount of professional skill, an inferior set of school-books, a vast deal of uninteresting task work, rules put into the memory with no explanation of their principles, no system of examination worthy of the name, a very false estimate of the relative value of the several kinds of acquirement, a reference to effect rather than to solid worth, a tendency to fill or adorn rather than strengthen the mind."[2]

The blame lies largely with the parents, who tend to believe that "girls are less capable of mental cultivation, and less in need of it, than boys; that accomplishments, and what is showy and superficially attractive, are what is really essential for them; and in particular, that as regards their relations with the other sex and the probabilities of marriage, more solid attainments are actually disadvantageous rather than the reverse."[3] It was therefore recommended that "in every town large enough to be worthy of a grammar school" there should also be a day school for girls under public management and with moderate fees. A more solid course of instruction should be adopted, including mathematics and, where possible, Latin. Moreover, there should be institutions "designed to hold, in relation to girls' schools and home training, a position analogous to that occupied by the Universities towards the public schools for boys."[4] This would make possible an adequate supply of properly qualified women teachers. "It is from the advent of more highly educated teachers that the first improvement in the education of girls is to be hoped for."

The agitation for an improvement in, and greater facilities for, the secondary education of girls led to a clause in the Endowed Schools Act of 1869, which laid it down that "in framing schemes under this Act, provision shall be made as far as conveniently may be for extending to girls the benefits of endowments."[5] Miss Alice Zimmern calls this clause 'the Magna Carta of girls' education.' To facilitate this requirement of the Act there was formed an Association for Promoting the Application of Endowments to

[1] Report of *Schools Inquiry Commission*, vol. i, pp. 548–9.
[2] *Op. cit.*, p. 552.   [3] *Op. cit.*, pp. 546–7.
[4] *Op. cit.*, p. 562; and see also 'Memorial' in vol. ii, pp. 194–7.
[5] Endowed Schools Act, 1869, § 12.

the Education of Women. It offered to assist trustees of schools and other persons interested in education, by supplying information and suggesting plans whereby available funds might best be applied to the education of women. Obviously, it was the girls of the middle classes who most needed educational facilities, because the passing of the 1870 Act brought State-aided schooling within the reach of the poorer children of both sexes indiscriminately. Where, therefore, the funds of educational trusts were not exhausted by existing boys' schools, new schools for girls were set up, or old ones revived, out of the surplus. One of the first was at Bradford, where part of the old grammar-school endowment was appropriated "to supply a liberal education for girls by means of a school or schools within the borough of Bradford." That is typical. Similar schools were founded at Bedford, Birmingham, Rochester, and many another town, large and small. St. Olave's and Dulwich saw the rise of sister schools on the same foundation. Christ's Hospital, though definitely founded in the time of King Edward VI for the benefit of children of either sex, was educating only eighteen girls as against 1,224 boys when it was investigated by the Schools Inquiry Commissioners in 1865. In spite of the Act of 1869, there was some delay in putting into operation a long-overdue reform of the foundation; and even to this day fewer girls than boys benefit from it.

The Endowed Schools Commission worked slowly—perhaps this was inevitable—and many of the schemes took some time to put into operation. This stimulated private enterprise to step in in order to supplement its efforts, which in any case were limited to existing endowments. One of the outstanding figures in this field of activity was Maria Grey (Mrs. William Grey), who had been a candidate for election to the newly formed London School Board and who was secretary of the Women's Educational Union.[1] In 1872 this body put forward a scheme for a "Public Day School for Girls, in the South-Western district of London,

---

[1] Its full title was 'The National Union for the Education of Girls of all Classes above the Elementary'—i.e. those for whom provision had not been made by the Act of 1870. See Magnus, *Jubilee Book of the G.P.D.S.T.*, p. 14.

the funds for which will be raised in shares of £5 each, by means
of a limited liability Company, capable of extending its operations
hereafter in various directions, wheresoever schools are wanted."[1]
This was the origin of the Girls' Public Day School Trust. It was
a commercial, as well as an educational venture, though its
dividends have never been high. The aim was to make the building and running of the schools "absolutely self-supporting." The
movement rapidly gathered strength, and it secured an imposing
number of illustrious supporters under the presidency and
patronage of Princess Louise, fourth daughter of Queen Victoria.
The first school was opened at Chelsea,[2] and it started work early
in 1873. Another school at Croydon followed in 1874. By 1891
thirty-six Girls' Public Day Schools had been founded, and they
were situated, not only in London and its neighbourhood, but
also in many of the chief provincial towns of England. They did
not all survive, but twenty-three of them still carry on the work.
They were modelled to some extent on Miss Buss's North London
Collegiate School; and they also adopted a scheme initiated by
Miss Beale at Cheltenham—that of having the main lessons in the
morning, and giving up the afternoon to what are still sometimes
regarded as 'extras'—e.g. music and art. Kindergarten work has
also been an integral part of the business of the G.P.D.S.T.
schools; while the Clapham High School also organised courses
of training for teachers. A similar trust to promote the secondary
education of girls, but on definitely Church of England lines, was
the Church Schools Company, started in 1883. It was less
successful than its prototype, but it still exists and maintains six
schools.

One of the by-products of the extension of schooling for girls
has been a development of co-education in the field of secondary
education. At the time of the Schools Inquiry Commission there
was already in existence at Upholland, in Lancashire, a small endowed school which had girls as well as boys among its pupils;
but the *Report* comments on this arrangement as being most unusual. Private co-educational schools for middle-class children

---

[1] Magnus, *Jubilee Book of the G.P.D.S.T.*, 1873–1923, p. 16.
[2] Its site was afterwards changed, and it became the Kensington High School.

were not unknown as early as the fifties and sixties of last century. In 1873 Lady Barn, one of the most interesting and effective schools of this type, was founded on the outskirts of Manchester by W. H. Herford and his wife.[1] The existence of such schools as these gave a fillip to the foundation of new mixed secondary schools. Especially after the Act of 1902, local authorities found that they were cheaper and more efficiently run in areas of small or scattered population than two small separate schools for boys and for girls. By 1919, out of 1,080 secondary schools recognised as efficient, 224 were mixed. It is only after the event that educational administrators tend to justify co-educational schools on the grounds of high principle; but it should be remembered that co-education has always been practised to a greater or less degree in the elementary schools of this country, and no one has shown undue alarm. Its advance in the sphere of secondary education within recent years has been due not simply to financial considerations on the part of local authorities, but also to the private enterprise of those who believed in it on educational grounds.[2] We now even have schools like Bedales (near Petersfield), St. George's, Harpenden, and Frensham Heights, organised on public-school lines as boarding schools for both boys and girls up to the age of eighteen.

[1] See Hicks, *Lady Barn House and the Work of W. H. Herford.*
[2] An account of some of the more important co-educational 'progressive' schools is given in *The Modern Schools' Handbook* (ed. Blewitt).

PART D

EDUCATION DURING THE LATTER PART OF THE NINETEENTH CENTURY

Chapter XIX

ELEMENTARY EDUCATION DURING THE SCHOOL BOARD PERIOD

Progress of the School Boards. The Sandon and Mundella Acts. The Influence of Froebel. The Cross Commission.

WE turn now to elementary education which we left at the passing of the 1870 Act. This, has been said, was a compromise, because it accepted the existing voluntary system and 'filled up the gaps' by providing secular schools where they were needed. Most of the school boards followed the example of the London School Board in making undenominational Bible teaching compulsory, on the lines suggested by Huxley, though they were not bound by the Act even to do this. Thus the 'religious difficulty' still continued and was emphasised by the triennial school board elections, which were often fought out with great bitterness. The provision of places in voluntary schools was greater than in board schools, though each was stimulated by the rivalry of the other. In 1880, out of 17,614 elementary schools, 14,181 were voluntary and 3,433 under school boards; but the board schools tended to be better equipped, larger, and more efficient, and the voluntary schools found the strain of competing with institutions aided by the rates heavier and heavier. The disproportion gradually decreased, but as late as 1897 the number of children in voluntary schools outnumbered those in board schools; and by 1900 they were still 46 per cent. of the total elementary-school population.

The 1870 Act had not made education compulsory, though it had compelled the school boards to provide schools where there were 'gaps.' School fees were still to be paid, but the Act had given school boards the power—if they wished to use it—to compel attendance by making by-laws to this effect. Fees of necessitous children could be remitted. Thus there remained the point of controversy as to whether elementary education should be universally enforced. The London School Board, soon after its formation, passed a by-law for compulsory school attendance of children between the ages of five and thirteen, with exemption to children over ten, who had passed Standard V, and half-time exemption to younger children who were adjudged to be 'beneficially and necessarily at work.' Other school boards in the large towns passed similar by-laws, but the country school boards were reluctant to apply compulsion. By 1876 50 per cent. of the whole population was under compulsion, but in the boroughs the percentage was as high as 84.

It should be remembered that a series of Factory and Mines Acts had for some time past made a modicum of school attendance a compulsory condition of the employment of children. The Factory Act of 1844, which was still in force in 1870, made it possible for children over the age of eight to be employed in factories and workshops half-time; when they reached the age of thirteen they could become full-time workers. A Factory Act of 1874 raised these ages to ten and fourteen. Thus for children below these ages and in employment education was compulsory, though no standard of education was prescribed. It was an unsatisfactory and confusing situation. A Factory and Workshops Act Commission, which reported in 1876, expressed the view that special legislation for the benefit of factory children was bound to be unsatisfactory; and it went on to say: "We consider that justice, expediency, and consistency alike require that the attendance at school of all children should be enforced by law, whether they are at work or not."[1] The problem of irregular attendance was also involved. The Act of 1870 had empowered school boards to appoint officers to enforce school attendance in areas where by-laws to this effect had been made. Lord Sandon's Act of 1876 set up school attendance committees in districts where there were no school boards. It also laid upon the parent the duty of seeing that his child should receive "efficient elementary instruction in reading, writing, and arithmetic";[2] penalties for neglect were provided. Thus the Act did imply compulsory

[1] *Report* of Factory and Workshops Act Commission (1876), lvii.
[2] *Elementary Education Act*, 1876, § 4.

education, although it did not compel the parent to send his child to school. At the same time it forbade the employment of any child under the age of ten, or of any between ten and fourteen, who had not reached certain specified educational attainments.[1] But there were loopholes. Children living more than two miles from a public elementary school were exempt from the provisions of the Act, and in rural areas they could be excused from attendance at school for a period up to six weeks in order to help with agricultural work. The employment of children out of school hours was also not forbidden. Sandon's Act increased the Education Department's grant so as to make it possible for voluntary schools to meet the increasing cost of education.

It was followed by Mundella's Act of 1880, which compelled all school boards and school attendance committees which had not already framed by-laws to enforce compulsory attendance to repair the omission. By it school attendance was made obligatory for all children between the ages of five and ten. Exemptions based on proficiency or attendance could be obtained up to fourteen. Thus the question of compulsion was at last settled, but fees were not at the same time entirely abolished and school pence continued in some cases to be paid, especially in the voluntary schools. With the introduction of compulsory schooling, it naturally became increasingly difficult to collect them. In 1891, therefore, a special fee-grant of 10s. a head was introduced, and this measure made elementary education virtually free; other provisions secured that there should be no areas which were entirely without fee schools. The Fisher Act of 1918 finally and definitely abolished fees in elementary schools.

The evolution of a system of compulsory and gratuitous education is of great importance, but its significance should not be overestimated. It value depends on the connotation given to the term 'education.' Even after the Mundella Act, the exemption by-laws varied considerably from one district to another. Standards of proficiency also varied; in some areas compulsory attendance ended at the age of ten, elsewhere at eleven or twelve.

---

[1] Standards of proficiency in the three 'R's' for the purpose of a certificate enabling a child to be employed were laid down in the First Schedule to the Act.

It was not always easy for officials to check irregular attendance, and in some cases children even succeeded in leaving school before the prescribed age. Truancy also was rife in some quarters, and, as grants were calculated partly on a basis of attendance, there was a temptation to teachers to falsify registers. 'Payment by results' did not disappear until 1900, but even as early as the seventies some modifications were made in the Code, and these somewhat mitigated its harshness. In 1875 children were allowed to qualify for grant on the result of examination, not only in 'obligatory' subjects—the three 'R's—but also in 'class' subjects taught throughout the school above Standard I. These included, for example, history, geography, and elementary science. Later the examination in obligatory subjects was required only of sample groups comprising not less than a third of the pupils of a school; while in 1895 even this attenuated form of examination was replaced by an inspection. But so long as it lasted—and particularly in its earlier days—the system had deleterious effects, and education in voluntary and board schools alike suffered by it. The passing of the 1870, 1876, and 1880 Acts had caused a large influx of new pupils into the elementary schools. Many of these children were utterly ignorant. They clogged up the schools and yet had to be coached and crammed for grant-earning purposes, instead of being dealt with according to their needs. All this encouraged mechanical rote-teaching. Moreover, the Revised Code of 1862 had cut off a supply of well-trained pupil-teachers, and that implied a deterioration in the quality of the teaching staff in elementary schools. The actual proportion of pupils who managed to qualify for grant even in the three 'R's' was surprisingly small; it was about 25 per cent. of those examined in 1874 and roughly the same in 1880.

None the less, there was some gradual improvement in the education given in public elementary schools. The general level of work was raised, and in 1882 a Seventh Standard was added. The Code of that year also assessed grants on the average attendance of a school and not on individual pupils. The method by which the total amount was estimated is rather complicated, but the sum included a fixed grant and a 'merit' grant. This latter was decided by the inspector's report of 'fair,' 'good,' or 'excellent,' "in respect of (1) the organisation and discipline; (2) the intelligence employed in instruction; and (3) the general quality of the work, especially in the elementary subjects." The bulk of the grant still depended on the examination results together with the 'merit' grant, which itself was in practice estimated largely by the examination; but a separate arrangement was made for infant schools where examination determined only a small proportion of the grant. The general result of these measures was that a well-supported and well-staffed school could earn high grants; but a poor school, with irregular attendance and inferior teachers, could qualify only for low grants and was therefore doubly penalised. The board schools, which could rely on rate aid, were as a rule in a stronger position than the voluntary schools. The best teachers tended to go to the board schools because these could offer better pay, and this was one reason for hostility towards such schools on the part of the supporters of voluntaryism. It is also true to say that in spite of its amendments the 1882 Code made for formalism in the schools for older children, but this was less marked in the infant schools because the system of 'payment by results' was less potent in them.

There was another influence which was beginning to affect the education of younger children. It was due to Froebel, whose educational principles—often, perhaps, much misunderstood—began to be applied in English schools from about the seventies onwards. Froebel (1782–1852) was a German and a disciple, though not an uncritical one, of Pestalozzi. To him the child is an organism, and education is the development of that organism. "The vigorous and complete development and cultivation of each successive stage depends on the vigorous, complete, and characteristic development of each and all preceding stages of life."[1] This development is spontaneous; Froebel calls it "self-activity." Pestalozzi in his doctrine of *Anschauung*[2] had over-emphasised receptivity; Froebel insists that observation must be combined with free expression. Thus the educator's part is not to

[1] Froebel, *The Education of Man* (trans. Hailmann), p. 28.
[2] See *supra*, p. 38.

interfere and prescribe, but to oversee and protect. The child's natural activity expresses itself in play. Thus childhood's play is not mere sport or amusement; it is full of meaning and serious import. "The plays of childhood are the germinal leaves of all later life. Play is the purest, most spiritual activity of man at this stage, and, at the same time, typical of human life as a whole —of the inner hidden natural life in man and all things."[1] To Froebel the school's function is to encourage this natural development, and his view is illustrated by the name he gave to it—the *Kindergarten*. This does not mean, as seems sometimes to be assumed, a garden in which the children play, but one in which the children are the plants, and where the teacher is the gardener who helps them to develop most effectively along the lines laid down by nature and not by the gardener himself. To encourage self-expression through play, Froebel introduced certain pieces of apparatus which he called 'gifts' and for which he claimed virtues which they probably do not possess.

As early as 1854 a private kindergarten was started in Bloomsbury by one of Froebel's disciples. The movement progressed very slowly, but during the next twenty years a few more schools of the type were opened in other parts of London and in some of the provincial towns. They were confined to children of well-to-do parents. But in 1874 a Froebel Society was founded, largely through the instrumentality of Maria Grey, who had done so much to bring the Girls' Public Day Schools into existence. A kindergarten was attached to one of these schools—the Croydon High School—and before long a department of this kind became an essential part of every school belonging to the Trust. The movement now spread rapidly. Kindergartens—or schools calling themselves by this name—were largely private schools for the young children of middle- and upper-class parents who were unwilling to send them to the public elementary schools. They varied very greatly in efficiency, but (as the writer can testify from personal experience) some were very good, and Froebelianism, however misunderstood, was the basis of their work and organisation. But it was less easily adaptable to the conditions in

[1] *The Education of Man*, p. 55.

the infants' departments of public elementary schools, even after they had been delivered from the worst effects of 'payment by results.' There, as Adamson says, "Froebelianism remained a misunderstood exotic."[1] The main business of such schools was still to teach the three 'R's.' 'Kindergarten' appeared on time-tables as a kind of extra subject, alongside of the more orthodox ones, in order to brighten the curriculum and afford some relief. That, of course, was very far from what Froebel intended. Writing early in the present century, Raymont says: "We do him a very questionable honour when we start children of four or five along the uninviting paths that lead to mastery of the three 'R's,' reserving a place in the time-table for exercises labelled 'Kindergarten' . . . When [the infant school and the private kindergarten] place the stress on teaching rather than on physical and moral culture, and when they are conducted by persons un-acquainted with the true principles of infant training, their value resides chiefly in the fact that they keep the children out of worse mischief."[2] Nevertheless, Froebelianism, even where it was mis-understood and misapplied, brought something of value into the education of young children. There were happy and progressive infant schools even in the eighties of last century. As the principles which Froebel enunciated have been better understood, more carefully developed, and more completely applied, such schools have been multiplied. Today our infant schools form one of the most effective and encouraging parts of the English educational system.[3]

In 1886 a Royal Commission, with Sir Richard Cross (after-wards Lord Cross) as chairman, was appointed to take stock of the working of elementary education since the 1870 Act. In 1888 it issued a majority and a minority report; but although there was noticeable difference of opinion, a considerable measure of agreement was secured on some important points. The Commissioners say that they "are unanimously of opinion that the present system of 'payment by results' is carried too far

---

[1] Adamson, *English Education, 1760–1902*, p. 340.
[2] Raymont, *The Principles of Education*, p. 31.
[3] Refer to *Friederich Froebel and English Education*, ed. Evelyn Lawrence.

and is too rigidly applied, and that it ought to be modified and relaxed in the interests equally of the scholars, of the teachers, and of education itself."[1] Both parties feel that there should be an extension of "school provision, with better buildings and adequate playgrounds. The age limit for exemption from attendance should also be raised. There should be greater facilities for the training of teachers; training departments should be established in university colleges and day students admitted to training colleges. The inspectorate should be opened to elementary-school teachers. More stress should be given to science teaching and to manual and technical instruction.

It was on the religious issue that the division of opinion between the two *Reports* was largely manifested. The majority were supporters of the voluntary system. They urged that voluntary effort should have equal right with the school boards to "fill up the gaps," and that, in order to achieve this, voluntary schools should be aided from the rates.[2] They wished to see the Cowper-Temple clause withdrawn, so that it might be possible to give denominational teaching in board schools. The minority believed that there should be an undenominational school available for every child whose parents wanted it. No rate aid should go to voluntary schools, because this should be accompanied by complete public control. The school boards had a prior right to supply deficiencies in school provision, and their schools had already proved their superiority over those of the voluntary bodies.[3] Another point of disagreement concerned the meaning of 'elementary' education and the extent to which it was being financed. Some school boards were already running 'higher-grade' schools which were in effect secondary schools and, as such, were doing excellent work. But the Cross Commission majority were alarmed that such schools should be financed by public money, because in them "a portion of the cost of the education of the children of wealthier persons would be defrayed out of the rates."[4] The minority saw no harm in such a situation, but it should be recognised and regularised. A system of higher

[1] *Final Report*, part vii, § 162.   [2] *Op. cit.*, § 183.
[3] *Op. cit.*, p. 340.   [4] *Op. cit.*, part vii, § 129.

N

elementary schools, as distinct from secondary schools of the normal type, was needed, and these should be aided by public funds. This assistance should not be restricted to the existing elementary schools, which did not keep pupils beyond the age of fourteen.

The division of opinion among the members of the Cross Commission, though it reflected the divergence of views on education among the public at large, weakened the force of the recommendations that were made. Steps were, however, taken to give effect to some of its suggestions. The Code of 1890 abolished grants in respect of the three 'R's,' and this was a heavy blow to the system of 'payment by results.' It was retained only for 'class' subjects and specific subjects, such as elementary science and physical geography, taught to older children. To quote Sir George Kekewich, who was the Secretary of the Education Department at the time, the aim of the 1890 Code was "to substitute for the bald teaching of facts, and the cramming which was then necessary in order that the children might pass the annual examination and earn the grant, the development of interest and intelligence, and the acquirement of real substantial knowledge."[1] Another important outcome of the Cross Commission was the establishment of day training colleges in universities and university colleges. These date from 1890. By 1900 there were sixteen of them, and the majority of their students were reading for degrees.

[1] Quoted by Frank Smith, *A History of English Elementary Education* (1760–1902), pp. 331–2.

Chapter XX

TECHNICAL AND FURTHER EDUCATION

The Devonshire Commission and its Results. 'South Kensington' Grants. The Polytechnics. Evening Classes. University Extension and Settlements.

WHILE the Continent was in confusion during the Napoleonic wars and the years which followed them, England had been developing her textile industries, her metal manufactures, and her mines. Thus she was able to turn to best advantage the invention of machinery for spinning and weaving, and the application of steam-power. As she had been first in the field, the only way by which her Continental rivals could overcome their handicap was by developing the skill of their workers. When the Great Exhibition was held in Hyde Park in 1851, it became apparent that this country was losing its lead, and in some respects falling behind other nations. The result was a demand for the technical instruction of workers and a development of the teaching of science. This, of course, had been the original aim of the mechanics' institutes; but, as has been pointed out, the character of most of them had tended to change. One of the results of the Great Exhibition had been the foundation in 1853 of the Science and Art Department,[1] which certainly did much to guide and encourage the teaching of scientific subjects; but it was less successful in co-ordinating the teaching of science with technology—i.e. in showing how science could be applied to industry; and that, after all, was the crux of the matter.

A commission, under the chairmanship of the Duke of Devonshire, was appointed in 1870; during the following five years it issued a series of reports which furnished a full account of the work of existing institutions giving scientific instruction; it also disseminated information on the progress in technology which was being made in foreign countries. In 1877, therefore, the

[1] See *supra*, p. 135.

Livery Companies of London, which for centuries had been interested in education, formed a committee to prepare a scheme for a system of technical education. The outcome of this was the foundation of the City and Guilds of London Institute. Its object was to "provide and encourage education adapted to the requirements of all classes of persons engaged, or preparing to engage, in manufacturing or other industries."[1] Its interest, therefore, was definitely in *applied* science. The Institute encouraged and subsidised evening classes for artisans and held examinations in technical subjects. Under its auspices also the Finsbury Technical College was opened in 1883. It was designed as "a model trade school for the instruction of artisans and other persons preparing for intermediate posts in industrial works."[2] Courses were held both in the evening and the day-time. They included not only basic subjects, like mathematics, science, and drawing, but also applied subjects, such as building, engineering, and design. The College became a pattern for technical colleges elsewhere. In 1884 a large Central Technical College was opened in South Kensington; it specialised in engineering. Other colleges were opened in the industrial towns of Northern England and were to a large extent financed by local manufacturing firms. In some cases (e.g. at Manchester) they were developed out of an existing mechanics' institute which had avoided the general decline and preserved something of its original purpose and function.

All this activity was followed by the appointment of another Royal Commission on Technical Instruction which reported finally in 1884. It gave an account of the facilities for technical instruction which were available in this country, and, as the Commissioners had also carried out investigations on the Continent and in America, they were able to draw the contrast. They saw the need for technical colleges of high standard, like the Polytechnikum at Zürich; but they realised that this was only part of the problem. Technical education was not a thing apart, but was closely bound up with other forms of education. The Commis-

---

[1] *Second Report* of the Royal Commissioners on Technical Instruction (1884), vol. i, p. 401.
[2] *Op. cit.*, p. 403.

sion emphasised the need for good secondary schools of the 'modern' type—they probably had in mind the 'third-grade' class of school advocated by the Taunton Commissioners; and they advised that local authorities (i.e. the school boards) should be empowered to establish and maintain such schools.[1] Similar recommendations were made by the Cross Commission. The Technical Instruction Act of 1889 did something to give effect to these suggestions. It gave local authorities the power to levy a penny rate in order to "supply or aid in supplying technical or manual instruction."[2] But it is noteworthy that these authorities are no longer the school boards. The Local Government Act of 1888 had brought into being the County and County Borough Councils, and it was to these that the power to aid technical education was given. They were to appoint Technical Instruction Committees which were to be represented on the governing body of any school, college, or institution which gave the instruction. All this implied that for the first time education other than elementary could be legally aided from the rates, and also that a branch of education was put into the hands of representative bodies elected for the general purposes of local government. These are moves of great significance in the light of the subsequent development of our national educational system.

The Technical Instruction Act was permissive, but it was largely adopted by the new Councils. They began to provide technical instruction in day and evening classes, and this work led up to more advanced courses in technical colleges, such as the City and Guilds of London Institute. The movement received assistance from a windfall which came in 1890. In that year a sum had been set aside to compensate publicans whose licences had not been renewed. It was an annually recurring contribution from the Customs and Excise. This "whisky money," as it was called, was diverted by Parliament to local authorities for assisting technical education or for the relief of rates, at their option. Most of them were sufficiently public-spirited to devote it to the

---

[1] *Second Report* of the Royal Commissioners on Technical Instruction, vol. i, p. 538.
[2] For a definition of these terms see § 8 of the Act.

first of these purposes. But the money was administered by the South Kensington Science and Art Department, which tended to be more interested in science than in technology. Thus, although the 'whisky money' did benefit technical instruction, it tended to be spent more on the encouragement of the teaching of pure science and less for the purposes for which it had originally been intended.

The mechanics' institutes were in some sense the forerunners of the technical colleges which began to develop in the latter part of the nineteenth century. But, as has been seen, they tended in many cases to fail of their original aim because they provided not so much vocational training for working men as general educational and social facilities for members of the lower middle class. Thus they may perhaps be regarded more appropriately as the prototypes of several other kinds of institution for continuative education which became available during this same period. Chief among these are the polytechnics. Their aim was primarily educational. The best known was started by Quintin Hogg and moved to Regent Street in 1880. He aimed at "the instruction of artisans and clerks in the principles and, to some extent, the practice of their breadwinning pursuits."[1] The fees were low, and the classes—run mainly in connection with the City and Guilds Institute—included instruction in bricklaying, plumbing, electrical work, watch-making, photography, printing, and tailoring. But the Polytechnic also developed a strong social side. The whole movement received considerable impetus as the result of City Parochial Charities Act of 1883. This Act released the accumulated charitable funds of most of the London parishes, totalling about £50,000 a year, to provide open spaces and free libraries and to promote polytechnics. A central governing body was established to supervise them, and when the London County Council came into existence as the result of the Local Government Act of 1888, it took over this work. Extra contributions came from City companies and private benefactors, and other polytechnics were established in different parts of the metropolis. The polytechnics have developed a wide range of activities—

[1] See E. M. Hogg, *Quintin Hogg*, chap. vi.

they run secondary schools and technical schools; they have domestic science and trade classes; they provide general educational courses for pupils engaged in work during the day; they have day technical classes for more advanced students; and they even prepare for university degrees. They are, in fact, as well as in name, *polytechnics*, for they teach 'many arts'; and they have developed far beyond their original purely industrial aim.

The work of evening schools of various types was an important form of further education. They had been in existence for many years. Some of them were held in elementary schools and taught elementary subjects. Since 1855 they had earned grants, like any ordinary elementary school, in respect of their pupils who passed the examination in the three 'R's.' They were, in fact, a means of giving elementary education to older persons whose schooling had been neglected.[1] But after 1870 these conditions were gradually modified. The Cross Commission, although it realised that the need still existed, felt that it was diminishing. It therefore looked to the evening classes of the future to be preliminary to institute classes, science and art classes, and university extension lectures. The Commissioners also stressed the possibilities of evening classes as an agency for moral and physical training. Other classes of this kind were held, not in schools, but in technical colleges and similar institutions (e.g. the polytechnics), and from 1861 onwards they were qualified to receive South Kensington grants. Most of the classes of the Working Men's College had always been held in the evening; so also were those of the Birmingham and Midland Institute, which dates from 1854; while in 1855 King's College, London, had opened an Evening Class Department. Birkbeck, from its foundation in 1823, has always devoted its main attention to evening-class work.[2] As time went on examples such as these were multiplied up and down the country. In some cases such institutions proved to be one of the factors which, at a later date, contributed to the development of a provincial university.

[1] There was a particularly marked increase in this type of adult education among unemployed workers in Lancashire during the cotton famine consequent upon the American Civil War of 1861–5. (See Binns, *A Century of Education*, p. 180 n.)

[2] The motto of the College is *In nocte consilium.*

Another of those factors was the university extension movement. It will be remembered that Miss Clough had organised courses of lectures for women to be given in the big towns of northern England.[1] In 1867 a committee, of which she was the leading spirit, invited James Stuart, fellow of Trinity College, Cambridge, to help them. He followed up his courses for ladies by lecturing to working men in several northern towns. A small fee was charged for these courses, written exercises were worked by those who attended them, and an examination was held at the end. Cambridge took up the movement in 1873, and it at once went ahead. London followed suit in 1876 and Oxford in 1878. Summer meetings, connected with the extension movement and held at a university town, date from 1888. At Reading and at Exeter the university extension classes formed the nucleus of a university college; and in each case it developed in due course into a university with a charter of its own and the power to grant degrees.[2] University extension lectures have dealt mainly with literary, historical, and economic subjects, and sometimes—though less often—with philosophy or science. But the history of the mechanics' institutes has in some measure been repeated in the case of these extension courses. Those who could best profit by them were those whose general education had already been carried some way. And so, at any rate in the early days, the extension lectures appealed less to working men than to people of leisure, and especially to those women whose intellectual needs had not been satisfied in the inefficient girls' schools, already described, in which they had been brought up. But while this is true, it is also true that the university extension movement did much to foster a new conception of the university's function in national life and a realisation of the university's responsibility in the field of social service.

F. D. Maurice, when he founded the Working Men's College in 1854, had already given expression to that realisation, and the growth of public-school missions, since Thring set the example,

---

[1] See *supra*, p. 159.
[2] The development at Reading from the holding of university extension lectures to the granting of a university charter is traced in Childs, *Making a University*.

is a somewhat similar phenomenon. A lineal successor of Maurice was Arnold Toynbee (1852–83). As an Oxford don he interested himself in social and economic questions and won many friends among the working classes in the East End of London. His weak constitution could not stand the strain of the work which he put upon himself, and he died young. In memory of him Toynbee Hall, the first university settlement, was opened in Whitechapel in 1884. Its aim was "to link the universities with East London and to direct the human sympathies, the energies, and the public spirit of Oxford and Cambridge to the actual conditions of town life." Under the wardenship of Canon Barnett, Toynbee Hall rapidly became a focus of varied social and educational activities. Its example has been extensively followed. Some of the settlements, such as Oxford House in Bethnal Green, Cambridge House in Lambeth, and the Manchester University Settlement at Ancoats, are—like Toynbee Hall—closely linked with universities. But there has also been a growth of settlements having a similar aim, but not directly of university origin. They have been founded by such bodies as the Wesleyans, the Jewish community, the Boy Scouts, and many other agencies. But their common purpose is that which both Toynbee and Maurice had at heart. It is, that those who have had greater opportunities of intellectual and cultural development may give practical expression to their responsibilities towards their less-privileged brethren, that mutual understanding and sympathy may be promoted, and that this may tend to the lessening of inequalities between class and class.

Chapter XXI

THE TRAINING OF TEACHERS

The Pupil-teacher System. Training Colleges. Training for Secondary-school Teaching. The Teachers' Register. Professional Associations.

THE provision of schools and the education of children pre-suppose a supply of teachers to carry on the work. In the case of the endowed schools and public schools it was not usually considered that a course of special professional training should be provided for those who were to teach in them. The headmaster almost always, and the members of his staff usually, held university degrees; and often he, and sometimes they, were in holy orders. So long as teaching in this kind of school meant gerund-grinding, and great reliance was placed on the character-training which was supposed to be imparted by the formularies of the Church of England, no other kind of preparation was felt to be necessary. But that was not quite the case with the elementary schools. Even in the first part of the nineteenth century, as we have seen, the two Societies, as well as individuals such as David Stow and Kay-Shuttleworth, had been training teachers, as teachers, for elementary schools.

In order to draw together the threads of this subject, it will be necessary to look back for a moment to the period before 1870, though it was the introduction of a national system of elementary education in that year that rendered more urgent than ever the problem of providing a sufficient number of qualified teachers to work it. The earliest training colleges had developed out of the monitorial system. Because Kay-Shuttleworth realised its short-comings, he introduced the pupil-teacher system to take its place. Pupil-teachers were children chosen at the age of thirteen, from among the most promising pupils in an elementary school. They were formally apprenticed to the headmaster for a term of five years, and were examined on a prescribed graded syllabus at the end of each year. If they acquitted themselves creditably, the

Government paid the headmaster a grant of £5 for one pupil-teacher, £9 for two, and £3 for each additional one. At the end of the apprenticeship—i.e. at the age of eighteen—the pupil-teachers could sit for a competitive examination. The successful candidates were awarded Queen's Scholarships, which entitled them to a three-year course at a training college. At the end of it they qualified as certificated teachers. This scheme had been introduced by Kay-Shuttleworth in 1846. In the following year there were 200 pupil-teachers; by 1861 their number had risen to 13,871 and the Newcastle Commission, although it criticised the arduousness and mechanical nature of their training, said that there could be no doubt that the pupil-teacher system was "upon the whole excellent."[1] Matthew Arnold in his *Report* on the state of education in France[2] went so far as to say that pupil-teachers were "the sinews of English primary instruction."

The pupil-teacher system suffered a setback owing to the introduction of the Revised Code in 1862. The syllabus of work was narrowed; intending teachers were encouraged to study just those subjects which they would afterwards have to teach. This syllabus was also applied to the training colleges, so that the student was still kept in the narrow range of subjects comprised in the elementary-school curriculum. The agreement of apprenticeship between pupil-teacher and headmaster was replaced by one between him and the school managers. By 1866 the number of pupil-teachers had fallen by more than a third and the standard of the Queen's Scholarships had to be lowered. In order to ward off a threatened shortage of teachers the Government was forced to increase its grants. The Act of 1870 did something to repair the ravages of the Revised Code and to render elementary-school teaching more attractive. But misgivings had already begun to arise as to the effectiveness of the whole system. The question was asked whether it was really wise to entrust the academic education of pupil-teachers to a headmaster, for so much depended on the effectiveness and conscientiousness of the individual who assumed this responsibility. The answer of the school boards was to develop pupil-teacher centres. Intending teachers were

[1] *Report* of Newcastle Commission, p. 106. [2] P. 74.

collected at these centres for instruction in classes, at first in the evenings and on Saturdays. In 1884 a further advance was made. Pupil-teachers were not required to teach for more than half-time in their schools; the other half could be given to day-time instruction in these centres which thus became in practice a specialised type of school. Some of them after the Act of 1902 were developed into county secondary schools.

In spite of these changes, it is obvious that by the middle of the eighties the pupil-teacher system was beginning to break up.[1] This is illustrated in the reports of the Cross Commission. The majority, although realising the weakness of the system, felt that it should be maintained and improved because there was "no other available, or as we prefer to say, equally trustworthy source from which an adequate supply of teachers is likely to be forthcoming."[2] The minority expressed the opinion that "the overwhelming mass of the evidence is that these young people are unsatisfactory as teachers and ill-taught and ill-trained as scholars. . . . The training colleges are unable to do all that they should for their students on account of the unprepared and crude state in which they receive them."[3]

The problem of the pupil-teachers was closely bound up with the problem of the training colleges. The whole system was a closed one. The pupil-teacher started as a member of an elementary school; he then became a pupil-teacher, probably in the same school; thence, if successful in the Queen's Scholarship examination, he went on to an elementary training college; and finally he returned to an elementary school as a teacher and spent the rest of his professional life in the elementary service. That system did not begin to give way until the nineties, and its doom was not sealed until the Act of 1902 had made possible the rise of a number of State-aided secondary schools. It then became more and more common to send boys and girls to these secondary schools before apprenticeship, rather than to train them in specialised pupil-teacher centres. In 1907 the pupil in a secondary school who in-

---

[1] A most interesting first-hand account of pupil-teaching at this period is given in Spencer, *An Inspector's Testament*, chap. iv.
[2] *Final Report*, p. 88.   [3] *Op. cit.*, p. 277.

tended to teach was allowed to remain there up to the age of seventeen or eighteen as a 'bursar' and then proceed direct to a training college, or he could become a 'student teacher,' spending half his time in actual practice in an elementary school and during the other half continuing his studies in his secondary school.

In the early days there had been some difference of opinion as to the length of the training-college course and the nature of its curriculum. At first the course in some colleges lasted only a few months; in others its length was one, two, or even three years. In some the staple of the curriculum was professional training; elsewhere general education was stressed. But too often the syllabus was shallow and ambitious; it tended to encourage memory work and superficiality and rule-of-thumb methods in teaching practice. For all that, the training colleges turned out a succession of teachers who, according to their lights, faced and overcame the severe handicaps under which they worked, and who deserved well of the community. Their salaries were low and there was little hope of public recognition or reward for their services. They tackled huge classes in ill-equipped premises, and they were perpetually exposed to the demoralising influences of 'payment by results.' But they laid the foundations of our national system of elementary education. Although, therefore, not all teachers were products of the training colleges, it is obvious that these institutions have played a most important part in the educational history of this country—a part that is not always fully recognised. At the time of the Cross Commission forty-three of these colleges were in existence. They were all residential and run by voluntary effort; most of them belonged to the Church of England, so that the facilities available for nonconformists or Roman Catholics were limited. The accommodation also was by no means sufficient for all the pupil-teachers who had passed the Queen's Scholarship examination and were therefore theoretically qualified for admission. This situation explains the Cross Commission minority's recommendation that day students should be admitted without denominational restrictions to training colleges which had hitherto been entirely residential; it also wished "to utilise the colleges and other places of higher instruction which are willing to aid in the training of teachers, and to encourage the formation of educational faculties in such colleges either in conjunction with or apart from the local school board."[1]

As we have seen,[2] this recommendation was put into effect in the year 1890, which for that reason is a date of great importance in the history of the training of teachers in this country. The Education Department authorised universities or university colleges to set up training departments in which students could read for degrees; selected students in training colleges could also take degree courses. 'University' departments were at once opened at King's College, London, and Owens College, Manchester, and in several other colleges. Cambridge had a 'university day training college' in 1891 and Oxford in 1892. By 1901 there were seventeen departments of this kind. As Adamson points out,[3] "they were not all non-residential, and none of them was a 'college' in the customary sense of the word." Their true *differentia* was that they formed an integral part of a university or university college.

In the field of elementary education the professional training of teachers has been bound up at every stage with the development of a national system of schools. But this has been far less the case with secondary education. As has already been pointed out, the possession of a degree—especially if it were reinforced by holy orders—was regarded as an entirely adequate qualification for teaching in an endowed or public school. Secondary-school masters doubtless tended to judge professional training by the type of training which was given in some of the elementary training colleges; and it is true that the teaching methods instilled into ex-monitors or pupil-teachers had often been extremely mechanical. If professional training in a special college for schoolmasters seemed to produce men of narrow views and superficial knowledge and unattractive personality, the inference which the secondary branch of the profession drew was that such training should be avoided. Thus during most of the nineteenth century secondary schools remained largely uninterested in the question

---

[1] *Final Report*, p. 290.   [2] See *supra*, p. 176.
[3] Adamson, *English Education*, 1789–1902, p. 380.

of professional training. The first impulse towards such training for secondary-school teachers came from women. Headmistresses believed in it and worked for it long before any headmaster did. The reason may be that women on the whole are more concerned about the details of technique and organisation than men are, and that the average headmaster may be more ready to think that so long as a man's discipline is sound, he can be left to work out his own salvation as a teacher.

Facilities for the professional training and qualification of secondary-school teachers were first afforded by the College of Preceptors, which was founded as early as 1846 and incorporated in 1849. One of its aims, as defined in its charter, was "promoting sound learning and advancing the interests of Education, more especially among the middle classes, by affording facilities to the teacher for the acquiring of a sound knowledge of his profession, and by providing for the periodical Session of a competent Board of Examiners to ascertain and give certificates of the acquirements and fitness for their office of persons engaged or desiring to be engaged in the Education of Youth." Any surplus funds which the College might possess were to be devoted *inter alia* "in or towards the founding or endowing of normal or training schools, or in instituting lectureships on any subject connected with the Theory or Practice of Education."[1] Diplomas for teachers, covering professional as well as academic competence, were instituted, and courses of lectures in educational theory and practice were arranged. In 1873 the first professorship in education in England was established by the College. Its occupant was Joseph Payne, who had already done much to interest English people in the educational ideas and experiments of Continental reformers. He was also an ardent advocate of the higher education of girls and women, and among those who attended his courses was Mrs. Sophie Bryant, who succeeded Miss Buss as headmistress of the North London Collegiate School. The professorship came to an end with Payne's death in 1876. An attempt to establish a Day Training College in connection with the College of Preceptors was made in 1895, but this also was discontinued in

[1] College of Preceptors, *Charter*, § 26.

1898. The College still continues to award professional diplomas and it organises courses of lectures on educational subjects.

The College of Preceptors diplomas were of value particularly to teachers in private schools, many of whom had not had the opportunity to obtain the more orthodox qualification of a university degree. The first university chairs of education were established in 1876 at Edinburgh and St. Andrew's out of funds left by Dr. Andrew Bell for educational purposes. A similar movement was in progress at Cambridge, and it led to the appointment in 1879 of a Teachers' Training Syndicate. Courses of lectures were arranged and an examination in the theory, history, and practice of education was introduced—but lecturing and examination do not constitute training in teaching. The success of these lectures and examinations was due to a considerable extent to the provision in 1885 of a Cambridge Training College for Women, largely with the support of Miss Buss. Miss Beale had also introduced a training department into the Ladies' College at Cheltenham; and the Girls' Public Day School Trust from the first aimed at providing facilities for student teachers to be trained for their profession under the direction of the headmistress. Maria Grey, who was largely responsible for the formation of the Trust, was also concerned with the founding in 1878 of a training college for women teachers. The main premises are now at Twickenham, though part of the College remains at Brondesbury, a suburb of London. The girls' secondary school which used to be annexed to it is now separate, though it is still used by students for teaching practice.

Thus 'professional training' remained largely a women's movement so far as secondary teaching was concerned. When, in 1894, Henry Sidgwick was giving evidence before a Royal Commission, he said of the Cambridge Training Syndicate that its scheme had "remained almost inoperative up to the present time so far as the schoolmasters for whose benefit it was primarily instituted are concerned; though it has been used to an important extent by women preparing for secondary teaching." But the opening of university day training departments from 1890 onwards, though they were designed primarily for the professional

training of elementary-school teachers, reacted in favour of training for secondary-school teachers also; and this affected men no
less than women. This was particularly noticeable after the opening of many new secondary schools, consequent upon the Education Act of 1902. These municipal or county schools were often
evolved from an older pupil-teacher centre or higher-grade
school. When this happened, the original staff was usually
absorbed into the new secondary school, and thus graduates who
had been trained as elementary-school teachers began to appear
on secondary-school staffs. The new schools also created a demand
for well-qualified graduate teachers, which could be supplied only
by drawing on the university day training colleges. All this
tended to break down the hard-and-fast line of demarcation which
had separated the elementary and secondary branches of the profession, and it helped to counter the old idea that, even if training
were necessary for the one class, it was not necessary for the other.

The question of professional training is bound up with that of
the registration of teachers. The law, medicine, dentistry, phar-
maceutical chemistry, accountancy, and many other professions
have their registers; and unless one's name appears there, one is
legally debarred from practising. But even to this day that condition does not exist as regards teaching. This has been due not
merely to public indifference and consequent lack of Government
support, but also to the great variety of types of teacher and the
want of homogeneity within the teaching profession itself. So
long, for example, as teachers in public, endowed, elementary,
and private schools regarded themselves as separate classes, hardly
at all over-lapping, there could be no register to contain them all
alike. There were, however, those who realised the importance
of the problem. The College of Preceptors from the beginning
advocated registration, and, owing to the action of its Council, a
'Scholastic Registration Association' was founded in 1866. The
Schools Inquiry Commission two years later recommended the
institution of certificates of competence to teach, granted after the
passing of an examination.[1] Perhaps it is understandable that no
effect was given to these recommendations.

[1] See *supra*, p. 132.

O

But the matter did not rest there, and other attempts were made to secure a register. In the *Report* of the Bryce Commission of 1894—which will be discussed more fully in a later chapter—the following passage occurs: "The formation of such a register has long been desired by a large number of the members of the teaching profession, and the evidence, which we have received during the course of our enquiry, shows that the need for some official test and standard of professional efficiency has now become a matter of general agreement."[1] In 1898 a Teachers' Registration Bill was introduced into Parliament. It was withdrawn; but by the Board of Education Act of 1899 an advisory or consultative committee was formed, and to it was given the duty of drawing up a register of teachers. This was to be divided into two 'columns'—A and B. Into column A went the certificated teachers in elementary schools; while in column B were placed those teachers in secondary schools who could fulfil certain requirements as to general attainments and show either training or adequate experience in recognised schools. There were to be supplementary registers for teachers of special subjects. The scheme broke down for various reasons. Column A was never printed, and therefore those on it were virtually excluded from recognition; elementary-school teachers not unnaturally resented the distinction between A and B; and it was found in practice that the regulations governing admission to column B did not encourage professional training for secondary schoolmasters in the way that had been hoped. A new Teachers' Registration Council was established by an Act of 1907.[2] Those admitted to its register appeared in one alphabetical list, and it could include teachers in all types of schools and institutions, including universities. In 1930 the teachers whose names appeared on this register were constituted the Royal Society of Teachers and entitled to append the letters M.R.S.T. to their names. Registration was voluntary, and by no means all of those who were entitled to register did so. Thus the register, though it deserved to succeed, achieved only a modified success. Neither the Board or Ministry of Education,

---

[1] *Report*, p. 318. See §§ 152-8.
[2] Education (Administrative Provisions) Act, 1907, § 16.

nor the local authorities, made any effective use of it—e.g. by requiring that teachers holding at least certain positions should be registered. Perhaps as the result of more recent legislation some at any rate of the effects of registration may be achieved in other ways.

An indication of the growth of what one may call professional consciousness is shown by the founding of teachers' associations, which is a feature of the second half of the nineteenth century. The activities of the Schools Inquiry Commission gave rise to some concern among the heads of the endowed schools and, as has been seen, one result of this was the establishment of the Headmasters' Conference in 1869. It has met regularly ever since. It tends to be a conservative body—what Professor Archer calls an 'educational House of Lords'—and to be distrustful of State interference. Its membership is in the main limited to headmasters of schools of the 'independent' type, which send a regular and adequate proportion of boys to Oxford and Cambridge. However, the Conference has helped the heads of these schools to get together, and it has also set up the Oxford and Cambridge Joint Board examination for the pupils of such schools. The headmistresses formed their own association in 1874, but it has been less exclusive. Its founder and first president was Miss Buss, and she was succeeded in 1894 by Miss Beale. Thring showed his goodwill towards this association by inviting its members to hold one of their meetings at Uppingham.

Meanwhile the elementary teachers had not been idle. In 1870 the National Union of Elementary Teachers was formed and the word 'Elementary' was dropped from its title in 1889. Other sectional societies have also come into existence—the Independent Schools Association (1883), the Headmasters' Association (1890), which admitted those secondary-school heads who were not eligible for the Conference, the Associations for secondary-school assistant mistresses (1884), and assistant masters (1891). Besides these there were endless professional or semi-professional societies concerned with purely educational matters, or with particular subjects of the curriculum and methods of teaching them. The very variety of these societies and associations is an indication of the sectionalism which has hampered the growth of the idea of a unified profession, and its expression in a teachers' register; but it has stimulated vigour and interest. The evolution of a more closely knit national system of education and the gradual obliteration of frontiers inside it, which have marked recent years, are shown in the formation of 'Joint-Four' or 'Joint-Six' committees, representative of several sectional societies, and in suggestions which have been made in some quarters for the absorption of all such societies in one comprehensive association.

Chapter XXII

UNIVERSITY AND SECONDARY EDUCATION

Progress at Oxford, Cambridge, and London. Rise of the 'Modern' Universities. New Types of Secondary School.

AS an outcome of the Oxford and Cambridge University Acts of 1854 and 1856[1] there was considerable progress at both universities. Religious tests for degrees (except in divinity) were not abolished till 1871, but in the same year the snobbish distinction between noblemen, gentlemen commoners, and commoners was swept away. New final honours schools or triposes were instituted. At Oxford Natural Science dates from 1853, Law and History from the same year—but they were separated in 1872—and Theology from 1870. Oriental languages, English language and literature, and mediæval and modern languages also became subjects for honours degrees. The development of science at Oxford and Cambridge dates mainly from the sixties and seventies of last century, as is evidenced by the foundation of the university laboratories and the establishment of new science professorships. The organisation of the two universities was affected by the activities of a Royal Commission on Oxford and Cambridge, with the Duke of Cleveland as chairman, which was appointed in 1872 and reported in 1874. An Oxford and Cambridge Act was passed in 1877 which gave the Commissioners power to frame statutes for the colleges, for the Acts of 1854 and 1856 had dealt only with *university* statutes. Other results were not inconsiderable. Life-fellowships were abolished and prize fellowships for research were instituted; fellowships involved teaching duties and the salaries attached to them were standardised. Celibacy was no longer required of college Fellows, and the result was a vast growth of suburban north Oxford. New professorships were founded and the endowments of existing chairs increased by the annexation to them of college fellowships. This

[1] See *supra*, pp. 123–124.

strengthened the link between the colleges and the professoriate.

These reforms, following on the abolition of religious tests, had the effect of transforming Oxford and Cambridge from a group of largely clerical institutions into modern universities. A system of inter-collegiate lectures was introduced, and this was gradually extended until they became available to all undergraduates who were reading for honours. Non-collegiate students were also admitted at Oxford in 1868 and at Cambridge in the following year—a step which had been suggested by the Commissioners of 1852.[1] Numbers increased and college buildings were enlarged. Two new colleges, both associated with the Church of England, also were opened—Keble at Oxford in 1870, and Selwyn at Cambridge in 1882. Other religious denominations moved their theological colleges to the universities. Some of them have become private halls and their students are able to benefit from the teaching and other amenities which the university affords. This too is the period of the opening of the women's colleges at both Oxford and Cambridge, to which reference has already been made. It marks also the growth of the university extension movement and the increasing university influence on secondary schools through the local, or 'middle class,' examinations, which had been in existence since 1858.

The second half of the nineteenth century saw not only a revival in the two ancient Universities, but also a multiplication of other institutions of university rank in various parts of the country. There are various reasons for this. In spite of reforms, there was still a tendency for many of the undergraduates at Oxford and Cambridge to be drawn from the 'upper classes,' or at any rate to be in easy financial circumstances. Life therefore tended to be expensive, though attempts had been made to reduce extravagance and increase scholarships. The poor student was certainly not excluded, but he was in the minority, and the success of Durham had shown the demand for university facilities of the Oxford and Cambridge type, but at a cheaper rate. Again, most of those who went to the older Universities were destined for the Church or teaching in public or endowed schools or the law or political

[1] See *supra*, p. 125.

or administrative careers. The bulk of the instruction given therefore tended to have the needs of such candidates in view. This is not to say that science and mathematics were neglected, as has already been indicated. But there was an increasing demand for teaching of an advanced university type in subjects which could be more definitely applied in the great manufacturing industries and which would be directly accessible to students living in the areas where they were carried on. Again, with the development of secondary education, not only in grammar schools, but in 'higher-grade' and similar schools, the demand for better-qualified teachers increased; and as women, as well as men, can be teachers, the need for giving university facilities to women was emphasised.

These needs had for some time to a great extent been met by the University of London—or rather by institutions, like University College and King's College, which submitted their students for London degrees. There was a good deal of criticism of a university which was an examining, but not a teaching, body, and which did not concern itself in the least with the origin or training of its students. The staffs of the colleges which submitted students for London degrees also complained that they had no hand in drawing up syllabuses or setting examination papers. As usual, this led eventually to the appointment of a Royal Commission (1888–9), with Lord Selborne as chairman, which endorsed the proposal that the University should become a teaching as well as an examining institution, but left the details undecided. A second Commission, known as the 'Gresham,' reporting in 1894, drew up a scheme which appeared in a modified form as the result of a University of London Act of 1898. The reconstituted University continued to examine 'external' students and did not concern itself with their training. They could work privately or in some institution along the lines of a syllabus prescribed by the University, and merely sit for the examinations, which were normally held in London. But the new constitution provided also for 'internal' students who attended courses in colleges which became constituent schools of the teaching University. They included twenty-four institutions of many different types, and one or two of them were not actually in London. In addition to University College and King's College, there were the great London teaching hospitals, a number of theological colleges belonging to various denominations, the London School of Economics (founded in 1895), and women's colleges like Bedford, and the Royal Holloway College at Egham which had been at work since 1886. The reconstituted University also included the Royal College of Science, the Central Technical College of the City and Guilds Institute, and the South-Eastern Agricultural College at Wye, in Kent. The organisation and administration of such an amorphous body were not easy.

With the exception of Durham, the first of the great provincial universities originated in Manchester. In 1851 a college had been opened as the result of a bequest by a local merchant, John Owens. Its aim was laid down as the provision of instruction "in such branches of learning and science as are now, and may be hereafter, usually taught in the English universities."[1] It had an uncertain start and much of its work was done in evening classes. But by 1864 there were 127 day and 312 evening students, and the corner was turned. Subscriptions flowed in and an Act of Parliament in 1871 gave Owens College a new constitution and power to admit women as students. It ran courses for London degrees, and there were, of course, no religious tests. Meanwhile Yorkshire was not being left behind. In 1874 a college of science and technology, called the Yorkshire College, was founded at Leeds. Liverpool University College dates from 1881, and was united in 1884 to Owens College, Manchester, in a federal university—Victoria—which granted its own degrees and was independent of London. Leeds joined the federation in 1887.

But federal universities tend to be unwieldy and their organisation is difficult. Victoria broke up in 1903, and since 1904 the three cities have had their separate universities, each with a full range of faculties, and each giving its own degrees. Birmingham University evolved from a college founded by Josiah Mason in 1880. Its original aims were frankly utilitarian, and they illustrate rather crudely the ideas in the minds of some of those who

[1] Fiddes, *Owens College and Manchester University*, p. 13.

were concerned in the founding of the colleges out of which the universities in the great industrial cities developed. Mason stipulated that his college should foster scientific education "to the exclusion of mere literary education and instruction, and of all teaching of theology and of subjects purely theological."[1] Subsequent developments led to a modification of Mason's scheme, and Birmingham now gives degrees in arts, and has instituted a chair in theology. The university's charter dates from 1900. Other universities have developed from University College, Bristol, Firth College, Sheffield, and the University Colleges of Reading, Nottingham, Southampton, Hull, Exeter, and Leicester. Originally they prepared their students for London degrees, but they now have charters and are independent. Armstrong College (afterwards King's College), Newcastle, which dates from 1871, has become an independent university. In Wales the University College at Aberystwyth was opened in 1872. Similar colleges were founded during the eighties at Cardiff and Bangor; and all three prepared for London degrees. But a charter of 1893 established a teaching University of Wales, with three constituent colleges, to which as a fourth the Swansea College was admitted in 1920.

It should be noted that none of these universities was founded as such—they gradually evolved out of colleges of various types. They were not able to obtain their charters as independent universities until they could satisfy the Privy Council that their financial position was such as to enable them to carry on university work in a proper manner. They owed their origin and growth largely to private benevolence and have been supported by business firms and municipalities. Treasury grants have also supplemented local resources. The first amount voted for this purpose was a sum of £15,000 devoted in 1889 to the needs of the university colleges. By 1902 the grant had risen to £24,000. The universities which have grown out of these provincial colleges are for the most part situated in industrial areas, and for that reason have tended to develop a scientific or technological bias. They have evolved new faculties and departments—

[1] Foundation deed, dated December 12th, 1870.

economics and commerce, engineering and metallurgy, textile and leather working, dyeing and brewing, agriculture and horticulture; but they realise now—even if they have not always done so in the past—that higher technological work can be built only on a basis of general education, and they all provide a full range of arts and pure science subjects. Their relative cheapness and their greater accessibility have opened university education, as never before since the Middle Ages, to the 'lower classes.' But there has been in the past a danger of their functioning simply as places of instruction rather than as societies. So long as students live at home or in lodgings and merely travel backwards and forwards to attend university classes, it is difficult to develop that community life which is perhaps the most educative thing that the university has to offer. This weakness of the provincial university system has been increasingly countered by the provision of halls of residence. At the University of Reading, which has never been a 'provincial' university in the ordinary sense, serving chiefly its own neighbourhood, the principle of residence in college for all students, as at Oxford and Cambridge, has been fully in operation from the first.

The result of the Endowed Schools Act of 1869 had been a gradual redistribution of the endowments of secondary schools. It was said that the Commissioners whom it appointed could turn a boys' school in Cornwall into a girls' school in Northumberland. But the Commissioners could not solve the whole of the problem. There was, in fact, no plan about the scheme, no framework of national or local organisation, and no aid from parliamentary grants or rates. As a whole, therefore, there was still a deficiency of secondary education, and private endeavour had not been able to supply the lack. To meet this situation some of the larger and more progressive school boards stepped into the breach. The Education Department had been giving grants not only for 'obligatory' and 'class' subjects, but also for what were called 'specific' subjects. These could be earned by children in the upper standards of elementary schools; and they included branches of mathematics and science, agriculture, languages, and commercial and domestic arts. Indirectly, therefore, education of a secondary type was being aided. Not only this, but Government assistance could be obtained from grants distributed on the result of examinations conducted by the Science and Art Department, independently of the Education Department; and this provided a further revenue for more advanced instruction in connection with elementary schools. In 1872 the Leeds School Board established what it called a higher-grade board school. Its example was followed by other large towns, including London. The movement progressed steadily in the eighties, and by 1894 there were in the country sixty-three of these higher-grade schools. Other progressive elementary schools developed 'higher tops,' consisting of pupils who had passed through Standard VII and were staying on to take more advanced work.

Education of this type was also encouraged by the offer by the Science and Art Department of grants for establishing what were called 'organised science schools'—i.e. grouped science classes, which might be held in the day-time or in the evening and which could meet in an elementary, higher-grade, or even an endowed school. The position of the higher-grade school was doubtless an irregular one, because the Education Act of 1870 gave the school boards control over elementary education only; but these schools were officially condoned, or even encouraged. The school boards had no power to organise or control secondary-school provision in their areas, and yet some of them were devoting rate aid to institutions which were giving an education quite as extended as that given in many of the smaller endowed schools, which received neither Government grant nor local rate aid; and this led to competition and controversy. There was no clear definition of the limits and nature of elementary and secondary education.[1] Yet few people really wished to raise the issues involved.

[1] The Cross Commission had drawn attention to this point. Cf. "As the meaning and limits of the term 'elementary' have not been defined in the Education Acts, nor by any judicial or authoritative interpretation, but depend only upon the annual codes of the Department, on whose power of framing such codes no limit has hitherto been imposed, it would appear to be of absolute necessity that some definition of the instruction to be paid for out of the rates and taxes should be put forth by the legislature. Until this is done, the limits of primary and secondary education cannot be defined." (*Final Report*, part vii, § 115.)

The big school boards realised that they were establishing a claim to control popular secondary education and did not wish to have this disputed; the opponents of the school boards did not want to provoke a situation which might result in the formal grant of local control and State aid to secondary schools. Thus, although Matthew Arnold's slogan had been "organise your secondary education," it was generally felt safer to let things slide. The Cross Commission of 1888, although appointed to review elementary education, could not, as things were, avoid some reference to secondary education. It suggested that if the curriculum of higher elementary schools were restricted within due limits, avoiding all attempts to invade the ground properly belonging to secondary schools, such schools might prove a useful addition to the existing school machinery for primary education. This was vague enough; but the minority report's recommendations were more definite. The provision of higher elementary schools was specifically advocated; and pupils would be drafted to them at the age of eleven or twelve. "The higher elementary school would satisfy the wants of an entirely different class from those who desire secondary education. Secondary education is for those who will be under continuous instruction till sixteen or eighteen, whether they go on afterwards to higher university instruction or not; whereas this higher elementary education is intended to teach more thoroughly those who must begin to earn their living, or at any rate begin to learn their trade, at fourteen or fifteen years."[1] This implied that these higher primary schools— to use a French term—would be assimilated to the elementary-school system of Government aid and Government control, rather than to the secondary-school system, which so far was virtually free from both.

It should be noted that in practice the term 'higher grade' was never very clearly defined.[2] The best of the schools of this type were fully organised, and some took pupils up to the age of sixteen; but others were ordinary elementary schools with 'tops,' and some of the voluntary schools had 'tops' of this kind. Moreover,

[1] Cross Commission, *Final Report*, p. 319.
[2] See Hadow *Report* on *The Education of the Adolescent*, pp. 23–4.

the higher-grade schools, assisted as they were by public funds, often competed severely with the endowed grammar schools, many of which—in spite of the 1869 Act—were still poverty-stricken and inefficient; and this helped to depress the grammar-school type of education to the advantage of schools which tended to emphasise—or even over-emphasise—instruction of a non-literary type. The whole situation was, in fact, becoming extremely complicated. Elementary education was still in the hands of the school boards which received Government grants and rate aid, and of the voluntary bodies which also received these grants but no rate aid. Some of the school boards were running higher-grade schools which were really secondary schools, although aided by the rates, supplemented as a rule by grants from the Science and Art Department. Technical education had been put into the hands of the newly formed county and county borough councils, and they also could levy a rate for this purpose. Secondary schools were still nominally free from control and were dependent on endowments or fees, or both; their authorities were boards of governors, companies like the G.P.D.S.T., or private proprietors. But in some cases these schools managed also to earn grants from the Science and Art Department, based on the results of examinations taken by their pupils; or they might be able to qualify for assistance from the technical-education funds administered by the county and county borough councils. In addition to this there was no organic relation between either the school boards or the councils and the new university colleges which were springing up in the big provincial cities. The *Report* of the Bryce Commission, which will be discussed in the next chapter, spoke of the confusion arising from this lack of organisation and of the "results of dispersed and unconnected forces, needless competition between the different agencies, and a frequent overlapping of effort, with much consequent waste of money, of time, and of labour."[1]

[1] *Report* of Bryce Commission, vol. i, p. 18.

Chapter XXIII

A NATIONAL SYSTEM OF EDUCATION

The Bryce Commission and the 1902 Act.

IT was obvious that the 'administrative muddle,' as Adamson calls it, could not continue indefinitely. In order to find some solution a Royal Commission on Secondary Education, with James Bryce[1] as chairman, was appointed in 1894 and reported in 1895. Its terms of reference were "to consider what are the best methods of establishing a well-organised system of Secondary Education in England, taking into account existing deficiencies, and having regard to such local sources of revenue from endowment or otherwise as are available or may be made available for this purpose, and to make recommendations accordingly."[2] The Commissioners conceived their task to be "nothing less than to complete the educational system of England, now confessedly defective in that part which lies between the elementary schools on the one hand and the Universities on the other, and to frame an organisation which shall be at once firm and flexible."[3] They examined a large number of witnesses and sent out a questionnaire to many "persons and bodies specially competent to supply information." They also examined the secondary-school systems of several European countries, the United States, and the self-governing colonies (as they then were) of Canada and the Australian States.

The recommendations of the Commission may be summarised as follows: There should be a unified Central Authority, including the existing Education Department, the Science and Art Department, and the Charity Commission so far as its activities were concerned with educational endowments. This authority "ought to consist of a Department of the Executive Government, pre-

[1] He had acted as an assistant commissioner for the Schools Inquiry Commission, and had emphasised the pressing need for educational co-ordination.
[2] *Report*, p. xxvi. [3] *Op. cit.*, p. 2.

sided over by a Minister responsible to Parliament, who would obviously be the same Minister as the one to whom the charge of elementary education is entrusted."[1] Its functions would be not "to control, but rather to supervise the Secondary Education of the country, not to override or supersede local action, but to endeavour to bring about among the various agencies which provide that education a harmony and a co-operation which are now wanting."[2] An advisory council of not more than twelve "persons specially conversant with education and holding an independent position"[3] should also be set up. In 1899 a Board of Education Act was passed which gave effect to these recommendations and which brought into existence a Consultative Committee, though the powers given to it were less than those recommended by the Bryce Commissioners.

The *Report* advocated that in every county and county borough there should be set up a local authority for *all* types of secondary education. The higher-grade schools and organised science schools were to be treated as if they were secondary. The majority of the members of each local authority would be appointed by the county council and others nominated by the Central Office or co-opted; but in the county boroughs the councils and the school boards were to appoint an equal number of representatives, together with co-opted members. Persons possessing educational experience as teachers were to be included. The local authorities would be required by the Central Office to take steps to make due provision for secondary education in any area where this was considered to be insufficient. They should have power to aid from the rates secondary schools, whether under their direct management or not; this would include existing endowed schools, as well as new schools to be established by the councils. The local authorities might also, with the sanction of the Central Office, acquire by agreement proprietary or private schools; while such schools as remained independent should be subject to recognition by the local authority and inspection by the Central Office. Fees, fixed in relation to the real cost of schooling, should be retained; but rate-aid, not exceeding 2*d*. in the £, should be extended for

[1] *Report*, p. 257.   [2] *Ibid.*   [3] *Op. cit.*, p. 258.

the benefit of secondary education. Whether it would be necessary to supplement this by Government grants must be left for
experience to decide. But "ample provision should be made by
every local authority for enabling selected children of the poorer
parents to climb the educational ladder."[1] To this end a sufficient
supply of scholarships should be made available. They should
cover the cost of instruction, and in some cases boarding fees as
well; and they should be fairly apportioned as between boys and
girls.

The Commissioners thought that the Central Office should
regulate, but not conduct, the examination of secondary schools.
This would leave intact the existing university 'locals' and similar
examinations; but the Central Office, aided by its advisory
council, should 'correlate' the examination certificates and 'make
them interchangeable.' "Such certificates might also well be accepted by the various professional examining bodies, as covering
the preliminary and general portions of their examinations."[2] In
the appointment of inspectors for secondary schools "great
weight ought to be given to previous experience in teaching;
and duly qualified women should be chosen where there is likely
to be sufficient work for them."[3] The appointment, conditions
of service, and payment of teachers should also be safeguarded,
and the advisory committee of the Central Authority "should
be charged with the duty of instituting and keeping a register of
teachers."[4] The *Report* also advocated professional training for
teachers in secondary schools. "To all reforms which can raise
the status and tone of the teaching profession, can draw abler men
and women into it by the prospects of a better career, can more
adequately fit them for their work by the provision of general
and special preparation, we attach the utmost importance."[5]
Those words might have been quoted from the report of the
McNair Committee issued nearly fifty years later.

In conclusion, it should be noted that the Bryce Commissioners seemed apprehensive lest the old grammar-school type of
secondary education might be too far replaced by technical and

[1] *Op. cit.*, p. 300.　　[2] *Op. cit.*, p. 305.　　[3] *Ibid.*
[4] *Op. cit.*, p. 318.　　[5] *Op. cit.*, p. 326.

scientific education. They were anxious to guard against this. "The importance of preserving all grammar schools which are, or can be, made efficient depends largely on the general ground that such schools represent especially the tradition of literary education. There is little danger at the present day that we shall fail to recognise the necessity for improving and extending scientific and technical instruction. It is less certain that we may not run some risk of a lop-sided development in education, in which the teaching of science, theoretical or applied, may so predominate as to entail comparative neglect of studies which are of less obvious and immediate utility, though not of less moment for the formation of mind and character. In efficient grammar schools, as existing examples prove, it is possible to harmonise modern requirements with the best elements of that older system which has produced good results in the past, and which in our own day still represents so much that is fundamental and indispensable in a properly liberal education."[1] The pendulum had indeed swung back since the Schools Inquiry Commission of 1867.

The *Report* of the Bryce Commission is of considerable interest because it contains the germs of much of the educational progress that has been made in this country since the beginning of the twentieth century. The Commission also was fortunate in that their work contributed to the passing of an Act of Parliament of outstanding importance. But meanwhile other influences were at work to make comprehensive legislation imperative. The Liberal Government, which had appointed the Bryce Commission, went out of power in 1895, and was succeeded by the Conservatives, under the leadership of Lord Salisbury. Many of them were concerned about the difficulties which the voluntary schools were encountering in their endeavour to compete with the rate-aided board schools. The Vice-President of the Committee of Council on Education, Sir John Gorst, prepared a Bill in 1896 which proposed to make an extra 'special-aid grant' of 4s. a head available for voluntary schools; and this was to be paid to the county and county borough councils for them to distribute.

[1] *Op. cit.*, p. 48.

The Cowper-Temple clause was to be abolished, and denominational religious instruction was to be allowed in board schools if
a reasonable number of parents demanded it. The Bill also proposed to make the councils themselves, and not independent composite bodies on which they had a majority of members, the local
authorities for secondary education. This was an improvement
on the Bryce recommendations, for they would have implied
three separate education authorities in each area—the school
boards, the new secondary 'local education authority,' and the
councils themselves for technical education. But the Bill encountered opposition from the supporters of the school boards,
and also from nonconformists who objected to increased State
grants for voluntary schools, and to denominational teaching in
board schools. It was therefore withdrawn; but the matter could
not rest there.

In 1895 an office of Special Inquiries and Reports had been
formed at the Education Department. One of its first acts was to
issue a series of reports on the educational systems of foreign
countries; the contrast between their logical and centralised
schemes and our own chaos was evident. The assistant director of
this office was Robert Morant, who was destined to play an important part in the educational fortunes of this country. He was determined to spare no effort to introduce some sort of order into
the organisation of English education. He realised clearly that
many of the larger school boards, aided by the rates, were giving
secondary education to advanced pupils, whereas they were
legally restricted to the field of elementary education. He drew
attention to this fact in a sentence which he inserted in a report on
education in Switzerland, of which he was the author; but it did
not attract public attention. But the matter was soon brought
to a head in another way. A Government auditor, named Cockerton, disallowed to the London School Board expenditure on
science and art classes in higher-grade schools, and on evening
continuation classes. He maintained that such expenditure was not
sanctioned by the 1870 and subsequent Elementary Education
Acts; and that a school board was competent to provide only
elementary education. This Cockerton judgment was upheld by

the Court of Appeal.[1] A special emergency Act in 1901, renewed in the following year, legalised the position; but it was obvious that such a situation could not continue. In 1899 the Board of Education had replaced the Education Department and become the sole central authority for primary, secondary, and technical education alike; but the question of local control remained to be settled.

The solution was provided in 1902. After the end of the Boer War, which incidentally did much to justify the products of English elementary education since 1870, the Conservatives won a sweeping victory. One of their first acts was to bring in an Education Bill. It was sponsored by the Prime Minister, A. J. Balfour, himself; and he was ably seconded behind the scenes by Morant, who became Permanent Secretary to the newly formed Board of Education. In spite of bitter opposition on the part of Liberals and nonconformists, the Bill became law on December 20th, 1902.

The Act reorganised education on a municipal basis. The school boards scattered up and down England and Wales, where they had been 'filling up the gaps' in the voluntary system, were swept away. They were replaced by the county and county borough councils—120 of them—which became responsible for both secondary and elementary education; but the oversight of elementary education only was given to 'Part III' authorities,[2] consisting of boroughs with a population of over 10,000, and urban districts the population of which exceeded 20,000; they numbered 180 all told. The Councils, whether 'Part II' or 'Part III,' became for the purposes of the Act the 'local education authorities'—often abbreviated to L.E.A. Each was instructed to appoint an education committee, to which would be referred "all matters relating to the exercise by the council of their powers under this Act, except the power of raising a rate or borrowing money."[3] The majority of this committee were to be members

[1] For the full story behind all this see Allen, *Sir Robert Morant*, pp. 138–145.

[2] Part III of the Act deals with elementary and Part II with secondary education; but it should be noted that what was called a 'Part II Authority' was concerned with both types of education. The term 'elementary' was limited to schools with pupils not over sixteen years of age, and evening schools were excluded. (See Act, § 22.)   [3] *Education Act*, 1902, § 17 (2).

of the Council, but other persons of educational or relevant experience were to be added and every education committee was required to include women members. It should be noted that the councils covered the whole country; there were no longer 'gaps' to fill. They had to supply elementary education in what had been board schools and were now called 'provided' schools, and to erect new schools where they were needed. But they had also—unlike the old school boards—to control and be responsible for secular instruction in what had hitherto been voluntary schools and were henceforth to be termed 'non-provided' schools. These non-provided, denominational schools were now eligible to receive rate aid, but the cost of capital expenditure on buildings, as well as of structural repairs and alterations, was thrown on the religious body to which the school belonged. The managers of a non-provided school retained the right of appointing and dismissing their teachers, subject to the approval of the L.E.A. on educational grounds; but one-third of the managers of a non-provided school had to be appointed by the authority. Religious instruction could be given in a provided school, as hitherto in a board school, subject to the Cowper-Temple clause. In a non-provided school it had to be "in accordance with the provisions (if any) of the trust deed relating thereto, and shall be under the control of the managers."[1] In both types of school there was to be a conscience clause and the possibility of withdrawal from religious worship or instruction.

As as been said, the Act of 1902, in accordance with the recommendations of the Bryce Commission, laid upon county and county borough councils a responsibility for secondary and higher education. Each local education authority was required to "consider the educational needs of their area and take such steps as seem to them desirable, after consultation with the Board of Education, to supply or aid the supply of education other than elementary, and to promote the general co-ordination of all forms of education."[2] They were to "have regard to any existing supply

[1] Op. cit., § 7 (6).
[2] Op. cit., § 2 (1). By the Welsh Intermediate Education Act of 1889, the Principality had already led the way in planning a national system of secondary schools linking the elementary schools with the university colleges.

of efficient schools and colleges, and to any steps already taken for the purposes of higher education under the Technical Instruction Acts, 1889 and 1891."[1] Their powers included the training of teachers, the providing of scholarships, and the paying of fees of students in colleges or hostels.

By the Act of 1902 a co-ordinated national system of education was at last introduced and the 'confusion arising from lack of organisation' was ended. But, like all Education Acts, it was largely a compromise. With its 'provided' and 'non-provided' schools it retained the 'dual system' which had been introduced by the 1870 Act. It also made a concession to local feeling and the supporters of school boards by setting up the distinction between Part II and Part III authorities. This may have helped to foster local enthusiasm for education, but it involved administrative difficulties; and these tended to increase as in course of time the frontiers between secondary and elementary education were gradually broken down.

[1] *Op. cit.*, § 2 (2).

PART E

EDUCATION SINCE 1902

Chapter XXIV

THE WORKING OF THE 1902 ACT

IT was only in the teeth of strong opposition and with the application of the closure that the Education Act of 1902 had become law. But the struggle did not end there. Opposition still was offered not only by those who deplored the passing of the school boards, but still more by nonconformists who strongly objected to the extension of rate aid to voluntary schools, though for many years past they had been supporting such schools through the medium of the taxes out of which the education grants were made. But most of the voluntary schools belonged to the Established Church; and in many rural areas especially the only available school was a Church of England school. Yet everyone had to pay rates for its support. The protagonist of the opposition in the House of Commons was David Lloyd George; outside he was seconded by a nonconformist minister named Dr. Clifford, who preached the doctrine of 'passive resistance.' Rather than pay the rates which aided voluntary schools, he and his followers suffered distraint to be made upon their goods. In Wales the counties and county boroughs went so far as to refuse to put the Act into operation. The situation had to be met by an Education (Local Authorities' Default) Act, passed in 1904, which provided that, if an authority failed to make adequate grants to voluntary schools in its area for maintaining their efficiency, the Board of Education could deduct from the grant payable to it such sums as were needed for the voluntary schools; and these sums would be paid over direct to the managers. This caused considerable ferment, and there was a danger that the whole educational system of Wales might be thrown into chaos; but Balfour stood his ground and the Welsh councils were compelled to yield.

By the end of 1905 the Act was practically everywhere in force.

But the return of the Liberals to power in the same year brought
the grievances of the passive resisters again to the forefront.
Lloyd George, now President of the Board of Trade, announced
that the first thing that the Government was going to do was to
remedy the wrongs of the Education Act. The new President of
the Board of Education, Augustine Birrell, whose father had been
a Baptist minister, introduced a Bill in 1906 which, while recognising the councils as the local authorities for elementary and
secondary education alike, proposed that "a school shall not be
recognised as a public elementary school unless it is a school provided by the local education authority." This implied the abolition of public aid to voluntary schools. They could carry on only
as private independent schools, unless they preferred to hand
themselves over to the control of the local education authority.
The only concession allowed was that 'special religious instruction' might be given in such schools on not more than two morn-
ings a week. The Bill was so fundamentally amended by the
House of Lords that the Government withdrew it. Another even
more drastic attempt to cut the knot, made by McKenna in 1908,
produced similar opposition and also proved abortive. But in
spite of all these difficulties and disagreements, it was increasingly
recognised, as the 1902 Act came gradually into force, that it had
inaugurated a new era in English education. The general advance
was so obvious that the difficulty of the 'religious question' died
down to some extent. Although even yet it has not disappeared
entirely, it has never since been so acute as it was in the early years
of the present century.

The Act put education under municipal control, but it did not
abolish the old 'dual system.' All the former board schools and
most of the 'British' and nonconformist voluntary schools were
transferred after 1902 to the local education authorities and became 'provided' schools. But the L.E.A.s were also responsible
for voluntary schools, except so far as the actual provision and
repair of their buildings were concerned. This laid on the
authorities a heavy burden, because they had to try to bring up
these 'non-provided' schools to the standard of their own council
schools. They were assisted by a rearrangement of the grant

system. The Code of 1900 had abolished the separate grants for subjects, attendance, discipline, efficiency, etc., and had substituted a single 'block grant.'[1] The new system made it possible to secure some sort of equality as between schools; the poorer ones were less likely to be penalised than they had been under the old system. The L.E.A.s also began to carry out systematic surveys of school accommodation and facilities in their areas. The Board of Education *Report* for 1904–5 stated that over fifty reports of this type had been issued since the beginning of 1903, and that among the most valuable of them were those prepared by Professor Michael Sadler, who had by this time left the Office of Special Inquiries and Reports and was Professor of Education in the University of Manchester. Sadler's investigations dealt primarily with secondary education, but they were of great general interest and were widely read; and they helped to make L.E.A.s conscious of their duty and to stimulate them to perform it. Thus improvements were made, though the task was difficult because L.E.As. had to deal with a very heterogeneous collection of schools. In 1908 the Board of Education exerted pressure on L.E.A.s by drawing up a 'Black List,' and encouraging them to eliminate their worst schools which were included in it. This has been a slow process. Too often school buildings, which were unsuitable to modern conditions, were so solidly built, or inconveniently placed, that they resisted adaptation. But, for all that, improvement was made until it was checked by the first World War. In 1924 the Black List scheme was revived.

In other ways a new spirit was infused into English education after 1902; and this was largely the work of Morant, who was knighted for his services in 1907. He issued a series of regulations, in each of which he included a prefatory memorandum signed by himself. These covered not only elementary and secondary schools, but also the training of pupil-teachers who were to receive a general education in a secondary school for three or four years, with schoolfellows intended for other careers. But it is perhaps in his introduction to the Elementary School Code of

[1] 'Subject' grants were retained for a few 'practical' courses, such as cooking and manual instruction.

1904 that the new official attitude to education was most clearly seen. It is too long to quote in full,[1] but its opening words strike a new note: "The purpose of the Public Elementary School is to form and strengthen the character and to develop the intelligence of the children entrusted to it, and to make the best use of the school years available, in assisting both girls and boys, according to their different needs, to fit themselves, practically as well as intellectually, for the work of life." The conception of elementary education as a charity provided for the 'lower classes' is gone for ever. *The Times*, in a leading article, made the following comment: "The change is a momentous one. It means that our English Board of Education has definitely abandoned the old crude idea that its functions were merely financial and administrative—viz. to devise means by which the country might get tangible value for an expenditure more or less grudgingly bestowed; and that it has finally shaken off the misleading associations of the theory of 'payment by results.' For the first time the child, rather than the official or the tax-payer, is recognised as the most important consideration."[2]

The Code of 1904 was followed in 1905 by a *Handbook of Suggestions for the Consideration of Teachers and others engaged in the Work of Public Elementary Schools*. The title is significant; it is not 'instructions' or 'regulations,' but 'suggestions.' In a comprehensive introduction, which was written by Morant himself, and which preceded detailed suggestions on teaching methods, he stresses the significance of the teacher's part in the training of character, the value of co-operation with other local social agencies and with the home, and the importance of physical welfare. The *Handbook* was periodically revised since its first appearance in 1905, and it was this—and not a set of official instructions—which gave the teacher guidance in his work. There is no country in which the teacher in the State schools has more freedom than he has in England; but as the *Handbook* wisely says: "Freedom implies a corresponding responsibility in its use." The virtual abolition of 'payment by results,' made possible by the

[1] It is given in Lowndes, *The Silent Social Revolution*, pp. 141-2.
[2] Quoted by Allen, *Sir Robert Morant*, pp. 213-14.

introduction of the 'block grant' in 1900, also involved a modification in the duties of the Board's inspectors. It was no longer their duty to examine children and assess grants on the results. They now had greater freedom to advise and help, and to disseminate new ideas. It took a long time to break down the old attitude of distrust and hostility to the H.M.I., which the old system had tended to encourage; but inspectors' visits are no longer regarded as inquisitorial visitations. As Mr. Lowndes, writing in 1937, said: "How great this change has been is only perhaps appreciated by the older members of H.M. Inspectorate and by teachers who began their career as pupil-teachers in the 1890's and are now retiring from the profession."[1]

In the field of secondary education the Act of 1902 perpetuated a 'dual system,' as well as in that of elementary education; but it was of a different kind. On the one hand were the old endowed grammar schools, which had hitherto received no assistance from public funds, but were now aided by L.E.A.s. After 1902 there also came into existence a number of municipal or county secondary schools, founded and maintained by the councils. In some cases such schools —as has already been said—were evolved out of existing higher-grade or organised science schools, or pupil-teacher centres. The fact that secondary schools were now eligible to receive grants made it necessary for the Board of Education to determine what exactly a 'secondary school' was. In the *Regulations for Secondary Schools* issued in 1904 it was defined as "a Day or Boarding School offering to each of its scholars, up to and beyond the age of 16, a general education, physical, mental and moral, given through a complete graded course of instruction, of wider scope and more advanced degree than that given in Elementary Schools." The course had to last not less than four years and was to include English subjects, at least one language other than English, mathematics and science, and drawing. Provision was also to be made for manual training and physical exercises. Music was not mentioned; but "where two languages other than English are taken, and Latin is not one of them, the Board will require to be satisfied that the omission of Latin is for

[1] *The Silent Social Revolution*, p.137.

the advantage of the School." Thus the curriculum prescribed for secondary schools of all types, including those which had recently been founded or had been evolved from forms of higher elementary or technical education, was "based wholly on the tradition of the Grammar Schools and the Public Schools. Furthermore, the concept of a general education which underlies these Regulations was divorced from the idea of technical or quasi-technical education, though in reality much of the education described as 'liberal' or 'general' was itself vocational education for the 'liberal' professions."[1] The 'academic' bias which was thus given to the concept of secondary education has tended to persist; and although much has been done since 1904 to widen this concept, progress has been slower than it might have been.

The founding of new secondary schools and the taking over of other schools of this type and making them efficient proved to be an expensive process. The L.E.A.s were anxious to keep fees low, but at first they were empowered to raise only a 2d. rate for higher education, except by special consent of the Local Government Board.[2] The situation was eased in 1907. In that year a scholarship system was introduced which greatly facilitated the access to secondary education of promising children from elementary schools. All grant-aided secondary schools were now to admit, as free-place scholars, pupils who had spent at least two years at a public elementary school. The number of such pupils was to be not less than 25 per cent. of the total entry to the secondary school in the previous year. A grant of £5 per pupil was payable. To ensure that this scholarship system would not have the effect of lowering the standard of work in the secondary schools it was provided that candidates for free places should pass an entrance test appropriate to their age and previous education. It was intended as a qualifying examination; but the subsequent development of the demand for secondary-school education made the test a highly competitive one. Its repercussions on both the work of the junior elementary school, and on the problem of selection for secondary education, were destined

[1] Young, Historical Introduction to Spens *Report*, pp. 66-7.
[2] See *Education Act*, 1902, § 2.

to cause many difficulties later on. The limit of 25 per cent. of the previous year's entry was subsequently raised; and even before fees were finally abolished in secondary schools by the 1944 Act, there were in existence some schools where this was the case. On the other hand, the economy campaign of 1932 involved a modification of the free-place system. In that year 'free places' became 'special places.' The parents of elementary-school pupils who had been selected by examination for admission to a secondary school were required to pay fees, if they could afford to do so; and L.E.A.s were instructed to draw up scales based on the parents' income. The free-place system caused some uneasiness at first, especially among schools and parents who were conscious of their own social exclusiveness; but on the whole the scheme worked well and the number of ex-elementary-school pupils in secondary schools rapidly increased. The introduction of the bursary system, whereby intending teachers in elementary schools were encouraged to attend a secondary school and stay there till the age of seventeen or eighteen,[1] also brought a large number of pupils into secondary schools aided or maintained by L.E.A.s.

Elderly critics, who base their censures of schools on vague recollections of their youth, do not always realise the very marked progress which has been made in curricula and methods of teaching since the beginning of the present century. This is, perhaps, particularly true of the secondary school. There are various reasons for this. The curriculum has been widened, and there may now even be a danger of sacrificing depth for breadth. New subjects, such as biology, Spanish, economics, civics, have been introduced. The reasons are partly social and partly economic, but they are due also in some measure to the reaction of the universities on secondary schools. The institution, for example, of new honours courses in geography or of degrees in commerce and agriculture has not been without its effect on schools. Again, the development of University Departments of Education, the improvement of training-college courses, the growing interest in educational psychology and in the theory of education, as well as in method—all this has led to greatly increased technical effi-

[1] See *supra*, p. 187.

ciency among teachers. It is noteworthy that nearly all treatises dealing specifically with the "special methods" of the various school subjects have been written since the beginning of the present century. Hitherto a chapter in a comprehensive manual was deemed sufficient.

The growth of new schools, not hampered by tradition, has also helped to foster experiment. The Dalton Plan and the Project Method, for example, even when they have not been adopted in their entirety, have diversified and vitalised the old routine of class-teaching. The use of broadcasts, the gramophone, and visual aids has also proved valuable. Experiments in self-government have helped to displace conventional methods of discipline and organisation. In fact, there has been in every department of the school's life a growth of freedom and flexibility. The Classics have lost much of their old predominance. Latin is no longer prescribed by official regulations as the second foreign language in a secondary school, and Greek, in particular, has lost much ground; but both subjects are taught more intelligently than they were under the régime of 'gerund-grinding.' Modern languages owe much to the use of phonetics and especially to the direct method. Geometry has replaced 'Euclid.' Natural science in the early days of South Kensington too often consisted largely of the memorising of text-books with little or no practical work; it is now taught in properly equipped laboratories. English grammar as a school subject is no longer formal, but functional. Geography, instead of being a subject which required little more than the getting by heart of lists of capes and bays, is now a scientific study of the interaction of man and his environment.

The broadening of the curriculum has been due largely to the influence and example of individual headmasters, such as Thring of Uppingham, Sanderson of Oundle, or Howson of Holt—and perhaps even more to the great headmistresses. Improvements in teaching method owe much to men like A. J. Herbertson, with his scheme of geographical 'regions,' M. W. Keatinge, who utilised documents in the teaching of history, and W. H. D. Rouse, who introduced the direct method into the teaching of Classics. The writings of Sir John Adams have also dealt largely with matters of technique.[1] The work of all these men was done in the first two or three decades of the twentieth century. The same period has also seen the most valuable co-operation of the Board of Education in the same field. Not only in their *Suggestions for Teachers* have they given detailed advice as to the teaching of various school subjects, but they have also issued a series of handbooks for specialist teachers in secondary schools. Four special committees[2] were set up to inquire into the position of natural science, modern languages, Classics and English, in the educational system. Those dealing with the first two subjects reported in 1918, and the other two in 1921. In addition to these reports the Board itself has issued from time to time numerous pamphlets dealing with method, organisation, and curriculum. The example has been followed by several of the professional societies. The Assistant Masters' Association, for instance, has issued admirable memoranda on the teaching of English, mathematics, history, modern languages, and geography. All this activity is at once an evidence of, and a stimulus to, that increasing efficiency of teaching technique and of school organisation which has marked English education since 1902.

[1] E.g. *Exposition and Illustration in Teaching* (1909); *The New Teaching* (1918); *Modern Developments in Educational Practice* (1922); *Errors in School* (1927).
[2] They were actually appointed by the Prime Minister.

Chapter XXV

THE DEVELOPMENT OF THE SPECIAL SERVICES

Special Schools and Health Education. Influence of Montessori. Nursery Schools.

ALONGSIDE the development of the national system of education there has been a notable expansion of subsidiary services dealing with the health and physical condition of the children in the nation's schools. But it was only gradually, after education had become compulsory, that administrators began to realise how many children were handicapped by ill-health, deformities, and malnutrition. For this reason school health services are a comparatively recent development, though they have made immense strides, especially since 1902.

As far back as 1893 an Elementary Education (Blind and Deaf Children) Act had empowered school boards to provide education for blind and deaf children, between the ages of seven and sixteen, resident in their areas. They were to be accommodated in schools certified by the Education Department as suitable for the purpose. As a result day schools and institutions for such children were established, and existing ones improved, in various parts of the country. Already, in 1892, schools for mental defectives had been opened in Leicester and London. In 1899 an Act empowered authorities to ascertain the number of children who were epileptic and mentally defective, and to provide special instruction for them. By further legislation in 1914 L.E.A.s were compelled to make suitable provision for mentally defective and epileptic children. Of recent years it has become a general practice to distinguish mental defectives from educationally 'backward' children, whose intelligence quotients may range from about seventy upwards.[1] A Mental Deficiency Committee, which issued its report in 1929, suggested that both types should be regarded as one unit, and, as far as possible, educated in ordinary schools. The sorting would be done by mental tests and the special school for

[1] See Burt, *The Backward Child*, pp. 84-5.

subnormal children would disappear; it would be replaced by 'special' forms in an ordinary school.[1] Segregation may be bad both for the mentally defective and for the dull or retarded child; and parents resent having to send their offspring to what they sometimes call the 'loony' school. But many teachers feel that there are serious difficulties in dealing with abnormal children in schools which are designed for those who are normal. What can be done in a 'special' school, when it is administered with vision and enthusiasm, is shown in the case of Lankhills School, near Winchester; and such achievements are not without their significance for the education of normal children.[2]

The mentally defective child and the blind or deaf-mute are so conspicuous and so difficult to deal with educationally that they have formed classes apart and have called for special treatment. But there remains the case of the child who can attend the ordinary school, but who is handicapped by bad health, neglect, lack of proper nourishment, poor physique, defective teeth or eyesight. School medical inspection was started in London in 1890 and in Bradford in 1893; but it was the Boer War (1899–1902) which forcefully directed public attention to the necessity for improving the national health. An Inter-Departmental Committee on Physical Deterioration in 1904 drew attention to the need for a systematic medical examination of school children. In 1907 a clause in the Education (Administrative Provisions) Act laid upon L.E.A.s "the duty to provide for the medical inspection of children immediately before, or at the time of, or as soon as possible after, their admission to a public elementary school, and on such other occasions as the Board of Education direct, and the power to make such arrangements as may be sanctioned by the Board of Education for attending to the health and physical condition of the children educated in public elementary schools."[3] Morant, who had always been interested in questions of public health and fully realised its educational implications, promptly established a Medi-

---

[1] See especially §§ 106 and 156–62 of *Report of the Mental Deficiency Committee* (1929).
[2] See Duncan, *The Education of the Ordinary Child.*
[3] Education (Administrative Provisions) Act, 1907, § 13 (b).

cal Branch of the Board of Education. This was put in the charge of Dr. (afterwards Sir George) Newman. The importance of the work which he did for the health of schoolchildren from the time of his appointment till his retirement in 1935 can hardly be over-estimated. His annual reports from 1908 onwards also did much to keep alive public interest in the school medical service.

Thus was developed a State system of school medical inspection and a regular school medical service. At first the work was confined to the *inspection* of schoolchildren, but the L.E.A.s were not called upon to provide treatment of any kind. Lowndes[1] says that this was due to the Victorian fear of 'pauperising' parents and still more to avoid antagonising private practitioners. But owing to the influence of teachers and the work of voluntary Care Committees much was done even without compulsion. A consolidating Education Act of 1921 turned the L.E.A.s' power of making arrangements for attending to the health and physical condition of schoolchildren into a duty; but any treatment provided was to be charged to the parents if their means permitted. The Fisher Act of 1918 carried medical inspection and treatment into the field of secondary and continuative education. The work of the school medical officer has been supplemented by the appointment of school nurses and dentists. This work was designed to be, so far as possible, preventive, and the central authority paid a 50 per cent. grant on expenditure which was incurred. The 1944 Education Act extended the system of health inspection to all types of secondary school; and with the institution of the National Health Service in 1946 it became possible for L.E.A.s to provide all forms of hospital treatment free of cost for the pupils in their schools.

If children are ill-nourished, they cannot profit by the teaching which is given them. It has therefore become increasingly evident that health treatment must be seconded, where necessary, by the provision of meals. An Act of 1906 laid it down that if children were unable, through lack of food to profit by the education given in a public elementary school, the local education authority might supply them with meals. Contributions were to be

[1] *The Silent Social Revolution*, p. 229.

collected, so far as was possible, from the parents, but this school feeding was not to be classed as poor-law relief. The scope of this Act was extended during the first World War, and it has been still further developed in recent years. By 1958 over three million pupils in maintained schools were taking dinner each day.

Health education should be not merely palliative, or even preventive, but still more positive. The increasing realisation of this fact has been shown by the development of all kinds of physical activity, designed not merely to strengthen the bodies of pupils, but also as an integral part of the 'education of the whole man.' Here again something is due to the influence of Morant. In a letter written in 1906 he says: "For myself I have for some time come to feel that for the good of the children and the people, what subjects are taught and how they are taught do not matter anything like so much as attention to the physical condition of the scholars and the teacher."[1] Military drill had appeared in the Code of 1871, and ex-soldiers were employed to give this kind of instruction. It survived in the secondary schools well into the twentieth century. But more sensible methods of physical education were suggested in a syllabus issued by the Board of Education in 1909. This was based largely on the practice of Sweden and Denmark, where the influence of P. H. Ling (1776–1839) had transformed the teaching of gymnastics. The Board also appointed special inspectors of 'physical exercises,' and under their expert guidance physical training has progressed along definitely educative lines. For long specialists had to go to Sweden or Denmark for training; but in 1885 a college for women who wished to become physical-training instructors was opened at Dartford. It was not until 1933 that a similar training college became available for men. But for the non-specialist student physical training has been a compulsory subject in all training colleges since 1909. The development of physical education in more recent years will be discussed later. It has been due not only to what have been by some people regarded as military necessities, but also to greater realisation of the fact that education is as much a matter of the body as of the mind, and that schools should be equally concerned

[1] Quoted by Allen, *Sir Robert Morant*, p. 231.

with both. We have, in fact, revived the teaching of the ancient Greeks on this matter.

The normal English method of physical education is not so much through set exercises, however scientifically these have been devised, but rather through games—whether 'organised' or not. In the early part of the nineteenth century these had been tolerated in the boarding schools as a method of keeping boys out of mischief in their spare time. But progressive headmasters, like Thring, saw the educative value of games; and this was more and more widely recognised in schools of all kinds. Most of the new secondary schools, which came into existence as a result of the 1902 Act, were provided with playing-fields and made full provision for organised games. This movement reacted on the elementary schools. In 1906 the Board of Education allowed organised games to be played during school hours, and public parks and open spaces have been utilised for the purpose. Instruction in swimming at the local baths has also been provided as part of the school curriculum. Some of the newer elementary schools, provided by L.E.A.s, have their own playing-fields; but even so there has been, and still is, a considerable shortage of facilities, not only for children at school, but even more for young people who are no longer under full-time instruction. It was to meet the needs of such as these, in particular, that the National Playing Fields Association was founded in 1925.

Another aspect of the same movement was the establishment of evening play-centres. A pioneer in this work was the Children's Happy Evenings Association, which had started its operations in 1888. By 1914 there were ninety-four centres in London and forty-one in the Provinces where children in poor districts could find opportunities for play after school hours. Later the Play Centres Association, due largely to Mrs. Humphry Ward, used school premises for two hours in the evening on five days a week, so as to provide play facilities. The Education (Administrative Provisions) Act of 1907 included a clause empowering L.E.A.s to provide such centres or to aid voluntary agencies in providing them; and in 1917 State grants were made available for this purpose. This led to an increase in the number of play centres, and by the end of March 1918 they totalled 171. These centres not only provided for organised games, but also for singing and dancing, and for painting, needlework, and handicrafts. Opportunities were also given for children to read or play quietly with toys on their own initiative.

It may not be out of place in this context to discuss another movement which has affinities with those which have already been described. This is the work and the influence in this country of Maria Montessori. Her theories owe much to those of Froebel, but she put them into practice at first among mentally defective children, and one of her chief interests is the health and physical freedom of children, especially those of the earliest age. After qualifying as a doctor at the University of Rome, she worked in a psychiatric clinic and became interested in feeble-minded children. She came to the conclusion that they needed education even more than medical treatment. For two years (1898–1900) she ran a school for such children, working in it herself and training teachers for the work. Her experience led her to the belief that the methods which she had found most successful in dealing with feeble-minded children would be quite applicable to those who were normal, and that ordinary schools needed the sort of transformation which she had accomplished in her own 'special' school.[1] At last there occurred an opportunity of putting her theories to the test. An association which was dealing with the housing problem in Rome proposed that each tenement should have attached to it a school in which the children, between the ages of three and seven, would be under the supervision of a teacher who would also live in the tenement. Dr. Montessori was invited to co-operate in the scheme. The first Casa dei Bambini, or 'Children's House,' was opened in 1907; and although the experiment lasted only till 1911, it amply proved the success of Montessori methods in the case of normal children. These methods are based on sense-training, and, like Froebel, Dr. Montessori lays stress on the use of pieces of apparatus which she has devised. The child is also given complete freedom and there are no class-methods. The teacher's part is to observe and direct,

[1] Compare the views of Mr. Duncan (see *The Education of the Ordinary Child*).

but not control. Dr. Montessori feels that under modern conditions, especially where the mother has to go out to work, the home cannot educate properly, and, if so, the school must make good the deficiencies. The Children's House was designed to "communise the maternal functions," as so many other social activities have been communised.

All these doctrines may—and indeed do—provoke criticism, but the work and theories of Dr. Montessori have stimulated much interest, particularly in this country and in America. They link up with a movement which has come increasingly into prominence since the beginning of the present century. The experience of the School Medical Service showed that little attention was available for children of pre-school age—i.e. from about two to five. Yet this is a stage at which medical supervision is of paramount importance. It is also a period when desirable habits, both personal and social, are most easily acquired. As Sir George Newman had repeatedly pointed out in his annual reports, the years below five are both physically and psychologically the crucial age. But there are many homes where conditions make adequate medical and educational supervision impossible. It is for reasons such as these that nursery schools and nursery classes have come into existence. The movement owes much to the two sisters, Rachel and Margaret McMillan. For years they worked, with little encouragement, to secure the provision of health centres for poor children, and of school meals and regular medical inspection. The passing of the Education (Provision of Meals) Act in 1906, and of the Act of 1907, which provided for medical inspection, was due in no small measure to their efforts. In 1914 Rachel McMillan started an open-air nursery school at Deptford. In such schools children from two to five years of age spend the whole day and are provided with meals. They are given full opportunity for play and rest and for the development of good and useful habits. There is, of course, no formal instruction, though some beginnings may be made informally; and perhaps the term 'nursery *school*' is somewhat misleading in this context. An alternative to the independent nursery school is the nursery class attached to an infant school.

Nursery schools in their early stages were fostered largely by voluntary effort. The Fisher Act of 1918 made it permissive for L.E.A.s to set up such schools, and grants for this purpose were offered in 1919; but not many of them availed themselves of this power. In 1933 the Consultative Committee of the Board of Education, under Sir W. H. Hadow's chairmanship, issued a *Report on Infant and Nursery Schools.*[1] It proposed to retain the statutory lower age limit for compulsory school attendance, but it regarded the nursery school as "a desirable adjunct to the national system of education. In districts where the housing and general economic conditions are seriously below the average, a nursery school should, if possible, be provided. . . . Apart from purely social and economic considerations model nursery schools for children from the age of two onwards are educationally desirable."[2] One of the members of the Committee, Miss Freda Hawtrey, in a note appended to the *Report*, expressed the view that the nursery school would be of more value if it could keep its children till seven, the age when they would pass into the upper department of a primary school.[3] This is a view which has gained increasing acceptance and is advocated by the Nursery School Association, which was first formed, with Margaret McMillan as its president, in 1923. The conditions obtaining during the second World War speeded up the nursery-school movement, and further reference will be made to it.[4] It is now felt in some quarters that nursery-school education should be available for children of all types and all classes. Teachers for nursery-school work are trained at the Rachel McMillan College, Deptford, and at the Froebel Educational Institute. Some other training colleges and some university training departments also provide special courses for preparing students to become teachers in nursery or infant schools.

[1] There is a good historical summary of the nursery-school movement in England in pp. 33–46 of this *Report*. See also Cusden, *The English Nursery School*.
[2] *Report on Infant and Nursery Schools*, pp. 187–8.
[3] *Op. cit.*, p. 196.   [4] See *infra*, pp. 232, 297–8, 319–20 and 332.

Chapter XXVI

A NEW CONCEPTION OF 'SECONDARY' EDUCATION

The Fisher Act and the Hadow *Report*. Reorganisation and the 1936 Act.

THE first World war of 1914–18 had considerable repercussions on national education. It altered the home conditions of many children; it weakened the staffing in many schools, because men teachers were taken away on military service; and it led to drastic economies in school building and equipment. But the schools rose to the occasion. Children gave help in social and agricultural work and formed war-savings associations. Perhaps their greatest contribution was 'business as usual' in spite of the great difficulties with which they had to contend. The whole population, which for the most part had been educated in the elementary schools, responded to the calls which the war made upon it, both in and out of the army; and this resulted in a more widely spread appreciation of the true value and significance of education. As Mr. H. A. L. Fisher said in his speech on the Education Estimates on April 19th, 1917: "If anyone had doubted the value of our elementary schools, that doubt must have been dispelled by the experience of the war."[1] Thus it was realised that education would play a leading part in the work of reconstruction when the war was over.

All these aspirations were gathered up in an Education Bill which was passed into law on August 8th, 1918—before the war was over and while its issue was still uncertain. The Fisher Act—for it is usually known by the name of the President of the Board of Education who sponsored it—affected many departments of the national system of education. It extended the powers of local authorities and gave them stimulus to co-operate. They "may and shall, when required by the Board of Education, submit to

[1] *Parliamentary Debates*, Fifth Series, vol. xcii, 1893. (Quoted by Birchenough, *History of Elementary Education*, p. 212.) The whole speech is worth reading.

the Board schemes showing the mode in which the duties and powers under the Education Acts are to be performed and exercised, whether separately or in co-operation with other authorities."[1] The system of grants was modified; "the total sums paid to a Local Education Authority . . . shall not be less than one-half of the net expenditure of the Authority recognised by the Board of Education."[2] Fees in elementary schools were abolished and—as has already been pointed out—L.E.A.s were empowered to supply, or aid the supply of, nursery schools and nursery classes "for children over two and under five years of age, or such later age as may be approved by the Board of Education, whose attendance at such a school is necessary or desirable for their healthy physical and mental development."[3] Local authorities were also permitted, with the Board's approval, to provide, maintain, or assist "(a) holiday or school camps, especially for young persons attending continuation schools; (b) centres and equipment for physical training, playing-fields . . . school baths, school swimming-baths; (c) other facilities for social and physical training in the day or evening."[4] The employment of children under the age of twelve was entirely forbidden; and the employment of those over this age—such as performers in entertainments or newspaper boys—was strictly regulated. Medical inspection was extended from elementary to secondary and continuative education.

But the most important provisions of the Act—which in the event remained almost entirely inoperative—were those empowering L.E.A.s to raise the upper age limit of compulsory full-time school attendance to fifteen,[5] and the institution of day continuation schools. The latter were to be available without fees for boys and girls up to the age of sixteen (after seven years, up to eighteen) who had left school. Attendance was to be compulsory for 320 hours in the year, though this total might during the preliminary seven years be reduced to 280 hours if the L.E.A.

---

[1] *Education Act*, 1918, § 1.   [2] *Op. cit.*, § 44.
[3] *Op. cit.*, § 19 (a).   [4] *Op. cit.*, § 17.
[5] Half-time and other exemptions were abolished, and attendance was everywhere made compulsory up to the end of the term in which the age of fourteen was reached.

so decided. Thus the 'young person' would spend part of his time in industry and part at an institution of continuative education. This would provide a valuable link between school and industry, and would ease the transition from the one to the other for the young worker. The scheme was to take effect from an 'appointed day,' which would be settled by the Board with each separate L.E.A., taking into account its preparedness to operate the system. But there were many difficulties. Employers were not always willing to co-operate, and it was not easy for L.E.A.s to find the necessary school accommodation and teachers. However, a start was made in some places. London and West Ham, for example, worked the scheme for a time, but generally it hung fire. Rugby alone succeeded in implementing this section of the Fisher Act and carrying it forward;[1] but several other big towns have run voluntary continuation schools, and some of the great industrial firms have also introduced continuation schemes for their young employees. But with exceptions such as these the project of part-time continuative education, like that of raising the school-leaving age, went into 'cold storage' for the time being.

The 1918 Act contains the seeds of reform which have begun to germinate after lying dormant for some time; in particular it adumbrated the nursery school and the day continuation school as integral parts of the national system of education, and it pointed the way to the raising of the leaving age. The fact that it remained in part ineffective was due largely to post-war financial stringency. In 1921 a Committee on National Expenditure, under the chairmanship of Sir Eric Geddes, recommended that grants to education should be reduced by about a third. This put an end to educational developments. Teachers were also made to suffer by having their salaries reduced and their pension scheme put on a contributory basis. The 'Geddes Axe,' as it was called, "led to a meticulous examination of local expenditure and the unnecessary holding up of the programmes of local authorities, to absurd economies on buildings and staff and to the indefinite postponement of continuation schools."[2]   In the event many of the

---

[1] See Kitchen, *From Learning to Earning.*
[2] Birchenough, *History of Elementary Education*, pp. 239–40.

so-called 'economies' proved ill-advised and expensive, and there was some reaction when the Labour Party came into power in 1924. This party has always regarded education as one of the most important agents of social reform; and as part of that reform it had advocated 'secondary education for all.' But 'secondary' in this context could not mean the academic type of education which was given in the endowed grammar or public schools. Dr. Tawney, a university teacher of economics and a prominent exponent of socialism, made clear the implications of the slogan. "The Labour Party," he says, "is convinced that the only policy which is at once educationally sound and suited to a democratic community is one under which primary education and secondary education are organised as two stages in a single continuous process; secondary education being the education of the adolescent and primary education being education preparatory thereto."[1]

To implement this scheme the Consultative Committee of the Board of Education were asked to review the experiments in post-primary education which had been made in the existing 'elementary' system, and "to consider and report upon the organisation, objective, and curriculum of courses of study suitable for children who will remain in full-time attendance at schools, other than Secondary Schools" (here the term was used in its contemporary sense), "up to the age of fifteen, regard being had on the one hand to the requirements of a good general education and the desirability of providing a reasonable variety of curriculum, so far as is practicable, for children of varying tastes and abilities, and on the other to the probable occupations of the pupils in commerce, industry, and agriculture."[2]

The *Report* on *The Education of the Adolescent*, which the Committee issued in 1926, is usually known by the name of the chairman, Sir W. H. Hadow. The essence of the Hadow plan was to make secondary education not, as hitherto, a privilege restricted to some 10 per cent. of the school population, but the normal course for all children between the ages of eleven and fourteen— or fifteen when the leaving age was raised. Thus there would be a

[1] Tawney, *Secondary Education for All*, p. 7.
[2] *Report* on *The Education of the Adolescent*, p. iv.

complete break in school life between the primary and the post-primary school; and this would occur at about the age of 'eleven plus.' The post-primary school would have a fresh organisation and curriculum, and the old sequence of standards from I to VII, ambling on without any fresh orientation from the ages of seven to fourteen, would be abolished. Thus children would leave the primary school at eleven plus and then be drafted to another type of school suited to their individual needs and attainments. For this reason several types of post-primary (or 'secondary' in the new sense[1]) school would be needed.

The first would be what the Hadow *Report* proposed to call the 'grammar school.' This would include all schools of the academic type, whether old endowed foundations, or municipal or county secondary schools such as had come into existence since the 1902 Act. These would "pursue in the main a predominantly literary or scientific curriculum."[2] Secondly, there would be 'modern schools,' analogous to the existing selective or non-selective central schools. These 'central schools' had been started in London in 1911 and in Manchester in the following year. They were designed as a kind of higher elementary school, fed by several contributory schools, for pupils aged eleven to fifteen, and their curriculum, although it had a commercial or industrial bias, was not narrowly vocational. The scheme had not spread, and it had not been encouraged by the Board of Education; but the Hadow Committee realised its importance. They suggested that the new 'modern' schools should give "at least a four-years course from the age of eleven plus, with a 'realistic' or practical trend in the last two years."[3] These schools could be either selective or non-selective. Finally, where conditions made the provision of such schools impossible, there should be "departments or classes within Public Elementary Schools, providing post-primary education for children who do not go to any of the above-mentioned types of Schools."[4] These would be known as 'senior classes.' In addition, there should be junior technical and trade schools, which the Hadow Committee considered to be "doing most valuable work

[1] Hadow *Report*, pp. 97–9.   [2] *Op. cit.*, p. 99.
[3] *Op. cit.*, p. 95.   [4] *Op. cit.*, p. 96.

and should be developed so far as is possible in accordance with the needs and requirements of certain local industries."[1] The normal age for entry to such schools would remain at thirteen plus. Schools of this type had been developing slowly since the early years of the twentieth century. In 1905 grants had been made available for 'day technical classes,' organised for pupils who had completed their elementary education. It was not until 1913, that the junior technical school was recognised as a separate type, giving a course lasting two or three years from the age of thirteen.

The Hadow *Report* thus proposed that primary education should end at eleven plus; the term 'elementary' would disappear. The Consultative Committee thought that "there is a tide which begins to rise in the veins of youth at the age of eleven or twelve,"[2] and it was for this reason that they proposed to make the transfer at that age. The wisdom of a hard-and-fast rule of this kind has frequently been questioned.[3] Mental and chronological ages frequently do not coincide; and in any case it has been felt by many competent critics[4] that another age of transfer would be indicated. However, the Hadow *Report* standardised the transfer at eleven plus—for better or worse. At that age the child would be drafted either to an academic grammar school or to a more realistic and practical modern school, whether selective or non-selective; if this was impossible, he would go into a senior class. The curriculum in the modern school or the senior class would not be rigid, and might admit of some 'bias' as determined by local conditions; but generally it would be of the same type. At the age of thirteen plus some pupils from these schools could be drafted to junior technical schools. The problem which immediately followed was how to make this selection. "For this purpose," says the *Report*, "a written examination should be held, and also, whenever possible, an oral examination. A written psychological test might also be specially employed in dealing with border-line

[1] *Op. cit.*, p. 66. For Junior Technical Schools see *infra*, pp. 271-273.
[2] Hadow *Report*, p. xix.
[3] See, for example, Burt, *British Journal of Educational Psychology*, November 1943, p. 126.
[4] E.g. Sir Fred Clarke (in *Education and Social Change*, pp. 50-3), who advocated two breaks, one about nine, and one about thirteen.

cases, or where a discrepancy has been observed between the result of the written examination and the teacher's estimate of proficiency."[1] Adequate arrangements should be made for transfer,
if it afterwards seemed indicated, from modern to grammar
schools at the age of twelve or thirteen, and conversely from
grammar schools to modern or junior technical schools. It was
also suggested that a new leaving examination should be "framed
to meet the needs of pupils in selective and non-selective Modern
Schools and in the Senior Classes which retain some of their pupils
to the age of fifteen."[2] All this meant that an entirely new meaning had been given to the term 'secondary.' Nothing is clearer
than the intention of the Hadow Committee to regard all types
of post-primary school as institutions of equal rank. "We regard
it as most important," they say, "that the new Modern Schools
and Senior Classes should not become inferior 'secondary'
schools";[3] and again: "This growth [i.e. of modern schools] will
run side by side with, but in no sense counter to, the growth of
secondary schools; and while it will differ in kind, it will not be
inferior in its promise or quality."[4] Much progress has been made
since 1926 in the popularisation of the contention, but we are still
far from realising it completely, and even farther from giving it
full expression.

The importance of the Hadow *Report* was generally recognised.
It was followed up in 1928 by a most helpful pamphlet issued by
the Board of Education and entitled *The New Prospect in Education*.
This dealt with the problems involved in reorganisation and gave
an account of schemes which were already in operation. But
there were difficulties in the way of implementing the Hadow
scheme. In order to reconstitute post-primary schools as separate
entities, L.E.A.s had to adapt existing buildings or provide new
ones; but a 50 per cent. Exchequer grant made for the purpose for
a period of three years from September 1st, 1929, had to be withdrawn in 1931 owing to financial stringency. However, the work
of reorganisation went ahead slowly, and by 1938 65·5 per cent.
of pupils over the age of eleven were in reorganised schools.[5] In

---

[1] Hadow *Report*, p. 178.   [2] *Op. cit.*, p. 179.   [3] *Op. cit.*, p. 108.
[4] *Ibid.*   [5] By 1958 this total had risen to over 93%.

country areas travelling was often a problem. If a small village all standard school were converted into a junior school, the post-primary school, which the elder children would have to attend, might be some distance away. Complications also arose out of the 'dual system.' If an all-standard Church of England school were 'decapitated' and became a junior school, and no senior Church of England school were accessible, those children who left at the age of eleven plus might have to be drafted to a post-primary council school. As the voluntary bodies had to provide the school buildings and carry out the necessary adaptations, reorganisation involved particularly heavy burdens for them, especially if, in addition to all this, the school-leaving age—as was generally hoped—were raised to fifteen.

There were many attempts to meet this situation. Finally, in 1936, an Education Act was passed to deal with these difficulties and make possible reorganisation in a complete form. The school-leaving age was to be raised to fifteen on September 1st, 1939; but the effect of this provision was largely nullified by allowing exemptions in the case of children over the age of fourteen who were entering what was called 'beneficial employment.' L.E.A.s were empowered to make grants of not less than 50 per cent., nor more than 75 per cent., of the cost of school buildings for non-provided schools "for the benefit of senior children." In these schools, which were to be known as 'special agreement schools,' denominational religious instruction was to be given by 're-served' teachers, who would have denominational qualifications for this work. They were to be appointed by the L.E.A., but school managers could veto such appointments if they were not satisfied as to the candidates' suitability in this respect. These new non-provided schools were at the same time to give non-de-nominational religious teaching on an 'agreed syllabus'[1] to chil-dren whose parents wished them to have it, but who could not conveniently attend a council school provided by the L.E.A. Conversely, if a denominational non-provided school were not

[1] I.e. a syllabus of religious instruction of a non-denominational character, agreed upon by local representatives of the Established Church and the Noncon-formist Churches.

available a parent might withdraw his child from religious instruction on an agreed syllabus, given in a council school, in order that he might receive denominational teaching of a kind not given in such a school. Voluntary bodies which desired to apply for building grants under this Act were required to submit their schemes by March 1st, 1938. Although this date was afterwards put forward, the events of the next few years rendered the 1936 Education Act much less successful than had been hoped.

Chapter XXVII

PUBLIC AND PRIVATE SCHOOLS

The Closed System and its Critics. The Fleming *Report*. Kindergartens; the
P.N.E.U.; Roman Catholic Schools; 'Progressive' Schools.

THE Act of 1902 brought the secondary schools into the
national system of education and the Hadow *Report* of
1926 greatly widened our conception of what secondary
education should mean. But, in spite of the expansion of the
national system since the beginning of the century, public and
private schools still flourish and still remain largely independent
of State control, though they have been more or less influenced
by ideas and movements from inside the State system. At the
beginning of 1963 there were in England and Wales over seven
million pupils in the various types of L.E.A. schools, but barely
seven per cent of this number in independent schools. The
public schools are for the most part boarding schools[1] and non-
local in character. During the latter part of the nineteenth century
they began, owing to pressure of numbers, to give up taking young
boys and to adopt an entry age of about thirteen. Some public
schools—as, for example, St. Paul's—have established separate
preparatory departments; but it is far more usual for these preparatory schools to be run by private enterprise as boarding establishments, and to be situated in healthy localities by the sea or in
the country. They take boys at the age of eight or nine and prepare them either for the 'Common Entrance Examination,'
established in 1903, which admits candidates to public schools, or
for scholarships at schools of this kind. The amenities which
preparatory schools provide are costly, and therefore high fees are
charged and admission is virtually restricted to the sons of well-to-
do parents. The Incorporated Association of Preparatory Schools,
which dates from 1892, links their headmasters and was represented on the Teachers' Registration Council The curriculum

[1] St. Paul's and Merchant Taylors' are conspicuous exceptions.

and general outlook of these schools are oriented towards the public schools for which their pupils are prepared. For example, a good deal of stress is laid on the teaching of Latin. Owing to these facts, and as the normal age of entry to a public school is thirteen, it was difficult to make the public school accessible to any boys who had not been educated along preparatory-school lines. This resulted in a closed private system, running parallel with the national system but having few points of contact with it.

But, although the public schools have perhaps tended to take too much for granted their superiority over the State secondary school, there has been a gradual breaking-down of their exclusiveness; and this has grown as the century progressed. The public schools share the first and second school examinations with all other types of 'grammar' school. They no longer secure the great majority of open scholarships at Oxford and Cambridge. Most of them have accepted inspection and have been recognised by the Board of Education. Some of their most distinguished headmasters—e.g. Sir Cyril Norwood, who was headmaster of Harrow, and Dr. Spencer Leeson, formerly of Winchester—have interested themselves in national education and have taken part fully in educational activities along with representatives of other types of education. At the same time State schools have learnt much of value from the public schools. Institutions such as organised games, prefects, and the house system have—with suitable modifications—been adopted not only by State secondary schools, but also by elementary schools. The public schools, being for the most part largely dependent on their fees, have encountered difficulties in the hard times which the twentieth century has brought; but the demand for public-school education has not diminished in spite of the development of the national system. New public schools were opened in 1923 at Stowe and Canford. Moreover, similar schools have been founded for girls. Roedean, for example, dates from 1885 and Wycombe Abbey from 1896, and there are numerous other schools of this type; but the preparatory-school system has not been to any great extent imitated for girls. A common entrance examination for girls' schools was established in 1947, but only a few schools so far have used it.

The public schools have been criticised ever since the days of Sydney Smith, and even before that. The narrowness of their curriculum and the harshness of their discipline and conditions of life were for long the chief charges levelled against them. These shortcomings were largely overcome during the nineteenth century; but with the great development of secondary education inside the State system, and with the spread of democratic ideas, the ground of criticism tended to change. It was urged that the public schools, with their high fees and their closed system, catered for a privileged class. It was only the wealthy—or, at any rate, the well-to-do—who could afford to send their sons to such schools. It was also argued that too much stress was laid on the desirability of public-school antecedents in appointing candidates to the highest posts in the State. Mr. Stanley Baldwin, when Prime Minister, in a speech-day address at Harrow, said: "When the call came for me to form a Government, one of my first thoughts was that it should be a Government of which Harrow should not be ashamed. I remembered how in previous Governments there had been four, or perhaps five, Harrovians, and I determined to have six." Remarks like this, even if made only half in earnest, occasioned much comment; and the assertion, not infrequently made, that the public schools afforded the best training for future 'leaders' was indignantly rebutted in some quarters. In short, it was argued that such schools were unfairly privileged, that they emphasised class distinctions, and that they were incompatible with a truly democratic régime.

But this is not merely the view of critics or opponents of the public-school system; it is a view which from time to time has also been expressed by headmasters of public schools. In 1919 the Headmasters' Conference, under the chairmanship of Sir Frank Fletcher, headmaster of the Charterhouse, told the President of the Board of Education that they were "prepared to offer as a voluntary service, or rather to claim as a privilege, that share in the education of ex-elementary schoolboys which was demanded by the State from other schools."[1] The offer was gratefully acknowledged, but no machinery was proposed to make it effective. But

[1] Fletcher, *After Many Days*, p. 272.

the matter was not allowed to rest there, and there were not wanting those who believed that the public-school type of education had something of value to offer, and that the real solution of the problems involved was to see that this kind of education should be made available to boys of any class, if they could profit by it.

At last, in 1942, the President of the Board of Education, Mr. R. A. Butler, appointed a committee, under the chairmanship of Lord Fleming. Its duty was "to consider means whereby the association between the Public Schools . . . and the general educational system of the country could be developed and extended."[1] The Fleming Committee recommended that the opportunities of education in public schools "should be made available to boys and girls capable of profiting thereby, irrespective of the income of their parents."[2] It suggested that two lists of schools should be drawn up working under conditions which were referred to as Scheme A and Scheme B. Schools admitted to the Scheme A list would be mainly those which are known as 'direct-grant schools.' In 1926 all grant-aided schools not under L.E.A.s were given the choice of receiving a capitation grant direct from the central authority instead of aid from the L.E.A. The majority opted for the L.E.A. grant, but 250 schools preferred the direct grant. The Fleming Committee proposed that under Scheme A these schools should be accepted by the Board of Education as 'associated schools.' They would be "required either to abolish tuition fees[3] or, if tuition fees are retained, to grade them according to an approved income scale which should provide for total remission if a parent's income requires it"; it was also recommended "that boarding charges should be similarly graded in all schools participating in the Scheme."[4] The local education authority (or authorities) should have the right to reserve places at such

---

[1] Report on The Public Schools and the General Educational System, p. 1.

[2] Op. cit., p. 100.

[3] In an interim report on the Abolition of Tuition Fees in Grant-aided Schools (1943), a majority of eleven members of the Fleming Committee advocated the abolition of fees in direct-grant schools; a minority of seven, including the chairman, was not in favour of this.

[4] Report, p. 64.

schools and would pay tuition fees for their pupils, and part or all of the boarding fee also according to the parents' means. Direct grant would continue to be paid in respect of the other pupils, and at least one-third of the governing body would be nominated by the L.E.A.s sending pupils to the school. Scheme B would apply only to "such Boarding Schools or schools taking a substantial number of boarders as the Board may accept, being schools recognised by the Board as efficient and not being conducted for private profit."[1] This class would cover public schools of the normal type and they also would become 'associated'—i.e. with the general educational system of the country. They would offer a minimum of 25 per cent. of their annual admissions to pupils who had been previously educated for at least two years at a grant-aided primary school. To these children the Board would grant bursaries to cover the total cost of boarding, tuition, and other necessary expenses, subject to a contribution from parents who could afford it. The bursars would be selected by a Regional Board, and parents would be free to apply for a child's admission to any school accepted under the scheme. If the governors of a Scheme A school made an agreement with an L.E.A. to reserve a certain number of places for its candidates, the L.E.A. was to be represented on the governing body.

The Fleming Committee's report, like so many other educational manifestos, was obviously a compromise. For that reason it was much criticised. It did little to satisfy those who believe that the public schools emphasise our existing social divisions and that they cater for a privileged class. Even if 25 per cent. of their pupils were admitted from primary schools on a bursary system, the remaining three-quarters of their places would still be reserved for the children of parents who could afford to pay high fees. It has also been suggested that so small a proportion of ex-elementary-school bursars might find it difficult to become an integral part of such schools; and the assumption by the advocates of the public schools that there is something of outstanding value in their educational system, which would warrant the enormous expenditure of public money involved in sending a few highly

[1] *Op. cit.*, p. 101.

selected bursars to them, is not everywhere regarded as axiomatic. But there already exist boarding schools which successfully bring together boys from different backgrounds under public-school conditions. At Rendcomb[1] in Gloucestershire, for example, about half of the pupils enter from preparatory schools and elsewhere on a fee-paying basis, while the rest are 'free placers' admitted on the results of the county special-place examination. Christ's Hospital affords a still more illustrious example. Here is a public school of unquestioned standing, an ancient endowed foundation, a boarding school with all the traditions of the 'old school tie' in the best sense, but reserved for those who are ostensibly best qualified to benefit by it, and admitting a large proportion of ex-public elementary-school scholars.

Perhaps if our public schools could be turned into institutions of this type we might secure the most suitable education for some of our best material, and there would no longer be any danger of the public school remaining a preserve for the wealthy or the snob. But there are still other considerations involved. There is a strong, and not unnatural, feeling in some of the State secondary schools that a 'creaming-off' of bursars to be sent to the public schools would react disadvantageously to them, and would in the long run fail of its purpose. This view has been clearly put by Mr. Claydon, the headmaster of Maidstone Grammar School. "It is," he says, "from the unhindered development of the Secondary day schools, opening the gates of opportunity to so many children and gaining each year the esteem and confidence of more and more parents, and from far freer access from them to universities and professions, that the resolution of our social divisions may be most hopefully expected, and not from the artificial association with them, on unequal terms, of schools whose evolution has been based on utterly different principles."[2] Thus the whole situation bristles with difficulties. There are extremists who would seek to cut the knot by abolishing the public schools, but there seems no immediate prospect of Eton being turned into a county college and Harrow into a training-college for teachers. The Fleming

[1] See Simpson, *Sane Schooling*, chap. i. (Here the school is called 'Churnside'.)
[2] Article in *Journal of Education*, September 1944; quoted by Lester Smith, *To Whom do Schools Belong?* (Second Edition), p. 231.

Committee's recommendations were reiterated and amplified by a Public Schools Commission, under the chairmanship of Sir John Newson, which reported in July 1968. No one can say that either body has finally solved the problem of the relation of the public schools to the State system of education, and there seems little immediate prospect of their recommendations being implemented. However, some solution along the lines which they have suggested may at length become possible.

The private schools, like the public schools, stand outside the national system. The latter have, for the most part, continued to flourish parallel with the development of State schools, but the private schools—as distinguished from the preparatory schools—have tended to decrease.[1] They vary enormously in efficiency. They are run for profit and are the property of individuals or groups of individuals. Unlike the preparatory schools, they are local schools, running parallel with the primary and secondary system and not normally catering for entrance to the public schools. They have laboured under increasing disadvantages. They receive no grants; teaching service in them is not pensionable; their buildings are too often improvised and their equipment poor. Yet some parents prefer them to the State schools because they are free from official interference and are more 'select.' The Board of Education Act of 1899 had given the Board power to inspect private schools if they asked for this. In 1930 a Departmental Committee of the Board was set up to investigate the private-school problem, and it reported in 1932. It recommended that the L.E.A. should inspect all private schools in its area, but mainly in order to see that the conditions were hygienic. Powers were to be given to the authority to close a school after warning if it remained unsatisfactory in this respect; but nothing was said about standards of work or the qualifications of teachers. Part III of the 1944 Education Act, however, provided for the inspection and registration of private schools.[2] It was some time before this work could be carried out; but, although in some cases the conditions were found to be unsatisfactory,[3] by the end of

[1] See Lowndes, *The Silent Social Revolution*, p. 165, and graphs on pp. 21 and 240.   [2] See *infra*, pp. 300–301.
[3] For examples see Ministry of Education *Report* for 1958, pp. 26–28.

1962 the great majority of independent schools had been accepted for registration and about two-thirds of them had been formally recognised by the ministry as "efficient."

Some of the most effective private schools are the kindergartens which, though private, are often conducted by women with Froebel qualifications. Mention must also be made of private schools under the ægis of the Parents' National Educational Union. This body was founded in 1888 by Miss Charlotte Mason, whose educational teachings are worthy of greater attention than they sometimes receive. She criticised the tendency to 'play down' to children, and emphasised their claim to be regarded as 'persons' and to be treated accordingly. She provided a curriculum based on the best literature and on contact with whatever was good and beautiful and interesting in the child's environment. The whole scheme was permeated with a deep religious spirit. Miss Mason laid stress on a teaching method, which she called 'narration' and which consists essentially in making the child reproduce in his own words the substance of what he has read or heard. In order to provide teachers and governesses to carry out her ideas she founded in 1892 a 'House of Education' at Ambleside. She also provided courses of instruction by correspondence for mothers who wished to educate their children at home.

Something more than a mere passing reference is also due to the schools run by Roman Catholic Orders, the importance of whose work in this country is also not always recognised as it should be by educational historians. Many of their schools are inside the State system and receive State aid; some of the Roman Catholic voluntary schools, for example, are staffed by 'religious.' But there are many convent schools for girls, in particular, conducted on the best secondary boarding or day-school lines, but independent of Government or L.E.A. assistance. The Jesuits and Benedictines also do much educational work and, *inter alia*, run public schools, such as Stonyhurst, and Beaumont, Downside, Ampleforth, and Douai. Worthy of note, too, are the Christian Brothers, whose Institute was founded in France by St. Jean-Baptiste de La Salle in 1684, and who have been at work in this country since 1855. They are responsible not only for

elementary and secondary schools, some of which are aided by
public funds, but also for five 'approved schools.'[1] Although, as
can be well understood, the schools maintained by Roman
Catholic Orders or Congregations have a very definite religious
character of their own, they include a fair percentage of non-
Catholics among their pupils.[2]

Midway between the private schools, which are run for profit,
and the public schools stands a group of schools which like to
call themselves 'progressive.' They are of many types and for that
reason are a little difficult to classify. They include schools so
widely different as Dartington Hall, Frensham Heights, A. S.
Neill's 'Dreadful School' in Suffolk, and King Alfred's School,
Hampstead. An idea of their scope and aims can be obtained by
consulting the *Modern Schools' Handbook*.[3] Many of these schools
are run by societies or groups of educational enthusiasts. They
experiment with 'free discipline' or 'self-government,' or unconventional curricula; and they often provide a useful challenge to
the traditional or stereotyped methods which are so difficult to
avoid in a school with large classes and prescribed syllabuses.
They are not usually conducted for private profit, even though
they are 'private,' or independent, schools; but because they are
often boarding schools and are expensive to run, and at the same
time are ineligible for any kind of grant from public money, they
tend to charge high fees. Thus they, again, are accessible only to
a certain class of the community—a class which hesitates, for
various reasons, to send its children to the ordinary State schools.
A few of these 'progressive' schools have been recognised by the
Board of Education, and many of them are willing to prepare
pupils for public examinations. But their chief aim is to be free
and unconventional and experimental; and they can be so largely
because they are entirely independent of any control by a local or
central authority. Thus they have made, and are still making, a
contribution to educational theory and practice which is sometimes beyond the scope of the ordinary State-supervised school.

[1] See *infra*, pp. 284–285.
[2] Reference should be made to Evennett, *The Catholic Schools*.
[3] See also W. A. C. Stewart, *The Educational Innovators*, Vol. 2.

Chapter XXVIII

UNIVERSITIES AND THE TRAINING OF TEACHERS

Development of University Education. The Reorganised University of London.
Universities and Training Colleges; the McNair *Report*. Teachers' Salaries.

IN 1902 England possessed six universities. In addition to Oxford and Cambridge, there were Durham and London, the federal Victoria University, and a separate university at Birmingham. The early years of the century saw a remarkable development of independent universities. Victoria ceased to be a federation; Manchester and Liverpool obtained separate charters in 1903, and Leeds in 1904. University College, Sheffield, attained university rank in 1905 and University College, Bristol, in 1909. Reading received its charter in 1926, Nottingham in 1948, Southampton in 1952, Hull in 1954, Exeter in 1955, and Leicester in 1957. The University of North Staffordshire (founded as a university college in 1949) conferred a B.A. degree after a four years' course. The first year, taken by all students alike, was concerned with the heritage of civilisation and the methods and influence of the sciences. St. David's College, Lampeter, granted a B.A. and a B.D.

The English universities have succeeded in remaining independent of State control. The Government does not dictate to a university what it should teach, nor does it control the syllabuses or organisation or examinations. It has no voice in the appointment of professors and it does not inspect university work. In spite of this, it gives the universities considerable financial help. The first annual Treasury grant to universities was made in 1889, and it amounted to £15,000; by 1961–2 the grant had risen to over eighty millions. In 1919 a University Grants Committee was set up, consisting not of officials, but of prominent men familiar with the work and needs of universities. To this body—and not to the Board of Education—was given the duty of allocating and distributing the Treasury grant for universities. Since 1922 Oxford and Cambridge, as well as the other British universities, have participated in this grant. But State aid is also given to universities for special services, and in particular for the training of teachers. Students recognised as 'teachers in training' receive tuition fees and a maintenance grant from the Ministry of Education, and a capitation fee is also paid to the university on their behalf. The modern university owes much to students of this type, even though the ear-marking of potential teachers during the actual degree course which had been introduced in 1911 was abandoned forty years later. L.E.A.s also often help universities by making grants or by giving scholarships to students coming up from their own schools. They are usually represented on the university governing body, but apart from this they have no control over university policy or organisation. All British universities still depend on fees and endowments to supplement the aid which they receive from public money.

With the increase in the number of universities in England and Wales and their individual development the number of full-time students has increased. It rose from 12,778 in 1908–9 to 40,465 in 1935–6.[1] The foundation of new secondary schools after the 1902 Act and the introduction of the 'free-place' system helped an ever-growing number of ex-elementary-school pupils to get through to the university. The institution of State scholarships in 1920, open equally to boys and girls from State-aided secondary grammar schools, also strengthened the connection between these schools and the universities. The opening of universities to women on the same terms as to men has again tended to increase student numbers; and the institution of grant-earning places for intending teachers has also contributed to this. Thus there has been of late years a considerable growth of university activity, and in it the 'modern' universities have played an increasingly important part. Yet Oxford and Cambridge still retain their old prestige and something of their old pre-eminence. But, while keeping what is best in their traditions, they have moved with the times. Compulsory Greek was abolished after the first Great

[1] See also *infra*, p. 326.

War. New honours schools and triposes have been instituted—
e.g. 'Modern Greats' (philosophy, politics, and economics) at
Oxford, and mechanical sciences at Cambridge. The Cavendish
laboratories at the latter University are among the best in the
country; the facilities for medical research at Oxford are un-
rivalled. All the English universities and university colleges—old
and new alike—have owed much to the private benefactor—
such as those whose names are commemorated in the titles of the
original colleges from which some of the universities have grown,
and more recently men like Nuffield, Wills, Trent, Palmer, and
Ferens.

The University of London is *sui generis* among English universities. As has been pointed out,[1] from 1858 onwards it became
purely an examining body. The high standard of its degrees—
and especially the pass degrees—and the variety of the courses
available gave it considerable prestige. The reconstitution of the
University at the end of the nineteenth century as a teaching, as
well as an examining, body was an important stage in its development, but it resulted in a complicated organisation of heterogeneous institutions, and this involved many difficulties of administration. The problem was worked out in successive stages
between the setting-up of a Royal Commission in 1909, under the
chairmanship of Lord Haldane, and the passing of a University of
London Act in 1926. The present constitution includes a Court,
which controls finance, and a Senate which is responsible for
academic matters and is assisted by five standing committees dealing with the various departments of university business. Another
important development has been the formation of a University
Quarter, by bringing the constituent colleges and university departments as far as possible together in one district, and grouping
them round the central buildings of the University. This scheme
was set in motion in 1920, when a considerable area in Bloomsbury was acquired by the University, and a large administrative
building was erected close to the British Museum and not far
from University College. All these things have helped to give
the University of London some sort of unity, and a soul of its

[1] See *supra*, p. 87.

own; but it can hardly be said that its constitutional problems have been fully solved.[1] It has a special significance among our universities in that, more perhaps than any other, it attracts students from all parts of the world. This helps to make it *par excellence* the imperial, or even the international, university; and that, after all, is one of the most characteristic traits of the university from its earliest origins in the Middle Ages.

The training of teachers has during the twentieth century become increasingly the concern of universities. The institution of 'day training colleges' in 1890 had given prospective elementary-school teachers a chance to read for degrees; though many of those who graduated by this means found their way, as we have seen, into the post-1902 secondary schools. At first the course was a 'concurrent' one and included both preparation for the degree and training in teaching. It was a system which bore heavily on the student and tended sometimes to encourage neglect of the professional part of the course. In 1911, therefore, a four-year course was introduced, which left the intending teacher free to study for a degree during the first three years, unhampered by professional work, and to devote the fourth year entirely to 'training.' This scheme was not adopted at once by all universities, but it is now the universal practice. Side by side with this development, the two-year (or three-year) course was maintained in the training colleges. The Act of 1902 gave L.E.A.s the power to train teachers; but they were unable to do much at first because all their efforts and available finance had to be devoted to the provision of elementary and secondary education. Training colleges also are not *local* institutions to the same extent as schools; and not unnaturally L.E.A.s were sometimes loath to spend their resources for the benefit of students from outside. Most of the existing training colleges were denominational; and in 1906, therefore, the Government offered to pay three-quarters of the cost of new undenominational training colleges to be provided

[1] Cf. Flexner, *Universities*, pp. 231–2: "I confess myself unable to understand in what sense the University of London is a university at all. It is a line drawn about an enormous number of different institutions of heterogeneous quality and purpose."

by L.E.A.s. Some of the more progressive of them responded; no less than twenty-two L.E.A. training colleges—most of them new foundations—came into being, all of them non-denominational and imposing no religious tests upon entrants. They included such well-known training colleges as that erected at Bingley by the West Riding County Council, and the Leeds City Training College.

The teacher's normal qualification, recognised by the Board of Education, was the 'certificate.' Up to 1926 it was awarded at the end of the training course on the result of an examination conducted by the Board of Education. The Board never made any sharp distinction between elementary and secondary training. As has been said, teachers trained in 'day training colleges' often went into secondary schools; and, conversely, a fair proportion of four-year-course candidates from university training departments had always taken posts in elementary schools. This situation was made clearer in 1926 when the Board gave its certificate to recognised candidates who had qualified for university diplomas in education. But in future the certificate examination for training-college students was to be conducted, not by the Board itself, but by Regional Boards, on which representatives of the universities, the training colleges, and the L.E.A.s were represented, while H.M. inspectors had the right to attend meetings in an advisory capacity. With each university, or with an association of universities, a group of training colleges was associated.

The primary duty of these 'Joint Examining Boards,' as they were called,[1] was to draw up courses of work for the training-college students and to conduct the examinations on which the certificate was awarded; but it was hoped that this purely examinational relationship between the university and its associated training colleges might develop into "some real measure of personal contact between training colleges and the university." In the event some Joint Boards went much farther in this direction than others. The fact that many of the training colleges are situated at a considerable distance from the nearest university has militated against close co-operation, though even under these

[1] See Board of Education Circular 1372 (December 11th, 1925).

conditions the handicap has to some extent been overcome. But in some places the training colleges have been near enough to be affiliated and for their students reading for degree courses to become ordinary undergraduates of the university. This has occurred, for example, at Durham. Bede College, St. Hild's, and Neville's Cross are at once training colleges and halls of residence in the University of Durham. Somewhat similarly Goldsmiths' College has been incorporated in the University of London.

Any expansion or improvement of the national system of education is most closely bound up with the recruitment and training of teachers. The complications introduced by the second World War and the renewal of plans to raise the school-leaving age and provide extended educational facilities for 'young persons'[1] made the problem of the supply of well-qualified teachers more urgent than ever. For this reason, in March 1942, Mr. R. A. Butler, the President of the Board of Education, appointed a committee which is usually known by the name of its chairman, Sir Arnold McNair. Its terms of reference were "to investigate the present sources of supply and the methods of recruitment and training of teachers and youth leaders, and to report what principles should guide the Board in these matters in the future."[2] Its report was presented in 1944.

The Committee, faced with the problem that some 70,000 additional teachers would be needed after the war, realised that conditions in the profession would have to be made more attractive and that the field from which teachers were drawn would have to be extended. "Education," said Mr. Butler in the House of Commons,[3] "is more than mere acquisition of knowledge, and it is my belief that after the war we could find young men and women with a wide experience of life, not necessarily academically inclined, who, if suitably trained, would welcome this form of service to the community and would add variety and richness to the teaching personnel." The McNair Committee

---

[1] This is the term normally used in Acts of Parliament to denote boys and girls who have left school, but are still under the age of eighteen. In the Children and Young Persons Act of 1933 the upper age limit is seventeen.

[2] *Report* on *Teachers and Youth Leaders*, p. 5.

[3] June 16th, 1942. *Parliamentary Debates*, Fifth Series, vol. 380, p. 1412.

therefore recommended that every encouragement and help should be given to pupils in all forms of post-primary school, and not merely in the academic grammar school, if they were willing "to consider preparation for the teaching profession and are provisionally judged suitable for it."[1] Facilities should also be offered to candidates of maturer years to become teachers. Conditions of service should be improved and salaries "substantially increased." The promise to enter teaching, which had hitherto been exacted of those admitted to grant-earning courses in universities or training colleges, should be abandoned, and the existing two-year course in training colleges should be extended to three. The four-year university course was left intact, though many people would have liked to see a more extended postgraduate diploma course. Recommendations were made for improving the status and quality of training college staffs and for "the secondment of teachers from schools for a period of service in training institutions."[2] The *Report* went on to deal with the training of 'youth leaders' and of teachers in technical colleges and schools; further reference will be made to these points.[3]

The McNair Committee agreed that there should be a Central Training Council for England and Wales, and that it should have the duty of "advising the Board of Education about bringing into being that form of area training service recommended in this Report which the Board may decide to adopt."[4] Unfortunately the members were equally divided as to what form the area training service should take, and they therefore submitted alternative schemes. The first proposed to set up University Schools of Education. It would lay on each university the responsibility for co-ordinating and organising the training of teachers of all kinds in its own area; and that, not only in the university itself, but also in training colleges and in any other kind of institution (e.g. technical or agricultural colleges, schools of art, music, or domestic science) which could contribute in any way towards the training of these teachers. The University School of Education would

[1] *Report* on *Teachers and Youth Leaders*, p. 141.
[2] *Op. cit.*, p. 146.   [3] See *infra*, pp. 289–90 and 332.
[4] *Report* on *Teachers and Youth Leaders*, p. 143.

S

be administered by a delegacy on which not only the university but the L.E.A.s and the training institutions would be represented; and it would be housed in a building which could be used to focus the general educational activities of the area, so far as both teachers and students in training of all kinds were concerned. The other scheme preferred to develop the existing Joint Board machinery. The University Department of Education and the training colleges would preserve their separate identity, but the Joint Board would link together both them and the other training facilities of the area, and would carry out the various educational activities involved.

These schemes provoked much discussion when the *Report* was issued. The majority of opinion outside the universities favoured the first scheme; but it was obvious that conditions in the different universities varied so much that a cast-iron system for all training areas in the country might be inadvisable. The universities also, not unnaturally, felt some misgivings about the 'major constitutional change' (as the authors of the first scheme described it) which they would undergo if this plan were adopted. In fact, the *Report* brought to a head a controversy on the value and function of the university, which had been developing with the growth of the newer universities. The American scholar, Flexner, writing in 1930, defines a university as "essentially a seat of learning, devoted to the conservation of knowledge, the increase of systematic knowledge and the training of students well above the secondary level"; and he says of our British university students in the arts and science faculties: "An excessive proportion become teachers. To be sure, teachers need to be educated. But a point is soon reached, where a university is saturated with prospective teachers; beyond that point, leisure and inclination for research suffer, and the university tends to deteriorate into a teacher-training establishment, though, of course, the right man will win through."[1] Thus the problem, not yet solved, is to bring the training of teachers of all kinds as fully as possible within the ambit of the university, without destroying the essential character of the university itself.

The recruitment of teachers must always be in some measure dependent on the remuneration which they are to receive. Teach-

[1] Flexner, *Universities*, p. 255.

ing has never offered more than a competence, and it affords far fewer highly paid posts than any other of the professions. Previous to 1921 there were no standard scales of pay; each school or L.E.A. made its own arrangements, and those which were most wealthy naturally attracted the best-qualified teachers. After the 1902 Act there had been some improvements; but even in 1909 some of the L.E.A.s and governing bodies paid their graduate assistant masters in secondary schools as little as £120, and the maximum rarely exceeded £200 a year.[1] The teachers in some of the elementary schools received a mere pittance. As late as 1914 the average salary for a certificated assistant teacher was £129 (man) and £96 (woman); for the uncertificated the figures were £76 and £69. In 1917 Mr. Fisher obtained an increased Exchequer contribution towards the cost of teachers' salaries. Two years later he set up a committee, including representatives of the L.E.A.s and the teachers, under the chairmanship of Lord Burnham. To them was entrusted the task of working out scales for elementary-school teachers on a national basis. Other committees did a similar service for secondary and technical teachers; and by 1921 a whole series of scales, accepted by all parties, was in operation. Subsequently there were some readjustments, and during the financial crisis following the year 1931 there was a considerable temporary 'cut'; but the principle of a national scale was never called in question. The great rise in the cost of living, due to the second World War, and the importance of attracting large numbers of additional teachers into the profession, brought the question of salaries again to the fore. As has been pointed out, the McNair Committee recommended substantial increases in the payment of teachers, and said that their salaries and prospects should be equated with those of the administrative and executive branches of the Civil Service. Accordingly the 'Burnham' Committee—now under the chairmanship of Lord Soulbury—completely recast its scales. Different rates of pay for teachers in 'elementary' and 'secondary' grades were abolished; but a single basic salary for all 'qualified' teachers was introduced, with extra allowances for special qualifications or duties. The initial salaries

[1] See Norwood and Hope, *Higher Education of Boys in England*, Appendix B.

were considerably increased; but the scheme was severely criticised on the ground that it gives inadequate reward to senior
and highly qualified members of the profession, and, in particular,
to the heads of 'grammar' schools. When therefore in 1963 a sum
became available for augmenting teachers' salaries, the Minister
of Education wished to distribute it so as to benefit particularly
teachers of this type. The professional associations, however,
were anxious to increase the salaries of entrants to the profession.
This led to much discussion and disagreement, but the Minister
stood firm. Finally the constitution of the Burnham Committee
was revised. Originally it had consisted merely of representatives
of the teachers' and educational authorities' associations and the
Minister only had the power to approve or reject their recommendations. Now, however, the Ministry is actually represented as
one of the partners on the Committee itself.

The institution of national salary scales implied the introduction also of a superannuation scheme for teachers. Even in
the days of Kay-Shuttleworth, small retiring pensions had been
available for teachers in grant-earning elementary schools. From
time to time these allowances were withdrawn, and, of course,
they were never available for secondary-school teachers who were
outside the State system. In 1898 a deferred annuity scheme was
introduced; and after the Act of 1902 some municipal authorities
included teachers in the superannuation schemes for their officials.
But the whole system was replaced by the Teachers Superannuation Acts of 1918, 1925 and 1956, which secured for all teachers,
serving in State-aided schools of any kind, a pension based on
length of service and the salary earned during the last five[1] years
of it, together with a lump sum calculated on a similar basis. At
first the scheme was non-contributory—as with Civil Service and
Army pensions; but after it had been working for a short time
teachers were required to contribute 5 per cent. per annum of
their salary towards superannuation. To this the State and the
L.E.A. or school governors together added another 5 per cent.[2]

[1] Later altered to three.
[2] For details see *Teachers (Superannuation) Act*, 1925, § 9. By a similar Act of
1956 the contribution of both teacher and employer was raised to 6 per cent.

Chapter XXIX

THE PROGRESS OF SECONDARY EDUCATION

The Spens *Report*. The Multilateral School and the School Base. The Norwood *Report*.

THE Hadow *Report* on *The Education of the Adolescent* had pointed the way to a new conception of post-primary education, some form of which was to be available for every child. It left intact the 'grammar' school with its rather academic course; but it also provided the modern school and the senior classes which would give a general education with some bias towards local industries. It also left the junior technical school with its two- or three-year course from about the age of thirteen. In theory all types of post-primary education were to be of equal status, and the modern schools were not to be treated less generously than the grammar schools. It was more easy to make these recommendations than to carry them out. As has already been seen, the administrative difficulties were considerable; but more fundamental is the fact that a national educational system reflects —though it may also in time modify—the national social outlook. An official report or an Act of Parliament cannot at once alter deep-seated social habits. The 'modern' school has inevitably inherited much of the long tradition of the old 'elementary' school; while the 'grammar' school, with its better equipment and its power (up to 1944) to charge fees, has tended to take a higher place in the social scale. To accustom the public mind to an entirely new outlook on secondary education will inevitably be a lengthy, and perhaps not an easy, process. But the work which the Hadow Committee began in 1926 has been diligently followed up. In 1938 the Consultative Committee, then under the chairmanship of Sir Will Spens, issued a *Report on Secondary Education*. Its terms of reference were: "To consider and report upon the organisation and inter-relation of schools, other than those administered under the Elementary Code, which provide education for pupils beyond the age of eleven plus; regard being had in particular to the framework and content of the education of pupils who do not remain at school beyond the age of about sixteen." Thus the *Report* was not directly concerned with 'modern' schools and it amplified the Hadow *Report* of 1926, which had given special attention to this subject.

The Spens *Report* points out that when, as a result of the 1902 Act, the State undertook for the first time the general reorganisation of secondary education, the ancient grammar school was adopted too exclusively as the model for the secondary school. The institution in 1917 of the first school examination (the school certificate), which was taken by the public and grammar schools, "had the effect of strengthening and intensifying this tendency towards uniformity."[1] But "schools of every type fulfil their proper purpose in so far as they foster the free growth of individuality, helping every boy and girl to achieve the highest degree of individual development of which he or she is capable in and through the life of a society."[2] Thus the secondary curriculum must cater for different interests and different needs; and it should be thought of in terms of activity and experience rather than of knowledge to be acquired and facts to be stored. The *Report* goes on to interpret this dictum in detail in terms of the grammar-school curriculum, and points out that hitherto it has been too much dominated by the requirements of the school certificate. It advocates greater freedom in the choice of subjects and a reduction in the content of examination syllabuses. But alongside of these grammar schools, which will continue to be the chief sources of candidates for the university and which will be distinguished by their Sixth Form work, the Spens Committee suggested a development of what might be called secondary technical education. It was proposed to retain the junior technical schools with their two- or three-year course and their entry age of thirteen plus; but the Committee also advocated "a new type of higher school of a technical character, wholly distinct from the traditional academic Grammar (Secondary) School."[3] Such schools would take in pupils at the age of eleven plus and would provide for

[1] Spens *Report*, p. 352.   [2] *Op. cit.*, p. 362.   [3] *Op. cit.*, p. 274.

them a five-year course; and to distinguish them from the junior technical schools, they would be called technical high schools.

To meet the criticism that eleven plus is too early an age at which to decide whether a child is best fitted for a technical career and to start him on a career of a vocational nature, the Spens Committee recommended that "the curriculum for pupils between the ages of eleven plus and thirteen plus in Technical High Schools should be broadly of the same character as the curriculum in other types of secondary school of equal status. For pupils above the age of thirteen the curriculum should be designed so as to provide a liberal education with Science and its applications as the core and inspiration."[1] Whenever possible technical high schools should be housed in technical colleges or technical institutes, so that staff and equipment may to some extent be shared. A new form of leaving certificate for technical high schools should be instituted, and this "should be given equal standing with School Certificates as fulfilling the first condition for matriculation."[2] There should be full opportunity for transfer as between grammar school and technical high school at about the age of thirteen. The Committee also reiterated the views expressed in the Hadow *Report* as to equality of status. "For the complete realisation of our recommendations regarding curriculum and the interrelation of schools, parity of schools in the secondary stage of education is essential. This principle was implicit in our Report on *The Education of the Adolescent* (1926), and we desire expressly to assert our conviction of its importance. If schools providing secondary education of different types are to be made equally acceptable to parents, and opportunities for entering the type of school which can best develop their particular abilities are to be made equally available to children, the establishment of parity between all types of secondary school is a fundamental requirement."[3] Nothing could be more definite than this.

The difficulty of ensuring this 'equality of status' led many to advocate what is known as the multilateral school. "The special characteristics of this type of school"—to quote the Spens *Report*[4]

[1] *Op. cit.*, p. 372.   [2] *Op. cit.*, p. 373.
[3] *Op. cit.*, p. 376.   [4] *Op. cit.*, pp. xix–xx.

—"are the provision of a good general education for two or three years for all pupils over eleven plus in a given area, and the organisation of four or five 'streams,' so that the pupils at the age of thirteen or fourteen years may follow courses that are suited to their individual needs and capacity. There would be a common core in these several courses, but they would differ in the time and emphasis given to certain groups of subjects." Thus, instead of having three or more kinds of secondary school, differentiated according to the 'type' of pupil for whom they catered, there would be only one kind—the multilateral school—but it would provide different 'sides' or courses for its older members. It would receive its pupils from the primary school at eleven plus, but for the first two years all would follow much the same course, and this would provide an exploratory or 'orientation' period to discover individual needs and proclivities. For pupils from about the age of thirteen onwards the multilateral school would provide academic, technical, 'modern,' and perhaps other kinds of course, each of which would have its own syllabus and special subjects, though certain classes could still be taken in common, and the school would still live together and play together as one society. Thus any question of 'status' would be obviated. The labourer who had been a pupil on the 'modern' side, the motor mechanic from the technical side, and the doctor or lawyer from the academic side would all wear the same old school tie. The Spens Committee, while believing that the 'multilateral idea' should permeate our system of secondary education, thought that administrative problems would make it difficult in practice. It was felt, *inter alia*, that multilateral schools would necessarily be very large and that therefore it would be impossible for the head to keep adequately in touch with the work of each 'side' and with individual pupils. It was also suggested that the numbers in the Sixth Form on the academic side would form so small a proportion of the total of pupils that the influence which it should exercise on the life and tradition of the school would be unduly diluted. The case for multilateralism was debated largely on *a priori* grounds, and issues other than the purely educational entered in to complicate it; but it was obvious that there was much room for experiment along these lines.[1]

Mr. J. Howard Whitehouse put forward an interesting scheme which might possibly achieve some of the benefits of multi-lateralism, while avoiding its alleged defects. He advocated what he called the 'School Base.' All the schools of every type, serving a given area, would be situated in close proximity to a large tract of open land, including if possible some woodland and water. In addition to the various schools there would be an art gallery, a concert room with a stage, craft rooms and gymnasia, a canteen and a chapel, medical inspection rooms with a full-time resident doctor and nurses. There would be ample playing-fields, swimming-baths, gardens, and agricultural land. There might also be facilities for adolescent activities and adult education. Residential accommodation might even be provided. On this 'base' each separate school or institution would retain its own in-dividuality, but there would be ample opportunity for the sharing of staff and equipment, and all schools alike would use the basic 'plant.' The transport needed to bring the pupils from the contri-butory areas would be provided by special buses or rail-cars. Here again we have a scheme which offers interesting possibilities and with which experiments have already been made.

The work of the Consultative Committee, under Sir Will Spens, was supplemented by a special committee set up by the President of the Board of Education in 1941. Its *Report*, which was issued in 1943, is usually named after its chairman, Sir Cyril Norwood. The Committee's duty was "to consider suggested changes in the Secondary School curriculum and the question of School Examinations in relation thereto"; but it interpreted its terms of reference in a wide sense, and the *Report* includes an out-line sketch of "the main features of a new secondary education which will cover the whole child population of the country and carry them on to part-time education."[2]

The *Report* begins by claiming that it is possible to divide children roughly into three types for the purpose of education. These "rough groupings, whatever may be their ground, have in

[1] See *infra*, pp. 328–30.   [2] Norwood *Report*, p. v.

fact established themselves in general educational experience, and the recognition of such groupings in educational practice has been justified both during the period of education and in the after-careers of the pupils."[1] According to the Norwood Committee there is first the pupil "who is interested in learning for its own sake, who can grasp an argument or follow a piece of connected reasoning, who is interested in causes." Secondly, there is the pupil "whose interests and abilities lie markedly in the field of applied science or applied art. . . . He often has an uncanny insight into the intricacies of mechanism, whereas the subtleties of language construction are too delicate for him."[2] And finally there is the type of pupil who "deals more easily with concrete things than with ideas. . . . His mind must turn its knowledge or its curiosity to immediate test: and his test is essentially practical. . . . Because he is interested only in the moment he may be incapable of a long series of connected steps; relevance to present concerns is the only way of awakening interest; abstractions mean little to him." The history of English education is full of examples of theoretical arguments advanced to justify an already existing state of affairs. The *a priori* classification outlined by the Norwood Committee fitted in excellently with the scheme of post-primary education laid down in the Spens *Report*; and that in turn had been modelled largely on a system which had grown up in this country and had been determined mainly by historical, political, and economic conditions. For the 'academic' child of the Norwood *Report* there would be the secondary grammar school; for the mechanically minded there would be the secondary technical school; while for the pupil with an 'essentially practical' bent there remained the secondary modern school. To all three kinds of school "should be accorded all the parity which amenities and conditions can bestow."[3] Transfer from one type of school to another should be rendered as easy as possible. Selection of pupils for the kind of secondary education appropriate to their 'type' should be made on the basis of the judgment of the teachers of the primary school, supplemented 'if desired' by intelligence, performance, or other tests. "Due consideration should be given

[1] *Op. cit.*, p. 2.   [2] *Op. cit.*, p. 3.   [3] *Op. cit.*, p. 139.

to the choice of the parent and the pupil."[1] The Norwood Committee agreed with the Spens Committee in suggesting that all types of secondary school should have a roughly common curriculum during the eleven plus to thirteen plus stage; and it was suggested that a 'lower school,' under the supervision of a special master or mistress, should be organised to deal with this. By such means it would be more easy to effect transfers at the age of thirteen plus, in cases where they were indicated, to the appropriate schools.

The division of children into three types, with three corresponding kinds of secondary school to which they can be drafted at the age of eleven plus, or possibly thirteen plus, is implicit in the recommendations of the Hadow *Report*; and this scheme has been merely applied and elaborated by the Spens and Norwood Committees. But it is a classification which has not passed unchallenged. As has already been indicated, the three types of mind seem to have been postulated so as to fit in conveniently with three existing types of school. The opinion has even been expressed that a scheme of this kind, if put into practice as completely as the Spens and Norwood *Reports* suggest, might intensify, rather than modify, social differences between 'types' of children and the schools which they attend. More convincing, perhaps, is the argument on psychological grounds which has been voiced, among others, by Sir Cyril Burt. In an article in *The British Journal of Educational Psychology*,[2] he discusses the belief that individual differences among pupils are chiefly due, not so much to an innate all-round capacity entering into every form of mental work, but rather to qualitatively different aptitudes producing qualitatively different types; and he says roundly: "This view entirely reverses the facts as they are known to us. The one thing which the analysis of mental measurements has demonstrated beyond all doubt is the supreme importance during childhood of the general factor of intelligence." This criticism, coming from an authority of such weight, has serious implications for the whole proposed set-up of post-primary education. We may wish, for reasons of administrative convenience, to have three main types of

[1] Norwood *Report*, p. 139.   [2] November 1943, p. 131.

secondary school and to give them all equal status. But a classification on the basis of general intelligence and not of 'type' may
in the end be the true solution. As Sir Cyril Burt says: "In the
interest of the nation as well as the child, the paramount need is
to discover which are the ablest pupils, no matter to what school
or social class they may belong, and generally to grade each child
according to the relative degree of his ability, and give him the
best education which his ability permits. . . . The proposed allo-
cation of all children to different types of school at the early age
of eleven cannot provide a sound psychological solution."[1]

The greater part of the Norwood *Report* was concerned—as
indeed its terms of reference implied—with the examinations
which so largely determined the curriculum of the secondary
grammar school. The 'local' examinations instituted by the Universities of Oxford and Cambridge date from the fifties of the
nineteenth century, and these were taken by pupils from both
endowed schools and private schools. In addition to the senior
local, which was virtually a school-leaving examination, junior,
or even preliminary, examinations were instituted to be taken by
younger candidates. The Oxford and Cambridge Joint Board
examinations date from 1874, and they were intended mainly for
the public schools which sent a fair proportion of their pupils to
these Universities. At first a higher certificate alone was instituted to be taken by candidates[2] aged eighteen or over. In 1884 a
a lower certificate was introduced for pupils leaving at the age of
about fifteen or sixteen, and in 1905 a school certificate for those
aged about sixteen or seventeen. In addition, many secondary
schools of all types entered their pupils for the London University
matriculation, which was originally intended as a preliminary
qualification for a degree course; but it became more and more
used as a school-leaving examination and was demanded as a
qualification by employers. As secondary education developed
after 1902 it became increasingly evident that the requirements of
this series of external examinations were having undesirable re-
actions on the work of many schools; they were, in fact, tending
to foster over-pressure and cramming.

[1] *Op. cit.*, p. 140.   [2] Girls were admitted from 1879.

The Board of Education made some attempts to deal with this problem, and finally referred it to the Consultative Committee. In a *Report*, published in 1911, this Committee expressed the opinion that the presentation of young and immature pupils for external examinations is mischievous, and that it was desirable that the various examinations should be co-ordinated. As a result the university examining bodies—there were seven of them by this time—recast or modified their schemes and there emerged two standard examinations—the first school (or school certificate) examination, with a general curriculum, and designed for pupils aged about sixteen; and a second school (or higher certificate) examination, offering more specialised groups, for pupils about eighteen. In 1917 the Board of Education set up a Secondary School Examinations Council to co-ordinate the standard of these examinations. Meanwhile the institution of 'advanced courses' for the Sixth Forms of 'secondary' (i.e. grammar) schools, for which a special grant of £400 a year might be obtained from the Board, had stimulated higher work for pupils who stayed on at school beyond the age of sixteen. In 1918 the Board issued a regulation that no external examination should be taken by pupils in grant-earning secondary schools below the standard of the school certificate, or first school, examination; and that those who stayed on to take an advanced course could enter for the second school examination normally two years later. This had the effect of forbidding schools of this type to enter pupils for the junior or preliminary examinations of the University Locals, or of the College of Preceptors. There were now eight university bodies running first and second school examinations which were approved by the Board and co-ordinated by the Secondary School Examinations Council. In 1920 a system of State scholarships was instituted in order to increase the opportunities for pupils in grant-aided secondary grammar schools to proceed to universities and institutions of higher education. Of these 178 went to candidates from England and 22 to those from Wales. The scholarships were awarded on the results of the second school examinations. Their value was determined by the candidate's other resources, but normally it covered tuition fees and a maintenance grant of £80 a year for the university course.

All these reforms brought some sort of order into the secondary-school examination system; but it was still criticised on various grounds. It was said that the syllabuses were not sufficiently flexible and that they still exerted too much influence on the curriculum and the teaching in the schools. Some of the universities also accepted the school certificate, under certain conditions, as qualifying for their matriculation; some were even willing to excuse the intermediate degree examination in the case of holders of such higher certificates as were of approximately equal standard. This had the effect of still further conditioning the work in school for these certificates by university requirements; and the fact that employers too often demanded 'matriculation exemption' from applicants for posts, as if it were a far superior qualification to the holding of a school certificate, had undesirable repercussions on 'secondary'-school work. It was to cope with such a situation as this that the Norwood Committee made a large part of its recommendations. It suggested that "in the interest of the individual child and of the increased freedom and responsibility of the teaching profession,"[1] the school certificate examination should be made an internal one. It should be based on a syllabus drawn up by the school itself and the papers should be set and marked by the teachers concerned. This would be a drastic change; but to ease the shock the Committee suggested that for a transitional period of seven years the examination should be carried on by the existing university bodies, with a strong representation of teachers, and that pupils should be allowed to offer "whatever subjects they wish to take." A certificate would be awarded to every candidate showing his performance in the examination, and to this the school authorities would add a statement of his school record.

The Norwood Committee also envisaged a 'school-leaving examination,' to be taken normally at the age of eighteen plus and designed to "give evidence of proficiency to pursue University or professional studies," and also to show that pupils had

[1] Norwood *Report*, p. 140.

"pursued a course of Sixth Form work with profit."[1] Its purpose would not be to provide evidence of a general or 'all-round' education, but the candidates would offer a limited number of subjects, as required for the particular purpose which they had in view. The existing higher certificate examination would be abolished.

There remained the question of State scholarships and other awards enabling candidates to take courses at some institution of higher education. The *Report* recommended that the winning of a scholarship offered by a university should give the scholar a "claim upon public funds for assistance towards the cost of living at the University, subject to evidence that such assistance is necessary."[2] But in addition there should be an examination, conducted each year in March, for the award of State and L.E.A. scholarships. On the result of this two lists of candidates would be issued. "Part A would contain those of high intellectual distinction, that is to say, capable of obtaining a first class or a good second class; part B would contain those of good intellectual attainment whose claims might be considered if there were other outstanding merits disclosed by the school record, but undiscoverable by written examination."[3] The recommendations of the university examining bodies would then be sent to the L.E.A.s from whose schools the candidates had come and would be reviewed by special boards, appointed for the purpose, who would take into account the candidates' performance in the examination and their school records. On these boards, which should be small, the universities, the L.E.A.s, and the teachers should be represented. The final award of the scholarships would be made by the Board of Education, and the State also would bear the cost. The amount granted should be sufficient to cover the entire expense of the university course. In addition to these State scholarships it would be open to L.E.A.s to make additional awards of their own to suitable candidates; and in this case the State would pay half the cost. The Norwood Committee deprecated a practice which had been adopted by some L.E.A.s—that of granting loans to students of merit to enable them to go on to advanced

[1] *Op. cit.*, p. 41.   [2] *Op. cit.*, p. 37.   [3] *Op. cit.*, p. 39.

education at a university or elsewhere. The obligation to repay such sums in the early stages of the recipient's salary-earning career often proved a very heavy burden; and the *Report* records the opinion that "encouragement should not be given to a young man or woman to borrow for any purpose."[1]

[1] *Op. cit.*, p. 41.

Chapter XXX

TECHNICAL AND CONTINUATIVE EDUCATION

Junior Technical Schools. Technical Colleges. Adult Education. The Community Centre and the Village College.

THE twentieth century has seen a great development in vocational and continuative education. This type of education includes full-time day courses, as well as part-time courses given mainly in the evening. Day courses for children of school age were provided by the junior technical schools, to which reference has already been made. Their forerunners were the trade schools which in the fifties of last century were started in connection with some of the larger and more effective mechanics' institutes at Manchester, Liverpool, Bristol, and elsewhere. These schools were designed to prepare boys for apprenticeship in the building, engineering, and manufacturing trades, by supplementing the work of the elementary school with practical mathematics and physical science as applied to industry.[1] The junior technical school owed something also to the organised science schools which were founded in the eighteen-seventies, and perhaps to the example of the German *Realschule*. It was not until 1913 that junior technical schools were recognised by the Board of Education as a distinct type of institution. They were described in the Board's Regulation as "definitely not intended to provide courses furnishing a preparation for the professions, the universities, or higher full-time technical work, or again, for commercial life; they are intended to prepare their pupils either for artisan or other industrial employment or for domestic employment."[2]

The junior technical school gave a two- or three-year course starting from the age of about thirteen or fourteen, and designed for children who normally came from the elementary school. In some of them fees were paid, but there was always a number of

[1] See article by Salter Davies in *The Schools of England*, p. 171.
[2] See Board of Education *Report* for 1912–13, p. 124.

free places. These schools had a strong vocational bias, determined by local needs, and they usually prepared for a group of allied trades, such as engineering or building. But some junior technical schools, especially in London, were more definitely 'trade schools,' and provided a more narrowly vocational training; for example, they might be oriented towards printing, the boot and shoe industry, tailoring, dressmaking. But at the same time all types of junior technical school gave a strong backing of general education, and in some of them even a foreign language was taught.

Junior commercial schools were also instituted to provide courses in shorthand, book-keeping, and allied subjects; but this kind of preparation, with a better general education behind it, was also given to senior pupils who wished for it in some 'secondary' schools of the normal type. For girls housewifery and pre-nursing courses were organised. Often a junior technical school contained two or three different departments of the kind described. Many of these schools developed a strong corporate life. Some of them entered candidates for the examinations of the Royal Society of Arts, or similar tests. Their teachers had a Burnham scale of salaries which, when it was first introduced in 1921, differed little from that for teachers in 'secondary' schools. It was provided, however, that a certain proportion of the staff in each junior technical school should have had industrial or workshop experience. As no special courses of professional training had been provided for teachers in technical schools, the McNair Committee turned its attention to this subject. It expressed the belief that "the training of the technical teacher, or at any rate the major part of it, should be undertaken after, rather than before, he has entered upon his work as a practising teacher";[1] and it suggested that "the area training authorities should report at frequent intervals to the Board of Education, so that systematic courses of training for technical teachers may be provided and recognised."[2] Much of the training would be provided in the technical colleges or schools themselves, and would be conducted by technical teachers; thus the technical institutions concerned would become

[1] McNair *Report*, p. 121.   [2] *Op. cit.*, p. 148.

part of the general training services of any given area. At the same time, some of the instruction given would be the same as that provided for other types of teacher and should be shared with them; and this would help to obviate the danger of segregating technical teachers in their training.

In most cases a junior technical school was included in a technical college for adolescents or adults; and junior art schools, run on junior technical school lines, were usually attached to a senior school of art. Junior technical schools, whatever form they took, proved of first-rate importance, and it seemed obvious that this type of education needed to be increased. Yet in 1937 there were in England and Wales only 220 junior technical schools of various kinds and 41 junior art departments in schools of art; the total of their pupils was 28,879.[1] With this we may contrast the provision of 'secondary' schools recognised by the Board of Education in the same year. There were 1,794 of these schools and they contained 558,097 pupils.[2] The relation of the junior technical school to other forms of post-primary education was rather ill-defined and unsatisfactory. So long as fees were payable in the 'grammar' schools and were higher than those in the junior technical schools, or if the latter did not charge any fees at all, parents tended to assume that a 'grammar'-school education was something intrinsically superior to that given in a junior technical school. The entry to the junior technical school at the age of thirteen also involved an awkward double break in the pupil's career, once the Hadow reorganisation, with its transfer to post-primary education at eleven plus, had been put into practice. One solution—which was adumbrated in the Spens *Report*—was to put grammar school and technical school on the same footing by abolishing fees in both and by making eleven plus the age of entry for *all* types of post-primary education. With the reorganisation of secondary education following on the 1944 Education Act the junior technical schools have become technical high schools or have been absorbed in some composite type of secondary school.

Continuative education, given in the evening after working

[1] See Spens *Report*, Table 16, p. 105.   [2] *Op. cit.*, Table 2, p. 91.

hours, has been available in various forms for the past hundred years or more.[1] The mechanics' institutes, for example, carried on their activities in the evening, and so did the evening continuation schools, which provided an elementary education for adolescents whose opportunities for ordinary schooling had been limited. Since 1926 the various types of school which give further education under these conditions have been officially known as "evening institutes." They cater either for adolescent or for adult students. In the case of the former—the junior evening institute—the pupils are usually under the age of sixteen or seventeen. Originally it was possible for students to take unco-ordinated subjects; but in 1907 the Board of Education suggested that a group system should be introduced by which each student followed a course composed of several allied subjects, including English. For adults the senior evening institute offers a wide variety of subjects, and there is no compulsion or persuasion to take grouped courses, except where examinations require this. Evening institute classes may often be held in the buildings of a day school or other educational institution. But there have also come into existence a number of colleges for further education, which have been specially built and equipped on a large scale; they often have enormous numbers of students and a staff adequate to meet all their requirements. They run full-time or part-time day courses for adolescents or adults; but they also cater fully for evening students. They even prepare for external degrees at London University, or in some cases have been affiliated to provincial universities. They provide courses for professional diplomas of many kinds and for the 'national certificates' which were instituted by the Board of Education in co-operation with various professional institutions—e.g. those of mechanical, electrical, and gas engineering, chemistry, and naval architecture. Sometimes employers have been willing to release their workers during the daytime to take courses at technical colleges of this kind; so that these have acted in such cases as a type of day continuation school. A good deal of technical education is also provided by the industrial firms themselves. Many of the larger

[1] See *supra*, p. 181.

engineering firms, for example, provide a systematic course of instruction for their trade apprentices who are taken straight from school. Thus there is often much co-operation between the firms which provide the 'internal' instruction in the works and the L.E.A.s which are responsible for the 'external' courses in the local technical colleges.[1]

The twentieth century has seen a great development in the institutions for advanced technical and scientific education which had been established in South Kensington. It will be remembered that these included the Royal College of Science and the Royal School of Mines, which traced their origin back to the period of the Great Exhibition. There was also the Central Technical College, which had been founded by the City and Guilds of London Institute in 1884, and which had devoted itself more particularly to the teaching of engineering. In 1904 the Board of Education appointed a departmental committee, under the chairmanship of Lord Haldane, to explore the possibilities of co-ordinating the work of these three institutions. Its *Report*, published in 1906, recommended "the establishment at South Kensington of an institution or group of associated colleges of science and technology where the highest specialised instruction should be given and where the fullest equipment for the most advanced training and research should be provided in various branches of science, especially in its application to industry, for which no sufficient provision exists elsewhere." The result was the establishment by Royal Charter in 1907 of the Imperial College of Science and Technology, which became a school of the University of London. Meanwhile the Normal School of Design, which had been founded as far back as 1837, had become—after the establishment of the Department of Practical Art in 1852—a National Training School of Art; and this in 1896 was renamed The Royal College of Art. It, like the Imperial College of Science and Technology, is situated in South Kensington. Its special object is "the training of Art Teachers of both sexes, of designers, and of Art workmen."

Many types of technical institution also afford opportunities for non-vocational continuative education; but this comes more

[1] See *infra*, p. 324.

particularly within the sphere of what since 1924 has been officially known as Adult Education. Hitherto this had not been separated from technical education; but in that year conditions of grant for the general and non-vocational education of adults were issued separately in the Regulations for Adult Education. The scope of these regulations was further enlarged in 1931. Adult education had been carried on by the universities ever since the 'extension' movement started in the seventies of the nineteenth century. It was in a way an outcome of the attempts which had been made to bring university education within the reach of women, and it owes much to the pioneer work of James Stuart of Cambridge.[1]

The movement has been supplemented by the foundation by Dr. Albert Mansbridge in 1903 of the Workers' Educational Association. Its aim was to bring together the co-operative societies, the trade unions, and the university extension authorities; and the scheme was first suggested in a series of articles which Mansbridge contributed to the *University Extension Journal*. But in the case of the W.E.A. the initiative has come rather from the side of the student than of the tutor. Its aim was to give working men and women opportunities of pursuing studies of a university type, under the direction of university teachers. Thus, in active co-operation with the universities, it has helped to develop adult education as an integral part of the national system, and to this end it receives assistance from the Ministry of Education. W.E.A. courses last in many cases for one year, though some may be continued as long as three years. The duration of a class is two hours, and a meeting is held normally once a week. The subjects of study cover a wide range, but economics, history, and literary topics are perhaps the most popular. The instruction includes lectures, discussions, and the preparation of essays. For students of the 'working class' who were able to take full-time courses lasting at least a year, Ruskin College was founded at Oxford in 1899. Its aim, in the words of one of its founders, was to "take men who have been merely condemning our institutions and to teach them, instead, to transform these institutions so that in place of talking against the world they will begin methodically and

[1] See *supra*, p. 182.

scientifically to possess the world." There was at first some confusion of aim and ideals, culminating in a split in 1909, when a separate Labour College was formed. Although this has since been closed, classes have been established in many industrial areas under the auspices of the 'Plebs League,' and a comprehensive organisation known as the National Council of Labour Colleges came into existence in 1921. This movement is less objective and more frankly sectional than that for which Ruskin College stands; it aims at providing instruction which will be of "practical usefulness to the workers in their class struggle."[1] Meanwhile Ruskin College continues the work for which it was first designed. It is a residential institution and since 1921 has been aided by public money. Although it does not, of course, form part of the University, some of its students read for university diplomas in such subjects as economics. Colleges of a somewhat similar type have been established at Harlech in Wales (Coleg Harlech), at Woodbrooke, Birmingham, and elsewhere.[2]

Sir Richard Livingstone has advocated the establishment of residential colleges for adult education, on the lines of the Danish People's High Schools. These would be run by L.E.A.s and would provide "for week-ends, or for weeks, of study." Their courses would be cultural and not vocational. They would, in fact, help to pull together our whole system of adult education, "to bring some order into the spiritual chaos of today and to create a democracy which had 'meat and raiment,' but in which the life was more than the meat and the body than the raiment."[3]

Another interesting form of adult education is provided by the women's institutes which are found particularly in country villages. They date from 1915 and they did admirable work during the first World War. By the end of 1932 there were some 5,000 institutes, with a membership of approximately 297,000. Every county in England and Wales had its own federation, and these were united in a National Federation of Women's Institutes. They arrange classes in cultural and recreational subjects, as well

[1] See J. F. and W. Horrabin, *Working-Class Education*.
[2] See *Residential Colleges for Adult Education*, published by the Educational Settlements Association.
[3] Livingstone, *The Future in Education*, p. 86.

as in domestic and other crafts; and they have usually a strong social side. For residents in urban areas the townswomen's guilds (started in 1933) perform a similar service.

A more fully developed attempt to focus the social and educational activities of an area is afforded by the community centre. In June 1929 a conference was held to consider what could be done to promote the growth of a healthy social life in the new housing estates which were being developed by local authorities. It was attended by representatives of the National Council of Social Service, the British Association of Residential Settlements, and the Educational Settlements Association. As a result of the conference a New Estates Community Committee (afterwards known as the Community Centres and Associations Committee) was set up, with Sir Ernest Barker as chairman. Within the next nine years other associations came into existence, not only in the larger cities, but also in some of the smaller towns, such as Reading and Taunton. By the summer of 1939 there were seventy Community Associations in existence, affiliated to the National Council of Social Service, and about two hundred schemes for the provision of community centres were in hand. Aid was given by the Carnegie Trustees, and in some cases by L.E.A.s. But these associations have sprung up and have been financed in many different ways. One of the largest and best equipped of them—that on the trading estate at Slough—was provided by the local employers whose workpeople benefited by the centre.

The object of a community association is the general well-being of the society which it serves. It aims at associating local authorities, voluntary organisations, and residents in a common effort to advance education, to promote health, and to foster a community spirit. To this end it establishes and maintains a community centre where its activities can be carried on. It includes such amenities as common rooms, a canteen, and a hall for lectures, meetings, dances, dramatic work, and the like. There should also be a gymnasium and craft rooms. At Slough there is a magnificent swimming-bath. It is possible that a branch library or a child welfare clinic will be accommodated in the centre; and it is sometimes advocated that a school should also be located on the site. Thus the centre aims at giving full expression to the social and cultural life of the community which it serves. It caters largely, but by no means exclusively, for the young men and women who live and work in its area; but it often includes also a junior membership for boys and girls between the ages of fourteen and eighteen. It is probable that the community centre will have points of contact with the day continuation school (or 'county college,' to give it the title conferred on it by the 1944 Education Act); but it has a rather wider outlook, although it is definitely associated with a specific community living together on a housing estate. It was hoped that one of the effects of the Education Act of 1944 would be to require L.E.A.s to play a greater part in relation to community centres than they have done hitherto, but owing to post-war difficulties a Ministry of Education circular of 1952 severely restricted building work at community centres, village halls, youth clubs and similar institutions. These restrictions have since been somewhat relaxed, but progress on the whole has been slow.

An important experiment in linking together the many-sided educational, cultural, and social activities of a definite region was provided by the Cambridgeshire village colleges. These owe their origin to the wisdom and vision of the County Education Secretary, Mr. Henry Morris. The first of these colleges was opened at Sawston in 1930, and others have since been erected in other parts of the county. Each serves a well-defined rural area. Its buildings house a secondary school, and the children are brought in by buses if they do not live in the village where the college happens to be. But in addition there is accommodation for adult education and all the amenities of a community centre. There are lecture rooms and common rooms for adults, a hall where concerts and dramatic performances and dances and cinematograph shows can be held, a branch of the county library, a workshop, a laboratory, a cookery room, a canteen, and adequate playing-fields. The parish council and the women's institute hold their meetings on the college premises. Thus the village college is at once a school, a club, and a cultural and recreational centre for old and young alike. If it is true, as a speaker at the British Association meeting in 1936 said,[1] "Education corporately administered is the principle of unity by which modern communities, whether urban or rural, can be significantly integrated at any stage of culture," then the village college provides an example of very far-reaching importance, and its implications are far from being confined to the purely rural area.

[1] See pp. 436–7 of B.A. *Report* for 1936.

Chapter XXXI

HELPING THE ADOLESCENT

Vocational Guidance. Juvenile Unemployment and Delinquency. Youth Service.

THE twentieth century has seen the development of many schemes to help the 'young person'—i.e. the boy or girl who has left school but has not yet attained the age of eighteen.[1] The chief problem facing the school-leaver is that of 'getting a job.' So long as this was left to chance, many square pegs got into round holes, and the State suffered thereby as well as the individuals concerned. To obviate this situation systems of 'vocational guidance' have been devised. This implies not only guiding the school-leaver into that particular occupation where he will find his greatest interest and realise his capacities to the utmost, but also giving him information about his duties and opportunities and the knowledge and training required in any particular sphere. In addition it necessitates acquainting him with the state of the labour market and his chances of obtaining the kind of post for which he seems best suited.

A good deal has always been done by the heads of post-primary schools, and in some such schools 'careers masters' have been appointed. But it is difficult for members of a school staff to get the leisure and the opportunities to carry out this work adequately; and for that reason the help of the school must be supplemented by specially constituted outside agencies. In 1910 the Education (Choice of Employment) Act enabled L.E.A.s "to give boys and girls information, advice, and assistance with respect to the choice of employment." But some of the labour exchanges, set up by an Act of 1909, had already established juvenile departments, and there was thus some overlapping of effort. This was increased when in 1920 unemployment insurance was extended to boys and girls of 16. In 1923, therefore, L.E.A.s were given the choice of administering their own juvenile employment service or leaving

[1] See *supra*, p. 254n.

it to the Ministry of Labour. This arrangement lasted until towards the end of the second World War. The *Report* of a Committee appointed to consider the situation resulted in the Employment and Training Act of 1948.[1] A Youth Employment Executive was formed, its function being to advise the Minister of Labour (who remained responsible) on all matters relating to the Service. Each L.E.A. could decide whether it would provide a Youth Employment Service; and 128 out of 181 had done so by 1953. In the remaining areas the Service was administered by the Ministry of Labour through the local employment exchanges. The scheme, though somewhat illogical, seems to work.

The bureaux and exchanges have done important work; but, in view of the large numbers of school-leavers with which they have to deal, they have had to work largely on empirical lines. A more ambitious and scientific method of vocational guidance is that given by the National Institute of Industrial Psychology, which was founded in 1921. A carefully thought-out series of psychological and other tests, lasting about three hours, is set to each candidate for guidance, and it is conducted by a team of experts. For this reason it is an expensive process, and it has therefore been used mainly for pupils leaving school at the age of sixteen to eighteen, whose parents can afford to pay the fees involved. It also takes account only of the suitability of the candidate, and is not concerned with the possibility of securing the kind of post to which he seems suited. At present, therefore, a system of this kind can be applied only to a limited extent; but it would be advantageous if some of the technique of the National Institute of Industrial Psychology could be combined with the activities of the youth employment bureau in giving vocational guidance. In this way the interests and capacities of the school-leaver might be so far as possible correlated with the occupational opportunities that happen to be available. A few L.E.A.s (e.g. Birmingham and Warrington) have actually experimented along these lines.

Reference may here be made to the attempts which were made after the first World War to deal with school-leavers who found difficulty in obtaining jobs. In November 1918 juvenile

[1] For details see *Report* of National Youth Employment Council, 1947–50.

unemployment centres, conducted by L.E.A.s, were set up to provide educational and recreative activities for young people who could not get work. Further schemes were tried out from time to time, and in 1929 the title was changed to 'junior instruction centres.' The whole matter was tied up with the question of unemployment insurance. Under Section 15 of the Unemployment Insurance Act of 1930 "the Minister [of Labour], after consultation with the Board of Education, shall . . . make arrangements with local education authorities for the provision, as far as is practicable, of approved courses of instruction for insured contributors under the age of eighteen years who claim benefit." But the minimum age for entry into unemployment insurance was sixteen, so that between leaving school and the age of sixteen there was a period when the 'young person' was non-insurable.

However, the Unemployment Act of 1934 carried the matter a stage farther. The Ministry of Labour, in an explanatory note on this Act, said: "The Unemployment Act provides for the establishment of courses of instruction for unemployed boys and girls between school-leaving age and eighteen years of age. For the first time a statutory obligation is imposed on education authorities to provide such courses as may be necessary. . . . For the first time also the Minister is empowered to require the attendance at an authorised course of instruction of any boy or girl between the school-leaving age and eighteen years of age who is capable of and available for work but has no work, or only part-time or intermittent work." Between 1918 and 1934 over a million young persons had passed through the junior instruction centres; and in December 1934 there were in Great Britain 111 centres and 13 classes for unemployed juveniles, with a total attendance of 18,887. In his *Report* on *Junior Instruction Centres and their Future*[1] Mr. Valentine Bell says that their object was "to guide young persons in the ways of spending their leisure time in order that their personalities may be developed or saved from the destruction of individuality wrought by modern methods of mechanisation. . . . It is the use of leisure time that is of such importance to the youth of today, for in the future this may be

[1] P. 77.

increased owing to the shortening of routine working hours, and the increase of part-time work." But the junior instruction centre was a palliative, and not a solution, for the problem of juvenile unemployment. It was difficult to organise coherent courses in them, for the membership was always fluctuating; and there also was no real incentive for boys and girls to attend an educational institution, so long as the work was regarded as a kind of penalty for being unemployed. A more satisfactory method of tackling the problem would have been the raising of the school-leaving age and the institution of day continuative education for all young persons, whether they happened to be employed or not.

Juvenile unemployment is one problem and another is juvenile delinquency. How far law-breaking by children is criminal, and how far due to bad home conditions or merely a manifestation of a spirit of adventure or mischief, may perhaps be debated. But it is obvious that treatment should be preventive and educational rather than penal. The practice of sending children under fourteen to prison was not abolished until the passing of the Children Act in 1908. This also set up special juvenile courts for dealing with offenders aged from seven to sixteen. The Children and Young Persons Act of 1933 raised the ages to eight and seventeen. Young offenders, awaiting the hearing of their case, were to be detained if necessary in what is known as a 'remand home'; but in the event the provision of such homes proved inadequate. A system of probation, by which delinquents are put under some form of supervision, has come extensively into use. If a child's home is considered to be unsuitable, he may be committed for a term of years to a hostel or home or "to the care of a fit person, whether relative or not, who is willing to undertake the care of him." But if it is decided that he needs institutional treatment, he may be sent back to a remand home until he can be admitted to an 'approved school'—i.e. one which has been approved by the Home Office for the reception of delinquents.[1] Approved schools are, of course, residential, and they cater for three age-

---

[1] A beginning has been made with a scheme for assessing delinquents in 'classifying schools' before deciding which particular approved schools are likely to be most suitable for them. See *Making Citizens* (H.M.S.O., 1945).

groups of delinquents—junior schools for those admitted under the age of thirteen; intermediate for entrants aged thirteen to fifteen, and senior for those aged fifteen to seventeen.[1] In the first group the curriculum is much the same as that of the ordinary school; in the intermediate approved school the work is partly vocational; while for the seniors many kinds of industrial and technical courses are provided. Delinquents are committed for a period of three years, but this is usually reduced; for, when it is considered advisable to do so, they may be released on 'licence' and sent out into some form of employment. They are 'followed up' for another three years, either by the head of the school or someone acting for him, or under the supervision of a local probation officer. How far this system is successful may be judged from the fact that about 20 per cent. of the boys, and rather less than this number of the girls, who have passed through an approved school have been found guilty of new offences within three years of leaving.[2]

For older and more serious offenders there are the Borstal institutions. In 1902 some convicted youths, aged sixteen to twenty-one, were sent to a disused prison at Borstal, near Rochester, to be trained on industrial lines apart from adult criminals. Their régime was designed to teach self-reliance and self-respect, and arrangements were made to find them work when they left the establishment. In 1964 there were twenty-four Borstal institutions for boys and two for girls. By Section 1 of the Prevention of Crime Act of 1908 the court, before sending an offender between the ages of sixteen and twenty-one to such an institution, must be "satisfied that the character, state of health, and mental condition of the offender, and the other circumstances of the case, are such that the offender is likely to profit by such instruction and discipline;"[3] and that "by reason of his criminal habits, or

[1] For girls there are normally only two types of approved school—junior, taking in delinquents under the age of fifteen, and senior for girls admitted between the ages of fifteen and seventeen.

[2] See Mayer, *Young People in Trouble*, p. 38. For details of more recent developments consult Hall, *The Social Services of the Modern England*, pt. III, and the White Paper *Penal Practice in a Changing Society* (1959).

[3] *Prevention of Crime Act*, 1908, § 1.

tendencies, or association with persons of bad character, it is expedient that he should be subject to detention." The length of the detention is not less than two, and not more than three, years, and its object is "training rather than punishment."[1] The Borstal system has been criticised on various grounds, but it is said to have proved beneficial, especially where the maximum period of detention has been imposed.[2]

Juvenile unemployment and delinquency are urgent problems and have called for serious attention; but a more fundamental consideration is how best to meet the needs of young people of all types, whether they be in trouble or not. It is from a realisation of this situation that the movement known as 'youth service' has grown. For many years past much had been done by voluntary effort, outside the schools, to meet the physical, mental, and spiritual needs of young people. The Young Men's Christian Association, for example, dates from as early as 1844. It started with twelve members and was founded to promote "the spiritual welfare of young men engaged in the drapery and other trades by the introduction of religious services among them." During the last 100 years the Y.M.C.A. has expanded enormously both in its numbers and in the range of its activities. The Y.W.CA. dates from 1855. The National Associations of Boys' Clubs and of Girls' and Mixed Clubs also have a large membership and many affiliated clubs, which provide social and intellectual opportunities, particularly for young workers. The pioneer of 'uniformed' organisations is the Boys' Brigade, founded in 1883. It has a semi-military organisation and is definitely religious in character. The Boy Scouts, which owe their origin in 1908 to the genius of Lord Baden-Powell, have since become a world-wide movement and have been followed by the Girl Guides, who came into existence in 1910. All these agencies have not only had a great social significance, but they have also helped to widen popular ideas as to what education really means, and they have thus reacted

[1] See chap. vi and Appendix E of *Prisons and Borstals* (H.M.S.O., 1945).
[2] A short-lived, but noteworthy, attempt to deal with the problem of juvenile delinquency was made by Homer Lane at Batcombe in Dorsetshire (1914–18). It was modelled on the Junior Republics started in America by W. R. George. Consult Bazeley, *Homer Lane and the Little Commonwealth*.

beneficially on the curriculum and organisation of schools. In estimating the development of 'youth service' in recent years it is important, therefore, not to overlook the contribution which, during so long a period, has been made by these, and many other, voluntary bodies.

So far as the State was concerned, its interest is of much more recent growth and at first was directed mainly towards the physical welfare of young people. This may not have been altogether unconnected with military considerations and with the deterioration of political conditions on the Continent of Europe. In 1935 the silver jubilee of King George V was commemorated by the establishment of the King George's Jubilee Trust. The funds raised were devoted largely to the purchase of playing-fields. The National Fitness Council was set up in 1937 to administer Government grants for improving physical training and providing facilities for recreation. But in September 1939 the National Fitness Council was replaced by the National Youth Committee, which took a wider view of what 'youth welfare' meant; and this was made clear in a circular (No. 1486) of more than usual importance, issued by the Board of Education in November of the same year. It pointed out that in spite of the efforts of the voluntary organisations and of the L.E.A.s there was still a lack of provision of opportunities for the social and physical development of boys and girls between the ages of fourteen and twenty, who had ceased full-time education. It urged every L.E.A. to "take steps to see that properly constituted Youth Committees exist in their areas." The duty of these committees would be to ascertain local needs and decide where assistance could best be given, and by so doing to strengthen the hands of local authorities and voluntary organisations. There was a large response to this appeal, and in a further circular (No. 1503) of March 1940 the Board made clear the grants which were available for youth service and the conditions under which they would be made. In June 1940 the Board issued yet another circular (1516), entitled *The Challenge of Youth*, which was designed to give some guidance to L.E.A. Youth Committees on the general aim and scope of their work. This was defined as "developing the whole personality of individual boys and girls to enable them to take their place as full members of a free community."

Thus youth welfare was recognised as a province of further education side by side with primary and secondary education. There was to be no State-controlled uniformity. The function of the State was to focus the efforts of youth service, and to supplement the resources of voluntary organisations. The L.E.A.s' part was to encourage existing organisations and fill up gaps where they existed. Thus there should be no clash between statutory and voluntary effort, but rather "variety of approach with a common purpose."

The situation had something in common with that in the field of elementary education in 1870; and it is obvious that the Board of Education was anxious to avoid any of the possible difficulties which the existence of a 'dual system' might involve. In November 1940 a circular (No. 1529), dealing with Youth, Physical Recreation, and Service, announced that a Directorate of Physical Recreation was to be set up in order "to strengthen the Service of Youth on a side on which it is at present liable to be increasingly handicapped," owing to the calling-up of many organisers and leaders of physical recreation, and the commandeering of premises and playing-fields. Reference was also made to the Youth Service Corps, which had been started in Suffolk under the title of 'Youth Squads,' in order to encourage young people, on their own initiative, to organise and undertake jobs of national importance. A further impulse to the youth organisations was given by the Government's decision at the end of 1941 that all boys and girls between the ages of sixteen and eighteen should be required to register. After doing this, those who had not already associated themselves with some youth organisation were interviewed and encouraged to do so.

Meanwhile, under the impact of the war, various types of pre-service training were becoming available. For many years past the public schools and other secondary schools had possessed contingents of the junior[1] Officers' Training Corps. This system had grown out of the volunteer movement of the 1860's, and the

[1] The senior O.T.C.s were attached to universities.

school 'cadet corps'—as they had been called—were reorganised as part of the Territorial Force in 1908. Their contingents were recognised by the War Office, and they received a grant in respect of every cadet who became 'efficient.' But the scheme had in view only the training of future officers, and it was restricted to the type of school from which a supply of such candidates would chiefly be recruited. The application of conscription, not only to men, but even to women, during the second World War, enormously increased the demand for pre-service training. In 1941 the Air Training Corps, for boys of sixteen (subsequently fourteen) to eighteen, came into existence, and it was supplemented by Sea Cadets and Army Cadets. Other pre-service organisations catered for girls. In some cases these pre-service units were actually attached to schools, as the original O.T.C.s had been. The pre-service organisations, though largely the outcome of wartime conditions, were not simply concerned with preparatory military training; they catered for the social and recreative needs of their members and they were in a very real sense 'youth organisations.'

In 1942 the National Youth Committee, which had been responsible for developing facilities for youth welfare and starting off the L.E.A.s on their activities in this field, was dissolved and replaced by the National Youth Advisory Council. It included representatives of all kinds of youth organisation—voluntary and statutory—as well as the pre-service corps and churches and employers. Its function was to consider and advise on problems remitted to it by the Board of Education, to act as a channel by which information concerning the Youth Service and its problems could reach the Board, and to train men to originate ideas for the improvement of the Youth Service and to put suggestions to the Board. One of the chief problems which youth organisations of all kinds have had to face is the training of those who, perhaps rather unfortunately, are called 'youth leaders.' Many of the voluntary bodies already have their own schemes, but much has also been done by universities and training colleges; and it is obvious that there must—or should—be a close relationship between the training of these 'leaders' and of those who are to teach

in schools. The McNair Committee gave considerable attention
to these problems. They recommended that three-year courses of
training should be provided to enable men and women to qualify
for full-time posts as youth leaders; but that in cases where a
candidate had already had adequate experience of this kind of
work, the course might be shorter, though not less than a year.
They further desired that service in youth organisations should
be linked up with ordinary teaching in schools. To this end they
suggested that the salaries of youth leaders should be comparable
with those paid to teachers and that service in a youth organisation should be made pensionable. To facilitate easy transference
from the one type of service to the other, it would be necessary
to link their superannuation schemes. It was hoped that the
training of youth leaders "during the first five years should be
regarded as experimental, and that before the end of that period
the Board of Education should review the experience of each area
with a view to systematising, so far as may be necessary, the
qualifications required for recognition as a youth leader and out-
lining the nature of the courses of training which they will recognise and aid."[1] It is obvious that an adequate supply of suitable and well-qualified leaders is essential to the successful development of youth service as an integral part of the national
system of education.[2]

[1] McNair *Report*, p. 147.   [2] See *infra*, p. 333.

Chapter XXXII

THE WAR AND THE 1944 ACT

Evacuation and its Effects. The Green Book and the White Paper. The Butler
Act and its Implications.

THE outbreak of the second World War in September 1939
had disastrous effects on the national system of education.
Before the actual declaration of hostilities a large proportion of children were evacuated from urban areas which it was
expected would be the object of enemy air attacks, and they were
moved to reception areas where it was hoped they would be safe.
It is difficult to make generalisations about so complex an operation, and conditions varied enormously as between one district
and another. The administration of the evacuation scheme was
shared between the Ministries of Health, of Transport, and of
Home Security, with the co-operation of the Board of Education.
The actual evacuating and transport were on the whole efficient
and successful; but most of the real difficulties arose in the reception areas. There was first the problem of billets for the children.
Even more difficult was the provision of school places for the
hosts of pupils who flowed into the reception areas. In some cases
a 'double-shift' system was put into force, by which the home
school and the visiting school used the same buildings at different
times. This cut down the actual hours of teaching in both schools,
but outdoor activities of some kind were arranged by the school
authorities for the off-sessions. Another method was to put the
evacuated school into some hall or similar building, which was
seldom well adapted to this purpose. Sometimes a school had to
work as best it could in several buildings situated at some distance
one from another. A third scheme for dealing with evacuated
children was to absorb them into existing schools in the reception
areas. This resulted in overcrowded classes and all kinds of time-
table difficulties. As the Permanent Secretary of the Board of

Education said in 1939:[1] "The type of senior school provided in a rural area is something very different, both in scope of buildings and in types of subjects taught, from a senior school provided in a highly urbanised area."

The general result has been roundly described as an "educational mess";[2] but the effects of it were minimised by the devoted work of inspectors of the Board of Education and of L.E.A. officials and of the heads and assistant teachers of evacuated and receiving schools alike. Their names were conspicuously absent from the Honours Lists, but no body of civilians served their country better during the stress of war. There were also some positive benefits to be gained from evacuation. Against the loss due to lack of proper buildings or equipment or grading may be set the claim that in many cases evacuated children benefited in body and mind alike by being moved from urban to rural areas. Town and country had for too long been "two Englands." Now they were brought together as never before. The children—and their teachers too—found new interests, new ways of approach to their work, new experiences, a new freedom from routine. But because evacuation was voluntary and not compulsory, a large number of children were kept in the danger zone. In January 1940 the percentage remaining in the evacuation areas varied from 62 per cent. in Liverpool to 97 per cent. in Rotherham. The average for all such areas was 80 per cent.[3] But in the so-called 'vulnerable' districts all State schools, after the evacuation had been completed, were closed by Government order, and the buildings were taken over for all kinds of 'civil defence' organisations, or by the military authorities. Thus the work of education practically ceased. Attempts were made in some places to provide a minimum of education for unevacuated children by sending peripatetic teachers to instruct them in their homes—a not very satisfactory expedient. The situation became so serious that on February 7th, 1940, L.E.A.s were instructed by the Board to prepare to resume the operation of compulsory school attendance.

[1] Sir Maurice Holmes in evidence before Select Committee on Estimates Minutes, p. 192).
[2] Padley and Cole, *Evacuation Survey*, p. 5.   [3] *Op. cit.*, table i, pp. 46–7.

By the end of the year the number of children left in London had been reduced to 80,000, of whom 30,000 were at school. But meanwhile incalculable damage had been done. It was said that many children had forgotten how to read, and that even those who remained in schools in evacuation areas had to spend a large part of their time in air-raid shelters, where no kind of satisfactory instruction could be given.

The national system of education, like our bombed cities, suffered grievously during the war; but those responsible for it and interested in it—like the inhabitants of those cities—carried on, improvising and repairing the damage wherever it was possible, and looking forward always to reconstruction on better lines than had ever been in the past. It is not without significance that the Education Acts of 1870, 1902, 1918, and 1944 were passed in a time of war; and it would seem that men's minds, in a revulsion against the folly and waste and false values of war, turn to education as the one hope for the future—though there are not wanting those also who are interested in education primarily as a means of promoting military efficiency. The great danger is that the lesson may be forgotten when the emergency is past. It is certainly true that public opinion during the war years was increasingly interested in education and increasingly determined to make educational facilities more adequate and more easily accessible to those who could profit by them. A scheme for putting these rather vague aspirations into practice was outlined in a tentative document issued in June 1941. It had been drawn up by some officials of the Board of Education and is usually known as the 'Green Book.'

The object of this memorandum was to serve as a basis of preliminary talks between the Board and the accredited representatives of local authorities, teachers' associations, and other local bodies with which the Board was associated in the educational service. The document was issued to the organisations concerned and was marked 'confidential'; but, as Professor Lester Smith observes,[1] "it was distributed in such a blaze of secrecy that it achieved an unusual degree of publicity." In answer to questions

[1] *To Whom do Schools Belong?*, p. 202.

in the House of Commons, the President of the Board, Mr. R. A. Butler, promised to publish a short statement indicating the major subjects covered by the memorandum. This summary appeared in October 1941; but, whereas the original document had made detailed and definite suggestions covering almost every aspect of national education, the so-called 'summary' consisted of a list of subjects for discussion, set largely in the form of questions. It included such topics as the raising of the school-leaving age and the allowing of exemptions, the re-defining of primary and secondary education, and the justification for retaining separate L.E.A.s for dealing only with primary education. Other subjects suggested for debate were free secondary schooling and one code for all types of secondary education; the promotion of the physical well-being of children and young people; youth service; an extended system of technical training; the provision of nursery schools; the recruitment, training, and remuneration of teachers; the working of the 'dual system'; the establishment of a unified system of aid to enable students to proceed to universities.

The appearance of the 'Green Book' provoked a considerable response from the organisations and authorities which received it, and there followed a spate of memoranda dealing with educational reform issued by organisations of many types—local authorities, political bodies, churches, and professional associations. Mr. Butler and Mr. Chuter Ede, the Parliamentary Secretary of the Board of Education, gave the fullest consideration to this response, interviewing deputations and touring the country. The results of their labours were shown in a parliamentary White Paper, issued in July 1943, and bearing the title *Educational Reconstruction*. *The Times*[1] not unjustly called it a landmark in English education, and said that it promised "the greatest and grandest educational advance since 1870." Its central proposal was that the statutory system of public education should be organised in three progressive stages—primary, secondary, and further education. This was indeed the logical outcome of the scheme first adumbrated in the Hadow *Report*. 'Elementary' education would disappear; there would be no longer 'elementary' schools taking children up to the

[1] July 24th, 1943.

age of fourteen or fifteen and overlapping with 'secondary' schools receiving pupils from the age of eleven or even younger. The system of local educational administration would also have to be adjusted to this new lay-out. The school-leaving age should be raised to fifteen without exceptions, and ultimately to sixteen; and fees should be abolished in all maintained secondary schools. Compulsory part-time education in working hours should be provided for young persons up to the age of sixteen. Nursery schools should be established wherever they were needed. The abolition of the special-place examination and the adoption of "other arrangements for the classification of the children when they passed from primary to secondary schools" would free junior schools from the evil effects of a competitive test and help them to foster "the potentialities of children at an age when their minds are nimble and receptive, their curiosity strong, their imagination fertile, and their spirits high"—a delightful phrase. The White Paper also dealt with provision for technical and adult education and for youth service. It referred to the need for reform in methods of recruiting and training teachers—a subject which was at the time being investigated by the McNair Committee—and to the problem of access to the universities, with which the Norwood Committee was also dealing. The administrative problems involved in the existence of the dual system were also discussed, and in order to give increased assistance to voluntary schools, with a corresponding extension of public control, it was proposed to revive the provisions of the Education Act of 1936.

The White Paper received a cordial welcome. In a two days' debate on educational reconstruction the House of Commons "showed itself of one mind to a degree rare in Parliamentary annals. . . . Not a single voice was raised in favour of holding up or whittling down any one of the proposals for educational advance."[1] Mr. Butler was thus able to carry on with his hands strengthened. There were inevitable practical difficulties in launching so vast and complex a scheme of reform—the problem of recruiting and training a large enough body of teachers to work

[1] *The Times*, July 31st, 1943.

the plan; the inevitable provision of new schools and the renovation of old ones at a time when the building industry was severely handicapped by war conditions; the "ancient and complicated problem of the dual system"—as Mr. Butler called it; the unwillingness of Part III authorities to forgo their control of elementary education. But patience and good-will smoothed out many of these difficulties, and when in January 1944 Mr. Butler laid his Education Bill before the House of Commons it was debated in an atmosphere very different from that in which most educational legislation had previously been carried through. The Bill became law on August 3rd, 1944; as Professor H. C. Dent has said, it "makes possible as important and substantial an advance in public education as this country has ever known."[1]

The Education Act of 1944 is set out in five parts, of which the last deals mainly with the bringing of the Act into operation and the definition of various terms used in it. An attempt will therefore be made to summarise only the other four parts which contain the gist of the reforms which the Act involves. The first clauses deal with the Central Administration. The Board was replaced by a Ministry of Education.[2] The duty of the Minister is "to promote the education of the people of England and Wales and the progressive development of institutions devoted to that purpose, and to secure the effective execution by local authorities, under his control and direction, of the national policy for providing a varied and comprehensive educational service in every area."[3] The Act also brought into existence two advisory councils, one for England and one for Wales, which would have wider scope than the old Consultative Committee; their duty would be to advise the Minister, not only upon questions referred to them by him, but also upon such matters connected with educational theory and practice as they thought fit.

The Act goes on to deal with the statutory system of education. The duty of L.E.A.s to maintain and keep efficient all public elementary schools in their areas was converted into a duty to

[1] Dent, *The Education Act*, 1944, p. 3.

[2] An Education Bill, introduced by the Duke of Marlborough in 1868, had proposed the appointment of a Minister of Education.

[3] *Education Act*, 1944, part I, § 1.

secure adequate provision of both primary and secondary schools. This meant that from April 1st, 1945, when this part of the Act came into operation, the 169 existing Part III authorities would be abolished. There had been much heartburning on this subject, and for this reason a compromise had been effected. It was set out in the first Schedule to the Act. Where two or more counties or county boroughs were too small to undertake by themselves the full educational responsibilities of their area, a joint education board might be created for this purpose. Moreover, bodies called 'divisional executives' could be set up in counties and empowered in their own areas to exercise on behalf of the L.E.A. "such functions relating to primary and secondary education as may be specified," [1] but the L.E.A. was not empowered to delegate to these divisional executives the power of borrowing money or raising a rate. Boroughs or urban districts with a total population of more than 60,000 could claim the status of 'excepted districts' which had rather more extended powers than divisional executives, but, like them, no financial ones.

By Section 11 of the Act every L.E.A. was required to survey the educational facilities and needs of its area and to submit, within a year of April 1st, 1945, a development plan covering the whole field of primary and secondary education. In doing so, it had to keep in view the new structure of the educational system. The category 'elementary' was abolished and, in the words of the Act, "the statutory system of public education shall be organised in three progressive stages to be known as primary education, secondary education, and further education; and it shall be the duty of the local education authority for every area, so far as their powers extend, to contribute towards the spiritual, moral, mental, and physical development of the community by securing that efficient education throughout those stages shall be available to meet the needs of the population of their area." [2] In order to do this L.E.A.s were required to secure an adequate provision of schools for primary and secondary education in separate institutions. They were also to see that nursery schools or nursery

[1] *Op. cit.*, First Schedule, part iii.
[2] *Op. cit.*, § 7.

classes were available for children under five, and that the needs of children suffering from any disability of mind or body should be met in special schools. The authorities were to have regard to "the expediency of securing the provision of boarding accommodation, either in boarding schools or otherwise, for pupils for whom education as boarders is considered by their parents and by the authority to be desirable."[1]

The thorny problem of 'dual control' was met by a compromise, which all the parties concerned agreed to accept—a striking example of the new spirit in which the Bill was debated. As all types of post-primary school now became 'secondary,' this implied an extension of the 'dual system.' Voluntary schools were divided into three classes. 'Aided' schools were eligible for a 50 per cent. grant towards external repairs and alterations, but the salaries of their teachers and the cost of other repairs were to be borne by the L.E.A. The second class—the 'special-agreement' schools—was a product of the 1936 Act. In order to aid voluntary schools in carrying out the reorganisation necessitated by the Hadow scheme and the proposed raising of the school-leaving age, L.E.A.s had been enabled to enter into agreements with managers to make grants of between 50 per cent. and 75 per cent. towards the cost of erecting or extending non-provided schools for senior pupils.[2] Five hundred and nineteen agreements had been made, but owing to the outbreak of war only thirty-seven had materialised. The 1944 Act provided that the remaining agreements could be revived and repeated the regulation of the 1936 Act with regard to 'reserved' teachers. Finally there was the class of 'controlled' schools. Here the whole cost of maintenance fell on the L.E.A. It was enacted that the L.E.A. must inform the managers or governors of a controlled voluntary school before appointing any particular candidate as head of it, and must consult them as to the appointment of reserved teachers for religious instruction.

The primary and secondary schools (other than nursery and special schools) which were maintained by an L.E.A., and which prior to the Act had been called 'provided,' were renamed county

[1] *Op. cit.*, § 8.   [2] See *supra*, p. 279.

schools. Here the appointment and dismissal of teachers would be in the hands of the authority, unless the rules of management or articles of government provided otherwise; so also as regards the instruction, both religious and secular. In addition to the primary and secondary schools—whether they were 'county' or voluntary (with its three subdivisions)—there were also the nursery schools and the special schools. The direct-grant schools, which received their aid direct from the central authority, and the independent schools remained apart. Thus the Act retained a variety of types of school, differing as to their administration and purpose, and in their relation to the local authorities. It laid down that in every county and voluntary school religious instruction should be given, and that the school day should begin with an act of collective worship; though, of course, the right of withdrawal on conscientious grounds was safeguarded. This is the first time in our educational history that religious instruction and 'school prayers' have been specifically enforced by Act of Parliament, and it affords striking evidence of our national unwillingness to add 'secular' to the formula 'universal, compulsory, and gratuitous,' which, as Adamson points out, was the "aim in the educational sphere which English Radicals and Liberals strove to attain throughout the nineteenth century."[1] But it was laid down in Clause 36 of the Act that in a county school the religious instruction should be in accordance with an 'agreed syllabus,'[2] and that the collective act of worship should not be distinctive of any particular denomination. In a controlled school denominational religious instruction might be given "during not more than two periods in each week."[3] In aided and special-agreement schools the religious teaching "shall be under the control of the managers or governors of the school and shall be in accordance with any provisions of the trust deed relating to the school, or, where provision for that purpose is not made by such a deed, in accordance with the practice observed in the school before it became a voluntary school."[4]

The Act went on to deal with the problem of school govern-

---

[1] *English Education*, 1760–1902, p. 7.   [2] See *supra*, p. 238.
[3] *Education Act*, 1944, § 27.   [4] *Op. cit.*, § 28.

ance. Primary schools were to have a body of not less than six 'managers,' while secondary schools would have 'governors' whose numbers were not limited in this way. The L.E.A. was to appoint the governing or managing body of a county school, and was to be represented on that of a voluntary school. If it appeared desirable, an L.E.A. could set up a single governing body for two or more of its maintained schools, whether county or voluntary. Other important provisions of the Act were the raising of the school-leaving age to fifteen without exemptions from a date which was decided to be April 1st, 1945, but which was subsequently postponed. The age was to be further raised to sixteen as soon as conditions made it possible. In addition, the provision of the Fisher Act with regard to day continuation schools were to be revived and fully implemented. A duty was laid on L.E.A.s to establish, not later than three years after the coming into operation of Part II of the Act, institutions which would be known as county colleges. These would give part-time education in working hours to young persons up to the age of eighteen for 330 hours in a year. The responsibility for attendance at such a college was laid upon the young person himself, and not upon his parents, and it would be the duty of the L.E.A. to direct him, by means of a 'college attendance order,' to attend at a specified centre. The Act further abolished fees for day pupils in schools maintained by L.E.A.s—secondary as well as primary —and charges for boarding could also be remitted. In spite of the recommendations of the Fleming Committee, fees were retained in direct-grant schools, except, of course, for those pupils who held 'free or reserved places.' L.E.A.s were empowered to provide boots and clothing for children who needed them, but the cost could be recovered from parents who were able to pay. In addition, meals, milk and other refreshments were to be provided. The conditions of employment of young people were also adapted so as to meet the new situation created by the raising of the school-leaving age and the institution of county colleges.

Part III of the Act (which was to come into effect on an 'appointed day') was concerned with 'independent' schools. It provided for the inspection and registration of private schools. If a school were regarded as unsatisfactory, it might be refused registration or removed from the register; but the proprietor would be given 'notice of complaint' before such a step was taken, and he would have the right of appeal to an Independent Schools Tribunal. Part IV, covered a number of general provisions. L.E.A.s were given power to defray the necessary incidental expenses of children attending maintained schools, and also the fees and expenses of pupils in fee-charging schools. They were empowered to grant scholarships and to aid educational research. The Minister was to see that salary scales for teachers, as recommended by the committee or committees appointed by him to deal with this matter and as approved by him, were duly paid by L.E.A.s. No woman was to be debarred from holding a post as a teacher by reason of marriage.

The 1944 Education Act contains 122 clauses and eight schedules. For this reason it is not easy to make a *précis* of it; but enough, perhaps, has been said to show its importance. The Acts of 1870, 1902, 1918, 1936, and 1944, taken together, afford an excellent example of what Dicey calls "our inveterate prejudice for fragmentary and gradual legislation."[1] We are now at last presented with a co-ordinated system of national education. Hitherto there had been a system of 'elementary' schools taking pupils up to the age of fourteen. These had gradually developed out of a plan to provide education of an inferior kind for children of the poorer classes, and, in spite of the great advance—especially since 1902—they had never entirely lost this stigma. Overlapping with this system were the 'secondary' schools taking in pupils at the age of about eleven and keeping them till sixteen or later. These had inherited the tradition of the old endowed schools with their more academic curriculum; and although this too had been greatly modified with the passage of time, they tended to retain something of their social superiority. The 1944 Act swept away the conception of 'elementary' education and provided a framework in which the recommendations of the Hadow *Report*, with its insistence on 'parity of status' for all forms of post-primary education, could be realised. But it said nothing about the 'types' of

[1] *Law and Opinion in England*, p. 28.

secondary school,[1] with which the Hadow, Spens, and Norwood Committees had been so much concerned; and therefore it did not raise the crucial problem of how to select children for post-primary education if the different types are retained. It is good to realise with Tacitus that a thing is not necessarily inferior because it is different;[2] but it is one thing to provide machinery and another thing to make it work. For example, it is not enough to rename a 'senior' school 'secondary,' so long as its buildings and equipment are far inferior to those of a neighbouring grammar school which has always enjoyed this title. The general public, who may not be particularly interested in educational legislation, tends to judge of these matters differently from the administrator.

There remained, moreover, after the passing of the Act some anomalies which seemed to many people to counteract its spirit. Fees in maintained secondary schools were abolished, but they were retained in direct-grant schools. Many of these latter schools at once raised their fees, and by so doing emphasised the spirit of social exclusiveness which the Act was designed to exorcise. The cleavage was now more marked than ever between the free maintained secondary school and the fee-charging direct-grant school. It is true that some of the direct-grant schools decided to become maintained schools; but a few, on the other hand, by raising endowment funds, gave up their direct grant and became independent schools. The continued existence of schools of this type, outside the national system, is also a problem which awaits solution. Even if, as the Fleming Report suggested, independent schools were to take 25 per cent. of their pupils as free-placers from the State-aided schools, it would still be possible for well-to-do parents to secure a majority of the places in such schools, solely by reason of their ability to pay the high fees which are charged. It would also, presumably, still be possible to enter a boy for such a school as soon as he is born; and, if so, the test of 'ability to profit' is meaningless. The criticism has therefore been made that the 'privileged' school still exists in spite of the Act; and in addition

---

[1] See *supra*, pp. 253–6.
[2] "Nec statim deterius esse quod diversum est." *Dialogus de Oratoribus*, chap. 18.

to the difficulty of making the public believe that there is 'parity of status' as between the various types of free secondary school, there may remain the further problem of making it clear that the maintained grammar school is not in some way an inferior type of institution to the direct-grant or independent school. As the *Journal of Education* has said,[1] "the maintained grammar schools now include very many of ancient and more recent foundation whose repute and academic standing are superior to those of many direct-grant and independent schools. . . . Parity of conditions is a means to an end; the end is equality of educational opportunity. But equality of opportunity will be further from realisation if the maintained grammar schools, through which alone the majority of able children can reach the universities and the professions, are less able than at present to compete on equal terms with the direct-grant and independent schools, above all for teachers of high academic attainments on whose quality depend the futures of their pupils." It will take time—as indeed past experience has shown—to convince the public that an education for which one pays is not intrinsically superior to one which is given free.

As in the case of the Education Bills of 1870 and 1902, the question of religious education took a prominent place in the debates on the Education Bill of 1944. In the White Paper it had been stated that "there has been a very general wish, not confined to representatives of the Churches, that religious education should be given a more defined place in the life and work of the schools." To meet this 'very general wish' the 1944 Act, as has been said, made it compulsory that every county school, as well as every voluntary school, should give religious instruction and begin its day with an act of collective worship. How far legislation of this kind will secure a religious basis for national education remains to be seen. Politicians and ecclesiastics do not always realise that school services and religious instruction, if they are perfunctory and uninspired, may—and often do—have the very opposite effect to that which is desired; and this applies quite as much to the churches themselves as to the schools. In both cases

---

[1] September 1945, pp. 426-7.

X

everything depends on the individual parsons or teachers concerned, for 'religion is caught, not taught.' It may have been politically expedient to include these provisions as to compulsory religious instruction and exercises in the Act, because they met the objections of those who believed that these things are in some sense a safeguard of a good education. But in actual fact they are no safeguard whatever. In the last resort the efficiency of machinery of this kind, whether provided by an Act of Parliament or not, depends on the teachers who work it.

Another difficulty which hampered the enforcement of the 1944 Act was a financial one. Many school buildings, especially those in rural areas and belonging to the voluntary bodies, were out of date and unsatisfactory. Dr. F. Spencer estimated that four out of every five 'elementary' schools should be pulled down and rebuilt. Moreover, owing to enemy action during the war of 1939–45, school accommodation for some 200,000 pupils was destroyed; and the raising of the school-leaving age to fifteen implied the provision of nearly 400,000 new school places. If it were raised to sixteen, double this number would be required. Thus a very large building programme was involved. But even more important was the recruitment of a sufficient number of trained teachers. To cope with the increase in pupils and to make possible the reduction in the size of classes it was estimated that some 70,000 extra teachers must be found; and these had also to be trained before the Act could become fully operative. The war had made large inroads in the teaching personnel; the entry of men, in particular, to the profession had fallen off very greatly. To meet this emergency a scheme was put forward in 1943 by which candidates considered suitable could be recruited from the Services or other walks of life and, after a one-year's intensive course in a specially organised college, could be launched as 'qualified' teachers. The emergency colleges were improvised by L.E.A.s acting as agents of the Minister of Education, and the full cost of them was met by the Exchequer. The scheme offered interesting possibilities, though the shortness of the training course, even if it were a necessity, was widely felt to be a regrettable feature. Hitherto the normal way of entry into the teaching profession had been via a secondary school and a training college or university. This may have tended to encourage too exclusively an academic outlook on the part of those who had been trained in this way, and it was felt that to draw teachers from a wider and more varied field of recruitment might have beneficial results. At the same time some of the advantages claimed for this emergency scheme were probably due to wishful thinking on the part of those at the Ministry of Education and elsewhere who were responsible for organising it.

It is obvious that the Education Act of 1944 offers opportunities of progress in national education such as have never been presented before; but subsequent experience has shown that to realise those opportunities will be an uphill task and will take time. The Act was passed owing to the co-operation of all political parties, and there was a noticeable absence of the sectarian bitterness and unwillingness to compromise which marked the passage of the 1870 and 1902 Acts. But, as the history of the 1918 Act reminds us, it is possible for provisions to remain on the Statute Book, but to be inoperative in practice. Professor H. C. Dent wisely reminded us that putting the Act into operation "will be the more difficult in that it will have to be carried out during a period of economic and social dislocation and simultaneously with other massive schemes of reconstruction."[1] We can agree with him also when he says that the Act "lays unprecedented obligations upon both public authorities and the private citizen. It may make all the difference between a happy and glorious future for our country and an unhappy and inglorious one. To make it a real success, the full co-operation of every citizen will be required."[2]

[1] Dent, *The Education Act*, 1944, p. 3.   [2] *Op. cit.*, p. 4.

Chapter XXXIII

RECENT EDUCATIONAL THEORY

The Work of the Specialists. The Individual and the Community. Mental Testing. Sir Percy Nunn and his Critics.

IN the second column of Appendix II will be found a list of books dealing with education and written by English authors during the period covered by the present volume. It reveals the interesting fact that the works which had most influence on educational thought in the nineteenth century date almost wholly from the eighteen-fifties and sixties. This is the period of Newman's *Idea of a University* and Darwin's *Origin of Species*, of many of the writings of J. S. Mill and Ruskin and Kingsley and Huxley and F. D. Maurice, of Spencer's *Education* and Matthew Arnold's *Culture and Anarchy*. It is, in fact, as Professor Archer has called it, an 'age of the prophets.' It was a period when Benthamite individualism was still the current political theory, and utilitarianism, as set forth in the writings of J. S. Mill and Herbert Spencer, had not yet lost its force. But the latter part of the period marks the beginnings of that collectivist trend of public opinion which has increased in force and volume from that time down to the present.[1] Some of our mid-century educational 'prophets' already show a break with the earlier individualism of the Bentham School.[2] Kingsley, for example, in a speech at Bristol in 1869, said: "It is the duty of the State, I hold, to educate all alike in those matters which are common to them as citizens."[3] Ruskin demands that "there should be training schools for youth established at Government cost and under Government discipline over the whole country; that every child born in the country should at

[1] Cf. "Socialistic ideas were, it is submitted, in no way part of dominant legislative opinion earlier than 1865, and their influence on legislation did not become perceptible till some years later, say till 1868 or 1870, or dominant till say 1880." Dicey, *Law and Opinion in England*, p. 66.

[2] For Huxley's position see *supra*, p. 143.

[3] *Life and Letters of Charles Kingsley*, vol. ii, p. 228.

the parents' wish be permitted (and, in certain cases, be under penalty required) to pass through them."[1] Forces of this kind played their part in the passing of the 1870 Act; but once a national system of elementary education is in being, the supply of seminal books on education seems to give out. The activity is now seen in the Legislature, and the Act of 1870 initiates a long series of further Acts dealing with national education or some aspect of it. In fact the progress of socialism is nowhere more marked than in the sphere of education. As Dicey says: "If a student once realises that the education of the English people was, during the earlier part of the nineteenth century, in no sense a national concern, he will see that our present system is a monument to the increasing predominance of collectivism."[2] He wrote those words in 1905, and the 'predominance' of which he speaks is today far more marked than it was at the beginning of the century.

But the existence of a great activity carried on to a large extent under public management is bound sooner or later to stimulate criticism or questioning as to its ultimate aim and the methods by which that aim may best be achieved. The educational literature of the last three decades of the nineteenth century consisted, to a considerable extent, of manuals of practice for the use of students in training colleges and teachers in State-aided schools. They did not, as a rule, raise any final issues about the problems of education, but they furnished techniques which could be applied forthwith in the class-room. So far as they concerned themselves with theory, they adopted a rather crude interpretation of the psychological theories which had been set forth by the German philosopher Herbart (1776–1841), and developed by his followers. They tended to overlook the philosophical and ethical implications of his doctrines and to concentrate rather on deducing from them a psychological justification for a technique of teaching. They therefore stressed the correlation and concentration of studies, and, in particular, they formalised five (or four) 'steps,' which formed a convenient frame for the setting-out of a lesson. A theoretical basis for these methods was found in the

[1] *Unto this Last*, Preface, § 6.
[2] Dicey, *Law and Opinion in England*, p. 278.

Herbartian doctrine of apperception; but its application tended to result in what was little better than a mechanical device. Whatever there is of value in the Herbartian system has been extracted by Sir John Adams in his enlightening and entertaining *Herbartian Psychology applied to Education*.[1]

Towards the end of the last century, however, 'education' began to emerge as a university 'subject.' The 'Day Training Colleges,' as they were called, began their work in the early nineties. The institution of post-graduate diplomas in education, awarded by universities, necessitated something more than a study of a text-book of method on neo-Herbartian lines, such as had hitherto been used in the two-year training colleges. But it was not very easy to determine satisfactorily what the content of the education diploma course should be; and it is more than possible that this problem has even yet not been solved. A study of what was called 'educational psychology,' of some outlines of educational history gathered from a collection of essays, such as Quick's *Educational Reformers*, and of a philosophical work—passages from Plato's *Republic* for choice—together with some information about school hygiene and teaching methods (largely borrowed from the training-college syllabus)—usually formed the staple of the diploma course. One can hardly call this 'educational science,' and it is very possible that there is no *science* of education. But a great deal has been done since the beginning of the present century to formulate some sort of philosophy—or philosophies—of education and to organise the knowledge that we have been able to acquire. This has been the work, not merely of philosophers and scientists who are outside the schools or training institutions—such as Prof. A. N. Whitehead, Sir Richard Livingstone, and Earl Russell—but to an even greater extent of professors of education and heads of university training-departments whom the new order of things brought into being. Among them a conspicuous part has been played by Sir John Adams, Sir Percy Nunn, and Sir Fred Clarke, of the London Institute of Education (London University), Dr. M. W. Keatinge of Oxford and Mr. Charles Fox of Cambridge, Prof. Findlay of Manchester,

[1] See also Adamson, *English Education*, 1760–1902, pp. 492–3.

Prof. Campagnac of Liverpool, Sir Godfrey Thomson of Edinburgh, and Prof. Valentine of Birmingham—to mention only a few.

It is a commonplace to say that education should imply the full development of the individual, and that this full development can be achieved only through the life of the community of which the individual forms part. That being so, modern English educational theory seems to have progressed along two lines which, if distinct, are very closely correlated. There has been firstly a close study of the individual to be educated—a process which has been assisted by methods which have been worked out by experimental psychologists; and secondly, a philosophical investigation of the social implications of education. A synthesis of these two lines of research may help us towards a determination of what should be the aim or aims of education in a community such as our own, so that the greatest benefit may accrue alike to society as a whole and to the individuals who comprise it.

The scientific study of the differences of individual minds has been made possible by the evolution of what is called 'mental testing.' We owe the conception of the mental test to Sir Francis Galton, a Cambridge scientist, whose *Inquiries into Human Faculty* first appeared in 1883. In this book he suggested statistical methods which he applied, for example, in an investigation into mental imagery.[1] He also designed pieces of apparatus for testing differences of sensation. Galton was for a time associated with J. McK. Cattell, who became professor of psychology in Columbia University. His pupil, Prof. E. C. Thorndike, whose work on mental testing is of outstanding importance, says that "Cattell refined Galton's methods and won recognition for the mental measurement of individuals as a standard division of psychology."[2] The work of Galton, although begun in this country, was for the time being taken over by investigators in other countries—notably America, France, and Germany. For example, the German psychologist Ebbinghaus (1850–1909) applied quantitative measurement to the testing of memory. At about the same

[1] See *Inquiries*, etc., pp. 57–79.
[2] See Board of Education pamphlet *Psychological Tests of Educable Capacity*, p. 5.

period—i.e. in the last decade of the nineteenth century—the Frenchman Binet was working at tests of memory, attention, and other mental processes. In America W. C. Bagley was employing tests to measure motor ability, and from the results he calculated what he called a 'motor index.' Thus by the beginning of the twentieth century much had already been done in the devising of mental tests. But hitherto the work had been largely of an academic type; the practical application of the tests has been the work mainly of the past fifty or sixty years. The process has been facilitated by the use of the correlation method extensively used by Prof. Spearman of the University of London. It furnishes a technique which, though at first criticised, has been widely accepted. One of the results of its application was the exposition of the theory of a general ability (called by psychologists 'g'), underlying all the various mental activities that can be tested. The correlation formula was also used by the English psychologist Sir Cyril Burt, who made tests of children in elementary schools in Oxford and Liverpool, and who directed his attention particularly to this problem of general intelligence. It appeared to be for the most part hereditary or inborn, and not acquired; and if this is so it has—as we have seen[1]—important implications for the educational administrator.

A contribution of great significance in the work of mental testing was made in 1908 by the Frenchmen Binet and Simon, when they put forward their Binet–Simon scale. In this scheme each test is classified under some age from three to thirteen, and the passing of the test for a specified age is correlated with the child's chronological age. If a child of five can manage to pass the tests for a child of seven, his mental age is two years in advance of his chronological age. The Binet–Simon scale was subsequently revised, but in principle it remained unchanged, and it gives us what Terman, the author of the 'Stanford Revision' (1916), called the 'Intelligence Quotient.' To obtain this, the mental age is multiplied by 100 and divided by the chronological age; so that the 'I.Q.' of the child mentioned above would be $\frac{700}{5} = 140$. But with the increasing use of psychological tests it has become

[1] See *supra*, pp. 265–6.

more and more common in recent years to set group tests. An impetus to this practice was given during the 1914–18 war, when mental testing was extensively used in the American Army for sorting recruits. It would have been impossible to handle the two million men involved if individual tests had been applied. Since that time the method of group testing has been increasingly employed in this country, especially in the selection of children for secondary education. It was first applied by the Bradford Education Authority in 1919 for their junior scholarship examination, and it has since become a standard practice. Group tests have been used by various colleges at the admission of students, and by the Civil Service and other public bodies. They also play their part in the technique of vocational guidance, and—as Sir Cyril Burt and Sir Fred Schonell have shown[1]—they are of great service in the investigation of backwardness and delinquency. Their importance can hardly be questioned. So far as they go, they have been brought to a high degree of reliability and they have considerable diagnostic value. It is well to remember that they have their limitations and that they test only certain features of the whole personality; but they do provide a tool which—if its use is properly understood—may be of the greatest value to the educator and the sociologist alike.

The application of educational psychology to the individual child who is to be educated is seen not only in the development of mental testing, but also in many more general ways. The nursery-school movement, the treatment of delinquency, child-guidance clinics, 'youth service,' altered conceptions of what is meant by 'discipline,' experimentation with curriculum and school organisation—all these and many other modern tendencies in education are to a large extent the outcome of an attempt to understand the psychology of the individual child, and to organise and make practical use of the knowledge which has been obtained by observation and experiment. This attempt has resulted in a spate of treatises dealing with 'educational psychology' which have appeared since the beginning of the present

---

[1] E.g. in Burt, *The Backward Child* and *The Young Delinquent*, and Schonell, *Backwardness in the Basic Subjects*.

century.[1] But the interest in, and emphasis on, individuality in education are shown particularly in one of the greatest of modern works on educational theory—*Education: its Data and First Principles*, by Sir Percy Nunn (1870–1944).

It first appeared in 1920, at a time when many progressive teachers in this country were much concerned about the educational implications of Hegelian views on State absolutism, which were gaining ground on the Continent of Europe. Against these doctrines Nunn roundly asserts that "Individuality is the ideal of life."[2] The main theme of his book is set out as follows: "We shall stand throughout on the position that nothing good enters into the human world except in and through the free activities of individual men and women, and that educational practice must be shaped to accord with that truth. This view does not deny or minimise the responsibilities of a man to his fellows; for the individual life can develop only in terms of its own nature, and that is social as truly as it is 'self-regarding.' Nor does it deny the value of tradition and discipline or exclude the influences of religion. But it does deny the reality of any super-personal entity of which the single life, taken by itself, is but an insignificant element. It reaffirms the infinite value of the individual person; it reasserts his ultimate responsibility for his own destiny; and it accepts all the practical corollaries that assertion implies."[3] The criticism has been made that the book 'dates'—but so does every important work on education, because it is written against the social and political background of its time. Shortly before his death in 1944 Nunn completed a revised edition of his treatise, with considerable alterations and additions. The history of Europe, however, since the end of the first World War had served only to strengthen the author's point of view. In this revised edition he says: "The central thesis of the book remains unchanged; it maintains that the primary aim of all educational effort should be to help boys and

[1] Among them may be mentioned: William James, *Talks to Teachers on Psychology* (1899); Lloyd Morgan, *Psychology for Teachers* (1907); Drever, *An Introduction to the Psychology of Education* (1922); Fox, *Educational Psychology* (1925); and Peel, *The Psychological Basis of Education* (1956).

[2] Nunn, *Education: its Data and First Principles* (First Edition), p. 11.

[3] *Op. cit.*, p. 5.

girls to achieve the highest degree of individual development of which they are capable."[1]

This 'central thesis' has not passed unchallenged, and the age-long problem of reconciling the claims of the individual and of society in education is once more raised. Prof. Campagnac, for example, in *Society and Solitude* examines critically the meaning of the term 'individuality';[2] and he goes on to say: "We are not ready to accept Individuality as the 'supreme educational end,' or to suppose that the end can be stated in any simple word or formula. The end when justly stated must also be illogically stated; it must be as various and as intolerant of strict definition as life itself. To seek individuality is good, but to lose it is good; to yield to society and to defy society are both proper tasks for men, who must be in the world and yet not of it; who must be themselves, but can only discover themselves by finding other selves than their own; who must die in order to live. It is granted, indeed, that the individual must make his contribution to the general welfare of the Society, the world, in which he lives; but the admission is followed by the claim that he must be free to make it as he chooses, in the form which he elects; and this is a freedom which the world cannot grant, because it would be a freedom without meaning."[3] Those are wise words; but though it may well be that Nunn lays less stress than some other educational thinkers on the social function of education, he obviously does not overlook it. "Individuality," he says, "develops only in a social atmosphere where it can be fed on common interests and common activities," but he safeguards his thesis by claiming that "the idea that a main function of the school is to socialise its pupils in no wise contradicts the view that its true aim is to cultivate individuality."[4]

To Nunn, then, the school's true aim was "to cultivate individuality," though it did so "within the common life." Other modern educational theorists have put the stress on the other side, and have contended that the school is primarily a place where the

[1] *Op. cit.* (Third Edition), p. 5.   [2] In chap. ix.
[3] Campagnac, *Society and Solitude*, p. 118.
[4] Nunn, *Education: Its Data and First Principles*, p. 249.

individual is socialised. If that is to be fully achieved, it cannot be shut off from the greater community, like a monastery hidden in a desert or among the mountains. In order to fulfil its functions it must be closely linked with the community and an integral part of it. Society, through the medium of the school, puts its past achievements at the service of its future citizens; but at the same time its whole future is bound up with the school. The school is, in fact, the growing-point of the community. No one has realised this fact and its implications more fully than John Dewey. Although he is an American professor, he has exercised a great influence in this country. "The school," he says, "has been so set apart, so isolated from the ordinary conditions and motives of life, that the place where children are sent for discipline is the one place in the world where it is most difficult to get experience—the mother of all discipline worth the name."[1] Dewey complains that the school is too much regarded as something between teacher and pupil, or teacher and parent. He also points out that the changes in educational methods and curricula, which have been brought about in recent times, are as much a product of social changes as are changes in industry or commerce. Thus Dewey finds the greatest value in those school activities which are productive—manual work, household arts, and co-operative activities. In practice we can import the economic life and conditions of the macrocosm of society into the microcosm of the school only to a limited extent; but, vast and complex as the social and economic system of the community is, the school must interpret it to the pupil.

The twentieth century has seen many political theories thrown into the melting-pot and the emergence of diverse types of community of a highly nationalistic kind. This has given added point to the questions: what should be the interrelation of the individual and the community, and what is the function of education in the State? Dewey makes the comment: "The so-called individualism of the eighteenth-century enlightenment was found to involve the notion of a society as broad as humanity, of whose progress the individual was to be the organ. But it lacked any agency for

[1] *The School and Society*, p. 15.

securing the development of its ideal, as was evidenced in its falling back upon Nature. The institutional idealistic philosophies of the nineteenth century supplied this lack by making the national State the agency, but in so doing narrowed the conception of the social aim to those who were members of the same political unit, and reintroduced the idea of the subordination of the individual to the institution."[1] Thus we have seen the employment of education in Nazi Germany and in Fascist Italy as frankly an instrument of State policy, and not as a means for the free development of the individual within the membership of the community. The States which called themselves 'democratic' were thus, as it were, challenged to rethink and restate their theory of education. Nunn's championship of individuality was one answer to the challenge. But it is also taken up in the Spens *Report*. "Speaking broadly," it says, "the interest of the State is to see that the schools provide the means by which the nation's life may be maintained in its integrity from generation to generation; to make sure that the young are prepared to preserve—and some of them to advance—its standards in all modes of activity which are important to the common weal. In a democratic community it must 'educate its masters'; in communities of other types it must see that the citizens are trained for obedient and willing service. Underneath this explicit, overt educational activity of the State, working through laws and regulations, there is the unformulated but very real demand of the community that the young shall grow up in conformity with the national *ethos*."[2]

What in this country that *ethos* is, and how it can be interpreted to meet the educational needs of a community profoundly affected by war conditions, are questions discussed by Sir Fred Clarke in his *Education and Social Change*.[3] This book, the small size of which is out of all proportion to its importance, first appeared in 1940. The author "accepts unreservedly" what he calls "the sociological standpoint," and he aims at exhibiting its

---

[1] *Democracy and Education*, pp. 115–16.   [2] Pp. 147–8.
[3] Cf. "The present argument assumes that the tradition is capable of the necessary degree of adaptation, granted a sufficient occasion, and an adequate measure both of intelligence to recognise and of will to execute the new applications of ancient principles that will be called for." (*Op. cit.*, p. 2.)

"concrete application to the field of English education." The book is governed by three main objectives: "(1) To provide some insight into the nature of the social influences by which the forms of English educational institutions have been determined and their practical objectives defined; (2) To formulate some analysis of the present situation in England . . . (3) To estimate the degree to which the existing order is capable of adaptation to the demands which have to be faced, the demands of a régime consciously planned and directed towards the guaranteeing of freedom for diversity of personality in a social order much more thoroughly collectivist in working than any of which we have yet had experience."[1] The author therefore proceeds from a discussion of the historical determinants of English education to a critical account of the existing agencies for education—schools, both primary and secondary, institutions of further education, and all the other 'informal organisations' which testify to "continuing social vitality, to a continuing power of adaptation and creation in response to need."[2] In looking to the future, Sir Fred Clarke contends that our "habit of thinking about education in terms of class . . . has made our educational categories and terminology the chaotic things they are. Our thinking is likely to be much more relevant both to actual social necessities and to the values of education as an instrument of social control and transformation if we keep it clear of any distracting ideas of a rigid class-structure."[3] For this reason "unification of the system over the whole range" is advocated.[4]

Since the book was published, the 1944 Education Act has given some expression to this scheme of unification; but it would seem that our national modes of thinking will have to be further modified if we are to divest ourselves entirely of "this habit of thinking about education in terms of class." The 1944 Act left intact the public school, the private school, and the preparatory school, which must inevitably make "unification over the whole range" difficult, if not impossible. The justification for leaving them independent was stated to be the desirability of retaining variety in

[1] *Op. cit.*, p. 7. [2] *Op. cit.*, p. 41.
[3] *Op. cit.*, p. 48. [4] *Ibid.*

educational provision or of safeguarding their 'freedom'; but it may conceivably be argued that the new scheme was devised so as not to interfere too drastically with the existing class structure of the community. Doubtless education in the long run influences public opinion; but there is a danger that it may fail of its effect if it tries too eagerly to outpace public opinion. However, Sir Fred Clarke contends that: "The development of a popular philosophy of education is perhaps the most relevant example that could be given of an urgently needed change in basic attitudes. It is unlikely, in England, that such a philosophy would be sharply antagonistic to that which has been dominant hitherto. Its function would be to preside over the process of unifying the values of culture and usefulness, and to secure that, in so far as the educational system is an instrument of social selection, the criteria it applies shall be purely educational and used with no irrelevant bias."[1] If this could be achieved, then, he argues, education would be the fundamental principle by which the cohesion and continuance of society would be secured.

It is even yet the fashion in some quarters to disparage 'educational theory.' But education cannot be occupied solely with means and never with ends. The average teacher or administrator is of necessity so much occupied with routine that he has little opportunity to stop and think whither he should go, or how he should get there. The educational philosophers from the time of Plato downwards have helped us to see our way. The Greatest of them all said: "I am come that they might have life, and that they might have it more abundantly." Unless our conception of education is informed by that kind of spirit, our legislation, codes, memoranda, curricula, and examinations may merely lead us into the wilderness. But if we regard education in terms of 'abundant life,' our aim becomes clearer; and an educational system drawn up and administered in that light will be our chief, and perhaps only real, safeguard in an age which otherwise can offer us only the destruction of our civilisation.

[1] *Op. cit.*, p. 66.

Chapter XXXIV

EDUCATION SINCE 1944

Post-war difficulties. School buildings and school places. Training and recruitment of teachers. Technological education. University expansion. Selection for secondary education and its problems. The General Certificate of Education. Juvenile delinquency and the Youth Service. The Newsom and Robbins *Reports*.

AT the end of chapter *XXXII* Professor H. C. Dent was quoted as saying that putting the 1944 Education Act into operation "will be the more difficult in that it will have to be carried out during a period of economic and social dislocation, and simultaneously with other schemes of reconstruction." In the event the difficulties have proved even greater perhaps than the writer realised at the time; and an account of English education since 1944 must inevitably be largely a record of these difficulties, and of how they have been tackled and to what extent they have been overcome.

In the immediate post-war period one of the chief problems concerned itself with school buildings. Not only had many school places been lost owing to enemy action, but the arrears caused by the War had to be made up—and that at a time when there was an enormous demand for new houses. Building materials and steel were in short supply and sufficient labour was difficult to obtain. In 1950 an increased 'defence' programme, in particular, caused a serious set-back, and it was some years before this situation was to some extent eased. All along the problem of building and equipment was complicated by a continual rise in costs, so that it was difficult to draw up estimates which would not afterwards need revision. But in spite of these and other handicaps a real and far-sighted attempt was made to give a fresh impetus to the educational system of the country and to make use of the opportunities afforded by the 1944 Act. As was said on p. 297, the Act required every L.E.A. to draw up a 'development plan', in which the educational facilities and needs of its area were to be surveyed. In most cases this proved an enormous task;

and in spite of the earnest efforts of administrators and their staffs, the majority of L.E.A.s were unable to submit their plans by April 1st, 1945, and they therefore had to ask for an extension of time. By the end of 1947, 126 L.E.A.s, out of a total of 146, had prepared their plans. These were worked through by the Ministry of Education and gradually approved. Section 42 of the 1944 Act had also required local authorities, 'at such times and in such form as the minister may direct,' to prepare and submit schemes of further education for their areas; and a circular of March 1947 asked for such schemes by March 31st, 1948. They were to include the provision of full-time and part-time education for persons over compulsory school age, and for cultural and recreative occupations; and in preparing these schemes L.E.A.s. were to take into consideration any facilities offered by voluntary associations and by universities or university colleges in their areas. It was fully expected at this period that the county colleges (see p. 300), referred to in § 43 of the Act, would be brought into existence within the prescribed three years after the coming into operation of Part II of the Act. In 1945 the Ministry of Education put out a pamphlet entitled *Youth's Opportunity*, which made recommendations in considerable detail as to the aims, organisation, equipment and curriculum of these proposed colleges. But in the event the 'opportunity' has not yet occurred. The provisions of the Act dealing with county colleges have so far remained inoperative, and there seems no immediate prospect of their being realised. There have been other educational needs and other demands made by the Act which have appeared more urgent—and that at a time when to supply them has been no easy task.

Another casualty of the 1944 Act has been the adequate provision of nursery schools. In § 8 of the Act, L.E.A.s. were instructed to have particular regard, amongst other things, to the 'need for securing that provision is made for pupils who have not attained the age of five years by the provision of nursery schools, or, where the authority consider the provision of such schools to be inexpedient, by the provision of nursery classes in other schools.' But the immediate need for places for children of compulsory school age has—in spite of a good deal of criticism—

Y

resulted in this clause remaining practically inoperative. At the beginning of 1947 there were 370 grant-aided nursery schools in England and Wales, with 19,048 pupils. By January 1965 the totals had risen only to 461 and 23,914. Moreover during the greater part of this period the number both of schools and pupils remained almost static, and in some years there was even a slight decline.

The implementation of the 1944 Act, so far as it goes, has been accomplished against an unfavourable background, which perhaps was hardly expected when the Act was passed. The development of nuclear research and its application to re-armament have resulted in an international situation which seems to illustrate the ancient proverb that those whom God wishes to destroy He first makes mad. But meanwhile these things have to be paid for, in spite of the enormous and ever-increasing expense. This has inevitably had its repercussions on the national educational system. The whole problem of the provision of school-places has been complicated by a phenomenon usually known as the 'bulge.' Towards the end of the War and in the years which immediately followed there was an increase in the marriage rate; and it was this that was partly responsible for the need of new houses. But it also entailed a rise in the number of children who became of compulsory school age towards the end of the 1940's— just at the time when the school-leaving age had been raised to 15 (April 1st, 1947). After working its way through the primary schools the 'bulge' entered the secondary schools; and in fact the whole programme of school building since the War has been largely dictated by this factor. To cope with the immediate demand for school places after the War use was made of what were called HORSA[1] huts. They were not beautiful and too often they encroached upon valuable playground space. But they were reasonably comfortable and warm and airy and light—and sometimes preferable to class-rooms in old-fashioned and ill-adaptable school buildings. It is perhaps surprising—and encouraging—

[1] *I.e.* Hut Operation Raising School-leaving Age. (See M. of E. Pamphlet No. 33. *The Story of Post-War School Building.*) There was also a SFORSA to deal with School Furniture.

that in spite of all the difficulties involved so much has been accomplished. Every year has seen the opening of new primary and secondary schools, the extension and adaptation of inadequate premises, and the progress—slow though it has been—of 're-organisation' (see pp. 237–8). In order to help in this expansion the maximum government grant to voluntary schools was raised by 25 per cent. as from 1959.[1] Since Roman Catholics and the Church of England stood to benefit chiefly by this, a Free Church manifesto expressed 'deep regret' at the government's action. One is reminded of the nonconformist attitude in 1902.

The difficulty of keeping pace with the 'bulge' is one of the reasons for the continued existence of over-sized classes. Regulations lay it down that in primary schools the maximum number of pupils allowed in a class is forty, and in a secondary school class thirty.[2] In practice these figures are often exceeded. In 1963, for example, there were in England and Wales 19,893 primary and secondary pupils in classes of over 40, and 42,643 secondary school pupils in classes of over 30. Classes containing over fifty children were not unknown. It is most certainly desirable that as many as possible of our youngsters should get their first impressions of school in a bright and airy building, set in pleasant, open surroundings. But even more important is a class small enough to enable the teacher to maintain close contact with, and interest in, every individual member of it. This is true at any stage, and there seems no sound educational reason why the maximum for the primary school should be higher than that for the secondary school. Teachers should be given the best possible conditions under which to do their job—not, of course, primarily for their benefit, but for that of the children. If a choice had to be made, reducing the size of classes should have the priority. Vita-glass windows, radiograms, television equipment and grand pianos

---

[1] On the other hand, in 1957 the 'specific' grant for education which had been made to local authorities was replaced by a 'general' grant into which the 'specific' grants were absorbed; so that local expenditure could be allocated as the authority pleased. It was felt in some quarters that the result might be to affect educational expenditure and progress adversely.

[2] See S.I. 1959, No. 364.

are excellent things to have; but ultimately an efficient extra teacher on the staff is far better.

This observation calls attention to yet another difficulty with which post-war education in this country had had to contend—and that is a shortage of teachers. The Emergency Training Scheme (see pp. 304–5) lasted until 1951, and during the six years or so of its existence it produced some 35,000 teachers. A course of training lasting only one year and with no rigid conditions as to the academic qualifications for entry was bound to raise some disquiet and give rise to fears of professional 'dilution.' But on the whole the products of the emergency scheme made a worth-while contribution and helped to carry the country's education through a difficult period. But it was rightly realised that such expedients can be only temporary. In spite of pressure from some quarters, the government remained constant in their intention to lengthen the ordinary training college course to three years, and this came into effect in 1960. This was a bold step because the staffing of schools has been in the nature of a holding operation, owing largely to the 'bulge' and the raising of the school-leaving age to 15. In order to equalise the strain the Ministry of Education introduced a 'quota' system by which L.E.A.s were assigned a total number of teachers which they were not allowed to exceed. This has been particularly necessary in the case of women teachers of whom there was a serious shortage and who were badly distributed. Some authorities—Birmingham is a conspicuous instance—were unable to recruit a sufficient minimum of teachers to staff their schools. It is not always easy to forecast the number of teachers who will be required at any particular point in the near future; but in July 1958 the National Advisory Council on the Training and Supply of Teachers (which had been set up in 1949) recommended that 16,000 additional training-college places should be provided. The Ministry of Education put the figure at 12,000; but it is obvious that the need for more teachers will be felt for some years to come.

In this connection a major problem is how to attract suitable candidates into the profession. Here obviously the question of salaries is involved. The incidence of inflation and the demand for labour greatly pushed up wages in many industries. A table published in 1950 gave the relative rise in wage-rates for twenty-one occupations. It showed that bricklayers' wages had risen from a 1924 level of 100 to 184. Graduate teachers were at the bottom of the list; their rate had risen from 100 to 124. Since the 'basic' salary scheme was introduced in 1945 (see p. 257), there have been several revisions of the Burnham scale, so as to bring it more into line with the increased cost of living.[1] 'Equal pay' for women teachers by seven annual instalments was introduced in 1955, to be completed by April 1st, 1961. The Burnham scales have been criticised on the ground that they tend to put a premium on mediocrity, because they provide automatic annual increments which, irrespective of other considerations, accrue regularly from the minimum to the maximum. It has been suggested that the most logical way of dealing with this situation would be to institute in the teaching profession a series of grades with efficiency bars, such as exists in the civil service, the local government service, the armed forces, and the universities. Annual increments inside a grade could be secured, but there would always be the incentive of promotion to a higher grade with an increased salary range. Something in this direction has already been accomplished by the greatly extended use of extra allowances above the basic scale for such posts as headships, departmental responsibilities and the like. By 1956 52 per cent. of all teachers in all types of school were receiving payments of this kind. Even so, we are very far from realising the recommendation of the McNair *Report*[2] that the salaries of the various grades of teachers should be equated with those of civil servants in the Executive and Administrative classes, or with those of the School Medical or Dental Services.

A particular difficulty has arisen since the War in connection with the supply of specialist teachers of mathematics and science, who of course would normally be university graduates. We appear to be entering upon a period of scientific and technological development which will either provide a 'brave new world,' or else result in a quite literal fulfilment of the prophecy of the *Dies Iræ*—"dies illa solvet sæclum in favilla." Scientific research

---

[1] See page 258.   [2] Pp. 34–38.

advances knowledge, but it does not always increase wisdom. Perhaps the right kind of education would help to ensure that the applications of science were used to benefit, and not to destroy, mankind. But there remains the problem of coping with the scientific régime, and here the schools are in a key position. Advanced work in science can be accomplished only on the basis of good all-round school education, including a thorough grounding in scientific subjects. This implies good science teaching. But the demand for science graduates in the Scientific Civil Service and in industry has been so great, and the financial inducements offered there have been so much more attractive than those in teaching, that the schools have often found it impossible to obtain adequate science staff. But, to quote one of the Ministry of Education's *Reports*,[1] "if the needs of the schools were not properly met there would be very serious adverse effects on the life of the nation as a whole." There has been a determined attempt by L.E.A.s. to extend the provision of facilities for teaching science in all types of secondary school. In 1955 also the Industrial Fund for the Advancement of Scientific Education in Schools was instituted, and from this generous grants have been made to a number of independent and direct-grant schools to enable them to build and equip scientific laboratories. But there remains the problem of finding the men and women to teach in them.

The spectacular advances that have been made by scientific research during and since the second World War, and their application to industry, account for a greatly augmented interest also in technical and technological education. In spite of acute accommodation difficulties considerable progress was made, and every year showed an increase in the number of students, whether fulltime or part-time, in technical colleges. There has been considerable expansion of apprenticeship schemes which include formal training at a technical college, usually on one day a week in working hours and with pay. Another scheme at a higher level is that of 'sandwich courses.' These combine periods of fulltime education, normally in a technical college, with alternating periods of full-time work in industry. But some of the most

[1] 1954, p. 11.

interesting developments concern the higher training of technologists. Following on the Percy *Report*,[1] a National Advisory
Council on Education for Industry and Commerce, set up in
1948, made recommendations in 1950 as to their training and
qualifications. In 1955 another Council on Technological Awards
was formed; its function was "to create and administer the award
of Diplomas in Technology." It was not an examining body, but
it was responsible for seeing that the conditions under which the
technical colleges taught and examined their students for the
Diploma were satisfactory. These courses should be equivalent in
standard to those of a degree in a British university; and they
could be taken either full-time or on a 'sandwich' basis. In 1959
the Council announced the establishment of a College of Technologists. It was to administer the award of 'membership' (M.C.T.)
which was to be a higher qualification than the Diploma in Technology. The college was to operate within the framework of the
National Council for Technological Awards. Candidates for
the M.C.T. would study in a recognised College of Advanced
Technology;[2] experience in industry would also be required. In
1964, however, a Council for National Academic Awards was set
up, with power to award degrees and other academic distinctions,
comparable with those given in universities, to students from
institutions of higher education which have no right to confer
their own degrees. This Council took over the Diploma in
Technology and the work of the College of Technologists.
Several Colleges of Advanced Technology have recently become
degree-granting universities.[3] Training of teachers in the various
types of technical college was discussed in the McNair *Report*,[4]
and since then has been frequently considered. Here again a
special committee was established.[5] The technical colleges at
Bolton, Huddersfield, and Garnett College, London, S.E.1,

[1] Report on *Higher Technological Education*, 1945. See also the Barlow Report
on Scientific Manpower, 1946.
[2] By 1959 the Ministry of Education had designated nine colleges of this type.
[3] See *infra*, p. 334. Manchester University has for many years past conferred
the degrees of B.Sc. Tech. and M.Sc.Tech.; the Manchester College of Technology
has been affiliated since 1905 to the faculty of Technology of the University.
Sheffield also gives technological degrees.
[4] Chapter 14.
[5] The Willis Jackson Committee which reported in 1957.

had been running training departments for some years and had successfully resisted a proposal to close them down. It was now recommended that their accommodation should be extended and should include residential quarters. Industry should be encouraged to transfer experienced members of staff to full-time teaching, and more use could be made of late entrants from the armed forces or the Scientific Civil Service.

The need for more and more highly-trained personnel to cope with the problems of the post-war world has led to a large expansion in the British universities. Between 1947–8 and 1966–7 the number of full-time students in the universities and university colleges of England and Wales rose from 63,063 to 142,784. Even before the War had ended the Further Education and Training Scheme for ex-service candidates had been brought into operation. It provided grants to cover all the expenses of a full-time course at a university or institution of higher education. By the end of 1952, when the scheme had almost worked itself out 86,308 men and women had benefited from it. About a quarter of them became teachers. In 1947 the number of state-scholarships was raised from 360 to 750, and after that substantial increases were made from time to time. For the academic year 1958–9 no less than 3,974 state awards of various types were taken up; and 28,107 new awards were also made by L.E.A.s. State-scholarships have now been abolished, but the great majority of all university students are in receipt of some kind of grant.

This expansion has not been without its problems, quite apart from the financial ones. It may be asked how far there is an inexhaustible supply of 'fit persons' who can profit from a university education, and whether there may not be a danger of reducing academic standards to the level of those in some of the American State Universities. Again, universities have to be staffed, and they demand for their teachers academic qualifications of an exceptionally high standard. It may well be that the number of such persons is even more limited than that of their potential students. There is also the question of the optimum size for a university. The English tradition of academic life is that it should be spent in a community, and that such a life is in its way quite as educative as any of the studies which a university provides. That tradition has not always been easy to maintain in some of the newer civic universities; but it is noteworthy that increased attempts have been made, and are being made, to bring more and more students into halls of residence. In 1964–5 roughly 36 per cent. of them were living in colleges. To enlarge universities and yet preserve the principle of community life will entail a considerable increase in the very expensive business of providing residential accommodation. As existing universities have expanded, new ones have been formed.[1] The University of North Staffordshire (see p. 249) is now the University of Keele and has a full range of degree courses. There are now in England alone over thirty universities, many of which were established only recently. This development would have been Committee. The amount derived from this source was £5,798,507 in 1946–7; in the year 1964–5 the universities of Great Britain received £89,601,536 as income grant, besides an additional £61,942,378 as capital expenditure grant. It should be noted that these post-war universities do not to any great extent owe their origin to the generosity of some public spirited benefactor. The days of John Owens (Manchester), Josiah Mason (Birmingham), H. R. Hartley (Southampton), Mark Firth (Sheffield), T. R. Ferens (Hull), the Palmer family and Lady Wantage (Reading), are past. The fear is sometimes expressed that increased subsidies from the State and local authorities and, in some cases, industry may ultimately result in an increase of outside control and dictation, and a loss of academic freedom. Fortunately we have not yet reached such a situation.

The reorganisation of national education brought about by the 1944 Act has raised two important and difficult problems which are closely inter-related. If 'primary' and 'secondary' are to be progressive stages in a system of education, we have to decide firstly how far and in what way secondary schools should provide

[1] There has also been a considerable development in Area Training Organisations (Institutes of Education) of the 'university type'. (See *supra*, pp. 255–6.) The National Foundation for Educational Research in England and Wales, founded in 1945, has done much to encourage the study of education.

varying types of course adapted to different aptitudes and abilities; and secondly by what means children should be selected for the particular school or course which is best suited to their needs. The Hadow, Spens and Norwood *Reports* had envisaged three types of child and three corresponding types of school; but, as has been indicated on page 265, this convenient classification seems to have been determined, to some extent, at least, by existing conditions; and the Act itself makes no reference to the three types. The situation is even yet complicated by tradition and by class-distinctions; and the issue has therefore become partly a political one and has been debated with a depth of feeling that recalls the religious educational controversies of the early 1900's. A suggested solution of the difficulty is the provision of 'comprehensive' schools in which the three (or more) types of school are combined in the same institution, without the rigidity of parallel 'sides,' as in the multilateral or bilateral school. Such schools admit all the children from the primary schools of a catchment area and provide whatever kind of education is considered to be best suited to each individual pupil; because "there are not three types of children, but only children with different needs."

Another argument in favour of the comprehensive school is that it obviates the necessity for a selection test at the 'eleven-plus' stage, in order to determine to which form of secondary education a particular primary-school pupil shall be transferred. The original form of this selection examination had consisted of questions in English and arithmetic, supplemented by an intelligence test and perhaps an interview. There is no doubt that this method of selection was something of a nightmare to children—and even more so to their parents; and its effectiveness was also open to doubt. A number of L.E.A.s therefore experimented with other ways of making the selection. For example, instead of having one determining examination, a number of tests may be spread over the last year or two of the primary course, and the child may not realise that he is being formally examined. Much weight may be given to school records and to head teachers' recommendations, and the parents' choice may be taken into consideration. Some authorities—London, for example—have adopted the 'comprehensive' scheme in its entirety; others have made tentative experiments along somewhat similar lines. Leicestershire, for instance, has tried out an interesting scheme. Under it all children at the age of 11 + are transferred without tests to a 'high school' which has a three-years' course. Four or more of these 'high schools' are grouped to serve a major grammar school. At the age of 14 any child whose parents wish it may be transferred to a grammar school without examination—though what exactly the term 'grammar school' will mean in this context remains to be seen. Thus the 'high school' is a link in the system, and does not (like the secondary modern school) run parallel with the grammar school.

All these schemes—and many others—are designed to secure "equality of opportunity" within the State system of education, and to get rid of the incubus of the formal 11 + examination. But they do not, of course, escape criticism. They inevitably involve major changes in the organisation of existing schools and may upset the whole educational system of an area. Schools are not just institutions. It may be possible to amalgamate industrial concerns without harming them; but a school is a community with its own life and tradition and personality. Some of our grammar schools, for example, have inherited a history stretching back for hundreds of years; and many people would regret to see their identity merged in a huge, impersonal institution, such as a comprehensive school appears to them to be. Consideration should also be given (though it never is) to the attitude of old pupils' societies and teams, whose loyalties are undermined by the abolition of their old school. Teachers, again, have complained that when these drastic reorganisations of schools are carried out, little or no consultation is made with the staffs. A teacher who by his qualifications and experience has deliberately chosen to work in a particular type of school may suddenly find that after many years of service he is transferred to a completely different type of environment. Professional associations have also expressed concern that the provision of comprehensive schools considerably reduces the chances of obtaining headships. As to the selection test: even if all children from the primary schools of a given area are admitted to the comprehensive school, some sort of selection inside the school itself will be necessary. In spite of these difficulties the Department of Education and Science in July 1965 issued a circular (10/65) in which it required local authorities to prepare and submit schemes for reorganising secondary education in their areas on comprehensive lines. It is obvious therefore that the whole situation bristles with difficulties, and equally that determined attempts have been made to deal with them. Perhaps the chief danger is that drastic and far-reaching decisions may be taken on grounds of theoretical principle or administrative convenience. If we are to experiment with comprehensive or other types of secondary school—and it is undoubtedly advisable that we should do so—it would be wise to proceed tentatively, as, for example, Leicestershire has done. Perhaps the best place for trying out the comprehensive school is in the new housing estates where one can start *de novo*, and where it will not be necessary to engulf or amalgamate well-established schools, each with its special characteristics and community tradition. Meanwhile there remains the abiding problem of achieving some sort of real 'parity of status' between existing types of secondary school.

Another question which has received much consideration during recent years is the nature and purpose of the school-leaving examination taken by secondary school pupils. In 1947 the Secondary School Examinations Council[1] recommended that an examination at Ordinary, Advanced and Scholarship levels should be instituted, and that all subjects at these three levels should be optional. A General Certificate of Education (G.C.E.) would be awarded, showing the subjects in which the candidate had passed and the level attained in each. The standard of the 'ordinary' level would be approximately that of a 'credit' in the old School Certificate. In this examination one had had normally to satisfy the examiners in five subjects including a language and a science; but it now became possible to obtain a 'G.C.E.' of sorts by passing in one subject at ordinary level. For university entrance,

[1] In 1964 the Department of Education and Science set up a Schools Council for the Curriculum and Examinations.

however, the requirements were still such as might be expected of a sixth-former in a grammar school. They may vary somewhat according to the faculty in which the degree course is to be taken, but usually they include passes in five subjects of which two must have been taken at advanced level. The General Certificate of Education, which came into operation in 1951, is still largely a grammar school type of examination, but it is being increasingly taken at ordinary level by secondary modern schools. Some L.E.A.s also instituted special leaving examinations of their own, designed particularly for the pupils of these schools. The standard was necessarily inferior to that of the ordinary level of the G.C.E., and the value of the certificate depends largely on the attitude of local employers; but it is claimed with some justice that such arrangements consolidate the work in the upper forms of secondary modern schools and furnish an incentive for pupils to stay on after the statutory leaving-age of fifteen. The Beloe *Report*, issued in 1960, recommended the institution of a specially-designed examination at a lower level than the ordinary G.C.E. Teachers were to be largely represented on the regional bodies responsible for this. The Minister of Education accepted the principle of a new school-leaving certificate obtained in this way, and it is called the Certificate of Secondary Education. This is an interesting development in view of the fact that, when secondary modern schools were first formed after the 1944 Act, one of the chief advantages claimed for them over the grammar school was that they would be free of the 'examination incubus.'

The great increase since the second World War in juvenile and adolescent delinquency, including crimes of violence, has caused much searching of heart.[1] All sorts of causes have been assigned and any, or all, of them may be responsible. In spite of a gradual increase in material prosperity we have been suffering from a post-war *malaise* and sense of insecurity, since force and fear are more than ever major instruments of international policy. A decline of moral standards and the growth of materialism are often deplored. Lack of parental control, the denial to children of a settled home-

---

[1] Refer to White Paper *Penal Practice in a Changing Society*. (1959.)

life and the neglect to set them a good example (as evidenced by the increase in divorce) are obviously contributory factors. Perhaps even more potent has been the utterly irresponsible exploitation of violence, crime, horror, and sex by the popular press, by some of the cinema and television programmes, and by other forms of entertainment. All this coincides with a demand for young people's labour which results in their being able to earn unprecedented wages while still in their 'teens. But, as Sir William Alexander has well said: "However good the schools may be, however effective the emphasis in the class-room or the need for worth-while standards and the importance of restraint and self-discipline, the schools must lose a battle in which so many agencies influence young people in other directions. In this problem of misbehaviour among young people the whole of our society must accept its full share of responsibility."[1] Perhaps the Institute of Criminology, established at Cambridge in 1959, will give its attention to this problem of juvenile and adolescent crime and will be able to indicate where any realistic endeavour to deal with its root-causes should start. It is possible that something could have been done by a whole-hearted development of the Youth Service, to which a great deal of attention was given during the War and just after (see pp. 287–90). But, as the Ministry of Education's *Report* in 1951 said, "The economy measures announced at the end of 1949 had a serious effect on the expansion of the youth service." One reason has been the difficulty of recruiting youth leaders—perhaps the incidence of conscription was partly responsible. Also the recommendations of the McNair *Report* as to the training of such leaders have been implemented in only a very small degree.

To sum up the story of English education since 1944 we can say that, in spite of difficulties, great progress has been made in the provision particularly of secondary and technical education. There has also been considerable university expansion. The problem of adequately staffing these services has been a stubborn one. Nursery schools and the Youth Service have suffered comparative neglect; and the County College scheme, which might

[1] *Education*, Feb. 6th, 1959, p. 258.

have done much to solve some of our social problems, has remained in abeyance. Some of these matters were dealt with in the Crowther *Report* which was published in December 1959. It stated that the raising of the school-leaving age to 16, and the creation of county colleges for compulsory part-time education to 18, "should be re-affirmed as objectives of national policy."[1] It considered that the most favourable period for raising the school-leaving age would be between 1965 and 1969, and that as soon as possible after that a beginning should be made with compulsory county college attendance. The Government subsequently decided that school leaving at 16 should come into force during the educational year 1970–1. The *Report* also made important recommendations with regard to the development of technical education and the recruitment of teachers. A ten-year development plan for the Youth Service was set out in the Albemarle *Report* which was published in February 1960. It adumbrated a service for young people aged 14 to 20, a large increase in the provision of full-time leaders, and arrangements for the training of part-time paid and voluntary workers. A training college for youth leaders has been opened at Leicester.

During the year 1963 two more *Reports* of considerable signicance were issued. That of the Central Advisory Council for Education (England),[2] under the chairmanship of Sir John Newsom, dealt with the education of average or less than average pupils between the ages of 13 and 16. It reiterated the recommendation to raise the school-leaving age to 16 and advocated a broader curriculum, especially for the senior pupils, not all of whom should be entered for the Certificate of Secondary Education. The school programme in the final year should be limited to the adult world of work and leisure, and schools should give guidance on sexual behaviour to adolescents. There should be adequate provision for practical work and audio-visual aids should be available. Finally there should be a revision of teacher-training courses, and all graduate teachers should be required to have taken a course of professional training.

[1] *15 to 18*: *Report* of the Central Advisory Council for Education—England.
[2] See *supra*, p. 296. The *Report* was entitled *Half our Future*.

The other *Report*, issued by a Committee appointed by the Prime Minister and chaired by Lord Robbins, reviewed full-time higher education and made some important and far-reaching recommendations. The number of full-time higher education students should be substantially increased and the extent and scope of university work greatly extended. More Colleges of Advanced Technology[1] (C.A.T.s) should be provided and their status raised. Teacher-training colleges should be renamed Colleges of Education and closely linked with universities. Students who take a four-year course in them should be eligible to receive a B.Ed. degree. The Robbins Committee also made recommendations as to a reorganisation of the Ministry of Education, and these gave rise to considerable discussion. The Government accepted the *Report* in principle, and finally the Ministry was renamed the Department of Education and Science. The Minister became Secretary of State for Education and Science and he had two colleagues, one of whom was particularly concerned with universities and higher education and the other with schools.

The Robbins *Report* has perhaps received more limelight than that of the Newsom Committee. In the present technological age politicians and administrators tend to be primarily concerned with the supply and training of scientists and highly skilled technicians in industry; and it was to such matters that the Robbins Committee devoted much of its attention. But it remains true that specialised training, whether in science or in any other department of knowledge, is impossible unless it is based on a sound general education such as is given in a good school. Moreover the primary school must always be the foundation of the whole system, and this fact was emphasised in the Plowden Committee's *Report* which was issued in 1967. The work of the school underlies all other techniques and specialised knowledge, and the progress of a civilised and organised community is closely bound up with it.

[1] See *supra*, p. 325.

Appendix I

(See page 14)

COPY OF SCHOOLMASTER'S LICENCE TO TEACH (1769) PRESERVED IN THE NORWICH MUSEUM

John Greene, Clerk, Master of Arts, Commissary of the Rt. Rev. Father in God Philip, by Divine permission Lord Bishop of Norwich lawfully constituted, to our beloved in Christ Joseph Buck of Mattishall in the County of Norfolk and diocese of Norwich sendeth greeting. Whereas by a creditable testimonial which we have received we are fully satisfied as well of your sober life and conversation as of your sufficient capacity to exercise the function of a schoolmaster, we do therefore by these presents, so far as by law we may or can, give and grant unto you the said Joseph Buck our licence and ffaculty to instruct teach and inform any children in Grammar and other lawful and honest Documents allowed of and established by the Laws, Statutes and Constitutions of this Realm of England within the parish of East Dereham in the said County of Norfolk and Diocese of Norwich or in any other Parish within the said Diocese to which you shall remove with the consent of your Ordinary, you having first before me subscribed and sworn to all things which the law in this case requires to be subscribed and sworn to. And this our licence to endure during our pleasure and your good demeanour but no longer or otherwise. In testimony whereof we have caused this Seal which in this behalf we use to be hereunto affixed.

Dated at Norwich the 23rd day of March in the year of Our Lord 1769.

Richard Moss
Deputy Registrar.

Appendix II

A LIST OF DATES

Date	Educational Events	Books dealing with or bearing on Education	Acts, Bills, Official Reports, etc.
1762.		Rousseau, Émile.	
1763.		La Chalotais, Essai d'Éducation Nationale.	
1765.		Priestley, Essay on a Course of Liberal Education.	
		Rolland, Compte Rendu.	
1768.	Priestley discovers oxygen.		
1774.	[American Independence.]		
1776.	Vicesimus Knox becomes H.M. of Tonbridge School.	Adam Smith, Wealth of Nations.	
1778.	Protestant Dissenters become legally free to teach.		
1779.			
1780.	Raikes opens Sunday schools at Gloucester.		
1781.		Knox, Liberal Education.	
		Pestalozzi, Leonard and Gertrude.	
1782.		Mme de Genlis, Adèle et Théodore.	
1783.		Day, Sandford and Merton.	
1787.		Wollstonecraft, Thoughts on the Education of a Daughter.	
1789.	[French Revolution begins.]	Knox, Letter to Lord North.	
1790.		Burke, Thoughts on the French Revolution.	
		Paine, Rights of Man.	
1791.	[Death of John Wesley.]	Wollstonecraft, Vindication of the Rights of Women.	
		Godwin, Enquiry concerning Political Justice.	
1793.			
1795.	[Speenhamland scheme.]		
1798.	Pestalozzi goes to Stans.	Edgeworth, Practical Education.	
	Butler becomes H.M. of Shrewsbury.	Malthus, Essay on Population.	
	Fellenberg starts work at Hofwyl.		
1799.	Robert Owen goes to New Lanark.		
	Birkbeck starts lectures in Glasgow.		

1800.	{ Royal Institution founded. { Oxford Public Examination Statute.		
1801.			General Enclosure Act.
1802.			Health and Morals of Apprentices Act (Peel).
1803.	Pestalozzi goes to Yverdon.	Lancaster, *Improvements in Education.*	
1805.	{ Leeds Grammar School decision.	Mrs. Trimmer, *Comparative View, etc.*	
1806.	[Abolition of the Slave Trade.]		
1807.			Parochial Schools Bill (Whitbread).
1809.		Edgeworth, *Essays on Professional Education.*	
1810.	Royal Lancastrian Assoc. (Brit. and For. Sch. Society) founded.		
1811.	National Society founded.		
1813.		Robert Owen, *A New View of Society.*	
1814.	[End of war with France.]	Wordsworth, *Excursion.*	
1815.	Robert Owen's Infant School opened at New Lanark.		Corn Law.
1816.	Hill's School at Hazelwood opened.	Bentham, *Chrestomathia.*	
1819.	[Peterloo. The Six Acts.]		Factory Act (Peel).
1820.	[Accession of George IV.]		Parish Schools Bill (Brougham).
1823.	Beginnings of Birkbeck College, London.	Wilderspin, *Education of Infant Children of the Poor.*	
1824.			Combination Laws repealed.
1825.	Society for the Diffusion of Useful Knowledge founded.	James Mill, "Education" (*Ency. Brit.*). Brougham, *Practical Observations on the Education of the People.*	
	[Stockton and Darlington Railway opened.]		
1826.	David Stow founds Glasgow Infant Sch. Soc.		
1827.	Faraday starts Christmas Lectures at the Royal Institution.		
1828.	{ Death of Pestalozzi. { Arnold becomes H.M. of Rugby. { 'University of London' founded.		{ Repeal of Test Acts. { Catholic Emancipation Act.
1830.	[Accession of William IV.]	Lyell, *Principles of Geology.*	
1831.	King's College, London, founded.		

	Educational Events	Books dealing with or bearing on Education	Acts, Bills, Official Reports, etc.
1832.	Durham University founded. [Beginning of Oxford Movement.]		Reform Act.
1833.	Foundation of the British Association for the Advancement of Science. [Abolition of Slavery.]	Tracts for the Times.	Factory Act (Shaftesbury). Education Bill (Roebuck). First Education Vote (£20,000).
1834.			Wood's Bill to open Universities to Dissenters.
1835.			Municipal Corporations Act.
1836.	Kennedy becomes H.M. of Shrewsbury. Home and Colonial Infant Sch. Soc. founded.		
1837.	Glasgow Normal Seminary (Stow) opened. Normal School of Design founded. [Accession of Queen Victoria.]		
1838.	Kay-Shuttleworth opens Training College at Norwood.		
1839.	Committee of Council for Education set up.		
1840.	Battersea Normal School opened.		Grammar Schools Act.
1841.	Cheltenham College founded.		
1843.	Governesses' Benevolent Inst. founded. Marlborough College founded.		Graham's Factory Bill.
1844.	Y.M.C.A. founded.		
1845.	Royal College of Chemistry founded.		
1846.	Pupil-teacher system introduced.	Whewell, Of a Liberal Education in General. Hook, On the Means of rendering More Efficient the Education of the People.	Repeal of the Corn Law.
1848.	Queen's College, London, founded. [Revolution and Reaction in Europe.]		
1849.	College of Preceptors incorporated. Bedford College, London, founded.		
1850.	North London Collegiate Sch. founded.		W. J. Fox's Education Bill.
1851.	The Great Exhibition. Govt. Sch. of Mines founded.		

Chartist agitation. (1838–1839)

Year	Events	Publications	Acts & Commissions
1852.	Department of Science and Art founded. [Charity Commission set up.]	Newman, *Idea of a University.* 'Cuthbert Bede,' *The Adventures of Mr. Verdant Green.*	Lord John Russell's Borough Bill.
1853.	Thring becomes H.M. of Uppingham. C. of P. local exams. instituted. Y.W.C.A. founded. Cheltenham Ladies' College founded. {Working Men's College Founded.		
1854.	[Crimean War, to 1856.] First Kindergarten opened in England.		Oxford University Act.
1855.	Oxford Museum founded.		
1856.	Education Department created.		Pakington's Education Bill. Cambridge University Act.
1857.	[Indian Mutiny.]	T. Hughes, *Tom Brown's Schooldays.*	
1858.	{Oxford and Cambridge Locals instituted. Dorothea Beale becomes H.M. of Cheltenham Ladies' College. {Medical Register instituted.		
1859.	Robert Lowe becomes V.P. of Educ. Dept. [Volunteer Movement.]	{Mill, *On Liberty.* {Darwin, *Origin of Species.* *Essays and Reviews.*	
1860.	London Univ. institutes degrees in Science.		
1861.	[American Civil War, to 1864.]	{Spencer, *Education.* {Faraday, *Chemical History of a Candle.* Ruskin, *Unto this Last.*	{Report of Newcastle Commission (Elementary Education).
1862.	The 'Revised Code.'		
1863.		{Mill, *Utilitarianism.* {Kingsley, *Water Babies.*	
1864.			Report of Clarendon Commission (Public Schools).
1866.	Cambridge locals opened to girls.	Mill, *Inaugural Address at St. Andrews.* Huxley, *Essay on a Liberal Education.*	
1867.			Reform Act. Public Schools Act. Report of Schools Inquiry Commission (Endowed Schools). Endowed Schools Act.
1868.	Non-collegiate students admitted at Oxford.		
1869.	{Cambridge higher local exam. instituted. {Beginnings of H.M. Conference.	{M. Arnold, *Culture and Anarchy.* {Kingsley, *Madame How and Lady Why.*	
1870.	N. Union of (Elem.) Teachers founded. [Franco-Prussian War.]		Education Act (Forster). Devonshire Commission appointed.

	Educational Events	Books dealing with or bearing on Education	Acts, Bills, Official Reports, etc.
1871.	G.P.D.S.T. founded.		University Tests Act.
1872.	Girton College founded.		Ballot Act.
1873.	Beginnings of Univ. Extension movement at Cambridge.		
1874.	Froebel Society founded. Oxf. and Camb. Joint Board exams. instituted.		{ Factory Act. Report of Royal Comm. on Oxford and Cambridge.
1875.	Newnham College, Cambridge, founded.		
1876.			Education Act (Sandon).
1877.	Maria Grey Training College founded.		Oxford and Cambridge Act.
1879.	City and Guilds of London Inst. founded. Somerville Coll. and Lady Margaret Hall founded.		Education Act (Mundella).
1880.	London Univ. admits women to degrees. Owens Coll., Manchester, becomes a University. Regent St. Polytechnic opened.		
1883.	Finsbury Technical College opened. Church Schools Company founded. Boys' Brigade founded.	Galton, Enquiries into Human Faculty.	City Parochial Charities Act.
1884.	Toynbee Hall opened. Central Technical College opened.		Report of Royal Comm. on Technical Instruction.
1885.	Cambridge Training College for Women founded. Dartford P.T. College for Women founded.		
1887.	Roedean founded. P.N.E.U. founded.		
1888.			{ Local Government Act. Report of Cross Commission.
1890.	Beginning of 'University Day Training Colleges.' 'Whisky Money' becomes available for Technical Education.		
1893.	Federal University of Wales formed.		Elem. Educ. (Blind and Deaf Children) Act. Report of Gresham Committee. Report of Bryce Commission.
1894.	London School of Economics founded.		
1895.	Morant goes to the Education Department.		

1896.	Royal College of Art established. Wycombe Abbey School founded.		Gorst's Education Bill.
1897.		Adams, *Herbartian Psychology applied to Education.*	
1898.			
1899.	Ruskin College, Oxford, opened. [Boer War, to 1902.]		
1900.	Block Grant system introduced. Cockerton Judgment. Mason Coll., Birmingham, becomes a University. [Accession of Edward VII.]	Dewey, *The School and Society.*	{ University of London Act. Teachers' Registration Bill. Board of Education Act.
1901.			
1902.	Borstal System started. W.E.A. founded.		Education Act (Balfour).
1903.	Victoria Univ. gives place to separate Univs. of Manchester, Liverpool, and Leeds. Common Entrance examination instituted.		
1904.			Education (Local Authorities' Default) Act.
1905.	Univ. Coll., Sheffield, becomes a University.		*Suggestions to Teachers* first issued. { Education (Provision of Meals) Act. Birrell's Education Bill. Haldane Comm.'s Report on Tech. Education.
1906.			Education (Administrative Provisions) Act.
1907.	{ Imperial College of Science established. 'Free-place' system started. Teachers' Registration Council established. Medical Branch of Board of Educ. established.		
1908.	{ Boy Scouts founded. The Binet-Simon Scale.		{ McKenna's Education Bill. Children Act. Prevention of Crimes Act.
1909.	Univ. Coll., Bristol, becomes a University.		
1910.	Girl Guides founded. [Accession of George V.]		
1912.		Montessori, *Method.*	
1913.	Regulations for Junior Technical Schools first issued.		Report of Royal Comm. on London University.

Year	Educational Events	Books dealing with or bearing on Education	Acts, Bills, Official Reports, etc.
1914.	Rachel McMillan opens Nursery Sch. at Deptford. [First World War, to 1918.]		
1915.	Women's Institutes started.		
1916.	Play Centres Association founded.	Dewey, *Democracy and Education*.	
1917.	Secondary Schools Examination Council set up.		
1918.	The 'Stanford Revision' test (Terman).		{Education Act (Fisher). Teachers (Superannuation) Act. Burnham Committee set up.
1919.	University Grants Committee set up.		
1920.	{Oxford University admits women to degrees. State Scholarships instituted.	Nunn, *Education—its Data and First Principles*.	
1921.	{The 'Geddes Axe.' National Council of Labour Colleges founded.		Education—Consolidating Act.
1923.	{Stowe and Canford founded. Nursery School Association formed.		
1924.	Regulations for Adult Education first issued.		
1925.	National Playing Fields Association founded.	Burt, *The Young Delinquent*.	Teachers (Superannuation) Act. Hadow Report—*The Education of the Adolescent*.
1926.	{Univ. Coll., Reading, becomes a University. Joint Examining Boards for training of teachers instituted.		University of London Act. B. of E. Pamphlet—*The New Prospect in Education*.
1928.	First Cambridgeshire Village College opened.	Adams: *The Evolution of Educational Theory*.	
1929.			Report of Mental Deficiency Committee.
1930.			Unemployment Insurance Act.
1931.			Hadow Report on the Primary School.
1932.	'Free places' become 'Special places.'		
1933.			{Children and Young Persons Act. Hadow Report on Infant and Nursery Schools.
1934.	[Hitler establishes the Third *Reich*.]		Unemployment Act.
1936.	[Accession of George VI.]		Education Act.
1937.	National Fitness Council.	Burt, *The Backward Child*.	
1938.	[Munich Conference.]		Spens Report.

Year	Events	Publications	Reports
1939.	[Second World War, to 1945.] ['Battle of Britain.']		B. of E. Circular 1486 on Youth Service.
1940.		Clarke, *Education and Social Change.*	B. of E. Circular 1516—*The Challenge of Youth.*
1941.	{ A.T.C. formed. Boys and girls of 16–18 required to register.		The 'Green Book.'
1942.	National Youth Advisory Council formed.	Lester Smith: *To Whom Do Schools Belong?*	
1943.	Further Education and Training Scheme introduced.		{ White Paper on *Educational Reconstruction.* Norwood Report.
1944.	L.C.C. adopt scheme for comprehensive schools.		{ Education Act (Butler). Final Report of Fleming Committee. McNair Report.
1945.	{ Emergency Training Scheme introduced. National Foundation for Educational Research set up. UNESCO constituted. HORSA introduced.	'Bruce Truscot': *Redbrick University.*	{ M. of E. pamphlet, *Youth's Opportunity.* Percy Report on *Higher Technical Education.*
1946.			{ Barlow Report on *Scientific Manpower.* Curtis report on *The Care of Children.*
1947.	{ Burnham 'basic' scale introduced. School-leaving age raised to 15. Cambridge admits women to full university membership.		{ M. of E. pamphlets—*Further Education* and *The New Secondary Education.*
1948.	Nottingham University College becomes a University. National Advisory Committee on Education for Industry and Commerce set up. [National Health Service introduced.]	Moberly: *The Crisis in the University.*	Children Act. Employment and Training Act.
1949.	{ University College of North Staffordshire founded. National Advisory Committee on Training and Supply of Teachers set up.		
1950.			{ N.A.C.E.I.C. Report on *The Future Development of Higher Technological Education.*
1951.	{ Emergency Training scheme ended. General Certificate of Education introduced.		

	Educational Events	Books dealing with or bearing on Education	Acts, Bills, Official Reports, etc.
1952.	Southampton University College becomes a university. M. of E. announces reductions in expenditure on school buildings.		
1953.	[H-bomb invented.]		
1954.	Hull University College becomes a university. Exeter University College becomes a university.		Report on *Graduate Teachers of Mathematics and Science.*
1955.	'Equal Pay' for women teachers (in seven instalments) National Council for Technological Awards set up. Industrial Fund for Scientific Education.		
1956.			Teachers (Superannuation) Act. White Paper on *Technical Education.*
1957.	Leicester University College becomes a university. ['General' grant to local authorities.]		Willis Jackson Report on *The Training of Technical Teachers.*
1958.			White Paper on *Secondary Education.*
1959.	Appointment of a Minister of Science.		Crowther *Report.* White Paper on *Penal Practice in a Changing Society.*
1960.			Albemarle and Beloe *Reports.*
1963.			Newsom and Robbins *Reports.*
1964.	Introduction of Certificate of Secondary Education. Ministry of Education becomes Department of Education and Science. Schools Council for the Curriculum and Examinations formed. Council for National Academic Awards formed.		
1965.			Circular 10/65 issued.
1967.			Plowden *Report.*

Appendix III

BIBLIOGRAPHY

THE following is a list of books which are quoted or to which reference is made in the text. Acts of Parliament and Reports of Commissions or Committees, which are mentioned in the list of dates (Appendix II), are not included in this Bibliography.

Adams, Sir John, *The Herbartian Psychology applied to Education* (1897).
    Exposition and Illustration in Teaching (1909).
    The New Teaching (1918).
    Modern Developments in Educational Practice (1922).
    Errors in School (1927).
Adamson, J. W., *English Education, 1760–1902* (1930).
Allen, B. M., *Sir Robert Morant* (1934).
Archer, R. L., *Secondary Education in the Nineteenth Century* (1921).
Arnold, Matthew, *Rugby Chapel* (1857).
    Popular Education in France (1861).
    A French Eton (1864).
    Higher Education and Universities in Germany (1868).
    Culture and Anarchy (1869).
    Reports on Elementary Schools, 1852–1882—ed. Marvin (1908).
Austen, Jane, *Emma* (1816).

Barnard, H. C., *The French Tradition in Education* (1922).
Bazeley, E. T., *Homer Lane and the Little Commonwealth* (1928).
'Bede, Cuthbert,' *The Adventures of Mr. Verdant Green* (1853).
Bell, Valentine, *Junior Instruction Centres and their Future* (1934).
Bellot, H. H., *University College, London, 1826–1926* (1929).
Bernard, Sir Thomas, *Of the Education of the Poor* (1809).
Binns, H. B., *A Century of Education* (1908).
Birchenough, C., *A History of Elementary Education in England and Wales* (1929).
Blewitt, T. (ed.), *The Modern Schools Handbook* (1934).
Brasenose Quatercentenary Monographs (1909).
Brodrick, G. C., *History of the University of Oxford* (1886).
Brontë, Charlotte, *Jane Eyre* (1847).
Brougham, Henry, *Observations on the Education of the People* (1825).

Browning, E. B., *Aurora Leigh* (1857).

Burke, Edmund, *Thoughts and Details on Scarcity* (in *Works*, vol. vii, 1826).

Burns, C. Delisle, *A Short History of Birkbeck College* (1924).

Burt, Sir Cyril, *The Young Delinquent* (1925).
   The Backward Child (1937).

Butler, Joseph, *The Analogy of Religion* (1736).

Butler, Samuel, *Life and Letters* (1896).

Campagnac, E. T., *Society and Solitude* (1922).

Childs, W. M., *Making a University* (1933).

Clarke, A. K., *A History of the Cheltenham Ladies' College, 1853–1953* (1953).

Clarke, Sir Fred, *Education and Social Change* (1940).

Corston, W., *Life of Lancaster* (1840).

Crabbe, G., *The Borough* (1810).

Cunningham, W., *The Growth of English Industry and Commerce* (1907).

Darwin, Charles, *Origin of Species* (1859).

Davies, J. L., *The Working Men's College, 1854–1904* (1904).

Day, Thomas, *Sandford and Merton* (1783).

Dent, H. C., *The Education Act, 1944* (1944).

Dewey, John, *The School and Society* (1900).
   Democracy and Education (1916).

Dicey, A. V., *Law and Opinion in England* (1905).

Dickens, Charles, *Sketches by Boz* (1836).

Duncan, J., *The Education of the Ordinary Child* (1942).

Edgeworth, R. L., *Practical Education* (1798).
   Essays on Professional Education (1809).

Encyclopédie (1751–65).

Essays and Reviews (1860).

Evennett, H. O., *The Catholic Schools of England and Wales* (1944).

Faraday, Michael, *The Chemical History of a Candle* (1861).
   On the Various Forces of Matter (1860).
      (In the second edition (1873) the title of this book was changed to *On the Various Forces of Nature*.)

Fiddes, E., *Owens College and Manchester University* (1937).

Findlay, J. J., *Arnold of Rugby* (1897).

Fletcher, Sir Frank, *After Many Days* (1937).
Flexner, Abraham, *Universities* (1930).
Froebel, F., *The Education of Man* (1826).

Galton, Sir Francis, *Inquiries into Human Faculty* (1883).
Genlis, Mme de, *Adèle et Théodore* (1782).
George, W. R., *The Junior Republic* (1911).
Godwin, William, *Enquiry concerning Political Justice* (1796).
Gray, Thomas, *Ode on a Distant Prospect of Eton College* (1748).
Green, J. A., *The Educational Ideas of Pestalozzi* (1905).
Green, T. R., *A Short History of the English People* (1874).
Green, V. H. H., *Oxford Common Room* (1957).

Hall, M. P., *The Social Services of Modern England* (1959).
Hansard, Parliamentary Debates.
Harrison, J. F. C., *A History of the Working Men's College, 1854–1954*
    (1954).
Hearnshaw, F., *Centenary History of King's College, London* (1929).
    (ed.) *Social and Political Ideas of the Age of Reaction and Reconstruction*
    (1932).
Hicks, W. C. R., *Lady Barn House and the Work of W. H. Herford* (1936).
Hogg, E. M., *Quintin Hogg* (1906).
Hook, W. F., *On the Means of rendering efficient the Education of the*
    People (1846).
Horrabin, J. F., and W., *Working Class Education* (1924).
How, F. D., *Six Great Schoolmasters* (1904).
Hudson, J. W., *History of Adult Education* (1850).
Hughes, T., *Tom Brown's Schooldays* (1856).
Huxley, T. H., *Collected Essays* (1906).

Jones, M. G., *The Charity School Movement* (1938).

Kennedy, B. H., *Public School Latin Primer* (1866).
Kingsley, Charles, *Alton Locke* (1850).
    Water Babies (1863).
    Madam How and Lady Why (1869).
    Life and Letters (1890).
Kitchen, P. L., *From Learning to Earning* (1944).
Knox, Vicesimus, *Essays* (1778–9).
    Liberal Education (1781).
    Letters to Lord North (1789).

La Chalotais, Louis-René de Caradeuc de, *Essai d'Éducation Nationale* (1763).

Lancaster, Joseph, *Improvements in Education* (1803).

Lawrence, Evelyn (ed.), *Friederich Froebel and English Education* (1952).

Leach, A. F., *Educational Charters* (1911).
  Schools of Mediæval England (1915).

Livingstone, Sir Richard, *The Future in Education* (1941).

Locke, John, *On Education* (1692–3).

Lowndes, G. A., *The Silent Social Revolution* (1937).

Lyell, Sir Charles, *Principles of Geology* (1830).

Lyte, H. C. Maxwell, *A History of Eton College* (1875).

Magnus, Laurie, *Jubilee Book of the Girls' Public Day School Trust* (1923).

Making Citizens (H.M.S.O., 1945).

Malthus, T. R., *Essay on Population* (1798).

Mangnall, Richmall, *Questions* (1800).

Marvin, F., *The Century of Hope* (1919).

Maurice, F. D., *Introductory Lecture on the Objects and Methods of Queen's College* (1848).
  Lectures to Ladies on Practical Subjects (1856).

Mayer, Sir Robert, *Young People in Trouble* (1945).

Mill, James, "Education"—article in *Encyclopædia Britannica* (1825).

Mill, J. S., *Utilitarianism* (1853).
  On Liberty (1859).
  Inaugural Address at St. Andrews (1867).
  Autobiography (1873).

Montesquieu, *Œuvres* (Laboulaye edition, 1875–9).

Montmorency, J. E. G. de, *State Intervention in English Education* (1902).

Napleton, John, *Considerations on the Exercises for the First and Second Degrees of the University of Oxford* (1773).

Newman, J. H., *Idea of a University* (1852).
  Apologia pro Vita Sua (1864).

Norwood, C., & Hope, A. H., *The Higher Education of Boys in England* (1909).

Nunn, Sir T. Percy, *Education: its Data and First Principles* (1920). Revised Edition 1945.

Owen, Robert, *A New View of Society* (1813).
  Life of Robert Owen (1857).

Padley, R., and Cole, M., *Evacuation Survey* (1940).

Paine, T., *Rights of Man* (1791).

Parkin, G. R., *Life and Letters of Edward Thring* (1904).

Pattison, Mark, *Suggestions on Academical Organisation* (1868).
  Memoirs (1885).

Percival, A. C., *The English Miss* (1939).

Pestalozzi, J. H., *Leonard and Gertrude* (1781).
  How Gertrude teaches her Children (1801).

Plato, *Republic*.

Priestley, Joseph, *Rudiments of English Grammar* (1761).
  Essay on a Course of Liberal Education (1765).
  Observations relating to Education (1778).

Prisons and Borstals (H.M.S.O., 1945).

Psychological Tests of Educable Capacity: B. of E. Pamphlet (1924).

Quick, *Educational Reformers* (1868).

Quintilian, *Institutiones Oratoriæ*.

Raikes, E., *Dorothea Beale of Cheltenham* (1908).

Rawnsley, W. F., *Edward Thring* (1926).

Raymont, T., *The Principles of Education* (1907).

Rogers, A. M. A. H., *Degrees by Degrees* (1938).

Rolland d'Erceville, *Compte Rendu* (1768).

Rouse, W. H. D., *A History of Rugby School* (1898).

Rousseau, J. J., *Émile* (1762).

Ruskin, John, *The Seven Lamps of Architecture* (1849).
  The Stones of Venice (1851–3).
  Unto this Last (1860).
  Sesame and Lilies (1865).
  Time and Tide (1867).

Salmon, D., *Joseph Lancaster* (1904).

Schonell, F., *Backwardness in the Basic Subjects* (1942).

Shenstone, W., *The School* (1742).

Simpson, J. H., *Sane Schooling* (1936).

Smith, Adam, *Wealth of Nations* (1776).

Smith, Frank, *Life of Sir James Kay-Shuttleworth* (1923).
  A History of English Elementary Education (1931).

Smith, Sydney, *Essays* (*Edinburgh Review* articles, 1802–27).

Smith, W. O. Lester, *To Whom do Schools Belong?* (1942).

Spencer, F. H., *An Inspector's Testament* (1938).

Spencer, Herbert, *Education—Intellectual, Moral and Physical* (1861).

Stanley, A. P., *Life of Arnold* (1844).

Storr, F., *Life and Remains of the Rev. R. H. Quick* (1899).

Stow, David, *The Training System* (1836).

Strachey, Lytton, *Eminent Victorians* (1924).

Suggestions for Teachers, B. of E. Handbook (1905 ff.).

Tawney, R. H., *Secondary Education for All* (1924).

Thackeray, W. M., *Vanity Fair* (1847).

Thomas, M. W., *Young People in Industry* (1945).

Thompson, W. D'Arcy, *Daydreams of a Schoolmaster* (1864).

Thring, Edward, *Education and School* (1864).
   Theory and Practice of Teaching (1883).

Toynbee, Arnold, *Lectures on the Industrial Revolution in England* (1884).

Trevelyan, G. M., *British History in the Nineteenth Century* (1922).

Trilling, L., *Matthew Arnold* (1939).

Trimmer, Sarah, *Reflections on the Education of Children in Charity
   Schools* (1792).
   *A Comparative View of the New Plan of Education promulgated by Mr.
   Joseph Lancaster* (1805).

'Truscot, Bruce,' *Redbrick University* (1943).

Tuckwell, W., *Reminiscences of Oxford* (1900).

Whewell, W., *On the Principles of English University Education* (1837).
   Of a Liberal Education in General (1845).

Wilderspin, Samuel, *Importance of Educating the Infant Children of the
   Poor* (1823).
   The Infant System (1840).
   A Manual for the Religious and Moral Instruction of Young Children
   (1845).

Wilson, J. Dover (ed.), *The Schools of England* (1928).

Wollstonecraft, Mary, *Thoughts on the Education of a Daughter* (1787).
   Vindication of the Rights of Women (1792).

Wordsworth, William, *The Excursion* (1814).
   The Prelude (1850).

Young, Arthur, *Annals of Agriculture* (1784–1808).

Zimmern, Alice, *The Renaissance of Girls' Education* (1898).

The following books, not listed in the Bibliography, are also suggested for further reading:

Curtis, S. J., *History of Education in Great Britain* (rev. ed., 1950).

Lester Smith, W. O., *Education in Great Britain* (3rd. ed., 1958).

Dent, H. C., *Education in Transition* (1944).
   Secondary Education for All (1949).
   Growth in English Education, 1946–1952 (1954).
   The Educational System of England and Wales (1961).

Leese, J., *Personalities and Power in English Education* (1950).

Judges, A. V. (ed.), *Pioneers of English Education* (1952).

Pollard, H. M., *Pioneers of Popular Education*, 1760–1850 (1956).

Graves, J., *Policy and Progress in Secondary Education*, 1902–42 (1943).

Moberly, Sir W., *The Crisis in the University* (1949).

Venables, P. F. R., *Technical Education* (1955).

Barnard, H. C., and Lauwerys, J. A., *A Handbook of British Educational Terms* (1963).

Annual *Reports* of the Ministry of Education. The Report for 1950 contains a summary of English educational history from 1900 to 1950.

INDEX

ACADEMIC freedom, 249, 327
Academies, nonconformist, 27–31
Accomplishments, 22–3, 157, 162–3
Acland, H., 82
Acts of Parliament, quoted or referred to:
  Board of Education, 205
  Cambridge University, 123
  Catholic Emancipation, 67
  Children Act, (1908, 1933 and 1948), 284
  City Parochial Charities, 180
  Education (1870), 116–19, 151, 164, 168, 201, 307; (1876), 169; (1880), 170; (1902), 191, 209–11, 214–18; (1918), 225, 230, 231–3, 301; (1936), 238–9; (1944), 279, 296–305, 316, 327
  Education (Administrative Provisions, 1907), 224, 227; (Choice of Employment), 281; (Local Authorities Default), 214; (Provision of Meals), 229
  Elementary Education (Blind and Deaf Children), 223.
  Enclosure, xiii–xiv
  Endowed Schools, 14–15, 116, 146, 163–4, 200
  Factory (1802), xv, 63–4; (1819), 65; (1844), 115, 169; (1874), 169
  Grammar Schools, 16
  Health and Morals of Apprentices, 63–4
  Local Government, 179
  Oxford and Cambridge, 195
  Oxford University, 123
  Prevention of Crime, 285
  Public Schools (1868), 128
  Reform (1832), 67, 116; (1867), 115–16, 119, 147
  Teachers (Superannuation) (1918, 1925 and 1956), 258
  Technical Instruction, 179, 211
  To prevent growth of schism, 28
  Unemployment Insurance, 283
  Uniformity, 28, 30
  University of London, 197
Adams, Sir John, 221–2, 308
Adamson, J. W., v, 16, 54, 67 n., 91, 174, 188 n., 204, 308 n.
Adèle et Théodore, 23
"Administrative muddle," 204, 211
Adult education, 89–92, 276–8
Advanced courses, 267
Advisory councils (Ministry of Education), 296
Age, school-leaving, 232–3, 238, 295, 300, 320, 323
Agreed syllabus, 238, 299
Agriculture, 115, 198, 200, 220

Aided schools, 210, 298
Air Training Corps, 289
Albemarle Report, 333
Alexander, Sir William, 332
"Almighty Wall," 153
Ambleside "House of Education," 247
Ampleforth College, 247
Anderson, John, 89
Anschauung, 38, 172
Apologia pro Vita Sua, 120
Apperception, 308
"Appointed day," 233, 301
Apprentices, 63, 64, 274–5, 324
Approved schools, 284–5
Area Training Organisations, 255–6, 327 n.
Archer, R. L., 81, 125, 151, 193
Arithmetic, 16, 61
Armstrong (King's) College, Newcastle, 199
Arnold, Matthew, 79, 113, 129, 146–8, 155, 185, 202, 306
Arnold, Thomas, 15, 74–80, 86, 116
Art, teaching of, 135–6, 149–50, 273, 275
Assistant Masters' Association, 193, 222
"Associate in Arts," 134 n.
Associated Schools, 244
Association for Education of Women, 160
Association of Preparatory Schools, 240
Aurora Leigh, 157 n.
Austen, Jane, 22
Autobiography (J. S. Mill), 144

Baden-Powell, Lord, 286
Bagley, W. C., 310
Baldwin, Stanley, 242
Balfour, A. J., 208, 214
Ball-frame, 60
"Barbarians," 147
Barker, Sir Ernest, 278
Barnett, Canon, 183
Battersea Normal School, 101–2
Beale, Dorothea, 161–2, 165, 189, 193
Beaumont College, 247
Bedales, 166
Bede College, Durham, 254
Bedford College, London, 158, 198
Bell, Andrew, 53–4, 55–7, 190
Bell, Valentine, 283
Beloe Report, 331
Benedictines, 247
"Beneficial employment," 238
Bentham, Jeremy, 71, 306
Biber, E., 140
Bible-reading, 7, 9, 11, 48–9
Binet, A., 310

Binet-Simon scale, 310
Bingley Training College, 253
Birchenough, C., 53 n., 233 n.
Birkbeck, G., 84, 89 n.
Birkbeck College, 92, 181
Birmingham and Midland Institute, 181
Birmingham L.E.A., 282, 322
Birmingham University, 198–9, 249
Birrell, Augustine, 215
"Black List," 216
Blake, William, 6
Block grant, 216, 218
Bloomsbury, 251
Board of Education, 205, 209, 218, 293
Board of Trade, 135
Board schools, 117–19, 168–72, 175–6, 210–11
Boarding schools, 14, 240, 243–4, 298
Boat-race, University, 125
Boer War, 209, 224
Bolton Technical College, 325
Borough Bill, 108
Borough Road School, 53–4
Borough Road Training College, 57, 102
Borstal, 285–6
Boy Scouts, 183, 286
Boys' Brigade, 286
Bradford Grammar School, 164
Bradford L.E.A., 224
Brighton University College, 327
Bristol University, 199, 249
British and Foreign School Society, 56–7, 66, 69, 102
Brontë, Charlotte, 156
Brougham, Henry, 38, 57, 59, 65–7, 84, 86, 90
Brown, Ford Madox, 151
Browning, E. B., 157 n.
Bryant, Sophie, 189
Bryce Commission, 192, 203, 204–8
Buckland, William, 93
Building programmes, 304, 318, 320–1
"Bulge," the, 320–1, 322
Bullying, 19, 77
Burke, Edmund, xvi, 4, 17, 46
Burnham scales, 257–8, 272, 323
Burt, Sir Cyril, 236 n., 265–6, 310, 311
"Business," 16
Buss, F. M., 161–2, 189, 193
Butler, Bishop, xiii n., 28
Butler, R. A., 243, 254, 294–6
Butler, Samuel, 18, 72–3

Cadet corps, 289
Cambridge University, 24, 26–7, 31, 82–3, 123–5, 158–9, 183, 188, 190, 195–6, 250–1
Cambridgeshire village colleges, 101, 279
Campagnac, E. T., 309, 313
Campbell, Thomas, 84

Camps, school, 232
Canford School, 241
Caput, 123
Careers masters, 281
Carlyle, Thomas, 72
Casa dei Bambini, 228
Catholic Emancipation Act, 67
Cattell, J. McK., 309
Cavendish laboratories, 251
Central Advisory Council for Education, 296, 333
Central schools, 235
Central Society of Education, 98
Central Technical College, 178, 198, 275
Central Training Council, 255
Certificate of Secondary Education, 331, 333
Certificate, Teacher's, 253
Challenge of Youth, 287
Charity Commission, 129, 131, 204
Charity schools, 5–7, 27
Charterhouse, 48, 126, 242
Chartism, 103, 150
Cheltenham College, 79, 129
Cheltenham Ladies' College, 161–2, 190
Child labour, xv–xvi, 8, 10, 63, 232
Children's Happy Evenings Association, 227–8
Chrestomathia, 67 n.
Christian Brothers, 247
Christian Socialism, 150, 151
Christ's Hospital, 34, 164, 245
Church of England, xii–xiii, 11, 48, 49, 83, 99
  and elementary education, 6, 53, 55–6, 65, 104, 108, 238
  and secondary education, 14, 80, 165
  and university education, 25–7, 82–3, 85–6, 196
  and training colleges, 187
Church Schools Company, 165
"Churnside," 245 n.
Circular 10/65, 330
Circulating schools (Wales), 11
Citizenship, education for, 139, 313–17
City and Guilds of London Institute, 178, 179, 180, 275
City Companies (London), 12, 178
City Parochial Charities Act, 180
Clapham High School, 165
Clarendon Commission, 126–8, 145
Clarke, Sir Fred, 236 n., 308, 315–17
Class distinctions and national education, 4–5, 40, 45–6, 49–50, 147, 148, 277, 301–3, 316–17, 328
Classes, size of, 321
Classics, the, 14–16, 34, 74, 78, 82, 94, 126, 127, 130, 142, 218–19, 221, 241
Claydon, W. A., 245
Clergy Daughters' School, 156, 161
Cleveland Commission, 195

Clifford, Dr. J., 214
Clough, A. J., 159, 182
Clubs, youth, 286
Cockerton judgment, 208–9
'Cockney College,' 84
Co-education, 23, 165–6
Coleg Harlech, 277
Collectivism, 306–7, 316
College attendance order, 300
College of Advanced Technology, 325, 334
College of Education, 334
Combined system, 103, 107
Comenius, 33
Commissions:
    Bryce, 192, 203, 204–8
    Clarendon, 126–8, 145
    Cleveland, 195
    Cross, 174–6, 179, 181, 186, 201 n.
    Devonshire, 177
    Gresham, 197
    Newcastle, 109–11, 146, 185
    Oxford and Cambridge (1852), 123; (Cleveland, 1874), 195
    Schools Inquiry (Taunton), 128–34, 146, 154, 162–3, 179, 191, 193, 207
    Selborne, 197
    Technical Instruction, 178–9
Committee of Privy Council on Education, 99, 104, 108
Common day schools, 3–4
Common entrance examination, 240, 241
Common Prayer, Book of, 14
Community centres, 278–9
Comprehensive schools, 262, 328–30
Comprehensive system, 103, 107
Compte rendu (Rolland), 43
Compulsory school attendance, 110, 168–70, 292
Conscription, 288
Consultative Committee, 205, 234–7, 259
Continuative education, 232–3, 273–80
Controlled schools, 298
Coplestone, E., 81
Correlation, 310
Council for National Academic Awards, 325
County colleges, 279, 300, 319, 333
County councils, 179, 203, 207–10
County school (before 1902), 129; (1902–44), 218; (after 1944), 298
Cowper, William, 49
Cowper-Temple clause, 118, 143, 175, 208, 210
Crabbe, George, 3, 4
Crimean War, 110
Cross Commission, 174–6, 179, 181, 186, 201 n.
Crowther Report, 333
Culture and Anarchy, 147, 306

Curriculum:
    approved schools, 284
    charity schools, 6
    elementary schools, 107, 142
    girls' schools, 22
    grammar schools, 14–17, 129, 145–6
    junior technical schools, 271–2
    nonconformist academies, 29–30
    private schools, 20–21, 247
    public schools, 72–80, 126–8, 152–4
    schools of industry, 7–9
    secondary schools, 216–17, 218–20, 260, 263–5
    Sunday schools, 9–11
    training colleges, 100, 101–2, 185
    technical high schools, 261

Dame schools, 2–3, 66
Dartford Physical Training College, 226
Dartington Hall, 248
Darwin, Charles, 136, 306
David, Herr, 153
Davies, Emily, 159, 162
Davy, Sir Humphry, 92, 94, 135
Day continuation schools, 232–3, 274, 279, 300
Day release, 324
Day, Thomas, 40
Day training colleges (university), 176, 252
Degrees, 25, 26–7, 82, 334
    external, 87, 197, 274
    internal, 197
    pass, 82, 122
    in science, 95, 199, 251
    for women, 159–61
Delinquency, juvenile, 284–6, 331–2
Democracy and the educational system, 234, 242–3, 244–5, 277, 315–17
Denison, Archdeacon, 103
Dent, H. C., 296, 305, 318
Department of Education and Science 334
Development plans, 297, 318–19
Devonshire Commission, 177
Dewey, John, 314–15
Dicey, A. V., xii, 124 n., 301, 306 n., 307
Dickens, Charles, 5, 20
Dickinson, C. Lowes, 151
Diderot, 42
Diploma in education, 189–90, 308
Diploma in technology, 325
Direct-grant schools, 243, 299, 300, 303, 324
Divisional executives, 297
"Dotheboys Hall," 20
Douai, 247
Downside, 247
D'Oyly, Dr., 85
Drever, James, 312 n.
Dual system, 118–19, 215, 238–9, 296, 298–9
Dublin University, 160

Dulwich College, 164
Durham University, 124, 196, 198, 199

Ebbinghaus, H., 309
Economics, London School of, 198
Ede, Chuter, 294
Edgeworth, R. L., and Maria, 41
Edinburgh Review, 17, 56, 81, 122
Edinburgh University, 190
Education:
 continuative, 232–3, 273–5
 elementary, 2–11, 98–101, 107–14, 168–
  76, 215, 236, 294, 297, 301
 part-time, 232–3, 295
 primary, 297, 298, 300
 secondary, 12–23, 71–80, 126–34, 146,
  186, 200–3, 204–7, 211, 294, 301
 technical, 88–93, 138, 177–81, 198–9,
  203, 211, 235–6, 261, 271–6
 university, 24–7, 81–7, 120–5, 195–200
 vocational, 83, 177–81, 271–5
Education and Social Change, 315–16
Education as a university subject, 188,
 190–1, 308–9
Education Department, 109
Education: its Data and First Principles,
 312–13
"Education-mad" party, 90, 98
Educational history, xi, 308
"Educational ladder," 134, 145, 206
Educational Reconstruction (White Paper),
 294
Eldon, Lord Chancellor, 16
Elementary education, 2–11, 98–101,
 107–14, 168–76, 201–3, 215, 236,
 294, 297, 301
"Eleven plus," 255–6, 273, 328, 329
Emergency training scheme, 304–5, 322
Émile, 33–7, 140
Eminent Victorians, 79
Emma, 22
Employment of children, xv–xvi, 7–8, 9,
 62, 232, 238
Enclosure Acts, xiii–xiv
Encyclopédie, 42–43
Endowed schools, 12–17, 128–34, 156
Endowed Schools Act, 14–15, 116, 146,
 163–4, 200
Engineering, 88, 90, 178, 274, 275
"Enlightenment," the, 42, 314
Enquiries into Human Faculty, 309
Enquiry concerning Political Justice, 47
"Equal pay," 324
Equality of opportunity, 329
Essai d' Éducation Nationale, 43
Essay on Population, 47–8
Essays and Reviews, 122
Eton College, 12, 17–19, 52, 77, 126, 152
Euclid, 131, 221
Evacuation, 291–3

Evangelicalism, 48–50, 71
Evening classes, 59, 89, 178, 179–81, 198,
 274
Evening Institutes, 274
Examinations:
 elementary schools, 110, 112–13, 171–2
 secondary schools: entrance, 240–1,
  264–5, 295, 311; leaving, 134, 193,
  206, 237, 260, 266–7
 university, 24–5, 26, 81–2
Excepted district, 297
Exeter University, 182, 199, 249
Expenses, university, 83, 84, 124, 196
Extension, university, 159, 182, 276
External degrees, 87, 197, 274
"Extras," 16, 165

Factory Acts (1802), xv, 63–4; (1819), 65;
 (1844), 115, 169; (1874), 169
Faraday, Michael, 86, 92, 94–5
Fees:
 elementary schools, 4, 65, 110, 117,
  170, 205
 secondary schools, 16, 219, 243, 259, 300
 junior technical schools, 271, 273
Fellenberg, P. E. von, 39–40, 59, 100
Fellowships, university, 123, 195
Ferens, T. R., 251, 327
Fights, 19
Findlay, J. J., 308
Finsbury Technical College, 178
Firth College, Sheffield, 199, 327
Fisher Act, 225, 230, 231–3, 301
"Five Steps," the, 307
Fleming Report, 243–5, 300
Fletcher, Sir Frank, 242
Flexner, A., 252 n., 256
Formal Training, 15–16, 145
Forster, W. E., 116–17, 146
Fox, Charles, 308, 312 n.
Fox, W. J., 107
Francke, A. H., 7
Free places, 219–20
French influence on English education,
 23, 42–5, 47, 68, 146, 147
Frensham Heights, 166, 248
Froebel, F., 172–4, 228
Froebel Society, 173

Galton, Sir Francis, 309
Games, 18, 60, 125, 141, 153, 227–8
Garnett Technical College, 325
Geddes, Sir Eric, 233
General ability, theory of, 265, 310
General Certificate of Education, 330–1
Genlis, Mme de, 23
Gentleman's Magazine, 9
Geography, 30, 36, 58, 73, 142, 220, 221
Geology, 93
George, W. R., 286 n.

Germany, education in, 7, 68, 84, 110–11, 119, 122, 128, 129, 146, 147, 271, 315
"Gerund-grinding," 72, 142, 221
Gibbon, Edward, 26
Giddy, Davies, 55
Gifts, Fröbelian, 173, 228
Girl Guides, 286
Girls and women, education of:
    school, 22–3, 132, 134, 141, 161–5
    university, 154, 156–66
    Rousseau, 37
Girls' Public Day School Trust, 164–5, 173, 190
Girton College, 159–60
Gladstone, W. E., 17, 19 n., 27, 116
Godwin, William, 47
Goldsmiths' College, 254
Gorst, Sir John, 103, 115
Governesses, 22, 156–7
Governing bodies, 298
Graham, Sir James, 103, 115
Grammar, learning of, 33, 72, 142, 221
"Grammar," meaning of term, 12, 16, 74
Grammar schools, 12–19, 71, 207, 219, 236, 259, 302–3, 329
Grants, government, for education:
    elementary schools, 69, 98, 105, 110, 142, 170, 171–2, 207, 214, 216, 238, 321
    health services, 224–5
    science and technology, 135–6, 179
    secondary schools, 201–3
    training colleges, 102, 105
    universities, 199, 249–50, 327
Gray, Thomas, 18
Great Exhibition, 126, 135, 177
Greek, compulsory, 250
"Green Book," 293–4
Green, J. R., 10
Gresham Commission, 197
Grey, Maria, 164, 173, 190
Grote, George, 84
Group tests, 311

Hadow Report:
    infant and nursery schools, 230
    education of the adolescent, 234–7, 260–1, 265, 294
Haldane, Lord, 254, 275
Halévy, Professor, 9
Halls of residence, 124–5, 202, 327
Hamilton, Sir William, 124
Handwork, educational value of, 148, 150
Harrow School, 13, 126, 242
Hartley, H. R., 327
Hatfield Hall, Durham, 124
Hawtrey, Freda, 230
Hazelwood School, 21
Headmasters' Conference, 154, 193

Health and Morals of Apprentices Act, 63–4
Hebdomadal Board, 123
Hebdomadal Council, 160
Hebrew, 15, 29
Hegelianism, 312
Helvétius, C. A., 58
Herbart, J. F., 307–8
Herbertson, A. J., 221
Herford, W. H., 166
Heurism, 36
Higher Certificate, 266, 268, 330
Higher Grade Schools, 175, 191, 201–3, 205, 208, 218
Higher local examination, 158, 159
"Higher tops," 201, 202
Hill, T. W., and M. D., 20–1
History, 30, 58, 73, 78, 139, 142, 221
Hofwyl, 39–40, 59, 100
Hogg, Quintin, 180
Home and Colonial Infant School Society, 60
Honours Schools (Oxford), 26–7, 81–2, 95, 195, 251
Hook, Dr. W. F., 107
Hook, Theodore, 84
HORSA, 320
House system, 241
How Gertrude Teaches her Children, 38
Howson, G. W. S., 221
Huddersfield Technical College, 325
Hughes, Tom, 150, 151
Hull University, 199, 249
Hullah, John, 151
Hume, Joseph, 84
Hurstpierpoint College, 129
Huxley, Thomas, 115, 137, 142–3, 306
Hygiene and health, 149, 152, 155, 223–7, 232, 278

Idea of a University, 120–1, 306
Illustrated London News, 126
Imperial College of Science and Technology, 275
Improvements in Education, 54
Inaugural Address (J. S. Mill), 145–6
Independent schools, 193, 240–8, 300–1, 342–3, 316, 324
Individual and society, 309, 312–13
Individualism, xvi–xvii, 83, 134, 142, 147, 306, 312–13
Industrial Fund for Science Education, 324
Industrial Revolution, xiv–xvi, 8, 10, 45, 88, 90, 99
Industry, schools of, 7–9, 37, 40, 69, 100
Infant schools, 58–62, 172–4
Infant System, 60
Inspectors, 100, 105, 110, 112–13, 131–2, 133, 146, 175, 206, 218
Institute of Criminology, 332

Institutes of Education, University, 255.
    327 n.
Intelligence quotient, 223, 310–11
Internal degrees, 197

James, William, 312 n.
Jesuits, 43, 247
Joint Examining Boards, 253, 256
Jones, M. G., 5
Jones, Rev. Griffith, 11
Junior commercial schools, 272
Junior instruction centres, 283
Junior Republic, 286 n.
Junior technical schools, 235–6, 259, 261,
    271–3
Juvenile delinquency, 284–6, 331–2
Juvenile Employment Bureaux, 282

Kay-Shuttleworth, Sir James (Dr. Kay),
    99–102, 104–5, 107, 111, 113, 114,
    134
Keate, John, 17
Keatinge, M. W., 221, 308
Keble College, 196
Kekewich, Sir George, 176
Kennedy, B. H., 73–4
Kenyon, Lord Chief Justice, 16
Kindergarten, 162, 165, 173–4
King Alfred's school, 248
King George's Jubilee Trust, 287
King's College:
    Cambridge, 12
    London, 85–7, 93, 150, 157, 181, 188
King's College School, 85–6, 129
King's School, Canterbury, 12–13
Kingsley, Charles, 3, 137, 150, 151–2,
    157, 306
Knox, Vicesimus, 25–6

La Chalotais, L.-R. de Caradeuc de, 43
La Salle, St. J.-B. de, 247
Labour colleges, 277
Labour exchanges, 281, 282
Labour party and education, 234, 276–7
Lady Barn School, 166
Lady Manners School, Bakewell, 12
Lady Margaret Hall, 160
Laissez-faire theory, xvi, 9, 63, 134
Lampeter, St. David's College, 249
Lancaster, Joseph, 4, 53–4, 56–7
Lancing College, 129
Lane, Homer, 286 n.
Lankhills School, 224
Latin grammar, 34, 72, 74, 142, 221
Lavoisier, A. L., 92
Leach, A. F., 13
Leeds City Training College, 253
Leeds Grammar School, 16
Leeds School Board, 201
Leeds University, 198, 249

Leeson, Dr. Spencer, 241
Leicester University, 199, 249
Leicestershire high school, 329, 330
Leonard and Gertrude, 38
Licence to teach, 14, 28, 335
Ling, P. H., 226
Lingen, 144
"Literæ Humániores," 82
Liverpool University, 198, 249
Livingstone, Sir Richard, 277, 308
Lloyd George, David, 219, 215
Loans to students, 269–70
Local administration of education, 131,
    179, 205
Local Education Authorities, 205, 208
    and 1902 Act, 215–16, 218
    and 1918 Act, 232–3
    and 1944 Act, 296–301
    and Fleming Report, 243–4
    and training of teachers, 252–3
    and universities, 250, 269, 327
    and youth service, 287
Local examinations, 133, 157, 206, 268–9
Local Government Act, 179
Locke, John, 7, 17, 33, 41, 42
London City Companies, 12, 173
London County Council, 130, 208
London Infant School Society, 59
London School Board, 143, 168, 208
London School of Economics, 198
London University, 31, 67, 78, 84–7, 95,
    121, 124, 158–9, 160, 181, 182, 197–8,
    251–2, 274
London University School, 86 n.
Lowe, Robert, 111–12, 116
Lowndes, G. A. N., 218 n., 225
"Lowood," 156 n.
Lyell, Sir Charles, 93

Macaulay, T. B., 106
Macaulay, Z., 59
Machinery, xv
Madam How and Lady Why, 137
Malthus, T. R., xvi, 47–8
Malvern College, 129
Management clauses, 105 n.
Managers, school, 119, 131, 238, 298
Manchester Grammar School, 80
Manchester University, 198–9, 216, 249
Mangnall's Questions, 20
Mansbridge, Albert, 276
Marlborough College, 79
Marvin, F. S., 71
Mason, Charlotte, 247
Mason, Josiah, 198–9, 327
Mathematics, 26, 29, 73, 74, 82, 95, 131,
    161, 221, 323
Matriculation, 261, 266, 268
Maurice, F. D., 150–1, 157–8, 182–3, 306
McKenna, Reginald, 215

McMillan, Rachel and Margaret, 229, 230
McNair Report, 254–7, 272, 290, 323, 325, 332
Meals, school, 225–6, 229, 300
Mechanics' institutes, 89–92, 135, 180, 271
Mechanics' Magazine, 89
Medical service, school, 224–5, 232
Mental defectives, 223–4, 228
Mental tests, 309–11
Merchant Taylors' School, 15, 126
"Merit grant," 171–2
Military drill, 226
Mill, James, 57, 59, 71, 144
Mill, J. S., xvi, 144–6, 306
Minister of Education, 69, 205, 296, 334
Missions, school, 154, 182–3
Moderations, 81
"Modern Greats," 251
Modern schools, 235, 259, 331
Modern Schools' Handbook, 166 n., 248
"Modern subjects," 20, 21–2, 29–30, 35, 130–1
Monitorial schools, 52–7, 105
Montaigne, M. Eyquem de, 146
Montesquieu, C. de S., xii–xiii, 42
Montessori, Maria, 228–9
Montmorency, de, J. E. G., 98
Moral education, 38, 141, 148, 149, 153
Morant, Sir Robert, 208, 209, 216–17, 224
More, Hannah and Martha, 10, 49
Morris, Henry, 279
Motor index, 310
Multilateral schools, 262, 328
Mundella, A. J., 170
Municipal schools, 191, 218
Museum, Oxford, 82
Music, 74, 142, 153

Napleton, John, 24–5
"Narration," 247
National Advisory Council on the Training of Teachers, 322
  for Industry and Commerce, 325
National certificates, 274
National consequences, doctrine of, 141
National Fitness Council, 287
National Institute of Industrial Psychology, 282
National Playing Fields Association, 227
National Public Schools Association, 107
National Society, 56, 57, 66, 69, 100, 132
National Union of Teachers, 193
National Youth Advisory Council, 289
National Youth Committee, 287, 289
"Natural education," 34–6, 38, 315
"Negative education," 34–6
Neill, A. S., 248
Neuhof, 37, 39
Neville's Cross College, 254
New College, Oxford, 12

New Lanark, 58–9
New Prospect in Education, 237
New View of Society, 59
Newcastle Commission, 109–11, 146, 155
Newcastle University, 199
Newman, Sir George, 225, 229
Newman, J. H., 120–1, 300
Newnham College, 159–60
Newsom *Report*, 246, 333
Newspapers, 91–2
Nightingale, Florence, 158
Noetics, 74–5, 120
Non-collegiate students, 125, 196
Nonconformists and education, 6, 27–31, 80, 108, 214, 321
Non-provided schools, 210, 238
Normal School of Design, 135, 275
North London Collegiate School, 161, 165, 189
North Staffordshire, University of (Keele), 249, 327
Norwood poor-law school, 100
Norwood *Report*, 263–6, 328
Norwood, Sir Cyril, 241, 263
Nottingham University, 199, 249
Nuffield, Lord, 251
Nunn, Sir Percy, 308, 312–14
Nursery schools and classes, 229–30, 232, 294, 295, 297–8, 319–20, 333
Nursery School Association, 230

Observations on the Education of the People, 67
Of a Liberal Education, 95
Officers' Training Corps, 288–9
Open-field system, xii–xiv
Organised science schools, 201, 218, 271
Oriel College, Oxford, 74, 82, 120
Origin of Species, 136–7, 306
Owen, Robert, 38, 57–9
Owens College, Manchester, 183, 198, 327
Oxford and Cambridge Joint Board, 193, 266
Oxford Movement, 82–3, 99, 120, 122
Oxford University, 24–7, 81–3, 95, 99, 121–5, 160, 162, 182, 183. 188, 195–6, 249–51

Paine, Tom, 4–5, 46–7
Pakington, Sir John, 108
Paley, Archdeacon, xii
Palmer, A. and G. W., 251, 327
Parenthood, education for, 137, 138
Parents' National Educational Union, 247
Parish Schools Bill, 65–6
"Parity of Status," 237, 261–2, 264, 301, 303, 330
Parochial schools, 5–7, 54, 64, 65–6
Parochial Schools Bill, 54–5, 64

Part II and III Authorities, 209 n., 211, 296, 297
Part-time education, 232–3
Pass degrees, 82, 122
Pattison, Mark, 121–3
Pauper children, 6–9, 64
"Pauperes et indigentes," 13
Payment by results, 112–14, 136, 171, 174, 217
Payne, Joseph, 189
Peel, Sir Robert:
    elder, 63, 65
    younger, 17, 27
People's High Schools (Denmark), 277
Percy Report, 325
Pestalozzi, J. H., 37–9, 59, 60, 140, 172
"Philistines," 147
Philosophy, educational, 308
Physical education, 46, 60, 141, 149–50, 151, 153, 224–5, 232
Pietism, 7
Pitt, William, 8, 17
Plato, 120, 149, 308, 317
Play, educational value of, 60, 141, 151, 153, 155, 173, 227–8
Play centres, 227
Playgrounds and playing-fields, 60, 227–8, 288
Plebs League, 277
Plowden Report, 334
Plumptre, Henry, 33
Polytechnics, 180–1
Poor relief, xiv, 8, 9
Population, xv–xvi, 47–8, 320
Practical Education, 41
Practical Observations on the Education of the People, 67, 90
Preceptors, College of, 132, 134, 189, 190, 191, 267
Prefects, 52, 73, 77
Preparatory schools, 240–1, 316
Prepostors, 19 n., 73
Pre-service organisations, 289
Prevention of Crime Act, 285
Priestley, Joseph, 29–30, 92
"Primary" and "Secondary," use of terms, 2
Primary schools, 234–5, 297, 298, 300, 327
Private Halls (Oxford), 125, 196
Private schools, 19–23, 156–7, 164–5, 248, 300–1, 316
Probation, 284
Professional associations, 193–4
Professional Education, 41
Professorships:
    university, 27, 122, 124, 189, 195–6
    of Education, 189, 216, 308
Progressive education, 34, 38, 172–3
"Progressive" schools, 19–21, 166 n., 248
Proprietary schools, 129

Protestantism, 9, 48–50
Provided schools, 210, 211, 215, 298
Prussia, education in, 68, 110–11, 119
Psychology and education, 307–8, 309–11
Public Examination Statute, 26, 81
Public schools, 12–19, 71–80, 126–8, 240–6, 316
Public Schools Act, 128
Public Schools Commission, 74
Punch, 6 n., 19, 148 n.
Punishments, 17, 21, 141
Pupil teacher centres, 185–6, 191, 218
Pupil teachers, 105, 109, 114, 171, 184–6

Quarterly Journal of Education, 77
Quarterly Review, 56, 73
Queen's College, London, 157–8, 161
Queen's scholarships, 105, 185, 186, 187
Quick, R. H., 113 n., 308
Quintilian, 72 n.
Quota system, 322

Radcliffe Observatory, 27
Ragged Schools, 70
Raikes, Robert, 9, 48
Rate-aid for education, 107, 117, 172, 175, 179, 203, 205, 219
Raymont, T., 174
Reading University, 182, 199, 200, 249
Realschule, 271
Rebellions, school, 18
Reform Act (1832), 67, 116; (1867), 115–16, 119, 147
Register Teachers', 132, 191–3, 206
Registration of boys and girls, 288
"Religious difficulty," 9, 27, 56, 62, 80, 99, 100, 102, 168, 214–15
Religious education and instruction, 36, 38–9, 99, 299, 303–4
    elementary schools, 5, 6, 7, 8, 9, 11, 100, 118, 168, 210, 239, 299, 303–4
    secondary schools, 76–7, 80
Religious tests, 26, 27, 28, 31, 67, 123, 195
Remand homes, 284
Rendcomb School, 245
Reorganisation, Hadow, 235–8
Repton School, 129
Republic, 120, 149, 308
Research, 95, 122
    educational, 301, 309–11
Reserved teachers, 238, 298
Residential universities, 120–1, 200, 327
Revised Code, 112–14, 146, 149, 171, 185
Revolution, French, 4–5, 18, 44–5, 46, 47, 88
Ricardo, David, xvi
Right of entry, 65, 98, 103, 107
Rights of Man, 5, 46
Robbins Report, 334

Robinson Crusoe, 36
Roebuck, J. A., 68–9
Roedean School, 241
Rolland d'Erceville, 43
Roman Catholic schools, 6, 105 n., 247–8
Rossall School, 79
Rossetti, D. G., 151
Rouse, W. H. D., 76, 221
Rousseau, J.-J., 33–7, 41, 42, 52, 141
Royal College of Art, 275
Royal College of Chemistry, 135
Royal College of Science, 136, 142, 198, 275
Royal Holloway College, 198
Royal Institution, 93–4, 135
Royal Lancasterian Association, 56
Royal School of Mines, 136, 275
Royal Society, 142
Royal Society of Teachers, 192
Rugby, L. E. A., 233
Rugby School, 13, 15, 18, 19, 75–80, 93, 126
Ruskin College, 276–7
Ruskin, John, 148–50, 157 n., 306
Russell, Bertrand, 308
Russell, Lord John, 108, 123
Rutherford, Mark, 147

Sadler, Sir Michael, 80, 143, 216
Salary scales, teachers', 257–8, 272, 322–3
Sanderson, F. W., 221
Sandford and Merton, 40
"Sandwich courses," 324
Schonell, Sir Fred, 311
Scholarships:
    school, 124, 206, 219–20, 267–8, 269, 311
    university, 123, 125, 269, 326
Scholastic Registration Association, 191
School Base, 263
School Board Chronicle, 3
School boards, 117–19, 168–72, 175, 201–3, 208–10
School certificate examination, 260, 266–8, 330
School-leaving age, 232–3, 238, 295, 300, 320, 333
School-leaving examination, 268, 330–1
School prayers, 299, 303–4
School, types of:
    aided, 210, 298
    approved, 248, 284
    associated, 244
    board, 117–19, 168–72, 175–6, 210–11
    boarding, 14, 240, 243–4, 298
    central, 235
    charity, 5–7, 27
    circulating, 11
    co-educational, 165–6, 248
    common day, 3–4

School, types of (*contd.*):
    comprehensive, 262, 328–30
    controlled, 298
    county (before 1902), 129; (1902–44), 218; (after 1944), 298
    dame, 2–3, 66
    day continuation, 232–3, 274, 279, 300
    direct-grant, 243, 299, 300, 303, 324
    elementary, 2–11, 27, 98–9, 168–72, 201–3, 215–17, 236, 294, 297, 301
    endowed, 12–17, 128–34, 156
    girls', 22–3, 141, 156–7, 161–5
    grammar, 12–19, 71, 207, 219, 236, 259, 302–3, 329
    higher grade, 175, 191, 201–3, 205, 208, 218
    independent, 193, 240–8, 300–1, 342–3, 316, 324
    industry, of, 7–9, 37, 40, 69, 100
    infant, 58–62, 172–4
    junior commercial, 272
    junior technical, 235–6, 259, 261, 271–3
    modern, 235, 259, 331
    monitorial, 52–7, 105
    multilateral, 262, 328
    municipal, 191, 218
    nonconformist, 26
    non-provided, 210, 238
    organised science, 201, 218, 271
    parochial, 5–7, 54, 64, 65–6
    People's High (Denmark), 277
    preparatory, 240–1, 316
    primary, 234–5, 297, 298, 300, 327
    private, 19–23, 156–7, 164–5, 248, 300–1, 316
    "progressive," 19–21, 166 n., 248
    proprietary, 129
    provided, 210, 211, 215, 298
    public, 12–19, 71–80, 126–8, 240–6, 316
    ragged, 70
    Roman Catholic, 6, 105 n., 247–8
    secondary, 12–23, 71–80, 153–5, 186, 201–3, 204–9, 211, 218–20, 235–7, 259–70, 294, 328–30
    special, 224, 228
    special agreement, 238, 298
    Sunday, 9–11, 27, 28, 48, 56
    technical high, 261, 264
    trade, 235, 272
    voluntary, 117–19, 168, 202, 209–10, 215, 239, 298–300, 303
Woodard, 129
Schools:
    Ampleforth College, 247
    Beaumont College, 247
    Bedales, 166
    Borough Road, 53–4
    Bradford Grammar, 164
    Canford, 241

Schools (*contd.*):
  Charterhouse, 48, 126, 242
  Cheltenham College, 79, 129
  Cheltenham Ladies' College, 161–2, 190
  Christ's Hospital, 34, 164, 245
  "Churnside," 245 n.
  Clapham High, 165
  Clergy Daughters', 156, 161
  Dartington Hall, 248
  "Dotheboys Hall," 20
  Douai, 247
  Downside, 247
  Dulwich College, 164
  Eton College, 12, 17, 17–19, 52, 77, 126, 152
  Frensham Heights, 166, 248
  Harrow, 13, 126, 242
  Hazelwood, 21
  Hurstpierpoint College, 129
  King Alfred's, 248
  King's College School, 85–6, 129
  King's, Canterbury, 12–13
  Lady Barn, 166
  Lady Manners, 12
  Lancing College, 129
  Lankhills, 224
  Leeds Grammar, 16
  "Lowood," 156 n.
  Malvern College, 129
  Manchester Grammar, 80
  Marlborough College, 18, 79
  Merchant Taylors', 15, 126
  North London Collegiate, 161, 165, 189
  Rendcomb, 245
  Repton, 129
  Roedean, 241
  Rossall, 79
  Rugby, 13, 15, 18, 19, 75–80, 93, 126
  Shrewsbury, 13, 18, 72–4, 126
  St. George's, Harpenden, 166
  St. Olave's, 164
  St. Paul's, 80, 127, 240
  Stonyhurst College, 247
  Stowe, 241
  Tonbridge, 25, 150
  University College School, 86 n., 129
  Upholland, 165
  Uppingham, 129, 152–5
  Wellington College, 79
  West Buckland, 129
  Westminster, 12, 126
  Whitgift, 16
  Winchester College, 12, 18, 52, 126
  Wycombe Abbey, 241
Schools Council for the Curriculum and Examinations, 330
Schools Inquiry Commission, 128–34, 146, 154, 162–3, 179, 191, 193, 207

Science, 15, 27, 89, 92–5, 135–43, 152, 195, 323–6
Science and Art Department, 135, 142, 177, 180, 201, 203, 204
Sea Cadets, 289
Secker, Thomas, 28
Secondary schools, 12–23, 71–80, 153–5, 186, 201–3, 204–9, 211, 218–20, 235–7, 259–70, 294, 328–30
Secondary School Examinations Council, 267, 330
Secularists, 43, 115, 299
Selborne Commission, 197
Selection for secondary education, 236–7, 264–6, 295, 311, 328–30
Self-government in schools, 21
Selwyn College, 196
Senior classes, 236
Settlements, 183
Seventh Standard, 171, 201
SFORSA, 320 n.
Shaftesbury, Earl of, 70
Sheffield University, 199, 249
Shenstone, William, 2–3
Sherriff, Lawrence, 13
Shrewsbury School, 13, 18, 72–4, 126
Sidgwick, Henry, 153, 159
Sixth forms, 77, 260, 262, 267, 269, 331
Sketches by Boz, 5
Slough Community Centre, 278
Smith, Adam, xvi, 45–6
Smith, Sydney, 17, 19, 23
Smith, W. O. Lester, 293
Society for Bettering the Condition of the Poor, 8
Society for Promoting Christian Knowledge, 5, 7, 11
Society for the Diffusion of Useful Knowledge, 67
Society for the Establishment of Sunday Schools, 9
Somerville College, 160
Soulbury, Lord, 257
South Kensington, 136, 178, 180, 181, 275
Southampton University, 199, 249
Spearman, C., 310
Special agreement schools, 238, 298
Special Inquiries and Reports, Office of, 208, 216
Special places, 220, 295
Special schools, 224, 228
Special services, 223–6
"Specific" grant, 321 n.
Speenhamland, xiv, 47
Spencer, Herbert, 115, 137–43, 145, 306
Spens Report, 259–63, 264–5, 315, 328
Sports (school), 18, 60; (university), 125
St. Andrew's University, 145, 190
St. David's College, Lampeter, 249

St. George's School, Harpenden, 166
St. Hild's College, 254
St. Hilda's College, 160, 162
St. Hugh's College, 160
St. Mark's Training College, 102
St. Olave's School, 164
St. Paul's School, 80, 127, 240
Standards, 113, 171, 235
Stanford revision, 310
Stanley, A. P., 79
Stans, 37
State Intervention in Education, 98
State scholarships, 250, 267-8, 269, 326
State, the, and education, 43-4, 63-4, 68-70, 73, 78, 80, 106, 107-14, 134, 145, 149, 306-7, 312-15
"Steam intellect society," 90
Stephenson, George, 90
"Stinkomalee," 84
Stonyhurst College, 247
Stow, David, 61-2, 100, 184
Stowe School, 241
Strachey, Lytton, 79
Stuart, James, 182, 276
Suggestions for Teachers, 217, 222
Sunday schools, 9-11, 27, 28, 48, 56
Superannuation, teachers', 258
Swimming, 227, 232

Tacitus, 302 n.
Taunton Commission, 128-34, 146, 154, 162-3, 179, 191, 193, 207
Tawney, R. H., 233
Teacher's Certificate, 185, 253
Teachers' Registration Council, 192, 240
Teachers' salaries and superannuation, 69 n., 132, 233, 257-8, 323
Teachers:
  training and qualification of, 250, 252-8, 304-5, 326, 333-4
  elementary schools, 57, 98, 100, 101-2, 105, 184-94
  nursery schools, 230
  secondary schools, 132-3, 136, 154, 163, 197
  technical schools, 272-3, 325-6
Technical education, 88-92, 135-6, 138, 177-81, 203, 236, 260-1, 271-3, 324-6, 334
Technical high schools, 261, 264
Technical Instruction Acts, 179, 211
Technique of teaching, 220-2, 307-8
Technological degrees, 325 n.
Technologists, College of, 325
Terman, L., 310
Test Act, repeal of, 67
Tests, mental, 309-11, 328
Tests, religious, 25, 26, 31, 67, 84, 124, 195
Thackeray, W. M., 20, 22

Theological colleges, 196, 198
Theology, 84, 120
Theory, educational, 15-16, 32-41, 144-52, 306-17
Thompson, D'Arcy, 34
Thompson, Godfrey, 309
Thorndike, E. C., 309
Thring, Edward, 19, 77, 152-5, 193, 221, 227
Times, The, 84, 217, 294, 295
Tom Brown's Schooldays, 15, 19, 77, 79, 150
Tonbridge School, 25, 150
Townswomen's Guilds, 278
Toynbee, Arnold, 183
Tractarianism, 82-3, 99, 120, 122, 129
Trade schools, 235, 271-2
Training colleges, 57, 98, 100, 101-2, 105, 200, 211, 230, 253-4, 322, 325-6
Transfer, inter-school, 236, 237, 244-5, 261, 265, 273, 302, 328
Transfer of training, 15-16
Trent, Lord, 251
Trevelyan, G. M., 49, 71, 119
Trimmer, Sarah, 7, 10, 55-6
Triposes, 26, 82, 95, 159, 195, 251
"Truscot, Bruce," 122
Tufnell, E. C., 101
Tutorial system, 122
Types, intellectual, 263-6, 301, 328

Unemployment, juvenile, 281-4
Uniformity, Act of, 28, 30
Unitarianism, 31
'Universal' education, 43-4
Universities:
  Birmingham, 198-9, 249
  Bristol, 199, 249
  Cambridge, 24, 26-7, 31, 82-3, 123-5, 158-9, 182, 183, 188, 190, 195-6, 250-1
  Dublin, 160
  Durham, 124, 196, 198, 199
  Edinburgh, 190
  Exeter, 182, 199, 249
  Hull, 199, 249
  Leeds, 198, 199
  Leicester, 199, 249
  Liverpool, 198, 249
  London, 31, 67, 78, 84-7, 95, 121, 124, 158-9, 160, 181-2, 197-8, 251-2, 274
  Manchester, 198-9, 216, 249
  Newcastle, 199
  Nottingham, 199, 249
  Oxford, 24-7, 81-3, 95, 99, 121-4, 160, 162, 182, 183, 188, 195-6, 249-51
  Reading, 182, 199, 200, 249
  Sheffield, 199, 249
  Southampton, 199, 249
  St. Andrew's, 145, 190

Universities: *(contd.)*:
  Victoria, 160, 198, 249
  Wales, 160, 199
University College, London, 84–5, 86–7, 158
University College School, 86 n., 129
University Colleges:
  Aberystwyth, 199
  Bangor, 199
  Cardiff, 199
  Lampeter (St. David's), 249
  Swansea, 199
University day training colleges, 176, 187–8, 190–1, 220, 308
University expenses, 83, 84, 124, 196
University extension, 159, 181–2, 276
University Grants Committee, 249–50, 327
University Schools of Education, 255–6
University, size of, 326
University standards, 326
Unwin, G., 10 n.
Upholland Grammar School, 165
Uppingham School, 129, 152–5
Utilitarianism, 71, 90, 142, 306

Valentine, C. W., 309
Van Mildert, Bishop, 124
Vanity Fair, 20, 22
Victoria University, 160, 198, 249
Village Colleges (Cambridgeshire), 101, 279–80
Vocational education, 83, 177–81, 271–5
Vocational guidance, 281–2, 311
Voltaire, 42
Voluntary Care Committees, 225
Voluntary schools, 117–19, 168, 202, 209–10, 214–15, 239, 298–300, 303, 321
Voluntaryists, 104, 115
Volunteer movement, 151, 288

Wales, education in, 11, 160, 199, 210 n., 214
Wales, University of, 160, 199
Wantage, Lady, 327
War and education, 110, 224, 226, 230, 231, 257, 291–3, 305, 320, 331–2
Ward, Mrs. Humphry, 227
Warrington Academy, 29, 30

Water Babies, 3
Wealth of Nations, 45–6
Wehrli, J. J., 100, 101
Wellington College, 79
Welsh Intermediate Schools, 210 n.
West Buckland School, 129
Wesley, John, 48–50
Westminster School, 12, 126
Wheat, price of, xiv
Whewell, William, 94–5
"Whisky money," 179
Whitbread, Samuel, 54, 55, 64–5
Whitehead, A. N., 308
Whitehouse, J. H., 263
Whitelands Training College, 102
Whitgift School, 16
Wilberforce, William, 49, 57
Wilderspin, Samuel, 59–61, 62
William of Wykeham, 12, 15
Willis Jackson Committee, 325 n.
Wills, W. H., 251
Wilson, J. M., 93
Winchester College, 12, 18, 52, 126
Wollstonecraft, Mary, 23, 47
Women, education of, 22–3, 154, 156–66
Women's Institutes, 277–8
Woodard, Nathaniel, 129
Woodbrooke, 277
Wooll, Dr., 76
Wordsworth, William, 44–5
Workers' Educational Association, 151, 276
Workhouse children, 8, 63
Working Men's College, 148, 150–1, 158, 181
Wycombe Abbey School, 241
Wye Agricultural College, 198

Yorkshire College, Leeds, 198
Young, Arthur, xiii
Young Men's Christian Association, 286
"Young persons," 233, 254 n., 300
Youth leaders, 254, 290, 332, 333
Youth Service, 287–90, 332, 333
"Youth squads," 288
Yverdon, 38, 59

Zimmern, Alice, 158 n., 163
Zürich Polytechnikum, 178